Around the Southern Table

Around the Southern Table

. . .

by S A R A H B E L K

GALAHAD BOOKS
NEW YORK

First Galahad Books edition published in 1997.

Galahad Books
A division of BBS Publishing Corporation
386 Park Avenue South
New York, NY 10016

Galahad Books is a registered trademark of BBS Publishing Corporation.

Published by arrangement with Simon & Schuster.

Library of Congress Catalog Card Number: 97-73422
ISBN: 0-88365-972-7
Permissions for quoted material can be found on pages 527-528.

Designed by Laurie Jewell.
Printed in the United States of America.

*In memory
of my grandmothers,
Carrie Jerome Anderson ("C. J.") and
Sarah Nesbit Belk ("Mother Belk"),
my first cooking teachers.*

Acknowledgments

I WOULD LIKE TO EXTEND my appreciation to the following people who helped make this book possible.

To my parents, Caroline Anderson Belk and Ralph Nesbit Belk, for teaching me not only about food, but also farming, flowers, and table manners, which all make dining a richer, more enjoyable experience.

To my brother, James Patrick Belk, and my sister, Jane Belk Hemingway, who ate some very experimental cooking (mine) the year the three of us lived together.

To Donald Alberti, who supported me unquestionably through the duration of this project and ate whatever I cooked with undying enthusiasm.

To the friends who continued to invite me to parties, movies, and for weekends in the country, in hopes that I'd take a break from this project. More often than not, I asked them to wait. They did. Susy Davidson, Vicki Poth, Amy Kaplan, Heidi Fleiss, Debbie Smith, Dorothy Zeidman, Jane Margolies, Susan Bell and Bradford Morrow, Elaine Smollin, Amanda Hewell, Diane Palmer, and Margaret Morgan: I love you all. Thanks for waiting.

To Carole Lalli, my former editor, who let me work at my own pace, trusting that I would produce the best book possible given the grace of time. To Kerri Conan, who gracefully intercepted the manuscript from Carole, and displayed incredible acts of empathy in winding up the details. Thanks, too, to her assistant, Karen Holden, who helped with last minute crises.

To my agent, Susan Lescher, for believing in this project and for pushing me in the right direction.

To fellow Southern authors, Susan Costner, Bethany Bultman, and Lucie T. Morton for loaning me research books. And to authors Paul Prudhomme, Edna Lewis, and Anne Willan for their kind words and encouragement.

To Rebecca Kimmons, for showing me West Virginia (it *is* almost heaven), and to Mimi Lewis for showing me Kentucky.

To my Southern friends and relatives for their support and suggestions:

Samuel E. Belk III; Adelaide, Herbert and George Simpson; Virginia and Benjamin Mayo; Ellen Lane; Ruth and Joe Polk; Betty Polk Snyder; Sybil Pope; Edith and Albert Williams; Thomas King; Frances King; Lottie Alexander; my brother-in-law, Jay Hemingway, and my sister-in-law, Kathleen Cabell Belk. A special thanks to Johnsie Alberti for sending the pokeweed and wild persimmons from her farm in Alabama.

To William Garry and Barbara Fairchild at *Bon Appétit* for hiring me, knowing I had a book on the way and that I might be somewhat distracted.

To JoAnn Barwick, Peggy Kennedy, and Betty Boote at *House Beautiful* for letting me work a 4-day week in the beginning.

To Michael Motta, Sal Marinello, Eric Ludlow, Pasquale Manocchia, Debbie Ercolino, John Alsop, and John Schmitt of Plus One Fitness Clinic for helping me stay fit, despite all the recipe testing.

To Heidi Fleiss, my gifted chiropractor and friend, who kept the stiff necks and headaches at bay.

To David Greenbaum for his clearheaded advice.

To Jeffrey Rian for ingesting more ham and fried chicken than I'm sure he ever dreamed of.

To Helen and Jim Bagley for loaning their car.

To those who helped with recipe testing, word processing, and research: Kathleen Nilon, Pamela Mitchell, Shirley Corriher, Andrea Israel, Susan Inglis, Susan Bernfield, Bonnie Slotnik, Penelope Green, Charles Pierce, Mindy Heiferling, Kim Brandt, Barbara Prisco, Jane Sanders, and especially Ann Frazier, who kept the office running smoothly under pressure.

To the experts who proofread various chapters: Beverages: Bill Samuels, Jr., at Maker's Mark, and authors Lucie T. Morton and Leon Adams; Beef: Marlyse Belunski; Pork: Robin Kline at the National Pork Producers Council; Lamb: Robin Ganse at the National Sheep Producers Council; Poultry: Steven Pretanik, William Roenigk, and Dot Tringali at the National Broiler Council; Fish and Shellfish: Clare Vanderbeck at the National Fisheries Institute, Jeanne Grasso at the National Fish and Seafood Promotional Council, and my friend, author Susan Hermann Loomis.

And finally to my nieces, Lauren, Kathleen, Meghan, and Carrie and my nephew, Sam, who fill a very special place in my heart.

Acknowledgments

■

Contents

• • •

$\mathcal{I}ntroduction$

. . .

$\mathcal{U}$NTIL I WAS ABOUT TWELVE, I figured everyone ate fried chicken on Sunday, drank iced tea sweetened, and ate bread—whether it was biscuits, cornbread, or yeasty pocketbook rolls—piping hot. I thought everyone knew that ambrosia was a holiday dessert and that across the country the word "barbecue" meant a smoky, shredded pork sandwich. It was only later—as I ventured beyond the Southeast—that I realized mealtime could include exotic things like hard, crusty (cold) rolls, wine, sausages made from veal (they were white!) instead of pork, and luxurious things like goose liver, caviar, and Champagne. I loved each and every adventurous bite, and for a brief, I'll-only-eat-French-food moment, I temporarily forgot how good the food was that I grew up with.

But I don't think I truly realized how good I had it until I moved to New York eleven years ago. The bagels are great, but you've got to search high and low for a decent ham hock. You can't find pure lard very easily, and you can just plain forget about self-rising flour. They grow excellent apples here in New York, and the local white potatoes—freshly dug from Long Island farms—are the best I've ever had. But Yankee sweet potatoes don't hold a candle to those grown in the South. And my first summer here, I had to wait until *July* for a local peach, and until *August* for a tomato! Imagine! I love New York, but sometimes I can't help but ache for a mess of fresh field peas and a quart of homemade fig preserves from a neighbor's backyard tree.

Mention the term "Southern cooking" to a non-Southerner and he or she will most likely think: "Ah, yes: pecan pie, mint juleps, ham biscuits, and those awful grits." And then there are others who think Southern food is only Cajun and Creole and to them, "Southern food" means jambalaya, gumbo, crawfish etouffée and blackened redfish. Period. Southern cooking is all of the aforementioned foods—and much, much more. It's the Anglo-Saxon fare—wine jellies, syllabubs, and Sally Lunn bread—inherited from our British ancestors. It's the French-inspired food and drink that evolved out of the Jeffersonian era. An even earlier Gallic influence dates back to the seventeenth century, when the religious-persecuted Huguenots settled in Virginia and the Carolinas and started one of the first vineyards in the the New World. Southern food includes the foods smuggled in and cultivated by African slaves—like sesame seeds and okra. But perhaps our greatest culinary debt is due to the native Americans, who taught us how to fish, grow corn, and, basically, how to keep from starving. Succotash and corn pone were two of their more lasting culinary contributions.

Southern cooking is not only a reflection and result of our ancestry, but of wars fought and independence won; of periods of plenty and times of want; of tables of almost embarrassing excess and of meager meals of salt pork and cornbread. Like other regional cuisines, Southern cooking is also a result of geography. This diverse region includes three major mountain ranges, over 3,000 miles of coastline, one of the most important rivers in the country, and the largest estuary in the world. Overall, the South has a temperate climate and therefore a long growing season, making it one of the most prolific food-producing regions in the country. But Southern agriculture is more than just pork, peaches, and pecans; farmers are branching out into new areas and cultivating jalapeño peppers and kiwi fruit, raising quail, "farming" crawfish, catfish, and shrimp, making goat cheese, and nursing *vinifera* grapes—not for juice, but for dry, European-style wines—through humid summers and cold winters.

The richly diverse region of which I write includes Maryland, Virginia, North Carolina, South Carolina, Georgia, Mississippi, Alabama, Arkansas, Tennessee, Kentucky, West Virginia, Florida, and Louisiana. But what about Texas? The cuisine of the Lone Star state is similar to the others, and most people consider Texas "Southern" in spirit. But to me, Texas fare is more "Southwestern" with its generous use of chili peppers, tortillas, and salsas.

How did I choose these states? My decision was not about the Mason-Dixon Line, although that certainly acts as a sort of vague border. It isn't about which states were part of the Confederacy and which remained loyal to the Union. The South that I deal with is roughly delineated by the boundaries of the former Confederate states, but edges over into some of the border states, like Maryland, Kentucky, and West Virginia. Despite these states' divided sentiments during the Civil War, their culture and cuisine is, by and large, Southern. But along with geography, the South is a state of mind. These states not only share a common geographical region, but their ancestry, culture, and spirit are unique and unlike any other region in the country.

The South is a place where good manners, going to church, and family life are still important. Chiggers, coon dogs and chewin' tobacco are alive and well but so are fancy debutante balls, full-dress fox hunts, and white-columned homes with formal gardens. The South is not just the languorous, drawl-laced, magnolia-scented region romanticized in books and the cinema. Yes, it does tend to be more relaxed than other parts of the country. And yes, in early summer, magnolias (and lilacs and roses) intoxicate the air. And indeed, the Southern tongue is one of the slowest—and one of the most beautiful—in the world, one that is in some remote areas tinged with Elizabethan English. But the South is also a vital, vigorous place, the birthplace of great presidents, astounding architecture, and noted writers, artists, and musicians. The bigger cities—like Richmond, Charlotte, and Atlanta—are thriving.

I have always loved studying the South's history, particularly its social history. How people farm, cook, serve, set the table, and eat gives us insight into other aspects of their lives and their world. Where did Sally Lunn bread come from? Why is a hoecake so named? Why was pork so popular? Why was melted butter used to dress salads in the eighteenth and nineteenth centuries? Why are traditional Southern vegetables cooked for so long? The answers give us insight into the evolution of a culture.

I love studying culinary history (or "foodways" as it is known in scholarly circles), and so in this book I include brief, relevant, historical background of Southern foods and ingredients. With the exception of two recipes (spoon bread and biscuits), the recipes are my own, original creations. These new recipes reflect my intention to explore the many possibilities of Southern ingredients and Southern dishes. In some cases, I've lightened a classic dish, taking out some of the fat, flour, or cream. In other cases—particularly desserts—I've reduced the sugar. For some dishes, I've added ingredients that have become widely available such as wild mushrooms, sun-dried tomatoes, pesto sauce, and fresh herbs.

Purists may think that some of my combinations—goat cheese with Smithfield ham, for instance—are unnecessary, and perhaps even a little blasphemous. Or that biscuits made with olive oil—instead of lard—is an affectation. My argument is this: generally, we no longer want food that is as salty, sweet, or fatty as it was a hundred years ago, so why not let dishes evolve? That doesn't mean do away with the classics, for that is what gives a region its particular personality, but there is a bounteous wealth of food to try. Mascarpone cheese, crème fraîche, cherimoya, chayotes, and chick peas. And what about those "forgotten" foods—parsnips, salsify, and rutabagas?

Introduction

■

I have not made changes just for the sake of making something new, but instead I have combined or changed ingredients where it is appropriate, and where the resulting dish will taste good. Although taste is subjective, I think most palates will agree: goat cheese does taste good with ham; caviar is good with spoon bread; ice cream made with sweet potatoes does work.

I have tried to give substitutions whenever possible for ingredients that may be hard to find, like fresh cilantro, or raspberry vinegar, or for wild foods, like pokeweed, and the small, native persimmon. Bacon and ham are cornerstones of the Southern table and I use them often. But I give suggestions when they can be omitted. The resulting dish will not taste like the pork-enriched original, but it will still be tasty. Although I am concerned with nutrition and health, this is not a diet book. Wherever appropriate, I have given a range for fats; I suggest substitutions whenever possible (yogurt for sour cream). Good lard can be difficult to find outside the South, so I don't call for it. If you can get pure, unadulterated lard and you like to cook with it, by all means, substitute it where I call for shortening.

I love peach pickles, chowchow, and damson preserves, but I haven't included a preserving chapter since these things are widely available at supermarkets, farmers' markets, at local farm stands, and by mail order.

I may be living in New York, but, as Woodrow Wilson once said, "A man's rootage is more important than his leafage." I grew up in Richmond, Virginia and spent summers in Monroe, North Carolina. The combined city/rural experience afforded me a mixed cultural background that included fancy, traditional Old Dominion parties where rich, sherry-scented crab concoctions filled tiny patty shells, and old-fashioned church suppers where devilled eggs and coleslaw and games like "crack the whip" were the attractions. My brother, sister, and I grew up on country-cooked greens, fried chicken, and field peas as well as crab imperial, shrimp Creole, wine jellies, and ambrosia. My mother hails from South Carolina, my father from North Carolina, so there was no chance for a Yankee dish—such as scrapple or doughnuts—to slip into our regular repertoire.

Whenever possible I have tried to promote ecologically sound recipes. I encourage the cook to use organically grown produce whenever possible, and to choose hormone-free beef and poultry when it is available. Humanely raised veal is the only kind I buy. It tastes terrific! All these efforts lead to a healthier planet, without which there will be no sweet potatoes, field peas, or oysters for the next generation of Southern eaters.

*I*f there were no other reason
to live in the South, Southern cooking
would be enough.

—MICHAEL ANDREW GRISSOM,
Southern by the Grace of God

Breads

Breads

"BREAD IS SO VITALLY IMPORTANT an element in our nourishment that I have assigned to it the first place in my work," states Marion Cabell Tyree, editor of *Housekeeping in Old Virginia* (1879). Indeed, one can hardly imagine a meal of fried catfish without cornbread or fried chicken without biscuits.

As in other cultures, bread has often been the main form of sustenance during the most desperate times, and in economically depressed areas of the South, cornbread or biscuits with gravy might constitute a meal. Southern breads fall into four main categories: biscuits, cornbreads, yeast breads (the simplest of which are called "light breads"), and skillet breads (for skillet breads, refer to section in "Breakfast," page 351). Cornbreads and biscuits—like other quick breads—are at their best just from the oven, a fact that probably led to the Southern preference for hot breads. Even the early colonists preferred their bread hot; the English toast rack would not find a home in America except, perhaps, for holding letters or postcards. According to Marjorie Kinnan Rawlings, author of *Cross Creek Cookery* (1942), ". . . part of the placidity of the South comes from the sense of well-being that follows the heart-and-body warming consumption of breads fresh from the oven. We serve cold breads only to our enemies." Breads continue to be an important part of the Southern diet, from the simplest cornbread and biscuits to the more refined spoon breads, Sally Lunns, and yeast rolls.

The earliest Southern breads were made from cornmeal. (In the seventeenth century, the word "corn" meant grain, so the early settlers referred to maize as Indian corn.) Corn remained the most important grain in the South until the eighteenth century, when the middle colonies began successfully growing wheat, the preferred grain of the middle and upper classes. Later in the century, wheat flour became Virginia's leading product, and by the nineteenth century flour milling had become such a large-scale industry in the state that Richmond was known as the flour capital of the nation. Farther South, wheat remained scarce, so cornmeal and rice flour continued to be the principal grains used in bread baking.

One of the earliest American breads was a wheat loaf, the recipe for which the colonists brought from England. Food historian Karen Hess states that from the beginning of recorded history, wheat has been the noble grain, not only because its unique qualities enabled the making of wonderfully light bread of dazzling whiteness, but also because it was the most expensive to produce by far. Nearly every other type of grain yields more per acre than wheat. Most wheat flour is bolted (sifted, to remove the bran) to make it white, reducing it in volume by about 30 percent, making it even more costly. White bread became a symbol of the upper class. The lower classes eventually demanded it in an increasingly prosperous and democratic society.

Today, as in colonial times, only soft wheat (wheat with a low-gluten content) is grown in the area of the thirteen colonies. Southerners prefer it (it makes a lighter, tenderer biscuit), and national brands of all-purpose flour sold in the South are generally softer than the same brands of all-purpose flour marketed in the North. "Today, hard wheat production in the United States is limited to the prairies, areas that were opened to large-scale transport only after mid-nineteenth century," says Hess. The use of low-gluten flour, plus the long fermentation and baking method of the South's early wheat bread, yielded a loaf much like hearty French loaves, such as that baked by the noted Parisian baker, Lionel Poilâne.

Sourdough breads seem to have fallen out of favor in the nineteenth century. Since they were time consuming to make (the dough must properly ferment), it comes as no surprise that with the end of slavery, Southerners preferred biscuits and other quick breads.

Biscuits

The importance of this branch of the intelligent, painstaking housekeeper's duties can scarcely be over-estimated. As there is no one article of food that enters so largely into our daily fare as bread, so no degree of skill in preparing other articles can compensate for lack of knowledge in the art of making good, palatable and nutritious bread. . . . A little earnest attention to the subject will enable any one [sic] to comprehend the theory, and then ordinary care in practice will make her familiar with the process.

—M.E. Porter, *Mrs. Porter's New Southern Cookery Book*

THIS CLASSIC BREAD appears in many forms in the South: from thin, crisp-as-a-cracker beaten biscuits to those that are thick and hunger quelling, to the yeast-leavened type, known as angel biscuits. Along with fried chicken, catfish, grits, and pecan pie, biscuits are synonymous with Southern eating.

There was a time when in many Southern households making biscuits was a three-times-a-day affair because, like cornbread and scones, biscuits—sometimes colloquially referred to as "hot 'uns" (as in, "have a hot 'un")—are best when hot. In fact, many Southern cooks keep a second—and even a third—batch of biscuits in the oven during the meal so no one is ever served a room-temperature biscuit or—heaven forbid—a cool one. (My mother is forever jumping up from the Thanksgiving or Christmas feast to present a piping-hot batch.)

In this section, I offer a variety of biscuits, from the most basic type for accompanying a meal or making shortcakes, to those made with whole wheat, rye, and buckwheat flours, to variations (much to the horror of biscuit purists) that include garlic butter, goat cheese, ham, and dried fruit and nuts. I find it worthwhile to have a set of biscuit cutters in various sizes since some biscuits—like Whole Wheat Raisin Pecan Biscuits—are large (2½ inches in diameter) while others—such as Ham Biscuits with Chèvre Butter and Buckwheat Biscuits with Crème Fraîche and Caviar—are better small, for serving with apéritifs or Champagne.

Basic Biscuits

Flour Biscuits at their most basic are made from flour, salt, baking powder, fat (lard or shortening), and milk or buttermilk. Southerners who bake biscuits with great regularity generally use the locally available self-rising flour made from soft winter wheat. The leavening and salt are already added to self-rising flour, so the cook has only to add fat and liquid. "Soft" wheat is planted in the fall and is often referred to as "winter" wheat. Flour made from soft winter wheat is lower in gluten (about 7 to 8 percent) than hard flour (which averages 13 to 16 percent), and it feels softer and powdery in comparison. Soft flour also weighs less than hard flour.

I have tried substituting cake flour and pastry flour (which are also low in gluten) for Southern soft winter wheat flour but without good results. Although cake flour and pastry flour produce biscuits with a texture similar to those made with soft Southern flour, the flavor is inferior and they do not seem to rise as well.

Biscuits made with soft wheat flour are lighter, fluffier, and rise higher than those made with standard all-purpose hard wheat flour. However, since soft wheat flour is difficult to find outside the South (see page 481 for mail-order source) I usually make my biscuits with all-purpose unbleached flour made from hard wheat. The recipes here can be made with either soft or hard wheat flour. (You may have to add a little more liquid to hard flour doughs.) However, for the ultimate biscuit, I heartily recommend soft flour. If you have friends traveling South, ask them to bring you back a 5-pound bag—in exchange for a batch of biscuits!

Fat Biscuits can be made with shortening, lard, or butter. Good-quality lard is hard to find these days, so I generally use shortening instead of lard. Butter may be used in place of shortening or lard to yield a rich, fine-crumbed biscuit, but shortening and lard produce a biscuit with more authentic flavor and flakier texture.

Liquid To my taste, the flavor difference between biscuits made with butter-milk and those made with "sweet" milk (regular, whole milk) is somewhat negligible. Since most households—including my own—are more likely to stock regular milk than buttermilk, the recipes that follow call for regular milk. If you prefer, buttermilk or plain yogurt may be substituted with a slight increase in the amount added. Low-fat, skim, or soy milk may also be substituted for whole milk.

Biscuits freeze well, and can be reheated in a microwave or standard oven with no discernible lack of flavor or texture. Just be sure to always serve biscuits piping hot!

Basic Biscuits

• • •

Do you know, Jason can already make biscuits? Mrs. Mullins has to make them twice a day for the old grandfather—he refuses to eat a warmed-over biscuit— and Jason has helped her so many times that, when he comes to our house, if I stand him on a chair and get out all the ingredients, he can mix them up all by himself. Then I roll them out for him—he's not quite strong enough to do that—and he cuts them out with a jelly glass, and they're the best biscuits I've ever eaten.

—Gail Godwin, *A Southern Family*

3 to 3¼ cups unbleached all-purpose flour (preferably flour made from soft wheat, such as Weisenberger's, White Lily™, or Red Band™)

4 teaspoons baking powder (omit if using self-rising flour)

1½ teaspoons salt (omit if using self-rising flour)

½ cup plus 2 tablespoons chilled shortening

¾ to 1 cup milk (or substitute 1 to 1¼ cups buttermilk or plain yogurt)

1. Preheat oven to 475° F.

2. In a large bowl sift the flour, baking powder, and salt. Cut in the shortening with your fingertips, a pastry blender, or two knives until the mixture resembles coarse meal. Add ¾ cup milk *all at once* and immediately stir with a fork 10 to 20 strokes to disperse the liquid evenly and to dissolve the salt and baking powder. Add additional milk if necessary to make a firm—but not sticky—dough.

3. Roll out the dough on a lightly floured work surface to a thickness of ½ inch. Cut out biscuits with a 2-inch-diameter floured cutter. (Do not "twist" the cutter; cut straight down through the dough.) You will have about 16 biscuits. Discard the dough scraps (rerolled scraps of dough will produce tougher biscuits), or save to make Maple Walnut Stickies (page 433).

4. Place biscuits an inch apart on unbuttered baking sheets and bake 8 to 12 minutes or until golden-brown on top. Serve immediately, piping hot, with sweet butter.

Makes 16 2-inch biscuits.

Marcene Rorie's "Pulled" Biscuits

• • •

CHILDHOOD SUMMERS spent on my parents' farm in rural North Carolina afforded me the pleasure of indulging in the ethereal, free-form biscuits made by our neighbor, Marcene Rorie. When Marcene was twelve, her mother suffered a stroke while in the kitchen making biscuits. Knowing that hungry men would soon be coming to the table for midday dinner, she pulled Marcene to her bedside and told her how to finish the biscuits. Marcene has made biscuits nearly every day since, and her foolproof method produces the fastest, lightest biscuits ever. Best of all, there is no rolling required; your hands are your only tools. And because there is no rolling, dough manipulation is minimized, so very little gluten develops (it is gluten that makes a stronger, somewhat tougher biscuit). This recipe is a good choice if soft, Southern flour is unavailable. Here is my version of Marcene's biscuits.

3 cups self-rising soft winter wheat flour, such as Weisenberger's, White Lily™, or Red Band™ (or substitute regular, unbleached all-purpose flour plus 4 teaspoons baking powder and 1½ teaspoons salt)
½ cup plus 2 tablespoons chilled shortening
1 cup milk

1. Preheat oven to 475° F.

2. Sift the flour into a medium bowl. (If not using self-rising flour, sift together the baking powder, salt, and flour.) Using your fingertips, cut the shortening into the flour until the mixture resembles coarse meal. Add the milk *all at once,* and immediately mix with a fork 10 to 20 strokes to disperse the liquid evenly and to dissolve the baking powder and salt.

3. On a lightly floured work surface, knead 2 or 3 times to form a smooth dough. Divide the dough in half, then divide each half into 8 to 10 equal pieces. Taking care not to overwork the dough, roll each piece into a ball, then flatten slightly to a thickness of ½ to ¾ inch. Place an inch apart on ungreased baking sheets (or place biscuits touching one another for soft-sided biscuits). Bake 10 to 12 minutes or until golden-brown. Serve immediately, piping hot, with sweet butter.

Makes 16 to 20 biscuits.

Ham Biscuits with Chèvre Butter

■ ■ ■

CLASSIC HAM BISCUITS are simply biscuits split and spread with a little butter and stuffed with thin slivers of dry-cured country ham. This version goes a step further, adding the mild flavor of soft goat cheese as a counterpoint to the salty ham. Serve with eggs for breakfast or brunch, as an hors d'oeuvre, or with soups and salads.

1 recipe Basic Biscuits (page 23)
½ cup (1 stick) unsalted butter,
   room temperature
2 tablespoons fresh, mild chèvre
   (goat cheese), such as Montrachet,

Bûcheron, or Southern goat cheese
   (see page 481 for mail-order
   source), room temperature
3 ounces thinly sliced Smithfield ham
   or other dry-cured country ham
   (see page 481 for mail-order source)

   1. Preheat oven to 475° F.

   2. Prepare biscuits as directed, but cut them into smaller circles, about 1½ inches in diameter. Bake as directed, then cool to room temperature.

   3. In a bowl, beat butter and goat cheese until well blended. Split biscuits and spread about ¼ teaspoon of the chèvre butter on the inside of the top and bottom of each biscuit. Place ham slice between biscuit halves. Serve at room temperature.

Makes about 24 biscuits.

Garlic Biscuits

■ ■ ■

SINCE THE GARLIC is cooked, there is no harsh, raw garlic taste. Serve with soups, salads, or any time you would serve garlic bread.

1 recipe Basic Biscuits (page 23)
6 cloves garlic, peeled
4 tablespoons unsalted butter, room
   temperature

3 tablespoons chopped fresh parsley,
   to garnish (optional)

Breads

■

1. Preheat oven to 475° F.

2. Prepare biscuits as directed, cutting them into 1½-inch circles for hors d'oeuvre–sized biscuits, 2¼ inches for supper-sized biscuits. Bake as directed.

3. In a small saucepan, bring cold, lightly salted water to a boil. Add whole garlic and boil for 20 minutes. With a slotted spoon remove the garlic and drain thoroughly.

4. Preheat broiler.

5. With the machine running, drop the garlic into a blender or food processor until chopped. Add butter and process until well blended.

6. Split biscuits. Place cut-side-up on ungreased baking sheet and spread with garlic butter. Broil 1 or 2 minutes or until bubbly. Sprinkle with parsley before serving, if desired.

Makes 10 to 12 medium (2¼ inches) biscuits or 24 small ones (1½ inches).

Buttermilk Angel Biscuits

• • •

THESE SOFT, tender little breads are a cross between a biscuit and a yeast roll. Angel biscuits differ from regular biscuits in three ways: first, yeast instead of baking powder or baking soda is used as a leavening agent; second, the dough is kneaded to develop the gluten; and third, the dough must rise before baking. Biscuits leavened with yeast have also been called Cream Biscuits or High Biscuits. Other leavened biscuits include nineteenth-century delights called French Biscuits (which also have eggs for lightness), and Light Biscuits (leavened with a sponge made from yeast and mashed potatoes). Some old South Carolina cookbooks have recipes for yeast biscuits with rice flour added.

Angel biscuits are not a spur-of-the-moment bread like classic baking powder biscuits, but because of their delicate taste and light texture they are worth the extra effort.

¼ cup warm (105° to 110° F) water
1 package active dry yeast
1 teaspoon sugar
1 cup buttermilk
½ cup (1 stick) unsalted butter

2¾ to 3¼ cups unbleached all-purpose flour
1½ teaspoons salt
1½ teaspoons baking powder
½ teaspoon baking soda

1. In a bowl, combine water, yeast, and a pinch of the sugar. Stir, and let stand until bubbly, about 5 minutes.

2. In a medium saucepan, heat buttermilk and butter over medium heat until butter melts. Cool to room temperature. (Note: This mixture may break into curds and whey. Do not worry; this will not affect the recipe.)

3. In a large bowl, combine 2½ cups flour, salt, baking powder, baking soda, and remaining sugar. Make a well in the center and add the cooled buttermilk mixture and the dissolved yeast. Stir to mix, adding enough additional flour to make a soft dough. Cover, and let rest 10 minutes. On a lightly floured work surface, knead dough for 5 minutes or until dough is smooth and elastic.

4. Roll out dough to ¼-inch thickness. Cut into 1½-inch rounds with a biscuit cutter and place an inch apart on lightly buttered baking sheets.

5. Place 4 small glasses or custard cups on each corner of the baking sheet and cover with a clean tea towel to make a "tent." (The glasses will keep the towel from touching the biscuits.) Let rise 1½ to 2 hours, or until doubled in bulk.

6. Preheat oven to 400° F.

7. Remove tea towel and glasses and bake biscuits 10 to 15 minutes or until light golden-brown on top.

Makes about 40 1½-inch biscuits.

Olive Oil Biscuits

∎ ∎ ∎

EXTRA-VIRGIN olive oil is used instead of butter or lard or shortening here for a quick, fragrant little bread. Serve Olive Oil Biscuits with any dish featuring Mediterranean flavors, including those from Greece, Spain, southern France, or Italy. Olive Oil Biscuits are also good with Fennel, Orange, and Pomegranate Salad with Raspberry Vinaigrette (page 109) and Corn, Hominy, and Lima Bean Salad with Jalapeño Peppers and Red Pepper Vinaigrette (page 128). To use them for Biscuit Pizzas with Two Toppings (page 58), undercook them slightly. For a unique hors d'oeuvre, cut the dough into tiny rounds (1½ inches in diameter), bake as directed, split and spread with softened goat cheese, Thyme Butter, or Sun-Dried Tomato Butter (see "Appetizers and Hors d'Oeuvres," page 65), and top with a fresh basil leaf to serve with apéritifs. You can adjust the flavor of the biscuits by the type of oil you use. The more assertive the olive oil, the stronger the flavor.

1 cup unbleached all-purpose flour
½ teaspoon salt
½ teaspoon baking powder

3 tablespoons olive oil
6 tablespoons milk

1. Preheat oven to 425° F.

2. In a medium bowl, mix flour, salt, and baking powder. Make a well in the center and add olive oil and milk. Stir until just blended; do not overwork dough or biscuits will be tough.

3. On a lightly floured surface, roll dough out to a ¼-inch thickness. Cut into 2-inch rounds and place on an unbuttered baking sheet. Bake 11 to 12 minutes or until biscuits are just beginning to turn a very pale golden on top. Do not overbake.

Makes about 10 2-inch biscuits.

Whole Wheat Raisin-Pecan Biscuits

■ ■ ■

THESE HEARTY BISCUITS, rich with nuts and naturally sweet with raisins and honey, make a quick breakfast or tea bread. Serve warm with sweet butter, ricotta or cream cheese, or indulge with crème fraîche and lavender honey.

½ cup plus 1 tablespoon milk
2 tablespoons honey
1½ cups unbleached all-purpose flour
½ cup whole wheat flour
1 tablespoon baking powder

1 teaspoon salt
7 tablespoons chilled unsalted butter
¾ cup golden raisins
½ cup coarsely chopped pecans

1. Preheat oven to 425° F.

2. In a small saucepan heat milk and honey just until honey melts. Remove from heat and cool to room temperature.

3. In a medium bowl, combine flours, baking powder, and salt. Using your fingertips, a pastry blender, or two knives cut in butter until mixture resembles coarse meal. Add cooled milk mixture and stir until just combined; do not overmix. Place dough on lightly floured surface and knead in raisins and pecans, being careful not to overwork dough. Pat or roll out to a thickness of ½ inch and cut into 2½-inch rounds. Place an inch apart on ungreased baking sheets and bake 12 to 14 minutes or until light golden-brown on top.

Makes 14 to 16 biscuits.

Caraway-Rye Biscuits

■ ■ ■

THE AMERICAN COLONISTS sometimes combined rye flour, wheat flour, and cornmeal to make what was called "thirded bread." This practice "stretched" the scarcer, more expensive wheat flour. Recipes appeared later in the South for rye wafers (baked in a waffle iron), rye griddle cakes (which also had wheat and corn flour), and rye yeast bread made with rye and wheat flours. Other than these, bread recipes using only rye or rye plus wheat do not exist in great numbers in Southern cookbooks.

This play on caraway-rye bread—a deliciously exotic food when I was growing up in Virginia—is as versatile as it is flavorful. Serve hot with butter, Muenster cheese, or smoked ham to accompany salads and soups. Or use to make Caraway-Rye Biscuits with Horseradish Cream and Smoked Trout (page 63), to serve with apéritifs.

1½ cups unbleached all-purpose flour
½ cup medium rye flour, preferably
* stone-ground*
1 tablespoon baking powder

1 tablespoon caraway seeds
1¼ teaspoons salt
7 tablespoons chilled unsalted butter
10 to 12 tablespoons cold milk

1. Preheat oven to 425° F.
2. In a medium-large bowl, combine flours, baking powder, caraway seeds, and salt. Cut in butter using your fingertips, a pastry blender, or two knives until

mixture resembles coarse meal. Add 10 tablespoons milk and toss with fork until just blended, adding more milk if necessary. Do not overmix.

3. Turn dough out onto lightly floured surface and knead 4 to 5 times to blend completely. Roll out to a ¼-inch thickness and cut into 2-inch rounds. Place an inch apart on unbuttered baking sheets and bake 10 to 12 minutes or until light golden on top. Serve piping hot with butter and jam.

Makes 24 2-inch biscuits.

Buckwheat Biscuits

. . .

Dars buckwheat cakes an' Injun batter,
Makes you fat and a little bit fatter . . .

—Daniel D. Emmett, "Dixie,"
written in 1859

WHILE BUCKWHEAT FLOUR was frequently used in the South for making buckwheat pancakes (sometimes in combinations with cornmeal and/or wheat flour), it is seldom found in other breads.

At one time buckwheat was grown in parts of Virginia, West Virginia, and North Carolina, but this fruit (botanically speaking, buckwheat is a fruit) grows best in cooler climates so it was never an important commercial crop in the South. Its past is still celebrated, however, every autumn in Preston County, West Virginia, in an annual buckwheat festival. (Preston County was named after James Payton Preston, Revolutionary War hero and governor of Virginia from 1816 to 1819.)

These biscuits are quick and easy to make. Serve them hot with butter and cherry preserves for breakfast or tea. Or, serve with butter or crème fraîche to accompany soups such as Ramp and Potato Soup with Caraway (page 83) and Sweet Potato Soup with Pine Nut Butter (page 94), or your favorite borscht recipe. For an easy, elegant hors d'oeuvre to accompany Champagne, cut into tiny rounds and top with crème fraîche and caviar (see recipe, page 64).

1¾ cups unbleached all-purpose flour
¼ cup buckwheat flour
1 tablespoon baking powder
1½ teaspoons salt

4 tablespoons chilled unsalted butter
3 tablespoons chilled shortening
10 to 12 tablespoons cold milk

1. Preheat oven to 425° F.

2. In a medium bowl, combine flours, baking powder, and salt. Using your fingertips, a pastry blender, or two knives cut in butter and shortening until mixture resembles coarse meal. Add 10 tablespoons of milk and toss with a fork until just blended, adding 2 tablespoons more milk if necessary. Knead dough on lightly floured surface 3 to 4 times. Roll out to ¼-inch thickness and cut into 2-inch rounds (see note). Place an inch apart on ungreased baking sheets and bake in upper third of oven 10 to 12 minutes or until bottoms are just beginning to turn pale golden.

Makes about 20 2-inch biscuits.

Cornmeal and Cornbreads

IT HAS BEEN SAID that in 1607 the Algonquins showed the Jamestown settlers how to plant corn, and by 1614 there were about 500 acres of the native grain. Imported European grains were scarce in the seventeenth century. Corn not only grew well in the Southeast, but it yielded more to the acre than European grains and it was easy to harvest and store, so, it wasn't long before almost all the wealthy planters in Virginia and Maryland were growing corn in the Chesapeake Bay area. Because of the scarcity of wheat, cornmeal naturally found its way into the bread baking of all classes. And, according to eighteenth-century Virginia historian Robert Beverley, there were wealthy planters who, even though they could obtain wheat for bread baking, ". . . rather chose the [corn] pone."

Many kinds of cornbread developed during the seventeenth and eighteenth centuries. At their simplest, they were made from cornmeal, salt, and water, then shaped and cooked a variety of ways. Corn pone was perhaps the very first cornbread. Its name comes from the Indian word *apone,* or *apan,* meaning

Breads

baked. Corn pone refers to the flat, broad cornmeal cakes the Native Americans baked in ashes, a cooking technique recorded as early as 1612. Local settlers adopted the method and soon it was called simply pone or corn pone. This bread has also been called ashcake, and the batter was sometimes wrapped in corn husks (like a tamale) before it was placed in the coals. This bread was also sometimes baked on the blade of a hoe, hence the name hoecakes. Because this dense, firm bread traveled well, some books suggest that the word Johnny cake is a derivation of the word "Journey." Others suggest that the word comes from *joniken,* a native word for a dish of flat, fried cornmeal cakes. In many old Southern cookbooks, Johnny cake made with cornmeal is called "corn Journey," differentiating it from "rice Journey," which was made with rice. Early cookbooks call for baking Johnny cakes before a fire, probably on a hoe, wooden plank, or stone. Names for these simple cornbreads varied from place to place, and what one area called an ashcake another called a Journey cake.

Later, with the advent of the stove, the breads were baked in the oven or on top of the stove in a skillet or on a griddle. One of these later breads was the corn dodger. Corn dodgers are usually made with the same ingredients as corn pones, ashcakes, hoecakes, and Johnny cakes, but their cooking technique isn't limited to baking. They can be fried in fat or boiled in water or broth like a dumpling. (To confuse matters even more, another colloquial name for this bread when it is baked or fried is dog bread.)

Recipes for Hot Water Cornbread do not appear in many Southern cookbooks. In fact, I never even tasted it until a recent visit to The Science Hill Inn in Shelbyville, Kentucky, where the Hot Water Cornbread is reason enough to travel to the Bluegrass State. This appropriately named bread has the same ingredients as the aforementioned cornbreads, but the water added to the cornmeal is boiling hot. This causes the grains of cornmeal to soften and expand more quickly than in cold water, so the texture of the bread is different.

As the New World evolved, so did these simple cornbreads. Butter, cream, and milk were added for richness and a more tender crumb. Rye, wheat, and rice flours added flavor and texture to the cornmeal mixture while eggs, baking soda (developed shortly after the Civil War), baking powder (devised in 1868), and commercial yeast acted as leavening agents. Sweeteners, such as sugar, honey, molasses, and sorghum syrup, and savory additions, such as onions, black pepper, and spices, took these breads into another dimension. What resulted was a wide array of cornmeal-based batter breads, spoon breads, muffins, loaf breads, fritters, hush puppies, and a variety of skillet breads.

White versus Yellow

Although yellow cornmeal nationally surpasses white by far in sales, in the South white cornmeal is—and has always been—the preferred choice. This may be because at one time there were fewer hybrid yellow corns, and people simply became accustomed to white meal. While some recipes in Southern cookbooks call for white cornmeal, most do not specify cornmeal color. But this may be because white was preferred in the South and authors may not have felt it necessary to specify. In his *Food and Drink in America: A History,* Edward Hooker states that, in the late nineteenth century, Northern millers—who used yellow corn—removed the germ. It is the germ that contains the fat, most of the minerals, and much of the flavor, so the result was a meal scorned by some Southerners, who prefer a more flavorful meal. In the recipes that follow, white and yellow cornmeal may be used interchangeably.

Some Southern mills grind white corn exclusively. My father, although raised on white cornmeal, recalls being taught that yellow meal was more nutritious. In fact, Dad was right: yellow cornmeal contains vitamin A, of which white cornmeal has none.

I think the difference in taste between yellow and white cornmeal is negligible. What is important is how the meal is ground: stone-ground meals have a stronger true corn flavor and aroma, and I heartily recommend it. (For more about cornmeal, see "Grits, Grains, and Beans," page 251.)

Self-Rising Cornmeal

Self-rising cornmeal is available throughout the South, and is a staple for making cornbread, dumplings, etc. Self-rising cornmeal mix (also called cornmeal mix) has flour added along with baking powder and salt. Some mixes also contain dehydrated buttermilk. Because of the added flour, cornmeal mixes yield baked goods with a slightly lighter texture than plain self-rising cornmeal. Since plain cornmeal is always available, that is what I call for in the recipes that follow.

Rich Buttermilk Cornbread

. . .

CLASSIC SOUTHERN CORNBREAD is made with white cornmeal, is never sweetened, and is often baked in a cast-iron skillet—heated and well greased with bacon drippings—which produces a satisfying, golden-brown crust. In many old Southern cookbooks, cornbread and corn muffins do not contain regular flour, but rather cornmeal, salt, fat, milk or buttermilk, egg, baking powder, and baking soda, which results in a simpler "cornier" flavor than those that combine cornmeal with flour. Here, I've used butter and buttermilk in place of lard and regular milk for richness and flavor, making this savory bread more than just a vehicle for gravy or pot liquor; it is flavorful enough to serve on its own with sweet butter and strawberry preserves for breakfast or tea. Regular milk can be substituted for the buttermilk, and vegetable oil can be used in place of the butter. It is also good with Shad Roe with Balsamic Vinegar and Capers (page 146), Grilled Catfish with Two Sauces (page 154), and Spicy Fried Chicken (page 182).

1 cup unbleached all-purpose flour
1 cup cornmeal, preferably stone-ground
4 teaspoons baking powder
1 teaspoon salt
½ teaspoon baking soda (omit if using regular milk)

1 large egg
1½ cups buttermilk (or 1¼ cups regular milk)
4 tablespoons unsalted butter, melted and cooled (or substitute vegetable oil)

1. Preheat oven to 425° F.

2. In a medium bowl, combine flour, cornmeal, baking powder, salt, and baking soda and whisk to blend thoroughly. In a separate bowl, beat egg with buttermilk, then beat in butter. Add liquid ingredients to dry ingredients and stir with a wooden spoon until just blended; do not overmix.

3. Turn batter into a greased 8-by-8-inch baking pan and bake in the center of the oven 20 to 25 minutes or until edges are golden-brown and bread is springy to the touch in the center. Serve hot with butter.

Makes 16 2-inch squares or 9 2¾-inch squares.

Note To make cornsticks, heat a well-greased cornstick pan in the preheated oven for at least 15 minutes. Add 1 rounded tablespoon of batter to each cornstick mold. Bake 10 to 12 minutes or until edges are golden-brown. Makes 14 to 18 cornsticks.

Whole Wheat Cornsticks
· · ·

SURPRISINGLY, very few Southern cookbooks mention cornsticks or give recipes for them. I suppose the authors assumed the readers knew that cornsticks could be made simply by spooning basic cornmeal batter into sizzling hot cornstick molds. The recipe here has whole wheat flour, which lends a subtle, earthy flavor, and a good amount of butter, which yields a delicate and refined crumb. These cornsticks wear a humble guise yet are elegant enough to accompany sophisticated party fare. Heating the pans before adding the batter makes their outsides crisp, the same effect as using a hot cast-iron skillet. Oil may be substituted for butter, but the results, to me, are not quite as tasty. Serve cornsticks warm with sweet butter and lemon or grapefruit marmalade for breakfast or brunch, or in lieu of or in addition to rolls or bread for lunch or dinner.

Bacon drippings, shortening, or vege-
  table oil, to grease molds
1 cup cornmeal, preferably stone-
  ground
½ cup whole wheat flour
½ cup unbleached all-purpose flour
1 tablespoon baking powder
1 teaspoon sugar

1 teaspoon salt
½ teaspoon baking soda
1 large egg, beaten
1½ cups milk
½ cup (1 stick) unsalted butter,
  melted and cooled (or substitute
  vegetable oil)

1. Preheat oven to 425° F.

2. Grease cornstick molds with drippings, shortening, or oil and place in preheated oven for at least 15 minutes to heat.

3. In a large bowl, mix cornmeal, flours, baking powder, sugar, salt, and baking soda. In a separate bowl, beat egg and milk together, then beat in the butter. Make a well in the center of the dry ingredients and add the liquid

Breads
■

ingredients. Beat the liquid ingredients with a fork, gradually incorporating the dry ingredients. Do not overmix.

4. Remove hot cornstick pans from the oven. Spoon a heaping tablespoon of batter into each mold. Bake in the center of the oven 10 to 12 minutes or until golden-brown on bottom and center springs back when pressed lightly. Cool in pans for 1 minute, then remove from molds with tip of a kitchen knife. Serve warm with butter.

Makes 16 to 18 cornsticks.

Note To make whole wheat cornbread, turn the batter into a greased 8-by-8-inch baking pan and bake 20 to 25 minutes or until golden-brown around the edges. To make whole wheat cornmeal madeleines, turn the batter into generously buttered madeleine molds and bake 8 to 10 minutes or until golden-brown on bottom. (Because this batter does not yield a bread as fine grained as a genuine madeleine batter, the madeleine molds will not leave as clear an imprint on the cornbread. The madeleine shape, however, is charming and a nice alternative to cornsticks and cornbread.) Makes about 18 madeleines.

Crusty Cornmeal Yeast Bread

• • •

THIS WAS ONE of the first recipes that I developed when I began this book. Why not, I asked myself, create a bread with a light cornmeal flavor with the crackling, crisp crust of a French baguette? It was a success, and has become one of my favorite recipes. This bread is denser than French bread, but has a lighter crumb than standard Southern corn muffins, cornsticks, and cornbread. Slice it on the diagonal and serve as you would French bread, to accompany lunch or dinner, or with butter and damson plum preserves for breakfast or afternoon tea. Or slice the loaf very thinly, toast, and serve as a vehicle for Southern liver pudding, or with pork rillettes, foie gras, or chicken liver mousse to accompany apéritifs. Or, top with finely grated cheese, broil until bubbly, and float on top of soups such as the Collard Greens and Black-Eyed Pea Soup (page 100).

2 packages active dry yeast
Pinch of sugar
1½ cups warm (105° to 110° F)
  water
3 to 3¾ cups unbleached all-purpose
  flour
1 cup yellow cornmeal, preferably
  stone-ground

4 teaspoons salt
1 egg yolk beaten with 1 tablespoon
  milk, for glazing (Note: Egg glaze
  results in a shiny golden crust.
  For a crackly crisp crust, omit the
  glaze and spritz the uncooked
  loaves with water just before baking)

1. In a small bowl, mix yeast and sugar with 1 cup of the water and let stand until bubbly, about 5 minutes.

2. In a large bowl mix 3 cups of the flour with the cornmeal and salt. Add the remaining ½ cup water and the dissolved yeast mixture and stir until well combined.

3. Turn the dough out onto a lightly floured work surface and knead 10 minutes or until smooth and elastic, kneading in additional flour as needed. Place dough in lightly oiled bowl and turn to coat. Cover and let rise in a warm place until doubled in bulk, about 2 hours.

4. Punch down dough, cover, and let rise again until doubled in bulk, about 1½ hours.

5. Preheat oven to 425° F.

6. Divide dough into 4 equal portions and use your palms to roll each portion into a 12-inch-long loaf. Place the loaves on a baking sheet that has been lightly sprinkled with cornmeal.

7. Brush tops of loaves with egg glaze, if desired. Using a sharp knife, cut diagonal slashes 2 inches apart along the length of the loaves. Let dough rest 5 minutes. Brush with another coat of egg glaze. (Or if using water, spritz loaves lightly at this point.) Bake in the center of the oven for 18 to 20 minutes, or until loaves sound hollow when tapped on the bottom.

Makes 4 12-inch loaves.

Note To make crusty cornmeal rolls, proceed as directed through step 5. Divide dough into 12 equal pieces. Roll each piece into a ball and place on a baking sheet lightly sprinkled with cornmeal. Let rise 30 minutes. Brush with water (for a crisp crust) or egg glaze (for a shiny, golden crust). With a sharp knife cut an "X" on top of each roll. Bake 12 to 14 minutes or until beginning to turn golden-brown on top. Serve hot with butter. Makes 1 dozen rolls.

Soft Cornmeal Buns

· · ·

WHILE A NUMBER OF RECIPES appear in Southern cookbooks for sweet potato buns (which were somewhat of a Virginia specialty at one time) and basic, wheat flour yeast rolls, there are very few recipes given for cornmeal yeast rolls. It might be assumed that the making of yeast rolls was reserved for the more refined wheat flour.

In her notes on Mary Randolph's *The Virginia House-wife* (1824), Karen Hess says that the author's recipe for basic wheat bread, which instructs that the dough be formed into rolls rather than large loaves, is "a telling note." According to Hess, in the mid-nineteenth century, large loaves were associated with the lower classes and since many Virginia colonists had an aristocratic heritage (or feigned one), it is natural that the author, a Virginia lady, would call for delicately sized individual rolls rather than a great, hulking, communal loaf.

Serve these soft, light, golden-colored buns warm with butter at lunch or dinner. Or, use in sandwiches. Try them with Lorraine Eppler's Crab Cakes with Smithfield Ham and Lemon-Caper Mayonnaise (page 170), pork barbecue, or sliced leftover pork roast with mustard, tomato, lettuce, and freshly cracked pepper. It also makes a terrific vehicle for a BLT, or a post-holiday country ham and turkey sandwich.

1 cup milk
4 tablespoons butter, diced
1 package active dry yeast
¼ cup warm (105° F to 110° F) water

2¾ cups unbleached all-purpose flour
½ cup cornmeal
1 tablespoon sugar
2 teaspoons salt

1. In a small saucepan scald milk. Remove from heat, add butter and stir until melted. Cool to 80° F.

2. In a cup sprinkle yeast over warm water. Stir to mix, then let stand 5 minutes or until bubbly. Add to cooled butter mixture and stir to blend.

3. In a bowl mix flour, cornmeal, sugar, and salt. Make a well in the center, add liquid ingredients, and stir well to mix.

4. On a lightly floured surface knead 10 minutes or until smooth and elastic.

5. Place in a lightly oiled bowl, cover, and let rise in a warm place 45 minutes or until doubled in bulk. Punch down, cover, and let rise again until doubled in bulk, about 20 minutes.

6. Divide dough into 10 equal pieces. Roll into balls and place several inches apart on lightly greased baking sheets. Invert 4 small glasses on the corners of the baking sheet and drape a tea towel over the dough balls to cover them without touching. Let rise in a warm place 1 hour.

7. Preheat oven to 375° F.

8. Remove tea towel and glasses. Bake rolls 15 minutes, or until they are light golden and sound hollow when tapped on the bottom.

Makes 10 buns.

Black Pepper Ham Bread with Herb Butter

• • •

Hog-chitlins and hot cracklin' bread. Must get some. The whole hog or none.

—Thomas Wolfe,
Look Homeward, Angel

THIS VARIATION on cracklin' cornbread (a Dixie favorite traditionally made in the fall at hog-killing time when cracklings are abundant) is a hearty accompaniment to composed salads and to soups such as Sweet Potato Soup with Pine Nut Butter (page 94), Jerusalem Artichoke Soup (page 92), or "Pot Likker" Soup (page 90). This bread can also be used for sandwiches. Spread with herbed butter (or herbed mayonnaise if you prefer) and top with thinly sliced Monterey Jack or cheddar for a variation on the basic ham and cheese sandwich.

Breads

■

HAM BREAD

1 package active dry yeast

½ cup warm (105° to 110° F) water

3 tablespoons unsalted butter, melted and cooled

2 cups buttermilk, room temperature

2 teaspoons salt

2 teaspoons freshly ground black pepper

2 tablespoons sugar

½ teaspoon ground red pepper (cayenne)

5½ to 6 cups unbleached all-purpose flour

1 cup yellow cornmeal, preferably stone-ground

2½ cups minced Smithfield or other dry-cured country ham (see page 481 for mail-order source)

HERB BUTTER

½ cup (1 stick) lightly salted butter, room temperature

½ cup chopped fresh chives (or ¼ cup chopped, dried chives) or ½ cup minced fresh parsley

1 tablespoon freshly squeezed lemon juice

Salt and freshly ground white pepper, to taste

1. To make bread: In a large bowl, sprinkle yeast into the water and stir to mix. Let stand 5 minutes or until bubbly. Add butter, buttermilk, salt, black pepper, sugar, and red pepper. Stir to blend and add 5 cups of the flour or just enough to make a soft dough that comes away from the sides of bowl and collects around a spoon (or dough hook, if using an electric mixer). Stir in cornmeal.

2. Turn out onto a lightly floured board and knead until dough is smooth and elastic, adding more flour if necessary. Knead in the minced ham. Place dough into a large, oiled bowl, and turn to coat. Cover and let rise in a warm place until doubled in bulk, about 2 hours.

3. Sprinkle 2 baking sheets with cornmeal. Punch down dough, shape into 2 rounds and place on baking sheets. Cover lightly and let rise until doubled in bulk, about 2 hours.

4. Preheat oven to 375° F.

5. Brush or spritz loaves with water and bake 30 to 40 minutes, or until loaves sound hollow when tapped on the bottom.

6. To make herb butter: In a bowl, beat together all the herb butter ingredients. Refrigerate until ready to use. Makes about ½ cup. Serve bread warm with the herb butter.

Makes 2 7-inch round loaves

Muffins

IN THE MID-1980S, muffin mania hit the country with a vengeance. Bakery concoctions that contained everything from zucchini to wild rice *looked* like muffins—nestled into their fluted paper cups—but were a far cry from their predecessors made by early American cooks.

Nineteenth-century muffin recipes generally call for flour, salt, yeast, water, and sometimes eggs. This batter was left to rise, then poured into ring-shaped forms on a hot griddle. They were cooked until puffed and golden-brown. These early muffins, English in origin, were similar to crumpets. Their difference was a subtle one, as described by Mrs. Beeton, the author of *Mrs. Beeton's Book of Household Management* (1859): "Crumpets . . . are made in the same manner as muffins; only, in making the mixture [for crumpets], let it be more like a batter than a dough."

The muffins made by nineteenth-century Southerners are more like what we now call "English muffins." The evolution of the muffins suggests that when baking powder was developed, it gradually replaced the yeast in the early muffin recipes. This process can be seen in *Housekeeping in Old Virginia* (1879) where some muffin recipes are leavened with yeast, others with baking soda, and one with egg whites. Nineteenth-century muffins were plain breads usually made of white flour. They had none of the nuts, fruits, and spices that we find in today's muffins. Savvy Southern cooks, however, often added leftover cooked rice to their muffin batter. These rice muffins were often called "Plantation Muffins."

Rye Muffins
with Figs and Black Walnuts

• • •

ALTHOUGH RYE is not a Southern-grown grain, I find it marries well with the earthy flavors of figs and black walnuts in this recipe. Substitute raisins for the figs, if you like, and use California walnuts if you aren't a black-walnut advocate. The resulting muffins will still be rich and deeply flavored.

1¼ cups unbleached all-purpose flour
¼ cup plus 1 tablespoon rye flour
1 teaspoon baking powder
¾ teaspoon baking soda
1 teaspoon salt
1 large egg
½ cup firmly packed brown sugar
¾ cup milk

5 tablespoons unsalted butter, melted
  and cooled (or substitute vegetable
  oil)
¾ cup diced dried figs (I prefer
  Calamyrna figs from California)
¼ cup chopped black walnuts (see
  page 481 for mail-order source)

1. Preheat oven to 375° F.
2. In a medium bowl, sift together all-purpose flour, ¼ cup rye flour, baking powder, baking soda, and salt. Set aside.
3. In a separate bowl, beat egg with sugar until smooth. Beat in milk, then the melted butter. Add to the dry ingredients and stir until just combined, about 15 strokes. (Batter will be lumpy; do not overmix.)
4. In a small bowl toss figs and walnuts with remaining tablespoon of rye flour. Fold into the batter.
5. Fill 10 greased or paper-lined muffin tins ⅔ full (about ⅓ cup batter in each) and bake 14 to 18 minutes or until golden-brown and a toothpick comes out clean when inserted in center. Cool 1 to 2 minutes in tins, then unmold and cool on racks. Serve warm or at room temperature with sweet butter.

Makes 10 muffins.

Whole Wheat Peanut Butter–Raisin Muffins

▪ ▪ ▪

THESE NOT-TOO-SWEET muffins are hearty and wholesome. Had George Washington Carver witnessed the muffin mania of the 1980s, he'd have surely added a muffin recipe to his peanut repertoire. Serve these with breakfast or as an afternoon snack with a glass of milk.

6 tablespoons butter (or vegetable oil, see note)

½ cup peanut butter, preferably crunchy (see note)

1½ cups unbleached all-purpose flour

1½ teaspoons baking powder

1 teaspoon baking soda

½ cup whole wheat flour

1¼ teaspoon salt

¾ teaspoon cinnamon

Generous pinch ground nutmeg

1 large egg

¾ cup firmly packed light brown sugar

1 cup milk

1 cup golden raisins

1. Preheat oven to 375° F.

2. In a medium saucepan melt butter over low heat. Add peanut butter and stir until smooth. Remove from heat and cool to room temperature. Set aside. (Note: If using vegetable oil instead of butter, melt peanut butter over low heat, add oil and whisk until smooth; cool.)

3. In a large bowl sift together all-purpose flour, baking powder, and baking soda. Stir in whole wheat flour, salt, cinnamon, and nutmeg. Set aside.

4. In a separate bowl, beat egg with sugar until smooth. Beat in milk, then beat in cooled peanut butter mixture. Add to dry ingredients and stir until just combined, about 15 to 20 strokes. (Batter will be slightly lumpy; do not overmix.) Fold in raisins. Divide batter among 12 buttered or paper-lined muffin tins (about ⅓ cup in each) and bake 15 to 18 minutes or until golden-brown and a toothpick comes out clean when inserted in center. Do not overcook. Cool 1 to 2 minutes in tins; unmold, then cool on racks. Serve warm or at room temperature with sweet butter (or more peanut butter).

Makes 12 muffins.

Note Although vegetable oil may be substituted for butter, the resulting muffins will not be as rich-tasting. If you don't have crunchy peanut butter on hand, add ½ cup chopped unsalted roasted peanuts along with the raisins.

Molasses
Cornmeal Muffins

• • •

LIKE CLASSIC SOUTHERN CORNBREAD, classic Southern cornmeal muffins are flourless, consisting only of cornmeal, eggs, milk or buttermilk, baking soda, lard or butter, and sometimes salt. They are simple and savory, and meant to accompany a meal. When I first moved to New York, I noticed the popularity of corn muffins for breakfast (usually taken on the run, at one's desk or at the bus stop), and I developed a taste for the sweeter, more refined Yankee-style bread. The recipe here is a compromise between the cakelike breads of the North and the coarse, crumbly muffins of the South. They have a distinct molasses flavor, and can stand on their own with coffee or tea and fresh fruit for a light breakfast.

1 cup yellow cornmeal, preferably stone-ground
1 cup unbleached all-purpose flour
1 tablespoon baking powder
1 teaspoon baking soda
3/4 teaspoon salt

4 tablespoons unsalted butter (or substitute vegetable oil)
1/2 cup molasses
1 cup buttermilk
1 large egg

1. Preheat oven to 400° F.
2. In a large bowl, combine dry ingredients.
3. In a medium saucepan, melt butter over low heat. Add molasses and stir until well mixed. Set aside. (Note: If using oil, whisk with molasses in a small bowl.)
4. In a medium bowl, beat buttermilk and egg. Beat in molasses mixture, then stir liquid ingredients into dry ingredients. Mix until just combined; do not overmix.
5. Fill buttered or paper-lined 2-inch muffin tins 2/3 full and bake 12 to 15 minutes or until toothpick comes out clean.

Makes 12 2-inch muffins.

Whole Wheat
Lemon Sally Lunn Bread
• • •

RECIPES FOR SALLY LUNN BREAD date at least as far back as 1770. During that same period, Sally Lunn buns were popular in Bath, England, where they were said to have been made by a young woman of that name who sold them in the streets. Others say that the recipe was created by George Washington's cook. Still others claim the bread's name is a corruption of the French "soleil et lune" (sun and moon), because of its bright, puffy appearance. Whatever its origins, Sally Lunn bread became very popular in the South—particularly in Virginia— during the nineteenth century. It was traditionally a rich yeast bread baked in a Turk's-head mold or muffin rings and served with tea. Later Sally Lunn recipes began to appear in the form of a quick bread, using baking powder instead of yeast. My recipe is an adaptation of one created by colleague and fellow Southerner Jean Anderson. Instead of granulated sugar, I use brown, and rather than all white flour, I use part whole wheat. The result is a hearty, wholesome bread—with a bit of zip from added lemon zest. And if you love homemade bread but hate to knead, you're in luck: simply stir this batter 100 strokes. Serve warm or toasted with sweet butter as a breakfast or a tea bread.

2 packages active dry yeast
6 tablespoons warm (105° to 110° F)
 water
¼ cup firmly packed light brown
 sugar
¾ cup milk, room temperature
1 teaspoon salt

½ cup (1 stick) unsalted butter,
 room temperature
4 large eggs, room temperature
2 teaspoons grated lemon zest
3 cups unbleached all-purpose flour
1 cup whole wheat flour
Juice of half a lemon

1. In a medium bowl, mix yeast, water, and a pinch of the sugar and let stand 5 minutes or until bubbly. Mix in milk and salt.

2. In a separate bowl, cream the butter and the remaining sugar. Beat in eggs one at a time. Beat in lemon zest.

Breads

■

3. In another bowl, combine the flours. Add flours to the butter mixture alternately with the yeast mixture; beat in lemon juice. Cover and let rise 1 hour in a warm place, or until doubled in bulk.

4. Beat 100 strokes then turn the dough into a buttered 9-by-5-inch loaf pan (or two 5¾-by-3-by-2⅛-inch pans) and let rise 30 minutes or until doubled in bulk.

5. Preheat oven to 350° F.

6. Bake 30 minutes (about 20 to 25 minutes for smaller loaves) or until loaf sounds hollow when tapped lightly on the bottom. Cool briefly in the pan; turn out onto a rack to cool completely.

Makes 1 9-by-5-inch loaf or 2 5¾-by-3-inch loaves.

Whole Wheat Brown Rice Philpy

■ ■ ■

IN *The Dictionary of American Food and Drink,* John Mariani defines *philpy* simply as a "South Carolina rice bread," implying that the name apparently has obscure origins.

Rice, which was planted in South Carolina near the end of the seventeenth century, became a principal crop. Many Southern nineteenth-century bread recipes often combine wheat flour with other farinaceous ingredients, such as cornmeal, mashed potatoes, hominy, or the ubiquitous grain, rice. Some examples include Plantation muffins (crumpet-like breads with rice), rice biscuits, rice drop cakes, and the deep South's version of Journey (or Johnny) cake, so-called "rice journey," which is made of rice and/or rice flour (instead of cornmeal), salt, and water. But perhaps the most prevalent of all the rice quick breads is philpy, which is usually made simply of cooked rice, rice flour or wheat flour, eggs, milk, and leavenings. It is baked in a shallow pan (usually a pie plate or skillet), cut into wedges, and served piping hot with plenty of butter. My version is made with brown rice and whole wheat flour, which yields more wholesome bread that has a heartier, nutty flavor. It is a very easy, very quick bread that makes delicious use of leftover rice. Split and serve piping hot with butter alongside eggs and bacon, soups, stews, or salads. Philpy is best served just after it is baked.

¾ cup cooked brown rice, room
   temperature
½ cup plus 2 tablespoons buttermilk
1 large egg
¾ cup unbleached all-purpose flour

¼ cup whole wheat flour
½ teaspoon salt
½ teaspoon baking powder
½ teaspoon baking soda

1. Preheat oven to 450° F.

2. In a blender or food processor, process rice with 2 tablespoons of the buttermilk for 1 minute. (Note: Mixture will be mealy.) Add remaining ½ cup buttermilk and process until blended. Add egg and process to mix.

3. In a bowl, combine flours, salt, baking powder, and baking soda. Fold in rice mixture until just blended. Turn the batter into a buttered 9-inch cake pan and bake in the center of the oven 25 minutes, or until deep golden-brown on top. Cut into 6 to 8 wedges and serve hot with sweet butter.

Serves 6 to 8.

Golden Buttermilk Scones

■ ■ ■

THESE RICHLY FLAVORED triangles are a cross between cornbread, buttermilk biscuits, and a classic scone. They're good for breakfast, brunch, or tea. Serve warm with butter and raspberry preserves.

1½ cups unbleached all-purpose flour
1 cup cake flour (not self-rising)
2 tablespoons plus 1 teaspoon baking
   powder
1 teaspoon baking soda
1 cup cornmeal, preferably stone-
   ground
6 tablespoons sugar

¼ teaspoon salt
10 tablespoons cold, unsalted butter,
   cut into small pieces
¾ to 1¼ cups buttermilk
1 cup golden raisins
1 egg yolk beaten with 1 tablespoon
   milk, to glaze

Breads

■

1. Preheat oven to 350° F.

2. In a medium bowl, sift flours, baking powder, and baking soda. Stir in cornmeal, sugar, and salt. Cut in butter with your fingertips, a pastry blender, or two knives until mixture resembles coarse meal. Add buttermilk in small amounts, stirring continuously until just combined, adding just enough buttermilk so that mixture comes together to form a dough. Do not overmix.

3. Turn dough onto lightly floured board and knead in raisins, being careful not to overwork the dough. Divide dough into 2 equal portions. (Note: To make smaller, tea-sized scones divide dough into 4 portions.) Roll or pat each portion into a circle about ½ inch thick. Using a floured knife, cut each circle into 8 equal wedges. Place wedges ½ inch apart on lightly floured baking sheets. Brush tops with glaze. Bake in the center of oven 12 to 18 minutes, or until tops are rich golden-brown.

Makes 16 3-inch scones, or 16 1½-inch, tea-sized scones.

Note Scones are best served immediately, but can be frozen and reheated (without thawing) in a moderate oven until warmed through.

Cornmeal Dropped Scones

• • •

TRADITIONALLY, scones are made either from a rich dough that is rolled and cut into wedges (see Golden Buttermilk Scones, page 47) or from a batter that is dropped onto a hot skillet or griddle to make dropped scones, also sometimes called Scotch Pancakes. The addition of cornmeal to this rather traditional dropped scone recipe adds a Southern touch, and also makes them a close cousin to the more savory hush puppies. Cornmeal Dropped Scones have a higher proportion of all-purpose flour to cornmeal than do hush puppies, so they are lighter and a bit more refined. Serve them hot as a bread, alongside grilled pork chops or roast chicken, or for breakfast or tea with crème fraîche and raspberry preserves. Alternately, fry the batter in fried-chicken drippings to make what are called "chicken biscuits" in some rural parts of the South.

⅓ cup cornmeal, preferably stone-
   ground
⅔ cup unbleached all-purpose flour
½ teaspoon sugar
½ teaspoon baking soda

½ teaspoon salt
½ teaspoon baking powder
1 large egg
½ cup buttermilk
Oil or drippings, for frying

1. In a medium bowl, combine dry ingredients. In a separate bowl, beat egg and buttermilk. Add liquid ingredients to dry ingredients and blend until just combined. Do not overmix.

2. In a large skillet, heat ¼ inch oil over medium-high heat. Drop batter by scant tablespoons and cook about 1 minute each side, or until golden-brown. Drain briefly on paper towels and serve hot.

Makes about 18 1½-inch scones.

Double Corn Hush Puppies

▪ ▪ ▪

WHEN THOSE LIVING NORTH of the Mason-Dixon line hear the term "Southern food," hush puppies are among the foods that come to mind. While hush puppies are without question a Southern classic, they actually are a relatively "new" dish, since few—if any—recipes for them appear until the twentieth century. Hush puppies are said to have originated at a fish fry, when a mound of cornmeal batter (for the fish) was dropped into bubbling hot fat then tossed to hungry yelping dogs with the admonishment, "Hush, puppy!"

Hush puppies are usually served at fish fries and are available at some hickory-pit barbecue joints. Recipes vary widely, and may contain an array of seasonings such as garlic, onion, bell peppers, herbs, ground red pepper (cayenne), beer, or cheddar cheese. Hush puppies are usually savory and even though they are deep-fried, Southerners like to gild the lily by spreading the split-open piping hot bread with butter.

The hush puppies here are an adaptation of a recipe from Nora Lee Rorie of Monroe, North Carolina. They are the most ethereal hush puppies I've ever eaten. While Nora Lee uses self-rising flour, I substitute the more widely available all-purpose flour. I also add fresh-cooked corn. Since I don't like to deep-fry, I cook these cornmeal fritters in only ⅛ inch of oil, a method I find safer and less costly than deep-frying. The variations provide extra serving ideas: try the cheese version to serve with cocktails, the fresh thyme hush puppies to accompany roast chicken, game, or chops.

Shortening, or oil, for frying
½ cup cornmeal, preferably stone-
  ground
6 tablespoons unbleached all-purpose
  flour
½ teaspoon baking powder
Scant ½ teaspoon baking soda
⅛ teaspoon salt

¼ cup very finely minced white on-
  ion
⅓ cup fresh, whole corn kernels (or
  substitute thawed frozen corn),
  parboiled and drained
½ cup plus 2 tablespoons buttermilk

Variations Add ¾ cup very finely shredded sharp cheddar cheese and a pinch of ground red pepper (cayenne).

Or add 1 tablespoon fresh thyme leaves or 1 teaspoon dried thyme.

1. In a large, heavy skillet, heat ⅛ inch shortening or oil until smoking.

2. In a bowl, combine cornmeal, flour, baking powder, baking soda, and salt. Stir in onion and corn, and the variation ingredients, if using. Make a well in the center and add buttermilk. Stir until just combined; do not overmix.

3. Drop batter by teaspoonfuls into the hot oil. (Note: Do not crowd the skillet; cook hush puppies in several batches if necessary.) Cook about 2½ to 3 minutes, turning several times, or until golden-brown. Drain briefly on paper towels and serve hot.

Makes 30 to 32 hush puppies.

Appetizers and Hors d'Oeuvres

· · ·

CLASSIC SOUTHERN HORS D'OEUVRES, like the rest of Southern cooking, tend to be uncomplicated and simply flavored. Cheese straws, celery stalks stuffed with pimiento cheese, cold shrimp to dip into cocktail sauce, and crackers topped with cream cheese and a dab of pepper jelly are just a few of the unpretentious offerings passed to accompany a bourbon on the rocks. Other regional specialties include ham biscuits, Chesapeake oysters on the half shell, and Benedictine canapés (toast or crackers spread with a favorite Kentucky mixture of cream cheese, grated cucumbers, onion, salt, mayonnaise, and Tabasco). The hors d'oeuvres here are just as easy as the old favorites. And because entertaining is trouble enough, all of the recipes here have make-ahead steps, so much of the work is out of the way before guests arrive.

Pimiento-Cheese Canapés

· · ·

There was, first, the problem with lunch. We stood in the church parking lot, considering our very limited options, since it was Christmas Day. Naturally, I didn't have a thing prepared, as I had no intentions of festivity for the day. I told Judson I had some pimiento cheese—homemade, mind you—in my refrigerator . . .

—Vicki Covington,
Bird of Paradise

THIS RECIPE was inspired by one of my favorite sandwich spreads: pimiento cheese. Southerners are great sandwich lovers, especially now that the big midday meal is all but a thing of the past. Favorite hot sandwiches include crab cakes, soft-shell crabs or pork barbecue served on soft buns; fried oysters on long loaves of hollowed-out crusty French bread, and the Hot Brown, an open-faced turkey, cheese, and bacon sandwich topped with béchamel sauce made famous by Louisville's Brown Hotel. Cold Southern sandwiches include the Po' Boy and the muffaletta from New Orleans (both of these big sandwiches are made with Italian meats and cheeses), the post-holiday combo of turkey and Smithfield ham. But my all-time favorite is pimiento cheese. It was only when I was in junior high school Spanish class—hundreds of pimiento cheese sandwiches into my life—that I realized that a pimiento is a pepper. The pimientos that we buy in supermarkets are simply roasted, peeled peppers packed in brine. (You can, of course, roast and peel your own peppers.) They add a marvelously sweet counterpoint to mayonnaise and the rich, tangy cheddar cheese that binds them.

Here, I've combined Pepper Jack cheese instead of the traditional cheddar, and used butter instead of mayonnaise. Red pepper and Tabasco sauce add zip.

6 ounces Pepper Jack cheese (Monterey Jack with jalapeño peppers, or substitute cheddar), coarsely grated
6 tablespoons unsalted butter, room temperature
3 tablespoons diced, well-drained pimientos (roasted, peeled red peppers)

Salt, to taste
Pinch of ground red pepper (cayenne)
Tabasco sauce, to taste
Unsalted tostaditas (tortilla chips), or substitute toast rounds

1. Preheat broiler.
2. In a blender or food processor, combine cheese and butter until smooth. Add half the pimientos and process until smooth.
3. Transfer mixture to a bowl. Fold in remaining pimientos, the salt, ground red pepper, and Tabasco sauce.
4. If using tostaditas, spread about ½ teaspoon of the cheese mixture on each tostadita. Place on baking sheet and broil 4 inches from broiler 1 minute or until bubbly. Serve hot. Makes about 1 cup spread; enough for about 48 tostadita canapés. If using toast rounds, use about 1½ teaspoons for each 2-inch toast round.

Makes about 36 toast canapés.

Herbed Chèvre Biscuit Thins

■ ■ ■

... it is herb seasoning which turns the prose of cooking into poetry. Without herbs a cook is like a painter with nothing but coarse brushes. Or a pianist when the soft pedal sticks.

—Virginia Moore,
Virginia Is a State of Mind

ACCORDING TO HIS JOURNAL, in 1773, George Washington was served "thin wafer biscuits" with crab as a starter at a Maryland dinner. Benne seeds brought by slaves from Africa flavored crisp, savory cocktail biscuits in 1880s Charleston (these were more of a cracker than a Southern-style biscuit). But the most popular classic Southern cocktail biscuits are made with cheese. Crisp, melt-in-your-mouth cheese straws (also called cheese pennies, crumbles, or thins) have a consistency that falls somewhere between shortbread and piecrust. They are made in different shapes (rounds, strips serrated around the edges or patterned on the top), sizes (wafer thin to a half-inch thickness, medallion to finger size), and colors (well browned, light brown, or not brown at all). Besides flour, butter, and a sharp cheese such as cheddar, spice is the most important ingredient in the rolled dough. Paprika or ground red pepper (cayenne) are the most common, but some cooks use Tabasco, mustard seed, or garlic salt. Pecans or ham are also frequent additions (an old Kentucky version features a double-decker cracker sandwiching devilled ham). The recipe here is a result of my efforts to make traditional Southern biscuits with chèvre instead of shortening. What resulted is something closer to a cheese straw than a bread. Serve these with cocktails or glasses of chilled California or Australian Sauvignon Blanc.

1½ cups unbleached all-purpose flour
2 teaspoons dried thyme
2 teaspoons dried rosemary, crumbled
1¼ teaspoons salt
8 tablespoons (1 stick) chilled unsalted butter, cut into small pieces
4 ounces mild chèvre (Note: I prefer to use Southern goat cheeses,
see page 481 for mail-order source, but you can substitute a French goat cheese such as Montrachet or Bûcheron, or one from California or New York State), well chilled and cut into small pieces
1 large egg yolk beaten with 2 tablespoons milk, for glaze (optional)
3 to 4 tablespoons ice water

1. In a blender or food processor, mix flour, herbs, and salt (see note below).

2. Add the butter and cheese and pulse until mixture resembles coarse meal. Add 3 tablespoons ice water and pulse, adding more water if necessary to form a dough that just holds together. Do not overprocess or biscuit thins will be tough.

3. On a lightly floured work surface form the dough into a log 12 inches long and 1½ inches in diameter. Wrap in waxed paper and chill at least 2 hours.

4. Preheat oven to 375° F.

5. Using a large heavy sharp knife, cut dough into ³⁄₁₆-inch-thick slices. Place rounds ½ inch apart on ungreased baking sheet. Brush with egg glaze, if desired, and bake 12 to 14 minutes or until edges turn golden-brown. Flip biscuits over with a spatula and bake 4 to 5 minutes on the other side or until both sides are golden. Cool on racks. These are best served the same day they are made, but can be stored up to 5 days in an airtight container.

Makes about 4 dozen biscuit thins.

Note To make dough by hand, in a medium bowl, combine flour, thyme, rosemary, and salt. Cut in butter and cheese with your fingertips, a pastry blender, or two knives until the mixture resembles coarse meal. Add 3 tablespoons ice water and toss with a fork, adding more water if necessary to form a dough that just holds together. Proceed to step 3.

Spicy Ham and Phyllo Triangles

■ ■ ■

SOUTHERN DRY-CURED HAM, fresh fennel, ginger, and garlic baked in mini-phyllo packages can be made in advance, frozen, and reheated just before serving.

10 tablespoons unsalted butter
⅔ cup minced scallions (about 6
  scallions)

4 cloves garlic, minced
1 teaspoon grated fresh gingerroot
½ cup minced red bell pepper

½ *cup minced fennel bulb (or substi-*
  tute celery plus ½ *teaspoon fennel*
  seeds)
½ *cup minced Smithfield ham or*
  other dry-cured country ham (see
  page 481 for mail-order source)

½ *pound frozen phyllo pastry dough,*
  thawed

1. In a small skillet, melt 2 tablespoons of the butter over low heat. Add scallions, garlic, and gingerroot and cook gently until tender but not brown, about 4 to 5 minutes. Raise heat to medium-high, add pepper and fennel. Cook, stirring constantly, until crisp-tender, about 3 minutes. Add ham and mix well. Remove from heat.

2. In a small saucepan, melt the remaining butter.

3. Lay 1 sheet of phyllo on a work surface and brush the entire sheet lightly with melted butter. Place a second sheet over the buttered sheet and brush with butter. Repeat with a third sheet, brushing it lightly with butter. The fourth and final sheet should be placed on top and remain unbuttered.

4. With a sharp knife, cut through the stack lengthwise and then widthwise to divide it into 4 portions. Cut each quadrangle into 4 strips, making a total of 16 4-layer strips, each measuring approximately 6 inches by 2 inches.

5. Working with 1 4-layer strip at a time (cover the remaining strips as you work to keep them from drying out), place 1½ teaspoons of filling at the lower left corner, and fold as you would a flag to make a triangular package. Lightly brush each completed triangle with butter and lay on buttered baking sheet. Continue with remaining 15 strips of phyllo and then repeat the entire procedure, starting at step 3.

6. Preheat oven to 375° F.

7. Bake until golden-brown and crisp, about 12 to 15 minutes. Serve warm.

Makes 32 triangles.

Note To make triangles in advance, prepare as directed and bake 10 minutes or until pale golden. Cool completely, wrap well, and refrigerate up to two days or freeze up to one month. Reheat (do not thaw, if frozen) until brown just before serving.

Biscuit Pizzas
with Two Toppings
...

PIZZA ISN'T SOUTHERN, but biscuits are, and when olive oil is used instead of lard or shortening, this Southern quick bread makes a great foundation for all sorts of toppings.

1 recipe Olive Oil Biscuits (page 27)

PESTO AND MOZZARELLA TOPPING

½ cup good-quality, thick pesto sauce, chilled (Note: If pesto sauce is not chilled, it tends to make the biscuits soggy)

3 firm, ripe, medium-sized plum tomatoes, thinly sliced

Salt and freshly ground black pepper, to taste

8 ounces fresh mozzarella cheese, thinly sliced or shredded

Good-quality olive oil

HERB AND FONTINA TOPPING

3 to 4 tablespoons fresh thyme leaves (or 1½ teaspoons dried thyme)

28 to 32 fresh basil leaves

3 firm, ripe, medium-sized plum tomatoes, thinly sliced

1 cup grated fontina

Good-quality olive oil

1. Preheat oven to 425° F.

2. Prepare and bake biscuits as directed. When cooled, split the biscuits using a serrated knife. (Note: If biscuits have been made in advance and frozen, thaw slightly, then split while still cold.)

3. Preheat broiler.

4. For pesto and mozzarella topping: Lay out the biscuit halves cut-side-up. Spread ¼ teaspoon pesto sauce on each. Add a tomato slice, sprinkle lightly with salt and pepper, and top with cheese. Drizzle lightly with olive oil and place on

ungreased baking sheet. Broil 4 inches from broiler about 1 minute or until bubbly. Serve hot.

5. For herb and fontina topping: Lay out the biscuit halves cut-side-up. Sprinkle thyme on each, add a basil leaf, a tomato slice, and top with cheese. Drizzle lightly with olive oil and place on ungreased baking sheet. Broil 4 inches from broiler 1 minute or until bubbly. Serve hot.

Makes about 20 hors d'oeuvre pizzas.

Cornmeal Pizza
with Greens and Fontina
∎ ∎ ∎

IN SOME PARTS OF ITALY it is not unusual for broccoli rabe or Swiss chard to find its way onto a pizza. Collards and other Southern greens provide the same pleasant bitterness as their Italian counterparts. Here, I use a cornmeal dough, which is crisp, light, and marries beautifully with the pungent greens.

CORNMEAL CRUST

2 packages active dry yeast
Pinch of sugar
1¼ cups warm (105° to 110° F) water

2¾ cups unbleached all-purpose flour
2 teaspoons salt
¾ cup yellow cornmeal

TOPPING

¼ cup plus 2 tablespoons extra-virgin olive oil
1 medium onion, finely chopped
2 large garlic cloves, minced
2 pounds watercress or arugula, tough stems removed (see note)
Pinch of hot red pepper flakes
2 ounces very thinly sliced dry-cured

country ham, such as Smithfield (see page 481 for mail-order source), or substitute prosciutto
½ pound Italian fontina cheese, shredded
¼ pound mozzarella cheese, shredded or cut into thin slices

Appetizers and Hors d'Oeuvres

∎

1. To make the crust: In a medium bowl, combine the yeast, sugar, and warm water. Stir gently to mix, then let stand until bubbly, about 5 minutes.

2. Add 1 cup of the flour and the salt and mix thoroughly. Add the cornmeal and another cup of the flour and mix well.

3. Sprinkle the remaining flour on a work surface. Turn out the dough and knead, incorporating the flour a little at a time, until smooth and elastic, 5 to 10 minutes. Place the dough in a lightly oiled bowl and turn to coat. Cover the bowl and let rise in a warm place until doubled in bulk, about 1 hour.

4. Punch the dough down, cover, and let rise until doubled in bulk, about 1 hour longer.

5. To prepare the topping: In a large skillet, heat 2 tablespoons of the olive oil over medium-low heat. Add the onion and cook until it begins to soften, about 5 minutes. Add the garlic and cook until fragrant, about 30 seconds. Increase the heat to medium. Add the greens and cook, partially covered, tossing frequently, until they are wilted and the liquid they exude has evaporated, about 5 minutes. Stir in the hot red pepper. Drain the greens in a colander and press with a wooden spoon to force out any excess liquid. When cool enough to handle, chop coarsely and set aside.

6. Preheat the oven to 500° F. Working quickly, divide the dough into 4 equal pieces. Form each piece of dough into a ball and roll it out on a floured surface to form a pizza round ¼ inch thick and 7 to 8 inches in diameter.

7. Heat a large, heavy, ungreased baking sheet, unglazed terra-cotta pizza dish, or bread tiles in the oven for 5 minutes. Place 2 dough rounds on the hot baking sheet, brush each lightly with 1½ teaspoons of the oil and return to the oven. Bake until pale golden-brown, 8 to 12 minutes. Repeat with the other 2 rounds.

8. Sprinkle the ham on the pizza crusts, leaving a ½-to-1-inch border. Divide the greens equally among the 4 pizzas, covering the ham. Top with the cheeses, distributing them evenly and covering the greens completely. Drizzle on the remaining 2 tablespoons oil. Bake the pizzas, two at a time, until the cheese is melted and bubbly and the crust is golden-brown, 5 to 8 minutes. Cut into wedges.

Serves 6 to 8 as a first course or 4 as a main course.

Note To substitute kale in the topping for the watercress or arugula, wash and trim 1 pound of kale. Stack the leaves and cut into ¼-inch-wide strips. Blanch for 1 minute in boiling salted water. Drain thoroughly, then squeeze out any excess water. Cook the onion and garlic as in step 5. Add the kale and hot red pepper flakes and toss over medium heat for 1 minute. Cool, chop coarsely, and set aside. Proceed with step 6.

Cornmeal Pizza
with Bacon, Tomatoes, and Peppers
• • •

I LIKE TO USE double-smoked bacon from Virginia on these pizzas for a deep, earthy flavor.

1 recipe for cornmeal crust (see page 59)
Olive oil
½ pound bacon, crisply cooked, drained, and cut into 1-inch-long pieces
1 7-ounce jar roasted red peppers, cut into very thin strips

¼ cup chopped fresh parsley
3 medium plum tomatoes, thinly sliced
¼ cup chopped fresh basil
2 cups shredded fontina, Bel Paese, or mozzarella cheese
Freshly ground black pepper

1. To make the crust: Proceed as for Cornmeal Pizza with Greens and Fontina, steps 1 through 4.

2. Divide dough into 2 (or 4) equal pieces. Roll out on a lightly floured cutting board to ¼-inch thickness to make 2 12-inch (or 4 7-inch) pies. Let rest 5 to 10 minutes. Brush lightly with olive oil.

3. Preheat oven to 500° F. Heat heavy baking sheet, unglazed terra-cotta pizza dish, or bread tiles in the oven for 5 minutes. Slide dough onto the hot baking sheet and bake 10 minutes or until light golden-brown and crusty.

4. Top 1 large or 2 small pizzas with half of the bacon, the peppers, and ¼ cup parsley. Top remaining pizza(s) with remaining bacon, the tomatoes, and ¼ cup basil. Sprinkle pizzas with cheese and black pepper. Bake 5 to 8 minutes or until bubbly.

Makes 2 12-inch or 4 7-inch pies.

Whole Wheat Cornmeal Pizza
with Vidalia "Marmalade," Ham, and Cheese
• • •

THIS TANGY-SWEET Vidalia "marmalade" is the perfect foil to salty, smoky ham and rich, nutty fontina cheese.

DOUGH

2 packages active dry yeast
1⅓ cups warm (105° to 110° F)
   water
Pinch of sugar
2 cups unbleached all-purpose flour

2 teaspoons salt
1 cup whole wheat flour
½ cup cornmeal
3 tablespoons olive oil

VIDALIA MARMALADE

3 tablespoons olive oil
4 cups thinly sliced Vidalia onions
   (or substitute other mild onions,
   such as Walla Walla, Maui, or Bermuda onions)

1 teaspoon sugar
2 teaspoons cider vinegar

TOPPING

Olive oil
4 ounces very thinly sliced dry-cured
   country ham, such as Smithfield
   (see page 481 for mail-order
   source)

1 cup thinly sliced plum tomatoes (2
   medium plum tomatoes)
1½ cups shredded Italian fontina
Freshly ground black pepper, to taste

    1. To make the dough: In a medium bowl combine yeast with the water and sugar. Stir gently to mix, then let stand 5 minutes or until bubbly.

    2. Add 1 cup of the all-purpose flour and the salt. Mix thoroughly. Add the whole wheat flour and the cornmeal and mix thoroughly.

    3. Sprinkle the remaining all-purpose flour on a clean work surface. Remove the dough from the bowl and knead in enough flour as necessary, a little at a time. Knead 5 to 10 minutes, or until dough is smooth and elastic.

4. Place in an oiled bowl, cover, and let rise in a warm place for 45 minutes or until doubled in bulk. Punch down, shape into a ball, cover, and let rise again until doubled, about 45 minutes to an hour.

5. To make the marmalade: In a heavy saucepan, heat oil over medium heat. Add onions and sprinkle with sugar. Cover and cook over medium-low heat, stirring frequently, 30 to 40 minutes, or until deep golden-brown. Remove from heat; stir in vinegar. Makes about 1 cup.

6. Preheat oven to 475° F. Heat heavy baking sheet, unglazed terra-cotta pizza dish, or bread tiles in the oven for 5 minutes.

7. Divide dough into 2 or 4 equal pieces. On a lightly floured cutting board, roll each piece of dough into 4 7-inch circles or 2 12-inch circles ¼ inch thick. Let rest 5 to 10 minutes. Slide dough onto the hot baking sheet.

8. Brush dough lightly with olive oil and bake 10 to 15 minutes or until light golden-brown and crusty.

9. While still warm, brush lightly again with olive oil. Top with ham, tomato slices, then the Vidalia marmalade. Sprinkle with shredded cheese. Bake 5 to 8 minutes, or until hot and bubbly. Season generously with black pepper.

Makes 2 12-inch pizzas or 4 7-inch pizzas.

Caraway-Rye Biscuits
with Horseradish Cream and Smoked Trout
· · ·

SMOKED FISH and horseradish are naturals together, and I find they're always a hit on these caraway-flavored rye biscuits. Southern smoked trout is delicious, and I urge the cook to try it.

1 recipe Caraway-Rye Biscuits (page 29)
¼ cup sour cream or crème fraîche
1 tablespoon freshly grated horseradish (or substitute drained, bottled horseradish)

8 ounces smoked trout, skinned, filleted, and broken into "chevrons" (see page 481 for mail-order source)
Fresh dill, to garnish

1. Preheat oven to 425° F.

2. Prepare biscuit dough as directed.

3. On a lightly floured surface, roll out dough to a thickness of ⅛ inch. Cut into 2-inch rounds with a floured biscuit cutter. Place on unbuttered baking sheets and bake 8 to 10 minutes or until light golden-brown on top. Do not overbake. Cool on a rack.

4. In a small bowl, combine sour cream, or crème fraîche, and horseradish. Top each whole, unsplit biscuit with ½ teaspoon horseradish sauce and then a chevron of trout. Garnish with fresh dill.

Makes about 24 hors d'oeuvres.

Buckwheat Biscuits with Crème Fraîche and Caviar

• ■ •

SINCE IN RUSSIA buckwheat blini are the classic accompaniment to caviar, it seems only natural that in the South caviar be served on a biscuit made with buckwheat flour. Try caviar from the Mississippi, if it's available. It's less expensive than the imported type, and it tastes terrific.

1 recipe Buckwheat Biscuits (page 30)
6 tablespoons crème fraîche or sour cream

¼ cup caviar, preferably American sturgeon (see page 481 for mail-order source)
Dill sprigs, to garnish

1. Preheat oven to 425° F.

2. Prepare dough as directed. Roll out to ⅛-inch thickness and cut into 1½-inch rounds. Place on ungreased baking sheets and bake 8 to 10 minutes or until light golden-brown. Cool.

3. Top each whole, unsplit biscuit with crème fraîche and caviar; garnish with dill sprig.

Makes about 40 1½-inch biscuits.

Olive Oil Biscuit Canapés with Thyme Butter
or Sun-Dried Tomato Butter

· · ·

THESE SIMPLE little hors d'oeuvres are good with apéritifs like Campari, Cinzano, and Lillet, or glasses of chilled Virginia Seyval Blanc or a sparkling wine.

1 recipe Olive Oil Biscuits (page 27)
½ cup (1 stick) unsalted butter,
  room temperature
2½ tablespoons fresh thyme leaves
  (or substitute 2½ teaspoons dried

thyme), or 2½ tablespoons very
  finely minced sun-dried tomatoes
Freshly ground black pepper, to taste

1. Preheat oven to 425° F.
2. Prepare and bake biscuits as directed. Cool slightly.
3. In a bowl beat butter with either thyme or sun-dried tomatoes. Season with pepper.
4. Split the biscuits open and spread the flavored butter on the cut sides of the biscuits while they are still warm.

Makes 20 open-faced canapés.

Note If bite-sized biscuits are desired, cut dough into 1½-inch circles.

First-Course Appetizers

MANY OF THE DISHES that follow are rather rich; therefore I've kept serving sizes conservative so appetites will not be spoiled before the main course arrives. (For other first course suggestions, see recipes in "Salads," and "Soups.") There are innumerable other ways to begin a meal; don't be shy about serving something out of the ordinary to start, such as Double Corn Hush Puppies (page 49; serve three or four with homemade catsup) or vegetable dishes such as Baked Yellow Squash with Chèvre and Corn Stuffing (page 321). Just remember that when planning a menu, it is advisable to serve only one course that has an abundance of cream, butter, or other rich ingredients. Basically, if the first course is a rich one, follow it with a simple main dish for the sake of health and digestion.

Spoon Bread Soufflé with Fresh Corn Sauce

• • •

THIS ETHEREAL "BREAD" made with cornmeal may have been named after an Indian predecessor—a porridge called *suppawn* or *suppone*—or perhaps because it is often eaten with a spoon. In any case, although the term spoon bread did not appear in print until 1906 (prior to that time it was known as batter bread, corn egg bread or bachelor's cake) the dish itself has been around since colonial times. It was a Monticello favorite and is still served in many of Virginia's historic taverns and gracious old hotel dining rooms.

There has always been controversy among Southern cooks over how spoon bread should be made. Since the Civil War, however, the basic recipe has usually involved beating eggs, milk, and butter into cornmeal mush, then baking the batter in a baking dish. It is served piping hot with more butter at the table. Although some spoon breads are firm enough to slice, hold, and eat as a true bread, spoon breads are usually very soft—almost like a soufflé—and are served as a side dish (often replacing rice or mashed potatoes) in the dish in which it was baked.

Some cooks insist upon stone-ground white meal, while others contend that commercially ground yellow meal is just fine. Early variations often substitute cooked grits for cornmeal, or they call for equal portions of grits and cornmeal. Some cooks even added cooked rice to the cornmeal batter. Before the mid-nineteenth-century invention of baking powder, beaten eggs were used for leavening. (Whole eggs are called for in early recipes, separated eggs in later recipes.) Many recipes, including mine, still omit baking powder and rely on eggs for lightness. It is because of this airiness that I call it a soufflé. This is my mother's recipe, to which I've added a sauce inspired by a North Carolina spoon bread recipe calling for fresh-cut corn. Try the ham and cheese variation when corn is not at its peak, or when you are in the mood for a change from basic spoon bread.

1¼ teaspoons salt

2 tablespoons unsalted butter

1 cup yellow cornmeal, preferably stone-ground

1 cup cold milk

3 large eggs, separated

SAUCE

3 cups fresh whole corn kernels, par-boiled and drained (or substitute thawed frozen whole corn kernels)

½ cup heavy cream

¼ cup unsalted butter

Salt and freshly ground black pepper, to taste

1. Preheat oven to 400° F.

2. To make the batter: In a large saucepan, bring 2 cups water, salt, and butter to boil. Add cornmeal slowly, whisking constantly. Bring to simmer: remove from heat. Whisk in cold milk and egg yolks.

3. In a separate bowl, beat egg whites until stiff but not dry. Fold into cornmeal mixture.

4. Quickly turn the mixture into a buttered 2-quart soufflé dish (or into 8 1-cup soufflé dishes). Place on a baking sheet and bake in the center of the oven for 30 minutes (25 minutes for 1-cup dishes) or until puffed and golden-brown on top.

5. While the soufflé bakes, make the sauce. In a food processor or blender, purée 2½ cups corn with the cream until very smooth. Press through a sieve set over a saucepan; discard solids (or add to soups or stews). Add remaining ½ cup corn, butter, salt, and pepper to the sieved corn; warm over low heat until butter melts. Serve spoon bread at the table and pour warm sauce on top of or beside each serving. (Or, for individual soufflés, let diners pour sauce directly into their own spoon bread.)

Serves 8.

Ham and Cheese Spoon Bread Use only ¾ teaspoon salt; stir into the batter ½ cup julienned Smithfield ham and 1 cup finely shredded medium-sharp cheddar cheese after adding milk and yolks. Proceed to step 3 and make sauce and serve as directed.

Asparagus on Toast Points
with Tarragon Butter

. . .

"HE LOVED FARMING and gardening, the fields, the orchards, and his asparagus beds," wrote Thomas Jefferson's granddaughter, Ellen Randolph Coolidge. Jefferson tended to his many eighty-foot beds of asparagus as soon as the ground had thawed enough to be worked, then kept close watch on its growth, measuring the height in inches, until sometime between March 23rd and April 14th it would be ready for his table. Asparagus still grows at Monticello, is planted in gardens throughout most of the South, and is a long-awaited edible rite of spring. It is mentioned in the diaries of Peter Kalm, who traveled around the colonies in the mid-1700s. Kalm doesn't speak of its flavor. But certainly Virginians have been enjoying asparagus at least since 1737, as can be noted in William Byrd's *The Natural History of Virginia, or The Newly Discovered Eden* in which he reports, ". . . very large and long asparagus of good flavor . . ."

It's no wonder that asparagus is a costly delicacy, and that commercial production has had a bumpy road in the South. Asparagus is a labor-intensive crop that is expensive to start up—it must be harvested by hand with the help of specialized machinery, and a good harvest can take up to three years. But tobacco farmers—especially in North Carolina and Kentucky—accustomed to a high-maintenance crop, are turning to asparagus as their primary market declines, and new varieties are making it possible for asparagus to grow in formerly prohibitively warm, humid Southernmost regions. Slowly but surely, more and more asparagus is being grown on Southern farms.

Old Southern recipes for asparagus are few, and those that exist show a simple treatment of this vegetable. It appears that the most popular way of serving asparagus was to boil it, then to serve it on toast drizzled with melted butter. Mary Randolph gives explicit instructions for preparing and cooking asparagus in her *The Virginia House-wife* (1824), especially in terms of timing. One hundred sixty years later, in reminiscing about the food of her youth, native Virginian Edna Lewis, author of *The Taste of Country Cooking*, spoke of asparagus: "The first asparagus of spring was treated as a great delicacy. They were served on toast with a cream sauce. What I remember most was the white sauce—how delicious it was, just a ribbon of sauce across the asparagus . . ."

The recipe here is my version of this classic Virginia preparation. A beurre blanc sauce with fresh tarragon dresses the asparagus for a rich and elegant first course. The tarragon underscores the herbaceous flavor of the asparagus.

4 slices firm-textured, good-quality, homemade-type white bread

12 medium-sized asparagus stalks (approximately 1 to 1½ pounds) tough ends trimmed and stalks peeled

2 medium-sized shallots, minced

16 to 20 fresh tarragon leaves (or substitute ½ teaspoon dried tarragon)

2 tablespoons white wine vinegar (or use tarragon vinegar and use only half the amount of fresh or dried tarragon called for above)

8 tablespoons (1 stick) unsalted butter, chilled, cut into very small pieces

Salt and freshly ground black pepper, to taste

Fresh tarragon sprigs, to garnish

1. Trim crusts from bread and discard or save for stuffing or bread crumbs. Toast the bread until light golden-brown. Set aside.

2. In a 10-inch skillet, bring lightly salted water to a boil. Add asparagus, shallots, and tarragon; simmer until asparagus is barely tender. Remove asparagus with a slotted spoon to a clean cutting board; reserve cooking liquid. Split each asparagus spear in half lengthwise, and set aside on a tea towel–lined plate; cover with foil to keep warm.

3. To make the tarragon butter: Transfer the reserved asparagus cooking liquid to a small heavy-bottomed, nonaluminum saucepan. Add the vinegar and boil until the liquid is reduced to 2 tablespoons. Discard tarragon leaves.

4. Over very low heat, briskly whisk in the butter, piece by piece, letting each piece of butter become incorporated before adding the next. Whisk constantly until mixture is thick and ivory-colored. Season with salt and pepper to taste.

5. To serve, place 6 asparagus halves on each slice of toast, trimming ends to fit neatly. Nap with a ribbon of sauce, leaving tips bare. Garnish with tarragon sprigs. Serve hot.

Serves 4 as a first course.

Fresh Figs with Smithfield Ham and Mustard Cream

• • •

WHEN THE SPANISH set out for the New World in the 1500s, they brought figs to plant alongside staple crops such as grapevines and sugar cane in their new colonies of St. Augustine and Jacksonville, Florida. Thomas Jefferson was another contributor to the spread of the ubiquitous fig tree throughout the South. He brought home from France three different varieties of fig. One type, the Marseilles, he pronounced "incomparably superior to any fig I have ever seen."

One hundred years ago figs were still a major crop in Florida, Virginia, and other Southern states. Times and tastes changed and commercial production stopped, but the fig has remained on the table and in the landscape. Trees—usually of the Turkish variety—are still a common sight in Florida, Georgia, Louisiana, Virginia, South Carolina, Tennessee, and Mississippi backyards. Figs grow well in the South—a backyard tree can yield very good fruit and a lot of it—but their perishability makes them a nonviable commercial crop in this region. Yet, while there are no fig orchards in these states (figs don't ripen all at once and an orchard would have to be quite large to be profitable), home-grown figs can be found at farmers' markets and roadside stands in much of the South. Fig trees sometimes yield both summer and fall crops. But the fact that they can grow more than ten feet tall in yards is not always a blessing; some fig-tree owners, concerned more with ornament than gastronomy, cut their plants back so far they never reap that wonderful fruit.

I have always adored figs—fresh, dried, in preserves and desserts—and feel they are underused in this country. Here I combine fresh figs with Smithfield ham, a nod to the traditional Italian combination of prosciutto and melon. A hint of Creole mustard in a cold, creamy sauce makes this no-cooking-required dish a refreshing summer starter. Don't let the combination of ingredients throw you; the marriage of soft, sweet fruit, smoky ham, tangy mustard, and fresh, cold cream is delightful.

¼ cup crème fraîche or sour cream
¼ cup heavy cream

2 teaspoons Creole mustard or
    whole-grain mustard

8 fresh, ripe figs (preferably white figs), gently washed and dried, stems trimmed	about 1 cup, loosely packed
	Freshly ground black pepper, to taste
	Fresh mint sprigs to garnish (optional)
¼ pound julienned Smithfield ham (or other dry-cured country ham see page 481 for mail-order source),	

1. In a small bowl, combine crème fraîche, cream, and mustard. Divide sauce evenly among 4 medium salad plates.

2. Cut each fig in half through the stem end. Gently stuff fig halves with all but 2 or 3 tablespoons of the ham. Place 4 fig halves cut side up with stem ends pointing toward the center on the mustard cream on each plate. Sprinkle with remaining ham and pepper to taste. Garnish with mint, if desired.

Serves 4 as a first course.

Duck Liver (Foie Gras de Canard) on a Bed of Dandelion Greens with Walnut Vinaigrette

• • •

FOIE GRAS, the fattened liver of force-fed geese for which southwestern France is famous, set the standard for good eating even in the old South: A menu from an 1860 Kentucky wedding suggests that guests were treated to "pattie des foi gras [sic]." Foie gras can be cooked whole, then sliced and served cold on toast. Or, uncooked, foie gras can be sliced and sautéed in a skillet. When it is made into a pâté, it may also include other ground meats or poultry, fat, spices, brandy or Madeira, onions, and sometimes, truffles.

But Southerners have interpreted pâté de foie gras in their own ways, combining available meats with favorite seasonings. One old Savannah recipe calls for boiled calves liver and tongue, rubbed into a paste and seasoned with cayenne, nutmeg, cloves, mustard, and onion, then packed in jars with more bits of tongue. A Charleston "mock" pâté de foie gras lists chicken livers, butter, garlic, brandy, and sherry among its ingredients. A Cajun liver pâté also uses chicken

Appetizers and Hors d'Oeuvres

■

livers, embellishing them with butter, shallots, thyme, bay leaf, Tabasco, and Cognac.

Among the pâté's most popular Southern relations is liver pudding, an old Dixie favorite described by one North Carolinian as "every bit as good as the best French pâté de fois [sic] gras." Neese's Country Sausage, Inc. distributes liver pudding to supermarkets in North Carolina, South Carolina, and Virginia. It is best described as a pork liver pâté sold in loaf form. It is similar to, but contains more liver than, its Northern cousin, scrapple. Liver pudding is traditionally eaten cold—plain or in a sandwich—but is often cooked like pork sausage, or dusted with flour and fried with onions. A homemade country dish with a consistency between liver pudding and pâté is Liverell, traditionally made in the fall when hogs are slaughtered. Liverell is made by cooking pork liver, pork, and seasonings, mashing the mixture with cornmeal, and setting it in loaf pans to chill. Liverell is usually sliced and fried in bacon drippings and served hot.

Since liver pudding and Liverell are regional products, I prefer to offer a recipe with ingredients that, while somewhat esoteric, are at least available in farmers' markets and by mail order. I love the rich, buttery texture of foie gras against the bitter dandelion greens. If you live in the South, try this recipe with Liverell or liver pudding.

¾ pound tender, very young dandelion greens (Do not use large, mature dandelion greens; to substitute other bitter greens, see note, below)
1 medium shallot, minced (or substitute 1 tablespoon minced onion)
3 tablespoons red wine vinegar
Small pinch of salt

1 tablespoon walnut oil
1 tablespoon light olive oil
1 tablespoon vegetable oil
8 ⅓-inch-thick slices (about 6 ounces) duck liver (see note, below)
Flour, for dredging
¼ cup coarsely chopped, lightly toasted walnuts

1. Wash dandelion greens well in 3 changes of lukewarm water. Discard all tough stems and any large or yellowed leaves. Set aside.

2. In a small saucepan simmer shallot with vinegar and salt for 1 minute; set aside.

3. Heat the oils in a large, nonaluminum skillet over medium-low heat. Add greens and cook uncovered, tossing occasionally, until crisp-tender, about 3 minutes. Keep warm.

4. Meanwhile, heat a large, heavy skillet over medium-high heat. Dust duck liver slices *very lightly* with flour; brush off excess flour. Add foie gras to a hot ungreased skillet, and cook 20 to 30 seconds on each side or just until exterior is crisp and golden-brown. Do not overcook.

5. Working quickly, divide the warm dandelion greens evenly among 4 warm salad plates. Top each serving with 2 slices foie gras. Spoon vinegar mixture over greens and sprinkle with 1 tablespoon walnuts. Serve immediately. If serving a rich first course or a large meal, serve only one slice of foie gras per person; it is very rich.

Serves 4.

Note Arugula or turnip greens may be substituted for the dandelion greens. If using arugula, trim tough stems from 6 ounces of leaves. Wash well, and proceed as for dandelion greens. If using turnip greens, discard any yellowed or discolored leaves from 8 ounces of tender, young turnip greens. Wash well then blanch in lightly salted boiling water 5 to 10 minutes or until greens are no longer bitter. Drain thoroughly in a sieve, pressing out excess water with back of wooden spoon. Chop greens coarsely, and proceed as directed.

Note Fresh duck liver (Foie gras de canard) is available in specialty food stores, or see page 481 for mail-order source.

Mini Corn Puddings with Caviar-Chive Cream

■ ■ ■

THOMAS JEFFERSON ate corn in pudding at Monticello, and the dish remains a Southern staple particularly in Kentucky, where it seems to appear on menus more than those in any other state. Originally made with so-called "green corn" (the first sweet corn of the season), corn pudding was a harbinger of summer's bounty. The classic dish combines fresh-cut kernels with butter, eggs, and milk or cream, into a rich, thick custard amenable to a variety of flavor variations.

Flour is added to some recipes as a thickener, but most cooks let the corn's own starch and the eggs do the trick. Other versions use cream-style corn instead of fresh kernels. More distinctive additions to the basic recipe have given the pudding many different characteristics. Sugar was sometimes used in great quantity to make a very sweet vegetable side dish. Virginia cooks sometimes topped their casserole-type "puddings" with cracker or bread crumbs. Other recipes include grated onion, vanilla, cinnamon, or the more classic flavoring, nutmeg. An elegant, more substantial addition—enjoyed in Charleston and elsewhere—is shrimp. The optional caviar in this recipe takes the idea a step further.

My Danish friend, Per Jensen, prepares this dish whenever guests from other countries come to his home for dinner. Rich as it is, Per always follows it with my Spicy Fried Chicken (page 182).

PUDDING

8 ears of corn, shucked	*1 teaspoon salt*
3 large eggs	*⅛ teaspoon white pepper*
1½ cups half-and-half	*Pinch of nutmeg*
1 teaspoon sugar	

CAVIAR-CHIVE CREAM

2 cups heavy cream	*3 tablespoons minced fresh chives*
2 tablespoons minced shallots	*2 ounces salmon roe (optional)*
Salt and freshly ground black pepper, to taste	*Chive blossoms to garnish (optional)*

1. Preheat oven to 350° F.

2. Using a small, sharp knife, and working over a large bowl, cut down the center of each row of corn kernels. Scrape off the kernels into the bowl. You will have about 4½ cups kernels.

3. In a separate bowl, beat eggs, half-and-half, sugar, salt, white pepper, and nutmeg. Stir this mixture into the corn. Divide mixture evenly among 6 buttered 8-ounce soufflé dishes.

4. Place dishes in a roasting pan and add enough hot water to the pan to come halfway up the sides of the dishes. Bake 30 to 35 minutes or until set. Do not overcook.

5. During the last 5 minutes of cooking, begin the sauce. In a medium skillet over high heat, boil the cream and shallots until reduced to 1½ cups or until thick enough to lightly coat the back of a spoon. Add salt and pepper; stir in chives. Cover and keep warm.

6. When puddings are just set, remove from water bath. Run a knife around the edge of each soufflé dish to loosen the pudding. Place a small plate (salad- or dessert-sized) over the pudding, then invert to unmold. Spoon 3 tablespoons sauce around each pudding, and 1 tablespoon on top. If desired, scatter 1 teaspoon salmon roe over each serving and garnish with a chive blossom. Serve warm.

Serves 6 as a first course.

Note For a lighter dish, make custards in 4-ounce soufflé dishes; reduce cooking time to 18 to 25 minutes, or until set.

Fresh Corn and Cornmeal Pancakes with Crème Fraîche and Caviar

• • •

RUSSIA AND IRAN share a reputation for the finest caviar, but America also has a competitive history of roe and caviar production. The roe of fish other than sturgeon (only eggs from the sturgeon should actually be called caviar)—including lumpfish, tuna, mullet, and salmon—are often processed and eaten the same way as sturgeon eggs. In the last quarter of the nineteenth century, in fact, the United States was the world's largest supplier of processed fish roe, producing 150,000 pounds yearly—much of which was exported to Europe and even Russia. But by 1900 overfishing, pollution, and dams wiped out the Atlantic sturgeon and depleted the fisheries. In the mid-1970s, the industry was reborn as entrepreneurs discovered excellent sturgeon, whitefish, and salmon roe in rivers in California, the Pacific Northwest, the Northeast, and the South. Today, the industry relies on the many rivers and ponds of the South, where several species of east coast Atlantic sturgeon such as paddlefish, hackleback, and boatfin are the source of some of the best American caviar.

From the start, sturgeon was everyday fare in the South, and the roe did not go wasted. For seventeenth-century settlers in Jamestown, Virginia, sturgeon roe was used to stretch meals when other foods were less plentiful. In the nineteenth century, Charlestonians ate grits with pickled fish roe and Carolinians ate the roe of mullet, menhaden, shad, and herring fried, baked, dried, or scrambled with eggs.

Processing caviar is a delicate, difficult matter. Technique can make more of a difference in the quality of caviar than a difference in types of roe. Most American companies have hired Iranian or Russian experts to teach them traditional—and very secret—processing methods. Today, not only is the caviar industry big business, but local products are abundant and high in quality. Southern caviar, much of which comes from the Tennessee, Missouri, and Mississippi rivers, is less expensive than its foreign competitors and of increasingly comparable quality. It is capturing a good portion of the caviar market as processors sell their products to companies who distribute it to specialty food stores throughout the country. For mail-order source, see page 481.

Corncakes with caviar has almost become a culinary cliché in the last decade as innovative chefs embraced American foods. But like many popular dishes there is a reason for the notoriety of this combination: it tastes terrific! I first tasted corncakes and caviar at New York's Arcadia restaurant, so I tip my hat to its chef, Anne Rosenzweig. These can be served as a first course, or passed as a hot hors d'oeuvre.

1 recipe Cornmeal Pancakes (page 355)
1 cup cooked, drained fresh whole corn kernels (or substitute thawed, frozen whole corn kernels)

6 to 8 tablespoons crème fraîche (or substitute sour cream)
3 to 4 tablespoons caviar

1. Prepare batter as directed, and fold in corn. Cook as directed.
2. Place 3 pancakes on each of 6 plates, and top each pancake with 1 teaspoon crème fraîche and ½ teaspoon (or more!) caviar. Serve immediately. Makes 18 2½- to 3-inch pancakes.

Serves 6 as a first course.

Note To serve these as an hors d'oeuvre, proceed as directed, but drop batter by level teaspoons to make bite-sized pancakes.

Avocado with Peach Vinaigrette
∎ ∎ ∎

"AVOCADO—ALLIGATOR PEAR—is of so mild and bland a flavor that it needs a pick-up" wrote Marjorie Rawlings in her *Cross Creek Cookery* (1942). Perhaps Ms. Rawlings never tasted a perfectly ripened avocado (which is doubtful, since she lived on a seventy-two-acre orange grove in Florida). In any case, I disagree with Ms. Rawlings. Subtle, yes; bland, no. Avocados have a wonderfully rich, nutty flavor, and a satiny texture that in my mind makes it one of the most sensual of all fruits.

The United States got its first taste of avocados after horticulturist Henry Petrine planted them in Florida in 1833, 2,000 years after the ancient Mayans, Aztecs, and Peruvians enjoyed them, and thirty-eight years before they reached California as well. The Florida avocado industry began seventy years later on just twenty acres. Judging from cookbooks, the avocado doesn't seem to have been popular until the 1950s, when it became a salad ingredient. Its popularity has grown to the extent that guacamole has become a household word. The industry has grown, too. Today, one million bushels of over sixty-seven varieties are grown annually on 12,000 Florida acres, mainly in the southern counties of Dade, Highlands, and Palm Beach. (Some home gardeners in southern Georgia grow avocados as well.) The avocado season runs from June until March, but fruit is most plentiful from August to December. West Indian and Guatemalan, two of the three kinds of avocado, grow in tropical Florida. Types are classified as summer, fall, and winter. Early harvest (summer) West Indian varieties, including Simmonds, Pollack, Fuchs, Tower 3, Waldin, and Windman, have smooth thick skins. Late harvest (fall and winter) Guatemalan varieties such as Choquette, Lula, and Taylor are darker, pebblier, smaller, and thicker skinned.

This starter is best served in summer when peaches are at their peak. The tangy vinaigrette would have no doubt been just the "pick-up" to please Marjorie Rawlings.

2 medium-sized ripe peaches
2 tablespoons freshly squeezed lemon juice
1 teaspoon white wine vinegar or red wine vinegar
1 tablespoon vegetable oil
1 tablespoon walnut oil, or light olive oil

Salt and freshly ground black pepper, to taste
3 medium-sized ripe avocados
6 tablespoons coarsely chopped walnuts

1. Peel, pit, and coarsely chop peaches. Purée in blender or food processor with lemon juice and vinegar. With machine running, add oils. Season with salt and pepper to taste.

2. Cut avocados in half lengthwise, moving the knife around the pit. Separate halves and remove the peel and pits. Place each avocado half cut-side-down and cut crosswise into slices ½ inch thick.

3. To serve, spoon 2 tablespoons of peach vinaigrette onto each of 6 salad plates. Place 1 cut avocado half in pool of sauce and fan out the slices. Repeat with remaining avocados. Garnish each serving with 1 tablespoon chopped walnuts. Sprinkle with freshly ground black pepper to taste. Serve immediately.

Serves 6 as a first course.

Soups

Soups

$\mathcal{T}$HE MAKING OF A GOOD SOUP is a simple art. And in the truest form of this art, there is probably no such thing as "a little soup"—at least not in the South. Historically, classic meat-and-vegetable stews, like Brunswick stew or Kentucky burgoo, are simmered for hours in large kettles over the coals of an open hickory fire and served to feed masses. Today these soups are still made in vast quantities for parties, picnics, fund-raisers, or any event that draws a large crowd. And the cook tending the soup pot at such a gathering is likely to insist that his or her version is the definitive one, for there are probably as many versions on a burgoo or a Brunswick stew as there are cooks in the South.

A Word about Gumbo

The recipe for gumbo, however, has perhaps been more thoroughly assimilated into the heritage of Southern soup making than even burgoo or Brunswick stew. There are hundreds of recorded recipes for gumbo, a South Louisiana favorite, which may have originated from the West Indian dish *gumbs* (okra stewed in water with butter and salt and pepper). Other sources say the word gumbo comes from the African *gambo*, meaning okra. Like burgoo and Brunswick stew, gumbo contains a variety of meats (and/or seafood) and vegetables—often depending upon what is fresh and at hand. Gumbo generally consists of some combination of tomatoes, bell peppers, okra, shrimp, sausage, and perhaps, chicken. It's usually thickened with filé powder— the finely ground leaves of the sassafras tree—or a roux, although some recipes rely strictly on okra as a thickening agent.

Other Southern Classics

While the exemplary stews of the region are a celebration of a wealth of fresh edibles—all in one soup pot—many distinctive Southern soups have also been created from the simple goodness of a single vegetable. The South's strong tie to the soil has been continually acknowledged with hearty okra and bean soups, tomato bisques and corn chowders. In lean times, soups like these have been the sustenance of many a Southerner.

But as often as Southerners have looked to the soil for the ingredients of a classic soup, they have also fished from the South's coastal and inland waters. The terrapin, or turtle, has been one of the more unusual catches. The recipe for terrapin stew—usually made with turtle meat, cream, sherry, a little butter, and salt and pepper—has appeared prominently in many old Maryland and Virginia cookbooks. Writing in 1940, Ferdinand C. Latrobe, the author of *The Chesapeake Bay Seafood Cookbook,* boasted of this delicacy as a "luscious but barbaric dish, which even today is the appreciation of the ultra-ultra circle that does not have to read Emily Post."

Although turtle soup is no longer made as frequently as it once was, soups, chowders, and bisques made from fish and shellfish are still popular. Fish muddles (thick fish stews) have been especially popular along the Southern Atlantic coastal region. "Rock muddle," made from rockfish, is a traditional Outer Banks stew of the coastal Carolinas. Pine Bark stew, another Carolina favorite, is a bacon, potato, and fish muddle traditionally made in a black iron pot over a pine-bark fire. Inland, fish stews have been made from freshwater catches, like catfish. And the deep South has been particularly known for its elegant shrimp, crab, and conch bisques and chowders. In Louisiana, court bouillon—fish soup often thickened with a roux and seasoned with tomatoes—is a favorite dish.

Here is a sampling of Southern soups—representative of the region but each with a unique twist. Most of them fare equally well as either a first or main course. But all you have to add is some cornbread or biscuits—and perhaps a light, green salad—and any one of them becomes a singularly satisfying meal.

Ramp and Potato Soup with Caraway

• • •

THIS IS A Southern vichyssoise, if you will, made with the wild onions that grow from March to mid-May from New England to Georgia, and west to Minnesota. Called "wild leeks" by Northerners and "ramps" (the word comes from the Elizabethan, *rams* or *ramson,* meaning wild garlic or wild leeks) in parts of Appalachia and the South, this pungent plant was considered a spring tonic, like dandelion, having medicinal qualities. No doubt it was a welcome change from a steady winter diet of potatoes and other tubers. Ramps—which look like scallions with wider leaves—are cause for celebration in West Virginia and Tennessee where festivals focusing on them (the foraging is as much of a rite as the cooking and eating) are held.

Country cooks prepare ramps as they do other greens: either boiled with salt pork or fried in bacon fat—often with potatoes. I love ramps boiled and fried, but they're also good sautéed and added to omelettes, pasta, and soup.

Scallions may be substituted if ramps are unavailable. Like other Southern greens, ramps develop very strong flavors during the summer months, so I suggest using ramps only in spring.

The caraway flavor here is subtle. Serve the soup as a first course or a light lunch or supper with cornbread or cornsticks.

6 slices bacon (optional)

3 tablespoons vegetable oil, butter, or bacon drippings

1 pound ramps, thoroughly cleaned, trimmed of root ends, chopped (include leaves); you should have about 2 to 2½ cups chopped ramps (Note: If ramps are unavailable, substitute scallions)

½ cup dry white wine

3½ cups chicken broth, preferably homemade

2½ cups water

1 herb bouquet, tied in cheesecloth, consisting of:
   1 teaspoon caraway seeds
   6 whole black peppercorns
   10 sprigs fresh parsley
   Generous pinch of red pepper flakes

¾ pound boiling potatoes (about 4 medium), cut into ½-inch chunks

Salt and freshly ground pepper, to taste

Crème fraîche, sour cream, or unsweetened whipped cream (optional)

1. In a deep, medium-sized saucepot, cook bacon, if using, over medium heat, turning frequently until crisp. Drain on paper towels and coarsely crumble. Reserve 3 tablespoons drippings.

2. Add ramps to the drippings (or, use oil or butter) and cook over medium-low heat stirring frequently, 10 minutes, or until they begin to soften. Do not brown.

3. Add wine and boil 1 minute. Add broth and water, and bring to a boil. Add herb bouquet to the soup. When soup has reached a boil, lower heat, partially cover, and simmer 15 minutes. Add potatoes and simmer uncovered 15 minutes or until potatoes are tender. Discard herb bouquet.

4. Pour the soup through a sieve set over another saucepan; reserve the solids.

5. In a blender or food processor, purée all but 1 cup of the reserved solids with some of the broth until very smooth, about 1 minute. Return the purée to the saucepan with the broth. Add the reserved 1 cup of solids and heat through. Season with salt and pepper to taste. Ladle into warm mugs or bowls and serve hot with a dollop of crème fraîche and crumbled bacon, if desired.

Serves 4 as a first course or light lunch or supper.

Fresh Pea Soup with Orange Mint

∎ ∎ ∎

THE ENGLISH at one time were rather skeptical toward the more Gallic tradition of soup making. Englishmen of the seventeenth and eighteenth centuries were particularly fond of meat and potatoes (and still are) and they considered soup somehow "less than honest" fare. Pease porridge, a thick soup made of boiled and strained peas, seems to have been an exception. And the recipe for this English favorite traveled across the Atlantic and found its way into several cookbooks. For example, *Martha Washington's Booke of Cookery and Booke of Sweetmeats*—a book representative of much eighteenth-century cooking in Virginia—features a recipe for a porridge of "old pease," consisting of mashed cooked white peas that are returned to the cooking broth to be seasoned with garlic, coriander seeds, salt and pepper, plus dried spearmint. Cooked onions, parsley, and butter are also added, and bread and butter are the recommended accompaniments. Another recipe in the same book calls for the addition of shredded marigold petals. Delicate soups made from tender lettuce leaves and new peas have also frequently appeared in many definitive historical Southern cookbooks—subtly suggesting everything that's new and clean about early summer.

Here, fresh green peas are made into a light soup that gets its lift not from the traditional mint (or lettuce) but from a bit of sweet citrusy orange zest. If you grow your own herbs, try orange bergamot mint, which has a slight citrus aroma, as a garnish.

4 cups fresh shelled peas (4 pounds in the shell), or substitute frozen peas
Pinch of sugar
3 cups chicken broth, preferably homemade (Note: Use 4 cups broth if you omit the ¾ cup heavy cream)
½ teaspoon grated orange zest

¾ cup heavy cream (optional)
Salt and freshly ground black pepper, to taste
4 tablespoons whipped heavy cream, to garnish (optional)
4 thin strips of orange peel, to garnish
4 sprigs orange bergamot mint, to garnish (optional)

1. In a small saucepan, simmer peas and sugar in chicken broth, uncovered, until peas are tender, about 10 minutes.

2. Strain peas, reserving broth. Purée peas in a blender or food processor.

3. Push puréed peas through a sieve and return the purée to the broth. Add orange zest, cream, if using, and salt and pepper to taste. Warm through or chill thoroughly. Serve hot or cold. Top each serving with a dollop of whipped cream, a twist of orange peel, and a mint sprig, if desired.

Makes 1 quart; serves 4 as a first course.

Crab Soup with Saffron

• • •

There were more crabs than crates, and the critters kept hopping out of the overfilled boxes like popcorn in a hot skillet. The floor crawled with their oblique scuttles for the nearest dark underside. . . . I started shuffling to avoid stepping on them.

—William Least Heat Moon, *Blue Highways*

THE SHE-CRAB found her way into a Charleston soup kettle sometime in the early nineteenth century, according to the culinary lore of this port city. And apparently she decided to stay for a while.

Although the she-crab is frequently served in the coastal regions of Maryland, Louisiana, and Alabama, it is associated with Charleston in a way that it's not with any other city in the South. Charleston may be she-crab soup's birthplace, but other cities along the eastern seaboard have adapted it and served crab-based soups for years.

She-crabs are prized for their roe, which are thought to impart an extra flavor to the soup. But male crabs are equally delectable. Also, frozen lump crabmeat is a fine substitution when fresh crabs are unavailable or if you don't have time to "pick" the crabs yourself.

Classic Charleston she-crab soup is generally finished with heavy cream and some versions are sometimes flavored with tomatoes. I have incorporated both cream and tomatoes, plus saffron—a spice that's often used to season the native fish and shellfish dishes of the Mediterranean.

2 tablespoons unsalted butter
1 medium yellow onion, finely chopped
2 cloves garlic, minced
1/4 teaspoon lightly crushed saffron threads
6 tablespoons dry white wine

3 cups homemade, lightly salted fish stock (or substitute bottled clam juice)
1 cup milk
1/2 pound backfin crabmeat
Pinch of white pepper
Salt, to taste

1 *herb bouquet, tied in cheesecloth,*   2 *teaspoons tomato paste*
  consisting of: 1 *cup heavy cream*
  5 *sprigs parsley*
  4 *2-inch-long strips of lemon peel*
  1 *small imported bay leaf*

1. In a large saucepan, heat butter over medium heat. Add onion and cook, stirring frequently, 5 minutes or until softened. Add garlic and cook 1 minute or until it just releases its fragrance. Stir in saffron and wine and simmer 1 minute.

2. Add stock or clam juice, milk, herb bouquet, and tomato paste and bring to a boil. Lower heat, cover, and simmer 15 minutes.

3. Add cream, crabmeat, and pepper. Cover and simmer 5 minutes longer to heat through. Season to taste with salt. Discard herb bouquet. Serve immediately.

Makes 5 to 6 cups; serves 4 as a first course.

Swirled Succotash Soup

■ ■ ■

SINCE CORN AND BEANS were the largest crops cultivated by the Native American tribes, it's not surprising that the two would end up simmered together in the same soup pot. But the history of Southern cooking is also rich with soups built from either corn or legumes: sweet, silky corn chowders scented with nutmeg or cayenne pepper, or earthy black-eyed pea soups stewed with a ham bone.

Msickquatash, a thick dried-bean and corn stew created by the Narragansett tribe of Rhode Island, became "succotash" as colonists North and South began to prepare the dish. In Mississippi, settlers called this classic combination Tom Fuller— an adaptation of *sofkee* which the Native Americans made there also.

The combination of corn and beans is a concept that's lasted. Many succotash recipes also call for tomato and okra. But here the two basics—corn and beans—are swirled together for an elegant, simple potage. Crème fraîche gives it a tangy richness, and a sprinkling of ham, a classic and just-right bit of saltiness.

Soups

■

3 cups chicken broth, preferably
    homemade
3 cups fresh baby lima beans (or sub-
    stitute 2 10-ounce packages frozen
    baby limas)
3 cups fresh whole corn kernels, cut
    from about 12 ears (or substitute 2
    10-ounce packages frozen whole
    corn kernels)

¼ cup crème fraîche or sour cream
Salt and freshly ground black pepper,
    to taste
¼ cup julienned, dry-cured country
    ham (such as Smithfield, see page
    481 for mail-order source) or sub-
    stitute cooked, crumbled bacon
    (optional)

1. Bring 1½ cups broth to a boil in each of 2 medium saucepans. Add limas to one, corn to the other. Return to a boil, lower heat, cover, and simmer until tender. (Frozen vegetables will be ready in about 5 minutes; fresh corn in about 3 minutes; fresh limas in about 5 to 10 minutes.)

2. In food processor or blender, purée limas and their broth for 1 minute or until smooth. Press mixture through a sieve set over the saucepan in which the beans cooked. Set aside.

3. In clean, dry food processor or blender, purée corn and its broth 1 minute or until smooth. Press through sieve set over the saucepan in which the corn cooked.

4. Stir in 2 tablespoons crème fraîche or sour cream to each mixture and heat through over medium-low heat. Season each mixture to taste with salt and pepper. (Note: If canned broth was used, salt may not be necessary. Note also that ham or bacon garnish will add some saltiness.)

5. To serve, divide lima mixture into 4 warm soup bowls or mugs, filling them only half full. Add corn mixture and swirl with a spoon. Sprinkle ham or bacon over each serving, if desired.

Serves 4 as a first course or light lunch or supper accompanied by bread, cheese, and a salad.

Cold Curried Benne Seed Soup

• • •

SOUPS MADE from nuts and seeds are actually less of a culinary novelty than they might seem to be—particularly in the South. African slaves brought with them the custom of making soup from peanuts, but even before that the Native Americans were thickening their soup with pounded nuts. In the Carolinas, low-country slaves often added ground benne seeds (sesame seeds) to a porridge of cooked hominy. And sesame seeds have also been a common ingredient in many oyster soups of the Piedmont region.

An interpretation of peanut soup, a specialty of Southeastern Virginia, this soup is made with tahini, a thick paste ground from hulled sesame seeds. The soup is reminiscent of mulligatawny soup, a popular Eastern Indian soup that also has a chicken-broth base and contains almonds and curry powder.

Tahini, which has a richness and texture similar to peanut butter, has become increasingly popular during the last few decades as health-conscious Americans have experimented with Middle Eastern cuisines and have turned to sources other than meat for protein. In fact, sesame seeds are today the number one U.S. import among spices. The sesame plant has been grown successfully in warmer-climate areas of this country. But because the fragile pods (which open easily, scattering the seeds—and providing the literal reference for the phrase "open sesame") require hand harvesting, most of our supply continues to be imported.

This cool, refreshing soup is rich, but very nutritious. Serve a mugful with toasted whole wheat pita triangles for a summer lunch, followed by fresh fruit.

2 tablespoons vegetable oil

2 tablespoons butter

2 carrots, peeled and finely chopped

1 medium yellow onion, peeled and finely chopped

1 stalk celery, finely chopped

2 tablespoons good-quality curry powder (such as Madras brand)

1 tablespoon all-purpose flour

½ cup dry white wine

3 cups chicken broth (preferably homemade)

1 to 1¼ cups milk

¾ to 1 cup plain yogurt

1 cup tahini (Middle Eastern sesame seed paste) or substitute smooth, unsalted peanut butter

½ cup toasted sesame seeds (substitute toasted crushed peanuts if using peanut butter instead of tahini)

Fresh cilantro or mint sprigs (optional)

1. In a medium saucepan, heat oil and butter over low heat. Add carrots, onion, and celery and cook stirring frequently, 5 minutes or until crisp-tender.

2. Add curry powder and flour. Cook 5 minutes more over very low heat, stirring frequently. Do not let mixture brown.

3. Add wine and broth and bring to boil. Lower heat, cover, and simmer 10 minutes.

4. Strain mixture into a bowl, reserving liquids and solids. Purée solids in a food processor or blender. Press this purée through a sieve into the reserved soup in the bowl. Cool mixture to room temperature.

5. Whisk in 1 cup milk and ½ cup yogurt until smooth. Add tahini slowly while whisking constantly, until smooth. Chill thoroughly. Taste for seasoning. Soup should be spicy, but if it seems too strong, add up to ¼ cup milk and ¼ cup yogurt to mellow flavors. Garnish each serving with a tablespoon-sized dollop of yogurt, sprinkle with sesame seeds, and add a sprig of fresh cilantro or mint, if desired.

Serves 4 to 5 as a first course.

Note This is a very rich soup: 6- to 8-ounce servings are sufficient. Keeps in refrigerator up to 4 days.

"Pot Likker" Soup

▪ ▪ ▪

"POT LIKKER" is the highly concentrated broth that results from the long boiling of greens (plus smoked pork and spices). It is, in other words, the "liquor" left in the pot. It's a nourishing potable that has often been consumed with nothing more than a chunk of cornbread. But it can also be the beginning of a sophisticated soup, like the assertive one here that's made with tender baby turnips and bacon, and thickened with a vegetable purée.

Southern greens are typically boiled for several hours but for this soup they're simmered only an hour—so that they retain more texture and flavor. And the turnips are cooked just until they are crisp-tender.

2 cups chicken broth, preferably
  homemade
1 pound unblemished turnip greens,
  trimmed of tough stems and any
  discolored leaves, washed and
  roughly chopped (about 9 cups
  loosely packed)
¼ pound bacon, preferably double
  smoked
2 medium carrots, peeled and
  coarsely chopped
2 medium yellow onions, peeled and
  halved
1 herb bouquet, tied in cheesecloth,
  consisting of:
    3 large cloves garlic, halved
    2 whole dried hot peppers (or ¼
      teaspoon hot pepper flakes)

6 whole black peppercorns
10 sprigs fresh parsley
2 sprigs fresh thyme (or ½ teaspoon dried)
1 small imported bay leaf
12 baby turnips (about 1 inch in diameter), trimmed and washed but
  not peeled (Note: If baby turnips
  are unavailable, substitute diced,
  peeled turnips)
¼ cup cooked, crumbled bacon, to
  garnish (optional)

1. Place all ingredients except turnips and cooked bacon in a large saucepot. Add enough water as necessary to just cover vegetables, and bring to a boil.
Lower heat and simmer 1 hour with cover askew, adding more water when
necessary to cover vegetables.

2. Set a colander or sieve over a large saucepan and strain the soup. Discard
pieces of onion, carrot, bacon, and the herb bouquet. Set greens aside.

3. Return the liquid to a boil and add the turnips. Lower heat and simmer
until turnips are crisp-tender, about 10 minutes. Remove turnips with a slotted
spoon and set aside. There should be 3 cups liquid; add water or boil to reduce
as necessary.

4. In a blender or food processor, purée half the greens with 1½ cups of the
broth. Return the purée, the turnips, and the reserved greens to the broth and
heat through. Ladle into bowls, and sprinkle with bacon, if desired.

*Makes about 4 cups; serves 4 as a first course or light main course
accompanied by Whole Wheat Cornsticks (page 35).*

Soups

■

Jerusalem Artichoke Soup

■ ■ ■

> . . . [A]fter the Yankees left, "all us had to thank them for was a hungry belly, and freedom," . . . With all the food and animals destroyed, slaves had to "scour de [*sic*] woods for hickory nuts, acorns, cane roots, and artichokes."
>
> —Paul D. Escott, *Slavery Remembered:*
> *A Record of Twentieth-Century Slave Narratives*

THE "ARTICHOKE" REFERRED to in this passage is not the green globe artichoke from California, but the gnarly root vegetable known in the South as Jerusalem artichoke. This indigenous North American plant was cultivated by Native Americans, but it also grows wild along the eastern seaboard, from Nova Scotia to Georgia. It is now grown commercially in many states. A golf-ball-sized, beige-skinned (sometimes purplish) vegetable, it is slightly sweet, and some say its flavor is similar to that of the globe artichoke. However, the plant is actually more closely related to the sunflower and has brilliant yellow flowers that bloom from August to October. You can often find Jerusalem artichokes labeled "sun chokes" at vegetable markets and in supermarket produce sections.

The Spanish word *girasol* and the Italian word *girasole,* both of which mean sunflower, are largely credited with giving this vegetable its name, "Jerusalem" being a corruption of *girasol.* The Jerusalem artichoke became popular in Europe after the Spanish and Portuguese first discovered it here in the seventeenth century. Two hundred years later, in England, recipes for "Palestine soup" appeared on restaurant menus—indicating the English assumed that the vegetable must have originated in Jerusalem (a common, but mistaken, association that is still made today).

In the South the Jerusalem artichoke is often pickled or shredded into salads. Here, smoky bacon and fragrant herbs and spices complement the delicate, rather haunting flavor of this humble tuber. Serve as a first course at Thanksgiving dinner, or any other harvest-season meal featuring poultry or game.

3 to 3½ pounds Jerusalem artichokes, scrubbed
1½ teaspoons dried thyme

1 large (or 2 medium) imported bay
   leaf
2 teaspoons whole coriander seeds

8 *whole black peppercorns*
15 *sprigs fresh parsley, tied in a bundle*
Salt and freshly ground black pepper, to taste
4 *slices thick-sliced bacon (or 6 slices regular bacon), cut crosswise into ½-inch-wide pieces*
2 *medium-sized yellow onions, finely chopped*
½ *cup dry white wine*

5 *cups rich, lightly salted homemade chicken broth (Note: Canned broth may be used but soup may be too salty for some tastes; add optional cream if soup is too salty)*
⅓ *to* ⅔ *cup heavy cream (optional)*
Fresh thyme sprigs (optional)

1. Place artichokes, thyme, bay leaf, coriander seeds, peppercorns, parsley, and pinch of salt in large saucepot. Add cold water to cover. Bring to a boil, and simmer partially covered 30 minutes or until artichokes are soft. Strain contents of pot, immerse the Jerusalem artichokes in cold water, and cool until easy to handle. Peel, and then purée the peeled artichokes in food processor or blender, leaving purée in the machine. Discard herbs and spices.

2. In a large skillet cook bacon over medium heat until crisp. Remove with a slotted spoon; drain on paper towels, and set aside. Reserve drippings.

3. Add onions to bacon drippings and cook over medium heat 5 to 10 minutes or until translucent. Remove onions with slotted spoon; drain on paper towels. Discard drippings. Add onions to the purée in the food processor or blender.

4. Add wine to the skillet and boil 1 minute. Add to the purée and process until smooth.

5. Return the purée to the saucepot and add broth; simmer. Adjust seasonings. Add cream if a richer soup is desired. Ladle into bowls and garnish with bacon and, if desired, fresh thyme sprigs.

Serves 6.

Sweet Potato Soup with Pine Nut Butter

• • •

OUT OF THE KITCHENS of New Orleans and Charleston have come many of the South's memorable vegetable soups—rich bisques made from tangy tomatoes or sweet pumpkins, for example. The sweet potato has not been overlooked. Like the pumpkin, it is an excellent soup vegetable because it lends body to a broth and can combine well with an array of seasonings. In Southern cooking the sweet potato is often mixed with sweet flavorings, such as sugar, marshmallows, and fruit juices, but here it meets with onions and chicken stock to take on a more complex, savory flavor. This soup is creamy—like a bisque—but without cream or flour. An optional garnish of rich pine nut butter dropped into the center of each soup bowl melts into a pinwheel of color and flavor.

This soup is a good first course for a Thanksgiving dinner or a warm retreat from the chill of any brisk fall or winter day. It can also be served cold in the warmer months. (To serve cold, omit Pine Nut Butter and top with a dollop of sour cream.)

SOUP

3 tablespoons unsalted butter (or substitute 3 tablespoons vegetable oil)

2 large carrots, peeled and diced

1 medium-sized yellow onion, peeled and chopped

1 large clove garlic, finely minced

1 quart chicken broth, preferably homemade

⅓ cup dry white wine

1 pound sweet potatoes (about 2 medium), peeled and cut into ½-inch dice (about 3 cups diced)

Pinch of white pepper

Pinch of ground red pepper (cayenne)

PINE NUT BUTTER

2 tablespoons pine nuts

4 tablespoons unsalted butter

Pinch of salt

1. To make the soup: Heat the butter in a large saucepan over medium heat. Add carrots and onions and cook, stirring occasionally, 10 minutes or until onions are translucent. Remove from heat, add garlic, and cook, stirring con-

stantly, for 1 minute or just until garlic releases its fragrance and turns golden. (Do not let garlic brown or it will taste bitter.)

2. Add broth, wine, and sweet potatoes. Bring to a boil, cover, and simmer 20 to 30 minutes or until vegetables are soft.

3. Meanwhile, make Pine Nut Butter by spreading pine nuts out on baking sheet and toasting in preheated 350° F oven 5 to 8 minutes, tossing frequently, or until golden-brown. (Or, toast nuts on a paper towel in a microwave oven.) Cool, then process in food processor or blender until smooth. Add the butter and process until well combined. Blend in salt.

4. Wash and dry food processor bowl. When vegetables are tender, use a slotted spoon to transfer solids from saucepan to food processor. Add ½ cup of the broth and purée until very smooth. Return purée to saucepan and stir to blend with remaining broth. Stir in white and red pepper. Ladle into bowls and top each with a level tablespoonful of Pine Nut Butter. Keeps 5 days in refrigerator.

Makes about 1 quart; serves 4 as a first course.

Brunswick Stew with Rabbit, Mushrooms, and Double-Smoked Bacon

■ ■ ■

I had always enjoyed my visits to Macon. But living there was a different proposition ... no entertainment but summer revivals at the two white churches, Methodist and Baptist; and once or twice a year, a fishfry or Brunswick stew.

—Reynolds Price, *Kate Vaiden*

THE AROMA OF BRUNSWICK STEW—whether it's simmering over an outdoor fire or in a simple stew pot in the kitchen—signals the onset of fall for many Southerners from Virginia to Georgia. Although both Brunswick County, North Carolina, and Brunswick, Georgia are pretenders to the soup kettle, Brunswick County, Virginia, is where this thick, filling stew is generally thought to have originated. Recipes for Brunswick stew date as far back as the early 1800s. It was originally made with squirrel, but now relies on rabbit for its gamey flavor. A classic Brunswick stew also usually contains beef, chicken, potatoes, tomatoes, and beans, and often okra or corn. Some recipes also call for tomato paste or catsup.

Soups

■

My version is a variation on the basic stew—but is equally hearty. A purée of sweet potatoes added as thickener is an excellent foil for the savory rabbit. The shiitake mushrooms contribute a smoky-woodsy flavor appropriate to this traditional hunter's stew.

The Southeast, incidentally, is the largest producing region in the United States for shiitake mushrooms—a brown Japanese mushroom that's become one of the most popular specialty mushrooms sold in food markets today. The shiitake grows well almost year-round in the Southeast—particularly in North Carolina—because of the warm, humid climate and the abundance of sweet gum and oak trees.

Serve this hearty stew with Savory Cabbage Coleslaw with Sweet and Tangy Yogurt Dressing (page 115), Basic Biscuits (page 23), Rich Buttermilk Cornbread (page 34), or Whole Wheat Cornsticks (page 35). For dessert, try Spiced Apple Stack Cakes with Cider Butter and Cream (page 389), or Baked Maple-Pecan Custard (page 414).

1 5-pound stewing chicken, quartered, giblets reserved

¾ pound fresh shiitake or other wild mushrooms, trimmed and diced into ½-inch pieces (optional)

3 large yellow onions, finely chopped

3 stalks celery, finely chopped

3 large carrots, peeled and finely chopped

1 herb bouquet, tied in cheesecloth, consisting of:

5 large sprigs parsley

2 large sprigs fresh thyme (or ½ teaspoon dried)

8 to 10 whole black peppercorns

2 2-inch pieces lemon peel

2 whole cloves garlic, lightly mashed with the broad side of a knife

2 small dried red peppers (or ½ teaspoon dried red pepper flakes)

1¼ teaspoons salt, or to taste

1 3- to 3½-pound rabbit, quartered, giblets reserved (Note: If rabbit is unavailable, it may be omitted)

½ pound thick-sliced bacon, cut into ½-inch pieces

2 large ripe tomatoes, peeled, seeded, and chopped

2 tablespoons tomato paste

2 tablespoons unsalted butter

2 cups fresh whole corn kernels (or substitute thawed frozen whole corn kernels)

2 cups fresh baby lima beans (or substitute frozen limas, thawed)

2 cups fresh okra, trimmed and sliced ¼ inch thick (optional)

*1½ cups sweet potato purée (cook 1
large sweet potato in microwave
oven 5 to 8 minutes on high power
or in preheated 375° F conventional oven one hour or until tender. Peel and purée in food processor or blender)
Freshly ground black pepper, to taste
Tabasco sauce, to taste*

1. Place chicken in large stockpot. Add ⅓ of the mushrooms, onions, celery, and carrots. Add the herb bouquet, salt, and add enough water to barely
cover the contents. Cover and bring slowly to boil (this can take as long as 45
minutes). Reduce heat and simmer partially covered for 30 minutes.

2. Add rabbit and simmer partially covered 1½ hours longer or until
chicken and rabbit are tender. Let them cool in the broth until easy enough to
handle. (This may take 1 to 2 hours.) Remove chicken and rabbit meat from
bones. Discard bones and cut meat into ½-inch pieces. Set aside.

3. Strain broth reserving liquid; discard solids. Return strained broth to the
stock pot. (Note: You should have about 10 cups liquid. Add water to make up
the difference if necessary.) Skim fat off top of the broth.

4. In a large skillet, cook the bacon over medium-low heat, until fat is
rendered and bacon is lightly crisped. Drain on paper towels and set aside.
Discard all but 2 tablespoons of the drippings. Add remaining carrots, onions,
and celery to the drippings in the pan along with the chicken and rabbit giblets
and cook over medium heat until vegetables are tender. Add tomatoes and
tomato paste.

5. In a separate large skillet melt butter over medium heat. Add remaining
mushrooms and cook, stirring frequently, until softened, about 5 minutes. Remove mushrooms and drain on paper towels. To the stock, add corn, lima
beans, okra, chicken and rabbit meat, the sautéed vegetables, giblets, bacon, and
mushrooms. Add sweet potato purée to thicken lightly, if desired, and heat
through. (Do not overcook or vegetables will be mushy.)

6. Season to taste with salt, pepper, and Tabasco sauce and serve over rice,
if desired. Freeze in airtight container up to 6 months. Thaw in microwave oven
(17 to 20 minutes on high for 1 quart), or thaw at room temperature until
loosened from sides of container, then place in double boiler over simmering
water until hot.

*Makes about 6 quarts (about 20 first-course servings or 10 to 12 main-course
servings).*

Lamb and Fennel Burgoo with Garlic Biscuits
. . .

ANYONE WHO'S BEEN to Churchill Downs for the Kentucky Derby has probably at least heard of burgoo, if not tasted this rich, meaty stew. There it's served as a concession-stand item—which says something about how far burgoo has evolved as a Bluegrass favorite. Burgoo is also standard fare at the Kentucky Colonels' Barbecue on the Sunday following the Derby each May, and at the Fancy Farm Picnic—the largest political gathering in the state —held each August in Fancy Farm, Kentucky. (The picnic began in 1880 as a church-sponsored event. Because at that time elections were held in August, politicians frequently turned up to make speeches. They still do.) And at the International Barbecue Festival in Owensville, Kentucky, about 1,500 gallons of burgoo are served every year.

Although the combination varies from soup pot to soup pot, burgoo generally contains beef, pork, veal, lamb, and chicken, a little Worcestershire sauce plus potatoes, corn, tomatoes, beans, and possibly onion, okra, cabbage or carrots. Lamb is what distinguishes this stew from other classic Southern dishes, since Southerners generally favor pork or beef over lamb.

Some burgoos are made of ground meats; however, I prefer versions in which the ingredients remain distinct—both to the eye and to the palate.

Fresh fennel contributes a very subtle anise-like flavor to this version. (Lamb and fennel are a classic pairing in many European and Middle Eastern cuisines.) I've also added fresh herbs and garlic for a more pungent, assertive flavor than that of a typical burgoo, which is usually seasoned only with salt, pepper, and ground red pepper.

2 tablespoons unsalted butter

2 tablespoons vegetable oil

3 pounds lean boneless lamb shoulder, completely trimmed of all fat and filmy white tissue, cut into 1½-inch cubes

1 large yellow onion, finely chopped

1 large carrot, peeled and coarsely chopped

4 large fresh fennel bulbs, 1 trimmed and finely chopped, 3 trimmed, quartered, and cut into thin bite-sized strips (reserve some of the feathery tops for garnish)

3 tablespoons unbleached all-purpose flour, seasoned with a generous pinch each of salt and pepper

1 large ripe tomato, peeled, seeded, and chopped

1 tablespoon tomato paste

1 *herb bouquet, tied in cheesecloth,*
  consisting of:
  2 *whole large cloves garlic, peeled*
    and lightly crushed
  2 *small dried hot red peppers (or*
    ½ teaspoon dried red pepper
    flakes)
  1 *medium-sized imported bay leaf*
  2 *large sprigs fresh thyme (or ¼*
    teaspoon dried)
  5 *large sprigs fresh parsley*
  2 *2-inch strips lemon peel*
  6 *to 8 whole black peppercorns*
  ½ *teaspoon fennel seeds*

2 *cups beef broth, preferably home-*
  made
½ *pound boiling potatoes, peeled (if*
  desired) and cut into 1-inch chunks
1½ *cups fresh whole corn kernels (or*
  substitute frozen whole corn ker-
  nels, thawed)
1½ *cups fresh baby lima beans (or*
  substitute frozen limas, thawed)
2 *tablespoons butter mixed with 2*
  tablespoons flour, to thicken the
  stew (optional)
Garlic Biscuits (page 25)

1. Heat half the butter and half the oil in a Dutch oven over medium-high heat. Pat lamb dry with paper towels. Add about half the lamb (do not crowd or lamb will not brown) and cook, tossing frequently, about 6 or 7 minutes or until well browned on all sides. Transfer browned lamb to a platter or bowl. Repeat with remaining lamb, adding additional butter and oil as needed; remove and set aside with the other lamb.

2. Add onions, carrots, and the finely chopped fennel and cook over medium heat 4 to 5 minutes or until softened. Add the browned lamb and sprinkle evenly with the seasoned flour. Cook over medium heat about 5 minutes, tossing often.

3. Add tomato, tomato paste, herb bouquet, broth, and enough water to barely cover lamb. Bring slowly to boil. Set cover slightly askew and simmer, skimming frequently, about 1 to 1¼ hours until lamb is very tender.

4. Remove cooked lamb pieces and keep warm. Set a sieve or colander over a large saucepot and strain the cooking liquid, pushing down on the vegetables to extract flavor. Skim off and discard as much fat as possible.

5. Return lamb to the cooking liquid. Add potatoes, corn, and lima beans. Cover and simmer 10 minutes or until vegetables are almost tender. Add fennel strips and simmer 10 minutes longer or until all vegetables are tender but not mushy.

Soups

6. If a thicker stew is desired, transfer 1 cup of the broth to a medium bowl. Add the butter-flour mixture little by little to the hot broth while whisking constantly until thickened. Return thickened broth to the stew and stir gently to blend. Serve hot with Garlic Biscuits.

Makes 3½ to 4 quarts.

Collard Greens and Black-Eyed Pea Soup with Cornmeal Croustades

• • •

IN THE SOUTH, bitter leafy greens—collards, kale, mustard, and turnip greens—are traditionally cooked in water with smoked pork and spices. This recipe respects the classic technique, however; the ratio of liquid to solids is greater, resulting in a soup instead of a side dish. White wine, herbs, and a final thickening with a purée of aromatic vegetables add depth of flavor without compromising the simplicity of honest Southern fare. Cooking time for the greens in this soup is about 1 hour; about 2 or 3 hours less than traditionally cooked greens! The shorter cooking time preserves the texture, flavor, and color of the greens; cooked longer and they tend to become a rather soft, grey-green mass, qualities only a Southerner can love. (Although greens are edible after 4 or 5 minutes of cooking, about an hour of simmering is needed to amply flavor the broth.)

The cornmeal croustades are a nod to a classic combination. In the South, a "mess" of greens is usually accompanied by cornbread or cornsticks to crumble into the pot liquor. Here, toasted rounds of Crusty Cornmeal Yeast Bread topped with melted cheese make a tasty, but somewhat more refined, presentation.

This thrifty, earthy soup can be served as a meal in itself for a simple lunch or supper, or as a first course to precede a fried chicken or catfish dinner. The soup improves if made a day in advance and can be frozen and reheated in the microwave oven, or in the top of a double boiler.

4 medium-sized carrots, trimmed,
  peeled, and halved crosswise
4 medium-sized celery stalks, halved
  crosswise
15 to 20 sprigs fresh parsley, tied in
  a bundle with kitchen twine
¾ pound smoked ham hock, hog
  jowl, or pork knuckles
1 teaspoon salt, or more to taste
4 whole cloves
4 medium-sized yellow onions, peeled
10 medium-sized garlic cloves, unpeeled
1 herb bouquet, tied in cheesecloth,
  consisting of:
  8 whole black peppercorns

6 small dried hot red chile peppers
2½ teaspoons dried thyme
2 medium-sized imported bay leaves
5 quarts (20 cups) water
2 cups dry white wine
½ pound dried black-eyed peas
1½ pounds collard greens (or substitute turnip greens, mustard greens,
  or kale)
12 to 16 thin slices of Crusty Cornmeal Yeast Bread (page 36), or
  substitute French bread, lightly
  buttered and toasted
½ cup finely grated cheddar cheese
Cider vinegar, hot pepper vinegar, or
  Tabasco sauce, to garnish

1. Place carrots, celery, parsley, ham hock, and salt in an 8-quart stock pot. Stick a clove into each onion and add to the pot. Skewer the garlic cloves onto toothpicks or short wooden skewers (for easy removal when soup is done) and add to the pot. Add herb bouquet, water, and wine and bring to a simmer. Simmer partially covered for one hour, skimming the surface as needed.

2. Meanwhile, rinse and drain the black-eyed peas. Place the peas in a large saucepan and add cold water to cover by at least 2 inches. Bring to a boil and boil for 2 minutes. Remove from the heat, cover tightly and let stand off the heat for 1 hour. Drain.

3. Wash the collard greens and discard any large, coarse stems. (You will have about ¾ pound trimmed greens.) Stack the leaves and cut into ½-inch squares.

4. When the broth has simmered for 1 hour, add the greens and simmer partially covered for 15 minutes. Add the black-eyed peas to the soup and simmer uncovered for 45 minutes or until peas are tender but not mushy.

5. Using tongs or a slotted spoon, remove onions, carrots, celery, garlic, and pork from the soup and set aside. Remove herb bouquet and parsley bundle and discard. Remove the cloves from the onions and discard cloves. Place on- ions, carrots, and celery in a blender or food processor. Remove garlic cloves

Soups

■

from toothpicks and squeeze the soft inside flesh of each garlic clove into the food processor; discard garlic skins. Process the vegetables with ½ cup broth for 30 seconds or until smooth. Strain, if desired, and transfer the purée to the soup.

6. Carefully pick over the pork. Crumble lean pieces with your fingertips and return them to the soup. Discard fat and bones.

7. Stir the soup and taste for seasonings, adding additional salt to taste.

8. Place toast on a baking sheet and sprinkle with cheese. Place 4 inches from preheated broiler and broil until cheese is melted and bubbly.

9. To serve, ladle soup into bowls and float 2 croustades on each serving. Add about ½ teaspoon vinegar and 1 or 2 drops Tabasco to each 1 cup serving. Pass cruets of vinegar and Tabasco sauce, letting each diner additionally season his or her own to taste.

Makes about 2 quarts, or 6 to 8 servings.

Salads

Salads

ALTHOUGH VERY FEW seventeenth-century salad recipes were written down, manuscripts reveal that the middle and upper classes in the new world settlements ate them. Englishmen who planned to emigrate were advised to bring vinegar and either butter or oil to their new home. These early colonists gathered wild greens in woods and fields and reaped cabbage, radishes, cresses, celery, endive, spinach, garlic, cucumbers, and an array of herbs from their gardens.

By the eighteenth century, middle and upper classes continued to gather and grow greens for salads that were dressed with melted butter or oil and vinegar. Thomas Jefferson grew a variety of lettuce, cabbage, and other salad greens in his Monticello garden. His European travels no doubt attributed to his interest in salad making. In the 1780s, when he was ambassador to Paris, he sent seven kinds of lettuce home, in the hopes that they would flourish and provide the new world with greater varieties. His diaries include drawings of two oil and vinegar cruets, one seen in Italy, the other in Germany. And in Provence, Jefferson observed, "With their vegetables they have always oil and vinegar."

Up until the time of the Civil War, Americans continued to enjoy green salads, as well as salads made of tomatoes and chicken. Tomato salads and chicken salads have survived with great popularity to this day. In her 1824 cookbook, *The Virginia House-wife,* Mary Randolph gives instructions for the proper handling of salad greens: "The lettuce, pepper grass, chervil, cress, etc. should be gathered early in the morning, nicely picked, washed and laid in cold water . . ." She suggests serving the salad with a simple boiled dressing.

For nearly a generation after the Civil War, the average Southerner probably did not eat many salads, if any at all. After the Reconstruction, when ingredients could once again be grown or transported into the area, the lower classes made salads of potatoes, cabbage, and tomatoes. The middle and upper classes once again enjoyed lettuce salads, and for special occasions, those made of oysters, crab, chicken, and turkey. The preferred dressings for green salads was vinegar and olive oil. However, olive oil was costly and hard to procure and was often rancid or adulterated with cottonseed oil. Butter was sometimes used as an oil substitute, as is noted by the author of *Housekeeping in Old Virginia*, who, in 1879, wrote: "Where oil cannot be obtained, fresh butter, drawn or melted, is an excellent substitute and is indeed preferable to oil by some persons, epicureans to the contrary notwithstanding."

Three other dressings of the day have flourished well into the present: One, made of hot bacon fat and vinegar for so-called "wilted" salads; sweet and sour dressings made with sugar and vinegar; and boiled dressings. All three continue to be made today in the South, despite the availability of good-quality domestic and imported oils.

Other popular salads of the late nineteenth century included those made of canned salmon, lobster, terrapin, turkey, chicken, celery, tomato, turnip, potato, oysters, and cabbage.

Toward the turn of the century the consumption of salad in middle-class homes and restaurants grew; they were no longer just a privilege of the upper class. Cookbooks' expanded salad sections reflected a new emphasis on healthy eating; salads were light and therefore well suited to a population that was becoming more urban and sedentary.

In the early twentieth century, as salad making become more common and experimental, salads suffered from the not-so-healthy addition of sugar, cream, and alcohol. Culinary history was made when, in 1905, a Pennsylvania housewife won a recipe contest sponsored by Knox gelatin. Inspired by her "perfection salad," American cooks everywhere showed an interest in salads. Despite their general lack of nutritional attributes, congealed salads were an instant hit, and continue to be popular. Some supermarkets in the South have entire sections of congealed salads, reflecting consumer demands. These rainbow-colored concoctions are not to my taste and are a vulgar substitute for the gentle aspics and savory jellies of yesteryear.

Dressing continued to pose a problem due in part to the lack of good olive oil. (Olive oil was perhaps more common in the Northeast, where more Italian and Greek immigrants resided.) What olive oil could be had was still frequently stretched with cottonseed oil, and vinegars were often adulterated with acetic acid. As a result, boiled dressings and mayonnaise maintained their popularity and frequently just about anything topped with a dollop of mayonnaise became a "salad."

It is interesting to note that in 1933, during this time of salad mania that Harriet Ross Colquitt, author of *The Savannah Cook Book* stood firm in her beliefs: "We agree with the French that nothing can improve the simple method of marinating with good dressing lettuce, escarole, or endive, and letting it go at that. Adding anything to this is but painting the lily."

In the 1950s, crab with Thousand Island or Louis dressing was popular as were carrot-raisin and three-bean salads. Composed salads such as Niçoise, chef, and spinach salads became common restaurant offerings. In the seventies, the whole-foods movement stressed the importance of vegetables and complex carbohydrates resulting in the popularization of legume and whole-grain salads, such as those composed of lentils, rice, bulgur, and kasha. In the 1980s, pasta salads took America by storm and salad bars became a favorite addition to many fast-food restaurants.

In France during the late 1970s and into the 1980s, chefs were advocating nouvelle cuisine and showing the world that salads could surpass the lettuce-oil-and-vinegar combination to include almost anything. Foie gras, truffles, pheasant, kiwi, hazelnut oil, and raspberry vinaigrette were waking up palates across the country. This vital culinary movement gave cooks the freedom to incorporate unorthodox fruits, vegetables, and other foods into salads.

In the South, as in the rest of America, salads are usually served as a first course. The American custom of serving a salad at the beginning of a meal is said to have stemmed from the fresh vegetable antipasto platters of the Italians. Even the most Gallic chefs in this country have adapted to the American way and offer a variety of salads for the first course.

To my mind, nothing beats a simple, mixed green salad as a palate refresher after the main course. I serve them often, as I believe they ease one into the cheese and/or dessert courses, giving pause after a serious main course. However, for starters and main course salads, I offer other combinations. All of the salads here, with the exception of the Bibb Salad with My Favorite Vinaigrette, and A Southern *Mesclun* Salad, are meant to be served as a first course or side dish. Some of them may be enjoyed as light lunch or supper dishes with soup, cheese, or bread.

Cucumber Salad with Lemon-Dill Cream

. . .

THE ENGLISH SETTLERS were no doubt already familiar with the cucumber, a native of northwest India introduced by the time the settlers landed on the shores of the Atlantic, and it was cultivated in the earliest gardens of the New World. According to James Beard, sliced cucumbers dressed with vinegar, salt, and pepper is probably one of the oldest American salad recipes. That simple dressing has essentially the same ingredients used in pickling cucumbers, which continues to be preserved in a similar manner by Southern cooks today. Later, lemon juice was sometimes substituted for vinegar, and sugar might be added for a sweet and tangy flavor.

Like the dressings used in making coleslaws (for more about slaw, see page 115) dressings for sliced cucumbers seem to have become richer with the passage of time. Some cooks still dress cucumbers with vinegar or lemon juice, salt, and sometimes sugar. Cucumbers appeared in molded salads and mousses of the 1950s, and were added to any number of tossed salads throughout the region. Cucumbers in sour cream—flavored with vinegar, salt, and sugar—is common in some parts of the South.

This cooling, watery vegetable is a bit humble and common, but it takes well to a sophisticated dressing of crème fraîche, lemon juice, and fresh dill. The resulting mélange is rich and silky, and best served with a low-fat main course such as grilled, broiled, or poached chicken or salmon. If crème fraîche is not available, substitute sour cream. If you are dieting, yogurt may be used, but be sure to add lemon juice accordingly—you will need less as the yogurt is naturally acidic.

2½ to 3 pounds cucumbers
¾ teaspoon salt
½ cup crème fraîche (or substitute sour cream or plain yogurt)
Grated zest of 1 lemon

2 to 3 tablespoons freshly squeezed lemon juice (or less, if using yogurt)
1 to 2 tablespoons chopped fresh dill, or 2 teaspoons dried dill

1. Peel cucumbers if desired and slice very thin. Place cucumber slices in colander and sprinkle with salt. Toss to coat. Let stand 30 minutes to release liquid. (Note: This liquid would otherwise water down the dressing.)

2. In a serving bowl, combine crème fraîche, lemon zest, lemon juice, and dill.

3. Shake cucumbers to drain, then press down with a wooden spoon to release liquid. Place cucumbers on double thickness of paper towels. Roll up and squeeze gently to dry. Add cucumbers to crème fraîche mixture and toss gently to coat. Chill at least one hour. Taste and adjust seasoning.

Serves 4 to 6.

Fennel, Orange, Pomegranate Salad
with Raspberry Vinaigrette
▪ ▪ ▪

THOMAS JEFFERSON planted pomegranates at Monticello in 1769. Today, although they grow wild in many areas of the South, they are grown commercially only in California. Fennel is as old as the Roman hills. This mild, anise-flavored, celery-like vegetable was introduced to this country from Europe and now grows wild in many parts of the United States. Juicy, sweet Florida oranges were also an inspiration in creating this recipe. (The sunshine state is the largest producer of oranges and grapefruits in the country, providing the east coast with a generous supply of fruit from October through July.) Oranges were brought into Florida between 1513, when Ponce de León first landed, and 1565, when St. Augustine, the first colony in Florida, was established. But it was not until 1870 that Florida orange growers realized the fruit's potential, and it was only at the turn of the century that commercial production began.

The Valencia orange (which originated in Spain) is the most widely grown Florida variety. Other popular varietals include the Washington, the Hamlin, and the Pineapple, which is named for its characteristic aroma. The glorious orange has become such a part of our lives that it is difficult to imagine its being rare. But every Christmas as we savored ambrosia (a classic Southern holiday mélange of orange sections, coconut, and sugar) my parents would tell us children about the days when oranges were a rarity and finding one in the toe of a Christmas stocking—a custom established well before the Civil War—was cause for excitement.

Salads

▪

This salad was inspired by one prepared by a Neapolitan artist friend, Baldo Diodato. Baldo's salad has only fennel, garlic, oranges, olive oil, vinegar, and salt. I love the addition of the pomegranate seeds; their sweet tanginess adds a flavor lift further enhanced by the addition of raspberry vinegar. Watercress adds a hint of contrasting bitterness. This salad makes a pleasing prelude to roast pork, veal, or poultry. I think it works particularly well as a first course or side dish to your own Thanksgiving dinner. Or, serve as a foil to rich, creamy Whole Wheat Spaghetti with Bel Paese, Cream, and Pecans (page 281).

DRESSING

2 large cloves garlic, minced

3 tablespoons raspberry vinegar (or, substitute 2 tablespoons red wine vinegar)

Pinch of salt

Freshly ground black pepper, to taste

6 tablespoons olive oil

SALAD

2 oranges, peeled and sliced into rounds 1/3 to 1/4 inch thick

2 medium fennel bulbs, trimmed (feathery greens reserved) and sliced 1/3 to 1/4 inch thick

1/4 cup pomegranate seeds, optional (see note below for how to extract seeds)

1 small bunch watercress, washed and trimmed of tough stems

In a serving bowl, combine dressing ingredients. Add oranges, fennel, pomegranate seeds, and watercress and toss to blend. Taste, adjusting flavors if necessary by adding more vinegar, oil, salt, or pepper. Serve immediately.

Serves 4 to 6.

Note To extract pomegranate seeds, cut out the blossom end of the fruit, removing some of the white pith but taking care not to pierce the seeds. With a sharp knife, score the fruit into quarters, from stem end to blossom end. Break the fruit into quarters along the scored lines. Bend back the rind and pull out the seeds. Seeds may be wrapped in a plastic bag and frozen up to a year for later use.

Pear, Ham, and Hazelnut Salad

. . .

IN 1807, Thomas Jefferson received a gift of cuttings and fruit of Seckel pears from Timothy Matlack, who wrote of them: ". . . a small pear to be gathered about the 10th of October—they are red upon the tree & ripen in about two weeks to a beautiful lemon colour—They are juicy and tender as the best of Burser pears, and much sweeter." Jefferson replied, "I duly received your present of Sickel's [sic] pears, most of them in their highest point of perfection, two or three just past it. they exceeded anything I have tasted since I left France, & equalled any pear I had seen there."

Seckel pears still grow in home gardens in Virginia. Other pears of course can be substituted for the Seckels in this salad, but the Seckels are particularly nice because of their diminutive size.

The American hazelnut, or filbert, is a tall shrub that grows in thickets and woodlands, producing hard-shelled nuts. It is found in the northern parts of Alabama, Arkansas, Georgia, and South Carolina as well as in Kentucky, Maryland, North Carolina, Tennessee, Virginia, and West Virginia. The Beaked hazelnut produces its thin-shelled nuts in West Virginia, northern Georgia, and eastern North Carolina. Hazelnuts are grown commercially only in Washington and Oregon.

This salad is a mélange that combines the natural sweetness of pears, the salty, smoky flavor of ham, and the rich toastiness of hazelnuts. Serve as a first course to precede Thanksgiving dinner or smoked poultry or game.

4 medium-sized Seckel pears, or 2 medium-sized ripe, firm Bartlett, Bosc, or Comice pears

2 tablespoons freshly squeezed lemon juice

4 to 6 cups mixed soft lettuces (choose from mâche, oakleaf, red leaf, Boston, or Bibb)

1 ounce Smithfield ham (see page 481 for mail-order source) or other dry-cured country ham, sliced

paper thin (about 3 or 4 slices), cut into 4-inch by 1-inch strips

½ cup hazelnuts, toasted, skinned, and coarsely chopped

1 tablespoon red wine vinegar

6 tablespoons hazelnut oil

2 tablespoons light olive oil

Salt and freshly ground black pepper, to taste

1. If using Seckel pears, cut each into fourths and drop into a bowl of acidulated water (2 tablespoons lemon juice to 1 cup water) to prevent browning. If using regular pears, wash, halve, and core. Cut each pear half into 4 wedges, then cut each wedge in half. Drop into acidulated water.

2. Heap 1 cup lettuce in center of each of 4 to 6 salad plates. Wrap 1 strip ham around each slice of pear. Arrange pear slices neatly on top of or around lettuce mound. Sprinkle with hazelnuts and any leftover ham.

3. In a screw-top jar, combine vinegar, oils, and salt to taste. Shake to mix and spoon 1 to 2 tablespoons dressing over each serving. Sprinkle generously with freshly ground black pepper.

Serves 4 to 6 as a first course or salad course.

Bibb Salad with My Favorite Vinaigrette
• • •

IN 1865, Bibb lettuce was propagated in Frankfort, Kentucky, by amateur horticulturist Judge John Bibb. Bibb lettuce is sometimes called Kentucky limestone or limestone lettuce because it was believed that the region's alkaline soil gave it its special flavor.

Bibb lettuce heads are small (one head is just right for a single serving), its leaves soft, and its flavor subtle, similar to Boston lettuce. It is an elegant salad green—and a costly one, probably due to its fragility. Bibb lettuce is best simply dressed so its delicate flavor and silky texture are not masked. Fresh herbs and a mere hint of garlic make this dressing special, but not overwhelming. If fresh chervil, tarragon, and chives are unavailable, use fresh parsley rather than substituting dried herbs since freshness here is the key.

¼ cup extra-virgin olive oil
¼ cup vegetable or safflower oil
2 teaspoons red wine vinegar
2 teaspoons freshly squeezed lemon juice
1 large clove garlic, slivered

Pinch of salt
1 teaspoon each fresh chervil, tarragon, and chives
Freshly ground black pepper, to taste
4 heads Bibb lettuce, leaves separated, washed and drained

1. In a screw-top jar, combine oils, vinegar, lemon juice, garlic, and salt. Cover tightly, shake, and let stand at least 1 hour, preferably overnight, to blend flavors.

2. Just before serving, discard garlic from dressing. Add herbs and black pepper and shake to blend. Toss with lettuce in serving bowl and serve immediately.

Serves 6.

Green Bean Salad
with Sesame Seed Dressing

■ ■ ■

GREEN BEAN SALADS do not appear with great frequency in Southern cookbooks. The regional preference for serving green beans seems to be to cook them until soft and well flavored with pork, then to serve them hot as a vegetable side dish. I was never served a cold green bean until my early twenties when I lived in Paris where slender, crisp-tender green beans were part of a Niçoise salad—I loved them!

Here they are tossed with a sesame-oil-based dressing flavored with garlic and ginger. Thomas Jefferson took great interest in the oil of the African Beni seed (called *sesamum* by botanists and known commonly as the sesame seed). In 1808, Jefferson was sent some sesame seed oil by Colonel Few. He responded:

I thank you for the specimen of Benni [*sic*] oil which you were so kind to send me. I did not believe before that there existed so perfect a substitute for olive oil. I tried it at table with many companies and their guesses between two dishes of a salad dressing, the one with the olive oil, & the other with Beni, shewed [*sic*] the quality of the latter in favor of which the greater number guessed. Certainly I would prefer to have it always fresh from my own fields to the other brought across the Atlantic and exposed in hot warehouses. I am therefore determined to go into the culture of it for domestic use, and should be thankful to you for the process of expressing the oil from the seed in which you appear to have succeeded so perfectly. All the minutiae in new processes give aid towards perfecting them.

His enthusiasm in benne seed oil was sustained by further knowledge of the little seeds, as can be seen in a letter to his eldest grandchild Anne Cary Randolph who attended the flowers when she was at Monticello:

> . . . an acre yields 10. bushels of seed, each bushel giving three gallons of oil. an acre, therefore, besides our sallad [*sic*] oil, would furnish all kitchen & family uses, most of them better than with lard or butter . . . the plant grows somewhat like hemp. it was brought to S. Carolina from Africa by the Negroes, who alone have hither to cultivated it in the Carolinas & Georgia. they bake it in their bread, boil it with greens, enrich their broth, &c. It is not doubted it will grow well as far North as Jersey. . . .

Serve this salad with any grilled or roasted poultry or meat. Or serve with other salads—such as those made with cracked wheat and chickpeas—for a vegetarian meal.

2 pounds young, tender green beans, trimmed and washed

6 tablespoons tahini (Middle Eastern sesame seed paste)

6 tablespoons light sesame oil or vegetable oil (do not use dark oriental sesame oil)

1 tablespoon freshly squeezed lemon juice

1 tablespoon red wine vinegar

2 large cloves garlic, minced

1 3-inch piece fresh gingerroot, peeled and very finely chopped

Salt, to taste

¼ cup sesame seeds, lightly toasted

1. In a large saucepot of lightly salted water cook beans 2 to 4 minutes or until crisp-tender. Refresh under cold running water to stop the cooking, and drain well.

2. In a bowl whisk together tahini, oil, lemon juice, vinegar, and garlic. Place minced ginger in a double-layer square of cheesecloth and wring it firmly over the bowl to extract juices. Discard gingerroot. (Note: If you don't have cheesecloth, squeeze the ginger in your hand.) Add salt to taste.

3. Just before serving, add dressing to beans and toss to coat. Sprinkle with sesame seeds and serve at room temperature or very lightly chilled.

Serves 4 to 6.

Salads

Savoy Cabbage Coleslaw
with Sweet and Tangy Yogurt Dressing

• • •

COLESLAW—from the Dutch, *koolsla* (meaning cabbage salad)—is at once identifiable with the South. No fish fry, picnic, or church supper would be complete without it. Coleslaw is the steady date to Brunswick stew and pork barbecue platters and in many parts of the South, restaurants, diners, and tea rooms are more likely to serve a small dish of coleslaw rather than a tossed salad as an accompaniment to lunch or supper.

Early slaw recipes call for a simple dressing of salt, vinegar, and pepper. Some Southern cooks still prefer this clear, straightforward mixture, sometimes adding sugar to it to make a sweet-and-sour solution. The creamy dressings more commonly used today appeared in an earlier form in the nineteenth century. *Housekeeping in Old Virginia* (1879) includes three coleslaw dressings: the richest is composed of cream, butter, and egg yolks, plus vinegar, mustard, sugar, and salt. Another recipe is similar, but omits the cream and butter and adds celery seed, a flavoring commonly used in Southern coleslaws today. A third recipe is a boiled dressing thickened with beurre manie (butter kneaded with flour). In rural areas, cooks made a dressing by mixing vinegar with the rich top cream skimmed from freshly drawn milk.

Boiled dressings are still used to dress slaw and there are also very good prepared slaw dressings available. Some cooks make a quick sauce using prepared mayonnaise, vinegar, plus chopped pickle relish and minced scallions. Sometimes chopped tomatoes, onions, and bell peppers may be added to the shredded cabbage.

Slaw keeps well and is hardy enough to survive long treks to the picnic spot (although if the dressing contains egg, cream, or mayonnaise, it must be kept cold). Its sharp, vinegary flavor makes it the perfect foil to the richness of fried foods; its assertive crunch is a satisfying contrast to soft, pork barbecue sandwiches.

Despite these attributes, coleslaw is sometimes too coarse, too rustic to be very versatile. So I like to make slaw with savoy cabbage, which has curly leaves (it is sometimes called curly cabbage) and is tenderer and has a milder flavor than regular cabbage. Although not as common as the hardier head cabbage,

Salads

■

savoy is not a newcomer to the South: Thomas Jefferson first planted it in his garden in 1774, and every year thereafter.

The tart yogurt dressing here stands up to traditional dishes; try it with Spicy Fried Chicken (page 182); Fried Catfish Fillets with Spicy Red Pepper Sauce (page 152) or Hickory Pit Pork Barbecue on Cornmeal Buns with Hot Sauce (page 228). But it also goes with more sophisticated main courses, such as Quick Pork Chops with Orange-Molasses Glaze (page 220); Steak with Bourbon-Ginger Sauce (page 235); sandwiches made with Spiced Beef with Two Sauces (page 232); Fried Oysters (or Clams) with Green Tomato Salsa (page 162); and Lorraine Eppler's Crab Cakes with Smithfield Ham and Lemon-Caper Mayonnaise (page 170). One caveat: savoy cabbage may be difficult to find during the summer months; substitute Nappa cabbage or regular cabbage.

1 cup plain yogurt
½ cup mayonnaise
4 teaspoons cider vinegar, or to taste
Salt and freshly ground black pepper, to taste

Pinch of ground red pepper (cayenne)
1 pound savoy cabbage (1 small head), shredded finely

In a serving bowl mix yogurt, mayonnaise, vinegar, salt, black pepper, and red pepper. Taste and adjust seasonings; mixture should be quite tangy. Add cabbage and toss to coat.

Makes 4 cups; serves 6.

A Southern Mesclun Salad

• • •

MESCLUN is an old Provençal word meaning mixed. In the culinary sense, the term refers to a salad of mixed baby lettuces, greens, herbs, and edible flowers. The *mesclun* here is composed of wild greens, herbs, and flowers found in most Southern states. Some farmers' markets and specialty food stores sell *mesclun* plants and cut *mesclun*, and seed catalogues offer packets of *mesclun* seeds. (For seeds, see mail-order source, page 481.)

Dress the salad with a light vinaigrette made with Japanese rice vinegar, which is low in acidity and has a clean, mild, faintly sweet taste, making it a good choice for this rather gay, but delicate mélange.

6 handfuls mesclun (*Choose a variety of tender young greens, herbs, and flowers such as purslane, poke-weed, dandelion, watercress, mustard greens, chickweed, creeping thyme, clover flowers, chicory flowers, chervil, and the tiny, inner leaves of Bibb lettuce heads.*)

½ cup light olive oil
¼ cup unseasoned Japanese rice wine vinegar (*see note*)
Salt and freshly ground black pepper, to taste

1. Remove tough stems from greens, herbs, and flowers and discard. Wash and dry carefully.
2. In the serving bowl, combine oil, vinegar, salt, and pepper. Add *mesclun* and toss to coat lightly.

Serves 6.

Note Chinese rice wine vinegar may be substituted for Japanese but it has a sharper, more acidic taste; adjust proportions accordingly.

Shrimp and Snow Pea Salad with Creamy Chèvre Dressing

■ ■ ■

SHELLFISH SALADS have been enjoyed in the South at least since the late 1800s when they were served at fancy parties, teas, and balls. In Southern cookbooks, recipes for crab, shrimp, and lobster salads are numerous, while those for oyster salads are scarcer.

Seafood salads were especially popular in the 1950s, when they appeared with great frequency at bridal or bridge luncheons and became a mainstay on country club menus. These salads were ladylike dishes usually consisting of cooked shellfish combined with chopped celery and mayonnaise on a bed of lettuce or stuffed into avocado halves or scooped-out tomatoes. Shrimp and crab was often added to mousses, aspics, and molds.

Cold, cooked shellfish have been served as a first course or appetizer up and down the southeastern seaboard. Three all-time classics include shrimp dressed with rémoulade or ravigote sauce, crab or lobster with Louis sauce (chili sauce, mayonnaise, cream, and spices) and in Mobile, Alabama, West Indies salad—crabmeat tossed with lemon juice and olive oil.

Here I combine cooked shrimp with snowpeas and dress them in a mild, creamy goat cheese dressing. Serve the salad as a first course to precede any simply prepared chicken, pork, or veal. Or, serve on a bed of tender greens (such as Bibb, Boston, or mâche) and serve as a light lunch or supper with crusty bread and glasses of chilled Sauvignon Blanc.

½ pound snow peas, trimmed
1 pound medium-sized shrimp,
* shelled and deveined*
6 tablespoons heavy cream
4 ounces fresh, mild chèvre, such as
* Bûcheron or Montrachet (or*
* Southern goat cheese, see page 481*
* for mail-order source)*

½ teaspoon minced fresh dill
Pinch of salt
5 tablespoons light olive oil or vege-
* table oil*
½ teaspoon white wine vinegar
Pinch of white pepper
Bibb or Boston lettuce leaves, or
* mâche*

1. In a small saucepan, blanch snow peas in boiling, salted water about 1 minute, strain, refresh under cold, running water, drain, and set aside.

2. Cook shrimp in boiling, salted water until just cooked, about 3 minutes, drain, and set aside.

3. To make the dressing: In a small bowl combine cream, half of the chèvre, dill, salt, oil, vinegar, and pepper and mash chèvre with a fork until dressing is smooth. Taste, and adjust seasonings.

4. Arrange lettuce leaves on 6 salad plates. Scatter reserved snow peas on top of lettuce and mound shrimp in the center. Spoon some of the dressing over each mound of shrimp. Crumble remaining chèvre and sprinkle over the salads. Serve at room temperature or lightly chilled.

Serves 6.

Celery and Celeriac Salad
with Creole Mustard Dressing

• • •

I FIND CELERY to be in much greater use in the South than in other areas of the United States. Southerners add celery stalks to broths, stocks, and soups right along with carrot, onion, and herbs. Celery is part of the "holy trinity" (as described by Paul Prudhomme) in Cajun cooking—the other two components being onion and green pepper. Celery is commonly found in Southern chicken, egg, crab, shrimp, and oyster salads. During the heyday of the congealed salad, celery was a common addition, along with marshmallows, nuts, squares of frozen cream cheese, and canned fruit cocktail. Many Southern salad dressings contain celery seed as do many pickles and relishes. Celery goes into poultry dressings and stuffings (see Roast Turkey with Herbed Cornbread Dressing, page 196 or Quail with Cornbread Stuffing, page 212) and celery stalks are usually part of a Southern crudité tray.

Inspired by a recipe for celery salad in *Housekeeping in Old Virginia* (1879), I combine this humble vegetable with celery root, that pale brown, gnarled root vegetable so popular in Western Europe. The recipe here is a quick, easy variation on the salad found in every French charcuterie, celeri-rave rémoulade. Blanching extracts the natural bitterness of the celery root; spicy Creole mustard adds a bit of zip without overpowering the celery. Serve as a side dish to warm or cold grilled poultry, veal, pork, or fish, or on a picnic with pâté, or Spiced Beef with Two Sauces (page 232), sliced tomatoes, cheese, and bread.

1¼ to 1½ pounds celeriac (1 large)
Juice of 1 lemon
⅓ cup mayonnaise, preferably homemade
2 to 3 tablespoons Creole mustard
  (or substitute Dijon mustard)

6 stalks celery, trimmed and julienned
2 tablespoons coarsely chopped fresh
  celery leaves
Salt and freshly ground black pepper,
  to taste

1. Peel the celeriac and cut into julienne strips, immersing it into acidulated water (2 cups water plus juice of one lemon) as you work to prevent browning.

2. Bring a medium saucepan of water to a boil. Add drained, julienned celeriac and blanch 30 seconds to extract bitterness. Strain, refresh with cold water to stop the cooking, then drain thoroughly and dry with paper towels.

3. In a medium bowl combine mayonnaise and mustard. Add celeriac, celery, celery leaves, and salt and pepper; toss to mix. Taste, and adjust seasoning if necessary.

Serves 4.

Chicken Salad
with Lemon-Chive "Boiled" Dressing
• • •

CHICKEN SALADS have been popular in the South at least since the 1700s when Thomas Jefferson popularized salmagundi, a salad of cold chicken (or turkey), grapes, onions, anchovies, capers, and sometimes ham, celery, and parsley. Salmagundi was an English import, a decorative so-called "made" dish.

Chicken salads maintained their status as a special dish, served at parties, teas, and balls. It was often molded in aspic (made with homemade calves-foot gelatin) preceding the early twentieth-century deluge of congealed salads.

Chicken salads were frequently dressed with boiled dressings, which were popular before the widespread availability of good oils and vinegars, prepared mayonnaise, and bottled dressings. (Boiled dressings, incidentally, are not really boiled, but cooked gently until thickened, like a hollandaise sauce.)

Boiled dressings are usually composed of vinegar, sugar and salt, milk or cream, and egg yolks, which thicken the sauce upon heating. Some recipes call for oil, butter, or flour for thickening, and paprika, cayenne, and dry mustard for seasoning.

Most classic boiled dressings are quite sharp and acidic. The dressing here is reduced in vinegar, and has lemon juice for added freshness. Just-snipped chives add a mildly pungent flavor. Serve this chicken salad on a bed of Belgian endive and watercress as part of a summer buffet. Or, add hard-boiled eggs, tomatoes, chopped bell peppers and celery, if desired, for a main-course salad. Chop chicken pieces smaller for sandwich fillings.

LEMON-CHIVE "BOILED" DRESSING

¼ cup white wine vinegar
¼ cup freshly squeezed lemon juice
⅛ teaspoon salt, or to taste
½ cup heavy cream
1 large egg, well beaten

1 tablespoon chopped fresh chives, or
   to taste
1 tablespoon chopped fresh tarragon,
   or to taste

SALAD

6 cups diced cooked chicken
Freshly ground black pepper, to taste
1 bunch watercress, trimmed, washed
   and dried
2 large heads Belgian endive or Bibb
   lettuce or 1 medium head Boston
   lettuce, washed and dried

1 to 2 tablespoons fresh chives, cut
   into 1-inch lengths to garnish (optional)
1 to 2 tablespoons fresh tarragon
   leaves, to garnish (optional)
2 to 3 teaspoons grated lemon zest,
   to garnish (optional)

1. To make the dressing: In a medium saucepan, bring vinegar, lemon juice, and salt to a boil. Reduce heat to low. Add cream, then the egg. Cook, stirring constantly, over low heat 2 to 5 minutes or until mixture thickens and coats the back of a wooden spoon. Do not overheat or mixture may curdle. Add chives and tarragon and cool to room temperature. Cover, and chill up to 2 weeks.

2. To assemble salad: In a bowl, toss chicken with ½ to ⅔ cup dressing or enough to coat lightly. Taste, adding more salt or herbs to taste. Season with pepper.

3. Line a platter or individual plates with watercress and endive or lettuce leaves. Top with chicken salad and garnish with herbs and lemon zest, if desired. Serve cool (not cold) or at room temperature, and pass remaining dressing on the side.

Serves 6 as a light lunch or part of a picnic buffet; serves 4 as a main course.

Note Sliced tomatoes, chopped bell peppers, diced celery, or hard-boiled eggs may be added to the chicken mixture, if desired.

Turnip, Rutabaga, and Beet Salad
with Black Walnut Vinaigrette
• • •

IN 1585 in his "A Brief and True Report of Virginia," Thomas Heriot said of walnuts: "There are two sorts of walnuts both holding oil: but the one far more plentiful than the other. When there are mills and other devices for the purpose, a commodity of them may be raised, because there are an indefinite store." One of the walnuts was the black walnut; the other "walnut" of which he spoke was probably the butternut, since the English walnut does not grow in southeastern United States.

Black walnut trees flourish in rich woods, bottomlands, and on flood plains and are commonly found in Alabama, Arkansas, Georgia, Kentucky, Maryland, Mississippi, North Carolina, Western South Carolina, Tennessee, Virginia, West Virginia, and the northern parts of Florida and Louisiana. Black walnuts can be expensive and hard to procure, mainly because they are literally a tough nut to crack. They are available in specialty food stores and by mail order.

Black walnuts have a strong, earthy flavor that for some is an acquired taste. I often like to combine them with California walnuts—as in the dressing here—for a lighter, more delicate taste that has wider appeal. The assertiveness of this nut marries well with earthy root vegetables.

In much of the South, turnips and rutabagas are often simmered with a piece of smoked or cured pork and a bit of sugar until very soft. Sometimes they are mashed.

Among other vegetables, turnips and beets were brought to the New World at the same time the New World foods were taken to Europe. They were similar to root vegetables the Native Americans already knew in the eighteenth century. Although considered plebeian, nearly everyone—even the upper class—ate turnips with mutton.

In the South, beets were traditionally pickled (usually dressed with a tart sugar and vinegar solution) or boiled in a solution of water, sugar, and vinegar.

In the seventeenth-century English terminology, this recipe could pass for a "boiled sallet," boiled vegetables dressed with oil and vinegar. Its rich red and golden color makes this salad a stunning addition to a fall or winter buffet. Or serve as a side dish with grilled, broiled, or roasted chicken, pork chops, or pork roast.

BLACK WALNUT VINAIGRETTE

¼ cup black walnuts, toasted and cooled (see page 481 for mail-order source)

¼ cup English walnuts, toasted and cooled

Generous pinch of salt, or to taste

¼ cup vegetable oil

1 tablespoon walnut oil, or more to taste

1 tablespoon light olive oil

2 teaspoons white wine vinegar

4 teaspoons freshly squeezed lemon juice, or more to taste

Grated zest of 1 lemon

Freshly ground black pepper

VEGETABLES

½ pound rutabaga (about ½ large rutabaga), peeled and diced into ½-inch cubes

½ pound turnips, trimmed, scrubbed (peeled if mature), and diced into ½-inch cubes

½ pound beets, trimmed, peeled, and diced into ½-inch cubes

2 tablespoons chopped fresh Italian parsley, to garnish (optional)

1. To make the vinaigrette: In blender or food processor, chop nuts with salt for about 3 seconds. Do not overprocess; nuts should be chunky. Add oils, vinegar, lemon juice, lemon zest, and pepper and process 1 second to blend. Taste, adjusting flavor with walnut oil, lemon juice, and salt. Set aside.

2. To prepare vegetables: In a large saucepan, bring 6 cups lightly salted water to a boil. Add rutabaga, return to boil and cook about 4 minutes or until just tender. Remove rutabaga with slotted spoon, drain thoroughly, and toss in a small bowl with 2 tablespoons Black Walnut Vinaigrette. Add turnips to the same water, and proceed as for rutabaga, keeping vegetables separate. Repeat with beets.

3. To serve, arrange vegetables on a platter separately in neat rows. Drizzle with remaining dressing and sprinkle with parsley, if desired. Serve warm or at room temperature.

Serves 6.

Red Cabbage Salad
with Sugar Snap Peas, Ham,
and Walnut Dressing

•••

CABBAGE SALADS don't have to mean slaw. Here, shredded red cabbage serves as a bed for crunchy sugar snap peas and smoky ham cloaked with a rich, nutty dressing. The cabbage and pork combination is no accident; the two go hand in hand in many classic Southern dishes. In 1884 a Virginia cookbook compiler said of cabbage served with ham, chine, or middling: "You have before you the daily and favorite dish of 9/10 of the country people, not only in Virginia, but throughout the South." Pork is frequently used in the cooking water to flavor boiled cabbage. Shredded or chopped cabbage is often tossed with hot bacon drippings in a big cast-iron skillet. This fried cabbage probably led to so-called "hot" or "wilted" slaws that, like wilted salads, are dressed with warm pork drippings, sugar, salt, and pepper. Camille Glenn, author of *The Heritage of Southern Cooking,* describes wilted slaws with bacon dressing as a "true country salad of the deep South." Mrs. Porter, in her book *Mrs. Porter's New Southern Cookery Book* (1871), says for warm slaws "red cabbage is best," which she says to shred, simmer 30 minutes, then dress with butter, vinegar, salt, and cayenne.

This salad is an update of the classic cabbage-and-pork combination. Because the dressing is made with a walnut oil instead of bacon drippings, which solidifies quickly and must be consumed promptly, the salad can be made partially in advance. Serve with roasted or grilled poultry or game.

SALAD

3/4 pound sugar snap peas or snow
    peas, trimmed
1 tablespoon red wine vinegar
6 cups shredded red cabbage (3/4
    pound)

1 1/4 cups julienned Smithfield or
    other dry-cured country ham (1/2
    pound) (see page 481 for mail-
    order source)

1 cup walnut oil
¼ cup vegetable oil
½ cup balsamic vinegar
½ teaspoon salt

¼ teaspoon freshly ground black pepper
½ cup chopped walnuts, lightly toasted

1. Bring a large pot of lightly salted water to a boil. Add peas and simmer until just tender, 3 to 5 minutes. Remove with slotted spoon. Add red wine vinegar and cabbage to the same water and boil until cabbage is just tender, 1 to 2 minutes. Strain, refresh under cold water, and drain well.

2. Arrange a small bed of cabbage on each of 6 to 8 salad plates. Put peas on top and a mound of ham in the center.

3. To make the dressing: Put dressing ingredients except toasted walnuts together in a jar and shake well to mix. Drizzle dressing over salad and sprinkle with toasted walnuts. Serve at room temperature.

Serves 6 to 8 as a side dish or first course.

Warm Potato Salad
with Green Beans and Bacon Dressing
· · ·

LIKE WARM SLAWS, warm potato salads probably grew out of the custom of cooking the vegetable in a skillet with bacon or ham drippings. Richard J. Hooker says in his *Food and Drink in America: A History* that by the end of the nineteenth century potato salads were being eaten cold, suggesting that prior to that they were eaten hot.

Potato salads do not date as far back as cabbage or lettuce salads primarily because potatoes did not come into popular use until the nineteenth century. There aren't many recipes for warm potato salads, except some called "German" potato salad, which are dressed with a sweetened oil-and-vinegar dressing. The classic Southern potato salad—eaten cold—is bound with mayonnaise and sometimes has chopped celery, hard-boiled eggs, or green peppers.

Salads

■

This salad of potatoes, bacon, and green beans is a humble but delicious one. Green beans and potatoes are a traditional Southern combination: green beans were quite often served with new potatoes as a hot vegetable side dish. The dressing is rich, so I suggest serving this as a side dish to a simple, clean main course, such as Grandmother's Roast Lemon Chicken (page 183), or broiled flounder, scrod, cod, halibut, or grouper.

2 pounds small red new potatoes,
  unpeeled
¼ pound green beans, trimmed
½ pound thick-sliced bacon (preferably double smoked), diced
3 tablespoons red wine vinegar

2 teaspoons Dijon mustard
Salt and freshly ground pepper, to
  taste
Chopped chives, to garnish (optional)

1. In a saucepan, cook potatoes in boiling, salted water in their skins until just tender, 12 to 14 minutes. Peel, if desired, cut into ¼-inch slices, and keep warm in covered, 2- to 3-quart ovenproof dish.

2. Blanch green beans in a saucepan of boiling, salted water until just tender, 3 to 5 minutes. Drain and keep warm along with potatoes.

3. In a heavy skillet, cook bacon until crisp and golden. Remove with a slotted spoon and drain on paper towels. Discard all but ½ cup bacon fat.

4. Over low heat, stir vinegar and mustard into bacon fat. Season with salt and pepper to taste and pour over potatoes and beans. Add reserved bacon, toss very gently, and sprinkle with chives, if desired. Serve immediately.

Serves 6 to 8 as a side dish.

Wilted Arugula and Spinach Salad with Bacon, Wild Mushrooms, and Thyme

. . .

"WILTED" SALADS—also sometimes known as "scalded lettuce" or "smoth-ered lettuce"—have probably been eaten in the South since bacon drippings from the first cured hog were poured over a mess of greens. Were these early American epicureans aware of similarly dressed salads in France? Perhaps the combination was simply a result of hunger, necessitating the use of ingredients at hand. Since there was a lack of good oils and vinegars, and prepared mayonnaise and bottled dressings were hundreds of years away, wilted salads were no doubt a tasty solution to the salad dilemma.

Put very simply, wilted salads consist of garden greens—spinach, lettuce, endive, and sometimes cabbage or wild greens, such as sorrel, cress, chickweed, mâche, or dandelion—tossed with a warm dressing based on the drippings from bacon, ham, or other fatty bits of cured pork. Vinegar and sometimes sugar, sieved hard-boiled egg yolks, salt, and red and black pepper were added. (Dressings of this type were also used to dress vegetables other than salad greens, such as potatoes and ramps, the wild leeks found in the mountains of Virginia and West Virginia.)

In this salad I use arugula, a cultivated "wild" green that is now widely available. Tender spinach, woodsy mushrooms, and a warm, thyme-scented dressing make this a gutsy, robust starter. Follow with roasted or grilled chicken, pork, veal, or beef. Or, add sliced hard-boiled eggs and croutons for a main-course salad. One word of caution: bacon fat congeals at room temperature so plates and salad greens should be warm, bacon fat should be hot.

6 slices bacon (about 3 ounces)
2 tablespoons olive oil
½ pound wild or cultivated mushrooms (such as shiitake, porcini, chanterelles, etc.), or substitute domestic mushrooms, wiped clean, trimmed of tough stems, caps cut into ¼-inch strips
1 tablespoon red wine vinegar

1 tablespoon lemon juice
1 teaspoon Dijon mustard
½ teaspoon sugar
1 tablespoon fresh thyme leaves (or substitute 1 teaspoon dried thyme)
1 large bunch arugula, well-washed
1 large bunch spinach, well-washed
Salt and freshly ground black pepper, to taste

1. In a large skillet cook bacon over medium heat until crisp and golden-brown. Remove and drain on paper towels. Set aside 2 tablespoons of the drippings in a small cup and discard the rest.

2. Add 1 tablespoon of the olive oil to the skillet. Add mushrooms and cook 3 to 4 minutes over medium heat or until tender. Remove mushrooms with a slotted spoon and set aside.

3. Add vinegar, lemon juice, mustard, and sugar to skillet and boil briefly over medium heat. Add the reserved bacon drippings, the remaining tablespoon olive oil, and the thyme and heat through. (May be made several hours in advance up to this point. Reheat before proceeding to the next step.) Add arugula, spinach, and mushrooms and toss over low heat just to coat. Season with salt and pepper, to taste. Serve on warm salad plates and crumble bacon on top. Serve immediately.

Serves 4 to 6 as a first course.

Note Add chopped hard-boiled eggs and croutons for a main-course salad for two.

Corn, Hominy, and Lima Bean Salad with Jalapeño Peppers and Red Pepper Vinaigrette

. . .

ONE DOES NOT FIND many recipes for corn, lima, or hominy salads in even the most contemporary Southern cookbooks, even though they are important regional ingredients. Traditionally, cooked corn kernels are served cold only in corn relish, a pickled mélange that usually includes diced red and green bell peppers, sugar, vinegar, celery seed, dry mustard, turmeric, and sometimes shredded cabbage. In rural areas pickled corn (cooked corn kernels packed in jars with salt) might sometimes be eaten at room temperature but is usually warmed in a skillet with bacon fat before serving. Like corn, whole hominy is usually eaten hot as a farinaceous side dish. An occasional three-bean salad can be found in Southern cookbooks but it rarely includes limas, the queen of Southern legumes.

The Southwest comes to mind when jalapeños are mentioned. However, in the mid-1980s, farmers in Virginia's South Boston area began growing jalapeño peppers as an alternative to tobacco. With the current interest in the food of the Southwest and spicy fare in general, these hot little capsicums may prove to be a successful alternative to the golden leaf that once was the pride and financial stability of the South. Jalapeños are a welcome foil to the mild-mannered corn, limas, and hominy. The flavor is perked up even more with a dressing made with hot pepper vinegar, commercially produced in the South. Pepper vinegar, made by infusing small hot chile peppers in vinegar, is commonly sprinkled on cooked greens. (My grandfather, Daddy Jim, sprinkled it on everything—except dessert.)

Pepper vinegar can be difficult to find outside the South, so I've devised a simple recipe using red wine vinegar and dried red pepper flakes.

DRESSING

¼ cup olive oil

¼ cup finely chopped fresh cilantro (*if cilantro is not available, substitute fresh parsley*)

1 tablespoon freshly squeezed lime juice

1 tablespoon hot pepper vinegar (or substitute red wine vinegar plus small pinch dried red pepper flakes)

1 large clove garlic, minced

Pinch of salt

Freshly ground black pepper, to taste

¼ teaspoon cumin

SALAD

15½- to 16-ounce can white hominy, drained (*about 2 cups*)

1 cup cooked fresh whole corn kernels (*or substitute thawed frozen whole corn kernels*)

1 cup cooked fresh baby lima beans (*or substitute thawed frozen lima beans*)

2 fresh jalepeño peppers, seeded and finely chopped (*retain seeds if a hotter flavor is desired*), or substitute a 4-ounce can chopped green chiles

2 tablespoons chopped red onion

1. In a medium bowl combine dressing ingredients and whisk to mix.

2. Add remaining ingredients and toss to blend. Cover and let stand at room temperature at least 1 hour to blend flavors. Taste, adding olive oil, lime juice, vinegar, salt, pepper, cumin, and cilantro, if desired. Serve lightly chilled or at room temperature with sliced tomatoes, if desired.

Serves 4 to 6.

Salads

■

Watercress Salad with Smoked Chicken and Walnut Croutons

...

WHEN I'M IN VIRGINIA at Christmastime I always stock up on wild watercress, colloquially known as "creasies," "creasy greens," or "cressies." It resembles cultivated watercress except the wild varieties tend to be hardier, darker in color, and rather "tangled" in appearance. Wild watercress has a stronger flavor, too—which I love in juxtaposition to the rest of the ingredients in this dish—but cultivated cress is a fine substitute.

The sweet-tangy mustard adds a welcome counterpoint to the bitter greens, while the walnut croutons add a toasty richness and crunch. Serve as a first course or main course along with Whole Wheat Cornsticks (page 35) or Madeleines (page 36).

CROUTONS

2 tablespoons walnut oil
1 tablespoon butter
3 large cloves garlic, slivered

3 slices stale, homemade-type white bread, cut into ½-inch cubes
Pinch of salt

DRESSING

2 teaspoons sweet mustard or spicy brown mustard
2 teaspoons freshly squeezed lemon juice
2 teaspoons red or white wine vinegar

Generous pinch of salt
3 tablespoons walnut oil
2 tablespoons light olive oil
1 tablespoon vegetable oil
Freshly ground black pepper, to taste

SALAD

12 ounces watercress, tough stems removed
6 ounces radicchio, torn into bite-sized pieces

6 ounces smoked chicken, shredded into bite-sized pieces

1. To make the croutons: In a large skillet heat walnut oil and butter over medium-low heat. Add garlic and cook gently 1 minute. Add bread cubes to the skillet and cook, tossing often, about 5 to 8 minutes or until crisp and golden-brown. (Note: Do not raise heat or garlic may burn and taste bitter.) Season with salt and set aside on paper towels.

2. To make the dressing: In a small bowl, whisk together mustard, lemon juice, vinegar, and salt. Whisk in oils and add pepper to taste.

3. To assemble the salad: In a bowl toss the watercress, radicchio, and chicken with the dressing. Top with croutons.

Serves 6 as a first course, 2 to 3 as a light main course.

Dandelion and Bacon Salad with Hard Cider Vinaigrette

■ ■ ■

WILTED DANDELION GREENS are a Southern classic. Served in spring, dandelion greens are a welcome addition to the diet after a long winter of root vegetables and sauerkraut. Here, hard cider and cider vinegar add a fruity note that I find quite pleasant with smoky bacon. Serve as a first course or main course with French bread and sparkling cider.

¾ pound small boiling potatoes, scrubbed
½ cup hard cider
½ pound bacon (preferably thick-sliced), cut into 1-inch pieces
1 to 2 tablespoons light olive oil, if needed
¼ cup cider vinegar

¾ pound tender, young dandelion greens (Note: If dandelion greens are large, buy 1 pound and trim away tough stems), or substitute other bitter greens, such as arugula, watercress, or chicory
Salt and freshly ground black pepper, to taste
Cider vinegar or hard cider, for sprinkling

1. Place potatoes in a large saucepan of lightly salted cold water and bring to a boil. Cook 20 minutes or until just tender. Drain. While still warm but cool enough to handle, peel and dice. Place in a bowl, toss with ¼ cup hard cider and cover to keep warm.

2. In a large skillet, cook the bacon, tossing frequently, until crisp. Drain bacon on paper towels and set aside. Set aside 7 tablespoons of the drippings in a cup or small bowl and discard the rest. (Note: If bacon has rendered less than 7 tablespoons, add enough olive oil to make up the difference.)

3. Add the remaining hard cider and the vinegar to the skillet and boil until reduced to ⅓ cup.

4. Add the dandelion greens to the bowl with the warm potatoes and toss with the warm bacon drippings. Add the hot cider reduction, and toss quickly. Season to taste, then serve immediately. Pass a cruet of cider vinegar or hard cider for diners to sprinkle over their servings.

Serves 6 as a first course, 3 as a main course.

Rice Salad with Pecans and Curry Vinaigrette

▪ ▪ ▪

DESPITE THE SOUTH'S ADORATION for rice (it continues to be the preferred farinaceous side dish of South Carolina and Louisiana) there are very few recipes for rice salad, and those that do exist appear in cookbooks published after 1950. Perhaps those rice salads were the result of the "salad mania" of that era, or cooks may have been inspired by the rice salads that were popular in France and Italy. For whatever reason, it seems that Southerners have always preferred their rice hot. Leftover rice was more likely to be added to bread, biscuit, waffle, or pancake batter than to be tossed with a dressing and eaten cold or at room temperature.

In this recipe I've combined nutty, rich-tasting Wild Pecan Rice™ with wild rice, raisins, pecans, and a curry dressing that is a variation on one in the *Charleston Receipts* (1950). The dressing adds a spicy but not overwhelming note. The toasted pecans add crunch and point up the nutty flavor of the rice.

Wild Pecan Rice™ is grown and processed by Conrad Rice Mill in New Iberia, Louisiana. The seed is actually a genetic hybrid of the one that came to this country after World War II from French Indo-China. The rice did not grow well, so it was crossed with domestic, long-grained varieties. An increased yield resulted.

Wild Pecan Rice™ is more nutritious than regular white rice since only 15 percent of the bran layer is removed. Despite its name, this rice is neither wild, nor flavored with pecans. It does, however, have a deep, hearty, nutty flavor that goes well with turkey, game, and other harvest fare. Serve this salad as a side dish to game, pork, poultry, or as part of a Thanksgiving dinner.

RICE SALAD

2¼ cups water
1 teaspoon salt, or to taste
7-ounce package (1 cup) uncooked Wild Pecan Rice™ (or substitute long-grain brown rice or brown basmati rice)

¼ cup uncooked wild rice
¼ cup golden raisins
3 tablespoons very finely minced scallions

DRESSING

¼ cup vegetable oil
2 tablespoons light olive oil
2 tablespoons white or red wine vinegar

¼ teaspoon curry powder
Salt and freshly ground black pepper, to taste
¼ cup coarsely chopped pecans

1. To make the rice salad: In a medium saucepan, bring water and the salt to boil. Add Wild Pecan Rice™ and wild rice. Lower heat; simmer, covered, 20 minutes. Remove from heat; let stand, covered, 5 minutes. Add raisins, fluff with fork to mix, then let cool to room temperature. When cooled, add scallions.

2. To make the dressing: In a small bowl, mix the oils, vinegar, curry powder, and salt and pepper. Add to the rice mixture and toss just until rice is lightly coated. Stir in pecans. Adjust seasoning.

Makes 4 cups.

Smoked Chicken Salad
with Dried Cherries and Walnuts
• • •

CHERRIES ARE NOT commercially produced in the South, but many types, including the tart Montmorency and several sweet varieties, can be grown in parts of the South. Thomas Jefferson's favorite cherry was the Carnation, a large, light red cherry highly esteemed for brandying and preserving. He planted over 200 cherry trees in 1774, 199 of which were Italian varieties.

For preserving, Mary Randolph, author of *The Virginia House-wife* (1824) was also partial to the Carnation as well as a variety she describes as "common, light red with short stems." For stewing, she calls for morello cherries.

Dried cherries have recently become available in specialty food stores and by mail order. While they may indeed be trendy, dried cherries are by no means "new." No doubt the Native Americans and early settlers dried cherries, just as they did other fruits. And Mary Randolph tells how to dry cherries in her cookbook: first the cherries are pitted, then they're stewed with sugar, drained, then dried in the sun. Of them she says, "They make excellent pies, puddings, and Charlottes."

You can dry cherries yourself, but I find it easier to let someone else do the work. Dried cherries—chewy and sweet like raisins, but with more tartness—are available in specialty food stores throughout the country and by mail order. (For source, see page 481.)

I like to serve this lusty, full-flavored salad as a first course to kick off a harvest meal (it's great as a starter to Thanksgiving dinner). Or serve alongside a bowl of Sweet Potato Soup with Pine Nut Butter (page 94) for lunch or supper.

3 tablespoons Madeira, port, marsala, or sweet sherry

⅓ cup dried cherries

⅓ cup light olive oil

3 tablespoons walnut oil

3 tablespoons cherry vinegar (available at specialty food stores) or red wine vinegar

3 tablespoons minced shallots (or substitute 1 tablespoon minced onion)

Salt and freshly ground black pepper, to taste

1 medium head red or green lettuce, washed, dried, and torn into bite-sized pieces

*1 medium head radicchio, washed,
dried, and torn into bite-sized
pieces*

*1¼ to 1½ pounds boneless smoked
chicken or duck breast cut into
thin slices*
½ cup toasted walnut halves

1. In a small saucepan bring Madeira and cherries to a simmer. Remove from heat and let stand 10 minutes. (Or heat in a bowl in microwave oven.)

2. In a separate bowl, combine oils, vinegar, shallots, and salt and pepper to taste. Add the cherry mixture.

3. Line each of 4 salad plates or bowls with lettuce and radicchio. Overlap chicken slices on top. Drizzle with dressing and sprinkle with walnuts.

Serves 4 as a light main course or 6 as a first course.

Parsnip and Carrot "Slaw" with Pecan Vinaigrette

∎ ∎ ∎

ON A RECENT TRIP to Georgia to witness the harvest and production of pecans, I asked producers why pecan oil—like the hazelnut oil and walnut oils on the market today—isn't made. The reply was that the oil-extracting process is too costly. Perhaps as the interest in American food flourishes, pecan oil will be produced in the near future. Until that time, I will use my own pecan vinaigrette as an alternative. Made of toasted, crushed pecans, olive oil, vegetable oil, mustard, and vinegar, it's easily made in a food processor and can dress grilled fish or meats as well as steamed vegetables.

I find it complements this "slaw" of carrots and parsnips. Serve as a side dish to roast turkey, chicken, game, or grilled pork chops.

If you have a julienne blade for the food processor or a mandolin, this salad is a breeze. Lacking both, the vegetables can be julienned by hand. If that seems too time consuming, you can grate the vegetables, but I find the texture less interesting than if they are julienned.

Salads
∎

½ cup lightly toasted pecans

1½ to 2 teaspoons white wine vinegar

1 teaspoon Dijon mustard

Generous pinch of salt

Freshly ground black pepper, to taste

3 tablespoons vegetable oil

3 tablespoons light olive oil

½ pound carrots (about 6 medium
carrots)

½ pound parsnips (about 4 medium
parsnips)

Toasted pecan halves to garnish, optional

1. In a blender or food processor, process the toasted pecans about 5 seconds. (Note: Do not grind to fine powder.) Add vinegar, mustard, salt, pepper, and the oils and process about 1 second just to mix. Taste; adjust seasonings.

2. Trim and peel the carrots and the parsnips and cut into julienne strips. (Do not peel the parsnips until ready to julienne and dress with the vinaigrette as it tends to turn brownish when exposed to air. The acidic ingredients in the vinaigrette will prohibit browning.) Place in a medium bowl, add dressing, and toss to coat. Taste, adding more vinegar, salt, and pepper as necessary. Garnish with pecan halves.

Serves 6.

Tabouli Salad with Okra, Tomatoes, and Walnuts

· · ·

THE CUISINE OF INDIA—which is as respectful of okra as is Southern cuisine—was the inspiration for this nutty grain and vegetable salad spiced with cumin and coriander.

Other than potato salads and a very occasional macaroni or rice salad, salads based on starches and grains were not widely consumed in the South until recently. Now many restaurants and most take-out shops sell pasta and grain salads of some sort, especially during the summer months.

Tabouli, a salad made with cracked wheat, is a cooling treat in warm weather when carbohydrates, which are easier to digest than heavy, meaty dishes, are often more appealing. The okra is cooked whole, and very quickly, so it is crisp-tender and not the least bit "stringy." Serve this spicy salad as a main course with sliced fresh mozzarella, feta, or goat cheese. Or serve as a side dish alongside grilled lamb, veal, pork, or hamburgers.

DRESSING

2 to 3 tablespoons lemon juice
1 teaspoon white or red wine vinegar
½ to ¾ teaspoon ground coriander
½ to ¾ teaspoon ground cumin
Salt and freshly ground black pepper, to taste
¼ cup light olive oil

1 tablespoon vegetable oil
¼ cup chopped fresh parsley
¼ cup chopped fresh basil or cilantro
¼ cup minced scallions
2 large cloves garlic, minced (optional)

SALAD

1 cup uncooked coarse bulgur, rinsed and drained (Note: Bulgur is wheatberries that have been steamed, dried, and cracked. It is available in supermarkets and in specialty food stores.)

¼ pound very tender, young okra
1 small ripe tomato, finely chopped
¼ cup walnut halves, toasted

1. To make the dressing: In a medium bowl, combine 2 tablespoons lemon juice, vinegar, ½ teaspoon coriander, ½ teaspoon cumin, salt, and pepper. Whisk in oils. Stir in parsley, basil, scallions, and garlic. Set aside ¼ cup dressing and leave the rest in the bowl.

2. To prepare the salad: In a medium bowl, pour 3 cups boiling water over bulgur. Cover and let stand 1 hour. Turn into a sieve and drain thoroughly, pressing bulgur with back of a wooden spoon.

3. Add the well-drained bulgur to the bowl of dressing. Toss to mix and let stand at least 1 hour to blend flavors (may be made a day in advance up to this point).

4. Trim the stems off the okra pods, leaving the caps intact. (This will keep the okra from becoming slimy. For more about okra, see page 315.) Drop okra

Salads

■

whole into a medium saucepan of lightly salted boiling water and cook 1 minute. Drain, refresh under cold water, and pat dry with paper towels. Place okra in a medium bowl along with reserved ¼ cup dressing and toss to mix. Let stand 1 hour at room temperature to blend flavors.

5. Taste the bulgur mixture for seasonings, adding more lemon juice, herbs, or spices to taste. On a serving plate, mound the bulgur in the center and surround with okra. Sprinkle top of bulgur with tomato and nuts.

Serves 2 as a main course or 4 as a side dish.

Steak and Potato Salad
with Vidalia Mayonnaise

• • •

BEEF SALADS are not particularly Southern. I've never seen one on a restaurant menu in the South, nor have I ever been served such a dish at a Southern table, other than my own.

Even in salads' heyday—the fifties—beef does not appear in cookbooks in salad form. Beef *was* eaten cold, however. In some parts of the South in the nineteenth century, boeuf à la mode (a braised-beef dish credited to Pierre de Lune, the French seventeenth-century author of *Le Cuisiner*) was sometimes served cold, often cloaked in natural gelatin made from calves' feet for boeuf à la mode en gelée. Spiced beef—a Christmas favorite—was also served cold.

Today, innovative chefs in urban areas are more likely to prepare sophisticated first-course salads with game, poultry, and foie gras rather than beef. One exception is the Italian carpaccio, razor-thin slices of raw beef drizzled with a mustardy dressing. Even this, although served cold and usually as a first course, is not a "salad" in the traditional sense.

With today's smaller families, single-person households, plus the tendency toward easy entertaining, I think beef salads are a good addition to the repertoire, as they utilize leftover beef.

The salad here presents sliced rare beef and new potatoes on a bed of arugula and romaine, drizzled with a simple dressing flavored with Vidalia onions. Serve as a light lunch or supper dish with a platter of sliced tomatoes and

Crusty Cornmeal Yeast Bread (page 36). Or, offer it as a part of a summer buffet, along with Tabouli Salad with Okra, Tomatoes, and Walnuts (page 136), Corn, Hominy, and Lima Bean Salad with Jalapeño Peppers and Red Pepper Vinaigrette (page 128), and Peaches and Cream Shortbread Tart (page 370) or Blackberry Roll (page 378).

VIDALIA MAYONNAISE

¼ cup very finely chopped Vidalia onion (or substitute 2 tablespoons finely chopped shallots, Bermuda, Spanish, or yellow onion)

¼ cup mayonnaise
¼ cup plain yogurt
1 teaspoon Dijon mustard
Pinch freshly ground white pepper

SALAD

1 pound unpeeled new potatoes, scrubbed and quartered
1 bunch arugula or watercress, trimmed of tough stems, washed and dried
1 very small head romaine (or use the very inner leaves of 1 medium head romaine), washed, dried, and torn into bite-sized pieces

1 pound lean steak, grilled or broiled to desired degree of doneness, cooled and thinly sliced
2 to 3 very thin slices Vidalia or other mild, sweet onion, separated into rings
Freshly ground black pepper, to taste

1. To make the Vidalia mayonnaise: In a small bowl mix the onions, mayonnaise, yogurt, mustard, and white pepper. Press through a stainless-steel sieve set over a medium bowl, pressing hard with wooden spoon or rubber spatula to release onion juices. Discard solids. Set 2 tablespoons of the dressing aside and leave the remainder in the bowl.

2. Steam potatoes over boiling water until tender but not mushy. Drain, refresh under cold running water to stop the cooking, and drain again. While potatoes are still somewhat warm, cut into ⅓-inch slices and add potatoes to the dressing in the bowl. Toss gently and, if time permits, let stand 30 minutes to blend flavors.

Salads

3. To serve, mound arugula and romaine in center of large serving platter. Mound potatoes on top of greens. Arrange beef in overlapping slices on or around lettuces. Scatter remaining Vidalia onion slices over beef and drizzle with the reserved 2 tablespoons dressing. Grind black pepper over all. Serve at room temperature or lightly chilled.

Serves 4 as a light supper or lunch, or 6 as part of a picnic buffet.

Fish and Shellfish

Fish and Shellfish

...

IN THE SEVENTEENTH CENTURY, Captain John Smith wrote that in Jamestown he found an ". . . abundance of fish, lying so thicke with their heads above the water, as for want of nets . . . we attempted to catch them with a frying-pan . . . neither better fish, more plentie, nor more varitie for small fish, had any of us seene in any place so swimming in the water . . . We tooke more in owne hour than we could eate in a day." Catfish, shad, bluefish, crabs, and oysters were just a few of the aquatic riches that the settlers eagerly embraced. And like pork, corn, and peanuts they have become a cornerstone of classic Southern cooking.

Fish and seafood dishes born along the Atlantic and Gulf coasts are many and varied, running the gamut from spicy boiled Chesapeake crabs—picked and eaten with sleeves rolled up and elbows on the table—to crawfish bisque elegant enough for the fanciest Crescent City dinner party. The fish fry and the various "boils"—shrimp boil, crab boil, or crawfish boil (Southern versions of the New England clambake)—have become social institutions, and a holiday menu without oysters is nearly unthinkable to most coastal Southerners.

The South's rich legacy of fish gathering and eating began with the Native American tribes, who had reputations for being excellent fishermen. Some fish were killed with spears or with bow and arrow. Others—like catfish—were often caught in underwater traps. (These were V-shaped rock formations that the Native Americans cleverly constructed on the bottoms of fast-moving streams. The "V" pointed downstream and the quick current forced the catfish into the enclosure.) Inland tribes depended less on fish for food than did coastal tribes, but both stalked catfish, which was considered a delicacy. The Florida tribes were perhaps the most adept fishermen of all the Southeastern tribes, and for them, sea life was a primary source of food. Everything from oysters to sharks to whales were taken for sustenance. Myth was an important part of daily life for most Native American tribes, and fishing was no exception. According to Native American lore, if it was a slow day at the fishing hole, spitting on the bait would up the chances of a large catch.

The Native American not only bestowed fish on the white man as a token of friendship, he gave him an even richer gift by teaching the settler how to fish. But even if the Native American hadn't been around, sooner or later colonists living on or near the Atlantic coastline would have begun eating fish. It was only natural to take from the variety of aquatic sources—both fresh and salt water—that were virtually brimming with life.

The Atlantic coastline and the Chesapeake Bay (the bay is North America's largest estuary) are two of the South's most dominant geographic features. Add to that the vast expanses of wetlands—such as the Louisiana bayous and the Florida Everglades—plus freshwater streams and rivers, and it is no wonder that aquatic life plays such an important role in Southern culture. The Chesapeake Bay alone gives life to over 2,700 species of animals, fish, and shellfish and today it is the source for 16 percent of the U.S. oyster catch and 36 percent of its hard crabs.

In *Growing Up in the 1850's: The Journal of Agnes Lee,* Agnes Lee writes: "Next morning we started for Balt.[imore] . . . we traveled by water. It was the first time I had been on the Chesapeake, it was fascinating to gaze down into the water. We had a delightful supper fresh perch was so like getting home!"

The perch that she enjoyed was probably pan-fried in lard and may have been served with melted butter or anchovy sauce, both typical accompaniments to fried fish in the nineteenth century.

Many earlier Southern fish dishes, however, tended to be simpler and the cooking techniques more rudimentary. Seventeenth- and eighteenth-century settlers cooked their catch on a spit or a gridiron over a fire or on a plank set alongside the heat source. Another favorite cooking method for fish, one that was also popular in England, was to boil it—often with a little vinegar and horseradish—or to stew it in white wine. Shellfish was also boiled or stewed, or parboiled in the shell, then sometimes dressed with butter, wine, anchovies, and/or spices. Oysters were fried or made into sauces and, like a lot of other fresh and saltwater seafood, they also appeared in soups and stews.

In the nineteenth century basic cooking methods—stewing, roasting, grilling, boiling—continued, but one also finds recipes for more elaborate preparations including fish and shellfish that was scalloped, devilled, or turned into pies, pâtés, sausages, and savory shortcake.

In the twentieth century, with increased industrialization and modes of transportation, American eating habits changed. People moved to the cities from farms; manual labor was replaced by machinery and automation. As a result, appetites shrank. Interestingly enough, the consumption of meat did not decline, but that of fish and shellfish did. Some coastal waters became polluted as a result of industrial waste and, for the first time, certain fish became temporarily unsafe for consumption. Some outbreaks of typhoid fever at the turn of the century were attributed to the unsanitary storage and transportation of shellfish. It was the beginning of the end of a once-thriving seafood industry, marked by the sudden drop in the popularity of the oyster, which had been copiously consumed in the nineteenth century.

Stricter controls over fishing, storage, and transportation have helped make seafood safe once again. Fish is naturally nutritious—low in fat and high in protein—and has always been the dieter's friend. And the recent discovery of Omega-3 is even more reason to enjoy fish. (Omega-3 is a polyunsaturated fatty acid present in certain fish that is said to possibly prevent hardening of the arteries. Fish with a high Omega-3 content include whitefish, salmon, lake trout, mackerel, herring, sardines, and anchovies. Fish with a moderate amount of Omega-3 include rainbow trout, smelt, pollock, halibut, bluefish, bass, and hake.) Aquaculture—the farming of aquatic plants and animals for commercial purposes—has also contributed to an increase in fish consumption.

Shad Roe
with Balsamic Vinegar and Capers

• • •

He remembered Johnny Clane and the old days at Sereno. He was no stranger—many a time he had been a guest at Sereno during the hunting season—and once he had even spent the night there. He had slept in a big four-poster bed with Johnny and at five in the morning they had gone down to the kitchen, and he still remembered the smell of fish roe and hot biscuits and the wet dog smell as they breakfasted before the hunt.

—Carson McCullers, *Clock Without Hands*

WE DON'T KNOW if the earliest settlers breakfasted on roe, but we do know that shad was one of the most abundant fish in the New World, and we can logically assume they enjoyed the eggs from this fish with which they were already familiar. Shad, from the old English *sceadd,* is any of a variety of the herring family in the genus *Alosa.* American shad (*Alosa sapidissima,* Latin for "most delicious") was indeed a tasty fish but it was so abundant in the early years that it wasn't particularly prized. The Native Americans even used it for fertilizer, a technique they recommended to Pilgrims. But by the time of the American Revolution, shad was greatly appreciated as a source of food: Washington's troops had it as part of their rations in 1776.

Shad season extends from December in the deep South—when the fish first appear in the St. John River in northern Florida—until late May further north. Today, Southern cooks who welcome spring with a shad roe supper are carrying out an old tradition: the Native American tribes celebrated the annual migration of shad as the harbinger of warm weather to come.

"Planking," a cooking method that continued throughout the nineteenth century, was one of the most popular methods for cooking this fish. In *Mrs. Porter's New Southern Cookery Book* (1871), Mrs. Porter instructs her readers as follows: "Procure at a house-furnishing store a shadboard of oak. It is better to purchase one ready-made, the cost being only about seventy-five cents." The reader is further instructed to secure the fish to the board and told how to cook it in front of hot coals.

Some early American cookbooks mention pickling shad, a technique that would preserve—as well as flavor—fish before the days of refrigeration. Shad was also baked. In fact, "boneless baked shad" was one of my grandmother's specialties. Although the name suggests that the bones are removed—something that even the most adept expert might find difficult since this fish is inordinately boney—in fact the fish is cooked for five to six hours or until the bones are soft and edible.

Although shad itself is a tasty fish, it is the delicate, mild tasting roe—the female egg sacs—that is the more sought-after delicacy. Shad roe is usually lightly floured and fried in lard or bacon drippings and it is often served for breakfast. It also makes a very special light lunch or supper dish. Mildly acidic, rich-tasting balsamic vinegar plus briny capers add zip to this otherwise traditionally prepared dish. Serve for any meal with eggs, bacon, or ham and grits or rice.

4 small pairs (8 to 10 ounces per pair) or 2 medium pairs (12 to 14 ounces per pair) fresh shad roe
4 to 6 slices bacon
Flour seasoned with salt and freshly ground black pepper, to taste, for dredging

½ cup balsamic vinegar
2 heaping tablespoons drained capers, chopped
Salt and freshly ground black pepper, to taste

1. Split the roe sacs to separate the pair into 2 separate sacs. Pat dry with paper towels.

2. In a large skillet cook bacon until very crisp. Drain on paper towels, then chop coarsely. Reserve bacon drippings.

3. Dredge the roe in flour. Heat the reserved drippings over medium heat. Add roe and cook 10 minutes, turning once. Transfer to a plate and keep warm.

4. Discard bacon drippings. Carefully pour vinegar into the hot skillet and boil while stirring constantly for 1 minute or until slightly thickened. Add capers and salt and pepper, to taste. Spoon sauce over each roe sac and top with bacon. Serve immediately.

Serves 4.

Baked Flounder
with Four Peppers

· · ·

FLOUNDER WAS AMONG the wide variety of fish that the Native Americans introduced to the early settlers. This lean, flat fish was close in color, size, and texture to European sole, with which the settlers were already familiar, so they soon made it a staple in their own diet. Abundant along the Atlantic shores, flounder is mentioned in virtually all eighteenth- and nineteenth-century Southern cookbooks. Recipes usually call for fried or broiled flounder, but American cooks may have also pickled it.

Flounder includes any of a variety in the families *Bothidae* and *Pleuronectidae*. The most common species in the South are the Southern flounder and the fluke, or summer flounder. The Southern flounder is caught from North Carolina to Texas, with the largest catch from the Gulf of Mexico. Fluke is slightly larger and is fished further north (fluke can be caught as far up the coast as Maine) and is most available, as its nickname implies, during the summer months.

According to a friend from Georgia, one popular method of catching flounder has turned into a popular Southern custom called "gigging." Using a torch (or nowadays a flashlight), good ol' boys gather together and with great ceremony lure curious fish to the boat in the dark of night. The unsuspecting flounder approaches and is promptly speared, providing a good catch as well as a good deal of fun.

Flounder is usually fried in the Southern kitchen, but its flesh is so mild and sweet, I see no reason to hide it in a cornmeal crust and a slather of catsup or tartar sauce. This baked dish is light and healthful, incorporating sweet bell peppers plus garlic, jalapeño pepper and lime juice for zip. Serve with rice or steamed new potatoes.

5 tablespoons light olive oil (or less, if using a nonstick skillet)

2 medium yellow onions, chopped

1 each green, red, and yellow bell pepper, cored, seeded, and cut into ½-inch rings

1 fresh or pickled jalapeño pepper, seeded and finely diced

2 large cloves garlic, minced

2 pounds flounder fillets (or substitute other lean, flat fish such as sole or turbot)

Juice of 1 lime
Salt and freshly ground black pepper,
   to taste

¼ cup finely chopped fresh cilantro
   plus extra sprigs to garnish (about
   1 medium bunch, total)
Lime wedges, to garnish

1. Preheat oven to 350° F.

2. In a large skillet, heat 4 tablespoons of the oil over medium-low heat. Add onion and cook 5 minutes or until softened. Add bell peppers and cook 3 minutes longer or until crisp-tender, stirring frequently. Add jalapeño pepper and garlic and cook, stirring constantly, 1 minute or until garlic releases its fragrance. Remove from heat.

3. Place fillets in 1 layer in a lightly oiled baking dish just large enough to hold them snugly in 1 layer. Season fish with lime juice, salt, and pepper. Drizzle with remaining tablespoon of oil and the ¼ cup chopped cilantro. Top with peppers and onions. Bake 10 to 12 minutes or until just opaque but not dry. Garnish with cilantro sprigs and lime wedges.

Serves 4.

Broiled Bluefish (or Pompano) on a Bed of Julienned Carrots and Fennel

■ ■ ■

Buck's (Open 24 Hours) Fish House in Manteo sat on pilings, its backside in the water. It smelled right: like fish. On mounds of ice lay crab slough oysters (fresh-shucked or in the shell), jimmy crabs, littleneck clams, croaker, mullet, flounder, bluefish.

—William Least Heat Moon, *Blue Highways*

THE BLUEFISH at Buck's may have been the only fish on the menu that wasn't fried. This soft, dark-fleshed fish has a naturally high oil content and is best cooked by a dry-heat method, such as baking, broiling, or grilling. Bluefish is rather rich tasting and needs little or no embellishment, something that hasn't

*Fish
and
Shellfish*

■

changed since 1622 when Englishman John Pory said of bluefish: ". . . [they are] of a taste requiring no addition of sauce."

Bluefish prefer water temperatures above 55° F and are found mostly in inlets, shoals, and inshore reefs off the Atlantic coast from Florida to Cape Cod. They prefer low-salt waters or mingled sea/fresh water like that around the Delmarva Peninsula, the tristate area of Delaware, Maryland, and Virginia that lies between the Chesapeake Bay and the Atlantic Ocean. Bluefish is mentioned in many eighteenth- and nineteenth-century Southern cookbooks, especially those from Virginia, Maryland, and the Carolinas.

In the following recipe, the natural sweetness of carrots, onions, and fennel is a refreshing contrast to the full-flavored bluefish. And fennel's natural anise-like flavor stands up nicely to the fish. This is a good dish for health-watchers not only because a small amount of oil is needed, but also because bluefish are rich in Omega-3 fatty acids. Pompano, another rich (but more delicately flavored) Southern fish, can be substituted for the bluefish, if desired.

2 to 4 tablespoons butter (or less, if using a nonstick skillet)

2 tablespoons light olive oil (or less if using a nonstick skillet)

2 medium yellow onions, julienned

3 large carrots, peeled and julienned (about 2½ cups)

2 large bulbs fennel, trimmed and julienned (about 4 cups), feathery greens reserved

2 large or 3 medium cloves garlic, minced

1½ pounds bluefish fillets, divided into 4 equal portions or substitute pompano, mackerel, or mullet

Salt and freshly ground black pepper, to taste

Lemon wedges and fennel greens, to garnish (optional)

1. Preheat the broiler.

2. In a large skillet, heat 2 tablespoons butter and the oil over medium heat. Add onions and carrots and cook 3 minutes. Add fennel and garlic and cook 2 to 3 minutes longer or until crisp-tender. Spread the mixture out evenly on a lightly oiled foil-lined broiler pan.

3. Sprinkle fillets with salt and pepper and place skin-side-up on top of vegetables. Tuck a fennel branch under each fillet. Dot with remaining 2 tablespoons butter, if desired.

4. Place 4 inches from broiler and broil 8 to 12 minutes or until skin is lightly crisp and deep golden-brown and flesh is opaque. Do not overcook. (Note: Timing will depend on thickness of fish—allow approximately 8 to 10 minutes per 1-inch thickness.)

5. Remove fennel branches and discard. To serve, arrange a bed of cooked vegetables on each of 4 plates, place fish on top, and pour pan juices over fish. Garnish with fennel greens and lemon wedges.

Serves 4.

Catfish

When fried catfish was served to the world's leaders at the 1983 Williamsburg Summit Conference, not a single piece of the entree, according to the observers, remained as leftovers. The South's lowly catfish has finally swum uptown.

New image and all, however, the catfish will probably never leave behind its down-home connections. Every Southern state proclaims at least one "catfish capitol of the world." To name but a few, Mississippi boasts Belzoni; Tennessee has Paris; and Arkansas declares Toad Suck as *the* spot for catfish. Most of these places and many more still hold annual festivals to celebrate their own hometown favorite—the catfish.

—Dianne Young, *Encyclopedia of Southern Culture,*
edited by C. R. Wilson and W. Ferris

CATFISH IS ONE of those foods whose basic goodness transcends all economic and social levels. Catfish suppers—complete with hush puppies, fries, coleslaw, and plenty of iced tea—create a kind of "get-down" comaraderie that is as warm and genuine as Southern hospitality itself.

Catfish, like fried chicken and watermelon, has become somewhat of a symbol of Southern cooking. In *Mrs. Porter's New Southern Cookery Book* (1871), the author lays down some rules for cooking catfish: "Catfish must be cooked fresh—if possible, directly out of the water. The larger ones are generally coarse and strong; the small-sized fish are the best. Wash and clean them . . .

score them . . . dredge them with flour, and fry them in plenty of lard . . ." Mrs. Porter goes on to say that "Indian meal" (cornmeal) can be used instead of flour for dredging and that "catfish are equally a breakfast or a supper dish."

A member of the family *Icataluridae,* the catfish is a scaleless, tough-skinned, whiskered fish that has a simple skeletal structure. There are over 2,000 species worldwide, ranging from tiny "madtoms" to huge blue catfish that can weigh as much as 150 pounds. North America can claim about thirty species but only three—the channel, the blue, and the white catfish—are found in sufficient quantities to be of commercial importance. All three species are commercially farmed—mostly in Mississippi, Arkansas, and Alabama—as well as fished for sport.

Once thought of as just a bottom-feeding creature of murky waters, the catfish is now considered a fish of some distinction. Rather than scavenging river bottoms in the wild, catfish that most of us enjoy today are from catfish farms, where man-made ponds are their habitat and vitamin-and-mineral-rich pellets are their food. Farm-raised catfish is mild and sweet, and is growing in popularity in a time when there is a trend toward eating less red meat and more fish and poultry.

Fried Catfish Fillets
with Spicy Red Pepper Sauce

. . .

SOUTHERNERS have a penchant for fried catfish and spicy sauces, usually catsup, hot cocktail sauce, or tangy tartar sauce. This taste for spicy foods was influenced partially by the food prepared by slaves from Africa or the West Indies, who had a taste for highly seasoned food.

Try this easy, sweet-and-tangy red pepper sauce when you want something a bit more sophisticated than catsup to accompany your catfish. (This sauce is also good with other fried Southern fish such as spot, brim, perch, bass, croaker, drum, mullet, smelts, or weakfish.) Serve with Double Corn Hush Puppies (page 49), coleslaw, and iced tea or beer.

RED PEPPER SAUCE

7-ounce jar roasted red peppers
  (pimientos), drained
2½ teaspoons sugar
4 teaspoons red wine vinegar
4 drops Tabasco sauce, or more, to
  taste

2 tablespoons tomato paste
Pinch of ground red pepper
  (cayenne)
⅛ teaspoon salt

FISH

⅔ cup vegetable oil
⅓ cup clarified butter (or substitute
  ⅓ cup vegetable oil)
6 6-ounce catfish fillets
Salt and freshly ground black pepper,
  to taste

2 eggs, beaten
1 cup cornmeal
Lemon wedges

1. Purée peppers in food processor or blender. Place in a small saucepan over low heat and add sugar, vinegar, Tabasco sauce, tomato paste, ground red pepper, and salt. Cook, stirring frequently, until warm and well blended, about 6 to 8 minutes. Set aside.

2. In a very large skillet (or two medium skillets) heat oil and clarified butter over medium heat.

3. Season fillets with salt and pepper then dip each into the egg and then the cornmeal.

4. When oil and butter are sizzling hot, add fillets, one by one, and cook over low heat until crisp and golden-brown, about 4 to 5 minutes on each side. Drain briefly on paper towels. Serve hot with Red Pepper Sauce on the side and lemon wedges.

Serves 6.

*Fish
and
Shellfish*

■

Grilled Catfish with Two Sauces

. . ▪

HERE IS A RECIPE for those who love the sweet, mild taste of catfish, but don't want it fried. Use an oiled, hinged basket or a stainless-steel mesh screen to hold the fish for easier handling. Make the sauces ahead of time and enjoy this easy dish in summer with corn on the cob, Sautéed Zucchini "Ribbons" with Bacon and Basil (page 322), or Sautéed Green Beans with Country Ham (page 324).

HERBED TOMATO SALSA

2 large, ripe tomatoes, diced (about 2 cups)
3 scallions, finely chopped
¼ cup light olive oil
1 tablespoon red wine vinegar

1 large clove garlic, minced
1 tablespoon fresh thyme leaves (or 1 teaspoon dried thyme)
⅛ teaspoon salt
Freshly ground black pepper, to taste

CELERY SAUCE

½ cup very finely minced celery
½ cup sour cream (or substitute plain yogurt)
½ cup mayonnaise

¼ cup very finely minced red onion
¼ cup freshly squeezed lemon juice
1 heaping teaspoon celery seed

FISH

4 to 6 whole catfish, cleaned and skinned

Olive oil or vegetable oil

1. In a bowl combine all the ingredients for herbed tomato salsa. In another bowl, combine all ingredients for celery sauce. Let sauces stand 1 hour at room temperature to blend flavors. Refrigerate up to 24 hours.

2. Place fish in lightly oiled hinged wire basket, brush lightly with oil, and grill 4 to 6 inches from medium-hot coals 4 to 5 minutes on each side or until fish flakes easily. (Or place fish on a foil-lined baking pan or broiling pan and broil 4 to 6 inches from preheated broiler.) Do not overcook. Serve hot with sauces on the side.

Serves 4 to 6.

Baked Grouper
with Mixed Herb Pesto

• • •

GROUPER is a member of the sea bass family, one that contains over 400 species. Of the many genera, only two, *Epinephelus* and *Mycteroperca*, are found in Southern waters, specifically, from the Carolinas down to Florida and across the Gulf of Mexico to Texas. Recipes for grouper are scarce in Southern cookbooks. This is perhaps because the fish are difficult to net and are usually caught with a hook and line. Since such catches are small, the fish tends to be costly, and therefore not as popular as the more abundant flounder or bluefish. The grouper's flesh is lean, white, succulent, and easily cut into fillets. Although grouper is often fried (as is most fish in the South), it is also excellent baked. The mixed herb pesto here adds a clean, zesty note, not unlike a squeeze of fresh lemon.

Buttered new potatoes and shredded carrot salad with walnut vinaigrette go especially well with this dish.

FISH

4 grouper fillets (about 2⅔ pounds), each about 2 inches thick (or substitute other lean fish such as scrod, monkfish, or tilefish)

Salt and freshly ground black pepper, to taste
1 tablespoon olive oil

MIXED HERB PESTO

3 large- or 4 medium-sized cloves garlic, peeled
1 cup firmly packed fresh, flat-leaf parsley leaves, washed and dried
½ cup firmly packed fresh mint leaves, washed and dried
½ cup firmly packed fresh dill leaves, washed and dried

½ cup (2 ounces) blanched slivered almonds
½ teaspoon salt, or more to taste
3 tablespoons lemon juice, or more to taste
6 tablespoons light olive oil
¼ cup vegetable oil

1. Preheat oven to 400° F.

2. Season fish on both sides with salt and pepper. Place in 1 layer in lightly oiled baking dish. Brush tops of fish with olive oil. Bake about 20 minutes or until just opaque but not dry.

3. Meanwhile, combine all the pesto ingredients in food processor or blender until well combined. Taste; adjust seasonings. (Note: Pesto may be made up to 1 week in advance. Pack in a jar and cover with olive oil. Cover and chill until 1 hour before serving.) To serve, place 1 to 2 tablespoons pesto on each grouper fillet. Serve hot.

Serves 4.

Poached Red Snapper with Double Tomato Bouillon

■ ■ ■

RED SNAPPER (*Lutjanus campechanus*), a warm water fish, is among the 250 species of snapper that exist worldwide. Fifteen species are fished in waters extending from Cape Hatteras, North Carolina, to Florida up and around the coastal areas of the Gulf of Mexico. The red snapper is a Southern delicacy of long standing. True red snapper is an expensive fish but well worth its price when fresh and properly cooked. It has lean, white, mildly sweet flesh that has wide appeal. Red snapper can grow to be quite large; the average weigh between 3 and 6 pounds. Look for specimens with distinctively bright red eyes, a feature that other species often sold as such do not have.

The following recipe involves poaching. An authentic fish poacher, while recommended, is not required. A fish poacher is an elongated pot with a removable rack that has handles on either side to facilitate lifting out the cooked fish. I've suggested an alternative poaching method. A cheesecloth "sling" cradles the fish, lifting it in and out of the poaching liquid easily.

Sweet, ripe red tomatoes, tangy tomatillos, herbs and spices, plus Florida limes make a light, elegant broth that complements this naturally sweet fish beautifully. It's simple to make, can be done a day in advance, and is easy on the waistline. This bouillon is a variation of one created by chef David Bouley of Restaurant Bouley in New York.

FISH AND POACHING LIQUID

¼ cup chopped yellow onions
1 large rib celery, chopped
1 large carrot, peeled and coarsely chopped
8 sprigs parsley
1 tablespoon salt

5 whole black peppercorns
1 cup dry white wine
2 quarts cold water
3- to 5-pound whole red snapper, or other lean fish (see note)

DOUBLE TOMATO BOUILLON

2 quarts cold water
1 pound ripe red tomatoes, diced
½ pound tomatillos, peeled and diced (or substitute red tomatoes, for a total of 1½ pounds)
6 whole cloves garlic, peeled but not chopped
1 small yellow onion, chopped
½ cup dry white wine
1 large carrot, peeled and chopped
10 sprigs parsley
2 tablespoons tomato paste

½ teaspoon dried thyme
½ teaspoon salt, or to taste
¼ teaspoon whole coriander seeds
8 whole black peppercorns
Zest of ½ of a lime (remove zest in strips with vegetable peeler)
Juice of ½ to 1 lime, or to taste
2 to 4 tablespoons extra-virgin olive oil, or to taste
¼ cup cooked fresh baby lima beans, or thawed frozen limas (optional)
Parsley sprigs, to garnish

1. To make the poaching liquid: In a fish poacher or a large, deep, non-aluminum flame-proof roasting pan or Dutch oven long enough to hold the whole fish, combine onions, celery, carrot, parsley, salt, peppercorns, wine, and water. Bring to a boil, lower heat and simmer uncovered 20 minutes. Strain; discard solids. Return broth to the fish poacher or Dutch oven.

2. To make the double tomato bouillon: In a large saucepot combine water, tomatoes, tomatillos, garlic, onion, wine, carrot, parsley, tomato paste, thyme, salt, coriander, peppercorns, lime zest, juice of ½ a lime, and 2 table-

Fish and Shellfish

■

spoons olive oil. Bring to a boil, lower heat so mixture simmers rapidly, and continue to cook partially covered for 1 hour, stirring occasionally.

3. Meanwhile, poach the fish by bringing the poaching liquid to a boil. Wash fish inside and out under cold running water. Place on the rack of the fish poacher and lower the rack into the boiling poaching liquid in the pan. (Note: If using a roasting pan or Dutch oven instead of a poacher, first wrap the fish in a double layer of clean cheesecloth, and tie at the ends with twine, leaving the ends long. You will need these long ends to grasp to lift out the fish when it is done. Lower the fish into the broth.) Add enough boiling water so that the fish is covered halfway by liquid.

4. Return the liquid to a boil, cover, lower heat, and simmer gently 45 minutes or until fish is opaque throughout. When the fish is done, carefully lift out of pan and drain. Remove cheesecloth and place fish on a platter. Cover to keep warm.

5. Place a strainer over the saucepan with the bouillon and strain the bouillon. Discard solids. You should have about 4 cups. (Add water, or boil to reduce to measure 4 cups.) Bring to a simmer and taste. Add lima beans, if desired. The bouillon should be quite tangy. Don't think of this as a soup, but as a light, citrusy, mildly acidic sauce to complement the fish. Add additional salt, olive oil, and lime juice, to taste.

6. To serve: Place about 6 ounces of skinless, boneless snapper fillet in each of 4 warm, shallow bowls. Ladle 1 cup hot bouillon over each serving. Garnish with parsley and serve immediately.

A 3-pound snapper serves 4 for a first course or for a light main course accompanied by side dishes and followed by a salad and cheese course. A 5-pound fish will serve 4 as a hearty main course.

Oysters and Clams

"Chesapeake oysters."
"A flavor that leaves you hanging between heaven and earth."
—William Least Heat Moon, *Blue Highways*

ANNUAL FESTIVALS in Louisiana, Maryland, and Virginia celebrate the oyster, the mollusk that has been a cornerstone in Southern cooking since the New World's beginnings. Oysters have been both a life-sustaining food—they kept Jamestown colonists from starving in the winter of 1609—as well as the raw material for elaborate gustatory specialties—including one that's even rich enough to be named Rockefeller. Early European settlers were amazed by the abundance of large oysters that Native Americans enjoyed as a basic food. Back home in Europe, oysters were small, expensive, and a precious commodity. That oysters were plentiful does not mean that they were undervalued. In 1632, Charles I granted part of Northern Virginia to his friend Lord Baltimore, thus making a gift to Maryland—at Virginia's expense—of much of the crabs and oysters of the region. Competitors in Virginia and Maryland are still fighting over the ever-dwindling harvests of oyster beds, three centuries later.

The pinnacle of oyster consumption came in the nineteenth century when the country went oyster crazy. As people moved westward, demand for oysters grew in the interior of the country. New shipping routes were established as oysters were sent by stagecoach on the "Oyster Line" from Baltimore to Ohio. Through the mid-nineteenth century oysters continued to be abundant. When other foods were scarce during the Civil War, Union soldiers in Savannah are said to have fed on buckets of oysters supplied by liberated slaves. The appetite for oysters became so great that by the 1880s Eastern beds began to be depleted. Natural disasters, overdevelopment, pollution, and demand that exceeded supply caused great reduction in the once-plentiful oyster beds of the Chesapeake. And by the turn of the century, many cultivators on the Chesapeake Bay went out of business. The industry moved southward to Florida, the Mississippi Delta, and New Orleans.

There are only four oyster species of culinary interest in the United States. One of the most common species (85 percent of total oyster production) in this country is the *Crassostrea virginica*, known by many names including Blue Point, Chincoteague, Apalachicola, and Kent Island. (According to Susan Hermann Loomis in her *The Great American Seafood Cookbook,* Blue Point is a generic term for the Atlantic oyster.) Oysters thrive in brackish waters with a relatively low salt content like the Chesapeake Bay.

Whether you eat them au naturel or in a fancy Creole guise, like Bienville (a shrimp and mushroom sauce) or Rockefeller (a parsley, spinach, and Herbsaint topping), there are some sound reasons for eating domestic oysters during the months that contain the letter "r" in their spellings. While refrigeration has all but done away with the problems of shipping during warmer months, fear of spoilage was one of the reasons for this time-honored rule of thumb. The other explanation is biological. Even though oysters are edible during the warmer months, they are usually soft and milky. This seasonal characteristic changes with the coming of fall when Northern oysters are at their best. Aficionados of Gulf oysters are likely better off waiting until December (or later) to be assured of plump, full-flavored oysters. It is perhaps for this reason that oysters have always been associated with the holidays in the South. In Baltimore, oysters appear on the Thanksgiving menu. Further down the coast, it's Christmas that signals the return of oyster stew and stuffing.

Susan Hermann Loomis, in her *The Great American Seafood Cookbook,* describes South Atlantic oysters as follows: *Alabama Gulf*: A mild, meaty oyster from Bayou La Batre and Mobile Bay. *Apalachicola*: A sweet, coppery tasting oyster from the Apalachicola Bay in Florida. *Black Bay*: A mild, deep-flavored oyster with a tinge of sweetness from Black Bay, Louisiana. *Blue Point*: The generic name for the Atlantic oyster. *Box*: From North Carolina and Long Island, this oyster has a slightly mild, muddy flavor, and is somewhat tough. *Chesapeake Bay (or Kent Island)*: An oyster with a mild, clean, and sweet flavor, from Maryland and Virginia. *Chincoteague*: There are two varieties of Chincoteague oysters. Those from the Chincoteague Bay are less consistent than those from the ocean side (which are also called Salts). Both varieties are sweet, crisp, and clean. *Emerald Point*: A small, delicate oyster from Emerald Point Bay, Mississippi. *Florida Gulf*: A medium-sized oyster with a mild, briny flavor from Horseshoe Beach, Wakulla Bay, Florida. *Hog Island Sweetwater*: A small oyster with a sweet, crisp flavor from Virginia. *Indian River*: A briny oyster from Cape Canaveral, Florida. *James River*: A fairly salty, but sweet oyster from Virginia. *Lake Borgnes*: A mild-flavored Atlantic oyster from Louisiana. *Louisiana Gulf*: A plump oyster with a brackish aftertaste from the Mississippi bayous. *Nelson Bay*: A meaty, mild-tasting oyster from Nelson Bay, Alabama.

A Word about Clams Clams never reached the popularity in the South that oysters did, although there are several kinds of clams found in southeast waters. The most popular are the hard clams—or, to the use the Algonquin name, quahogs—found from Canada to Florida. Their Latin name, *Mercenaria mercenaria*, evolved from an earlier Latin name, *Venus mercenaria* or "money-conscious goddess of love." Quahog shells were used for wampum, which served for money in the eastern colonies until the end of the seventeenth century.

The hard clam is sold in three different sizes: The chowder clam is the largest and least expensive. It is usually chopped and used for chowders or fritters. The Cherrystone clam (named after Cherrystone Creek in Virginia) is a moderately priced, medium-sized hard clam, usually served raw or steamed. The Little Neck is the smallest of the hard clams. It is also the most expensive, and is usually served raw, on the half shell, or steamed.

Softshell clams (*Mya arenaria*) are found from the Arctic Ocean to Cape Hatteras. They are usually fried or steamed. The eastern razor clam (*Ensis directus*), also known as the Atlantic Jacknife or Common Jacknife clam is found from Canada to South Carolina. They are eaten steamed, frittered, or in soups and stews.

Oysters and Leeks on Corn Pancakes

* * *

THESE GENTLY COOKED OYSTERS—swathed with cream—and silky-tender leeks on a corn pancake is my idea of oyster heaven. Serve for a light lunch or a late-night supper, or offer a smaller portion to begin a meal. A sparkling wine is the appropriate accompaniment—try a Virginia sparkler, or any brut from California, France, Italy, or Spain.

Fish and Shellfish

2 large leeks, washed, trimmed, and
  julienned
2 ounces pancetta (Italian-style bacon), or 4 slices thin-sliced bacon,
  diced into ½-inch by ½-inch pieces
2 tablespoons unsalted butter

½ cup oyster liquor or clam juice
¼ cup dry white wine
12 freshly shucked oysters
1 cup heavy cream
1 recipe Cornmeal Pancakes (page
  355), kept warm in a low oven

1. Drop leeks into a large saucepan of boiling water and cook 2 to 3 minutes or until crisp-tender. Drain thoroughly.

2. In a large skillet, cook pancetta or bacon over medium-low heat, stirring frequently, until crisp. Remove pancetta with a slotted spoon and drain on paper towels. Discard all but 1 tablespoon of the pan drippings. Add the butter and the leeks to the skillet and cook over low heat 8 to 10 minutes or until very tender. Transfer the leeks to an ovenproof baking dish and cover to keep warm. Add oyster liquor and the wine to the skillet and bring to a simmer. Add oysters and simmer 2 to 4 minutes or until oysters are heated through. With a slotted spoon, transfer oysters to the baking dish with leeks.

3. Boil the cooking liquid in the skillet until reduced to ¼ cup. Add cream and boil until lightly thickened and reduced to about ¾ cup. Remove from heat. Add oysters and leeks to the sauce and toss gently. Heat through over low heat if necessary. If serving as a main course, place 6 pancakes on each of 2 plates. If serving as a first course, place 3 pancakes on each of 4 plates. Spoon an oyster and some of the leeks neatly onto each pancake. Pour a tablespoon or so of the sauce in the center of the pancakes. Sprinkle with bacon and serve immediately.

Serves 2 as a supper or lunch; serves 4 as a first course.

Fried Oysters (or Clams) with Green Tomato Salsa

• • •

What usually keeps me from eating on an airplane is not anxiety but the food I'm served. I cannot say I have ever had a good meal off the ground. Once, just before we left New Orleans, Alice had the inspired idea of stopping at Buster Holmes' restaurant, on Burgundy Street, to pick up some garlic chicken for the flight. It occurred to me that while we were about it we might as well stop at the Acme for an oyster loaf—a half-dozen succulent oysters freshly fried and installed in buttered French bread.

"Aren't you always saying that oyster loaves won't travel more than twenty yards from the kitchen?" Alice said. "They would be awful on the plane."

"Who's talking about the plane?" I said. "Have you given any thought to what we're going to eat on the way to the airport?" Every theory needs a corollary.

—Calvin Trillin, *Alice, Let's Eat*

NINETEENTH-CENTURY COOKBOOKS include recipes for fried oysters and for oyster fritters. Fried oysters are usually dipped into flour, cracker crumbs, or cornmeal then fried in lard, butter, or a mixture of the two. Sometimes the oysters are dipped into beaten eggs mixed with milk or cream before dredging in seasoned flour. Fritter batter usually consisted of milk, flour, eggs, cream of tartar, and leavening. There are also old Southern recipes for oyster patties, which seem to be similar to fritters but have a thicker batter.

Fried oysters are usually eaten with a squeeze of lemon or catsup. In Louisiana and Alabama, fried oysters often appear in sandwich form called an "oyster loaf," which at one time was also known as a "peacemaker." Lore has it that a man who'd stayed out too late would bring a warm fried oyster sandwich home to his wife to distract her eyes from the clock's hands (or from the whiskey on his breath). The classic oyster loaf consists of fried oysters stuffed into hollowed-out loaves of French bread. But Southerners didn't invent the sandwich: this dish was enjoyed in seventeenth-century England. In her book, *The Virginia House-wife* (1824), author Mary Randolph's elegant "oyster loaf" may have been the predecessor for that dish of Louisiana fame. Mary Randolph's dish consists of hollowed-out rolls filled with stewed oysters, butter, and cream, then topped with a bread "lid."

The oysters in this recipe can be served in a sandwich (I like to use a French or Italian loaf, halved lengthwise and scooped out slightly), or you can serve it without bread. The accompanying relish is a refreshing change from the bottled tomato catsup or cocktail sauce that seems to follow fried oysters wherever they go. This sauce has a clean, tangy taste that cuts through the richness of the fried oysters beautifully—and is a great way to use end-of-season tomatoes and the first "r" month oysters.

2 cups (about 1 pound) diced green tomatoes (Note: If green tomatoes are not in season, substitute fresh or canned tomatillos [Mexican green tomatoes])

2½ teaspoons salt, or to taste

½ cup finely chopped cilantro

1 to 3 teaspoons red wine vinegar

¼ cup finely chopped Bermuda or other sweet onion, or more, to taste

Juice of 1 lime

Tabasco, to taste

1 cup yellow cornmeal

Vegetable oil, for frying

16 medium-sized shucked fresh oysters (about ¼ pound), or substitute ¼ pound (shucked weight) softshell clams

1 ripe avocado, peeled, pitted, and cut into 12 wedges

Lettuce leaves

1. Preheat oven to 200° F.

2. In a bowl, mix the green tomatoes with 2 teaspoons of the salt, the cilantro, 1 teaspoon vinegar, onion, lime juice, and Tabasco to taste. Toss gently. Taste, adding more vinegar if desired. Makes about 2 cups salsa. Set aside. (May be made a day in advance and refrigerated.)

3. In a separate bowl mix cornmeal with remaining salt.

4. Add enough oil to wok, deep skillet, or deep fryer to cover oysters completely. Heat oil to 375° F. Roll oysters one at a time in the cornmeal mixture. Drop into hot oil and fry 2 to 5 minutes or until golden-brown. Drain on paper towels and keep warm in the preheated oven until all oysters are fried. Serve with salsa and avocado slices on a lettuce leaf.

Serves 2 as a light lunch or supper dish; serves 4 as a first course.

Note I love having leftover salsa, so I call for making plenty. Use it the next day with corn chips, tortillas, on sandwiches, or in omelettes.

Shrimp and Crawfish

FROM THE CHESAPEAKE BAY to Mobile Bay shrimp is probably the most popular of all shellfish. This crustacean has been part of Southern cooking at least since the eighteenth century when the Native Americans and the early settlers in the Carolina low country and around great ports like Charleston, Savannah, and New Orleans made it an important part of their diet.

Eighteenth- and nineteenth-century sources suggest that shrimp was prepared very simply. It was often just boiled and dressed with butter. A more elaborate dish involved stewing the shrimp with butter and anchovies to make a sauce for salmon or other fish. Twentieth-century cookbooks, especially those from South Carolina and Georgia, feature shrimp in a variety of ways. South Carolinians show a penchant for shrimp that is fried, pickled, stewed in butter and vinegar, or sautéed in bacon fat. They put shrimp in casseroles, pilaus, savory pies and puddings, and made shrimp paste—a spread made of boiled, ground shrimp mixed with butter and spices. And perhaps because of their love for rice, South Carolinians adapted the Louisiana dish, shrimp Creole—shrimp cooked with Creole tomatoes and spices served over rice. Louisiana cooks are known for their barbecued shrimp (which I hear is neither cooked on a barbecue grill nor flavored with barbecue sauce, but baked with butter and hot spices). They also serve shrimp with rémoulade sauce, add it to jambalaya and gumbo, and stuff it into eggplant, avocadoes, artichokes, and mirlitons, a green pear-shaped vegetable that is a member of the cucumber family. You'll find it in Latin markets labeled chayotes. And not to be overlooked is that celebrated institution popular throughout the coastal South, the "shrimp boil." This gustatory rite, featuring great vessels of shrimp boiled in highly seasoned water, may have originally been the creation of cooks from Africa or the West Indies where hot, spicy food is legendary. The shrimp boil—like crab boils, pig pickin's, and fish fries—is a Southern institution where good eats mingle with a "let your hair down" atmosphere. Corn on the cob, coleslaw, biscuits, and iced tea are common accompaniments to the shrimp boil.

A Word about Crawfish Crawfish can be substituted for shrimp in many recipes. Crawfish are technically known as crayfish, but are locally known as crawfish, crawdads, or "mudbugs." These lobster-like fresh-water crustaceans were at one time considered rather humble fare, but, like catfish and many other regional favorites, they have recently acquired a new kind of respect and cachet. Fresh crawfish can be difficult to procure outside of Louisiana and Texas (90 percent of the world's crawfish comes from Cajun country). Like catfish, crawfish are being farmed in several Southern states (such as South Carolina), thus increasing availability. Frozen crawfish can be found in some markets outside of the South. However, they are considered by most Cajun and Creole cooks to be not as tasty as the fresh product.

If using live crawfish, first wash crawfish thoroughly in several changes of water. Drop clean crawfish into a kettle of boiling water and boil several seconds, or just until they turn red. When cool enough to handle, separate the heads from the tails. Remove the orange fat (actually the liver and pancreas) from the head and reserve it. (Use it to flavor the crawfish dish you are cooking.) Remove shells from the tails, and reserve the meat. You will need five to eight pounds of live crawfish to yield one pound of meat.

Shrimp (or Crawfish) with Spicy Chile-Saffron Sauce and Cucumber-Melon Relish

■ ■ ■

TODAY, most of the country's shrimp comes from the Gulf, with the greatest concentration extending from North Carolina to Florida and into the Gulf of Mexico. Shrimp have an affinity for spicy flavors, but in this recipe, instead of the traditional red and black peppers, I use chiles and garlic. The saffron adds a fragrant note. Serve with white rice or grits, two of the most popular accompaniments to shrimp in the South.

CUCUMBER-MELON RELISH

¾ cup diced honeydew melon

¾ cup diced, peeled, seeded cucumber

¾ cup diced mango, papaya, or cantaloupe

Juice of 2 limes, or to taste

1½ teaspoons red wine vinegar, or to
  taste
Small pinch salt, or to taste
2 to 3 tablespoons finely chopped
  fresh mint or cilantro

2 large (about 4- to 5-inches long)
  dried chiles pasillas (or substitute
  ancho or poblano chiles), available
  in specialty food stores

COURT BOUILLON

8 cups cold water
2 large cloves garlic, peeled and slivered
1 medium-sized yellow onion, peeled
  and chopped

1 large carrot, peeled and chopped
1 stalk celery, chopped
10 large sprigs fresh parsley, tied in
  kitchen twine
Generous pinch of salt

SAFFRON-CHILE SAUCE

1 cup heavy cream
½ teaspoon saffron threads
3 large cloves garlic, peeled
2 to 3 tablespoons tomato paste
Generous pinch of salt

¼ to ¾ teaspoon Tabasco sauce
2 pounds large shrimp, peeled and
  deveined
4 lettuce leaves, for serving relish

1. To make the relish: In a bowl combine all the relish ingredients. Toss gently, cover and chill at least 1 hour to blend flavors.

2. Bring a small saucepan of water to a boil. Plunge in chile peppers, remove from heat, and let stand at least 15 minutes. Remove chile peppers from water and drain. Using a small knife, slit chiles open and scrape out seeds. Reserve seeds. Cut chiles into 1-inch pieces and set aside.

3. To make the court bouillon: In a large, deep skillet, combine water, reserved chile pepper seeds, garlic, onion, carrot, celery, parsley, and salt. Bring to a boil, then lower heat and simmer uncovered 30 minutes. Set aside. (Note: This may be made 1 day in advance. Do not strain. Cover tightly and refrigerate overnight. Reheat when ready to cook shrimp.)

4. To make the sauce: In a medium saucepan, simmer cream and saffron uncovered until reduced to ¾ cup. Do not reduce more than this or sauce will be thick and cloying. In a food processor or blender with the machine running,

*Fish
and
Shellfish*

■

drop garlic and reserved chiles down feed tube until finely chopped. Add the warm cream mixture, 2 tablespoons tomato paste, salt, and ¼ teaspoon Tabasco sauce. Taste for seasoning. Mixture should be very spicy and tangy. If it is not, add more salt, tomato paste, and Tabasco sauce.

5. Bring the court bouillon to a boil. Add shrimp and lower heat. Simmer shrimp uncovered 2 minutes or until opaque and cooked through. Drain briefly, reserve court bouillon.

6. To serve, reheat saffron-chile sauce if necessary, adding 2 to 3 tablespoons of the court bouillon if mixture seems too thick. Divide shrimp among 4 warm dinner plates and spoon 2 tablespoons of sauce over each serving. Place a lettuce leaf on each plate and serve with Cucumber-Melon Relish on the lettuce.

Serves 4 as a main course; serves 6 to 8 as a first course.

Note There is just enough sauce here to lightly coat each serving. If you are serving this over rice or simply wish to offer more sauce at the table, double the sauce recipe. Sauce may be made 1 day in advance. Reheat when ready to serve.

Broiled Soft-Shell Crabs with Vidalia-Butter Sauce

■ ■ ■

"What's a pailer?"

"Peeler. Here they say 'pailer' and 'dredging' is 'drudgin.' The pailer is a metamorphosis, but the watermen don't call it that . . . The pailer splits his shell like a spider so he can grow. 'Softshell crab,' restaurants call them. Crabbing begins early in the spring when the jimmies start walking up the bay to look for the sooks—the females. Mating season. Sometimes you catch a 'doubler'—a mister and missus arm in arm . . . Once the crab peels, you have to pull him out directly or the water will start him to hardening again. That is, if another doesn't eat him first, soft morsel that he is for a few hours."

—William Least Heat Moon, *Blue Highways*

SOFT-SHELL CRABS are hard crabs that have molted and not yet grown their new shell. The peak season for Chesapeake soft-shells is May, so growing up in Virginia, we always welcomed spring with the first soft-shell crabs of the season, fresh asparagus, and strawberry shortcake. Vidalia onions from Georgia are harvested about the same time that soft-shell crabs peak, so I have incorporated them into this recipe. In the South, soft-shell crabs are traditionally floured or breaded and fried—often served on a soft bun—and served with tartar sauce. But I find their sweet, delicate flesh takes well to broiling. The butter sauce is optional; serve with a squeeze of lemon if you prefer a lighter dish.

CRABS

4 soft-shelled crabs

4 tablespoons melted unsalted butter, or less if desired

Salt and freshly ground black pepper, to taste

VIDALIA-BUTTER SAUCE

3 tablespoons dry white wine

3 tablespoons white wine vinegar or cider vinegar

½ cup finely chopped Vidalia onions (or substitute other sweet, mild onions such as Maui, Walla Walla, or Bermuda onions)

12 tablespoons cold, unsalted butter, diced into ¼-inch cubes

Salt and freshly ground black pepper, to taste

2 tablespoons chopped fresh parsley

1. Preheat the broiler.

2. To prepare the crabs: Wash crabs thoroughly. Working with 1 crab at a time, turn the crab belly-side-up and with a sharp knife remove the apron or flap that folds under the rear of the body. Turn the crab over. Lift the large spines of the top shell and scrap away the grayish gills. Using kitchen shears, cut just behind the eyes; remove eyes and mouth. Wash the crab again under cold running water and pat dry with paper towels.

3. Place cleaned crabs belly-side-up on lightly oiled broiler pan or foil-lined baking sheet. Brush crabs with half the melted butter and season with salt and

pepper to taste. Place under the preheated broiler and broil 4 minutes. Turn crabs over, brush with remaining butter, and broil 4 minutes longer or until outside is deep golden-brown and center of crab is opaque. Remove from oven. Cover and keep warm while you make the sauce.

4. In a small skillet or small saucepan over medium-high heat, boil the wine, vinegar, and onions until reduced to about 2 tablespoons.

5. Reduce heat to low and whisk in the butter piece by piece, letting each piece become incorporated before adding the next. Season with salt and pepper to taste. Just before serving, stir in the parsley. Spoon some of the butter sauce on 2 warm plates and top with 2 crabs. Serve hot.

Serves 2 as a light main course or 4 as a first course.

Lorraine Eppler's Crab Cakes with Smithfield Ham and Lemon-Caper Mayonnaise

■ ■ ■

From the darkness, a man with legs like masts and arms like spars and great blue-ebony lips walked up. Griggs called him Big Man. Never had I heard speech like his. "We been oat since yahstudy. Got mebbee leven hunred pounds o' blues."

—William Least Heat Moon, *Blue Highways*

THE "BLUES" BIG MAN was referring to weren't bluefish, but blue crabs (their Latin name, *Callinectes sapidus*, means "beautiful swimmer"), the most common of all crab species in the United States. Blue crabs are most abundant in the brackish waters of the Chesapeake Bay and, as a result, Virginia and Maryland are the largest commercial suppliers of blue crabs in the nation. Stone crabs—found from the Gulf of Mexico, around Florida, and up to the Carolinas—are another favorite Southern species, known for their sweet, succulent claw meat.

The meat from hard-shell blue crabs has found its way to the Southern table in many guises. At their simplest, crabs are boiled in or steamed over water (sometimes mixed with beer) that has been liberally seasoned with hot spices. Then their flesh is "picked," and dipped in drawn butter or cocktail sauce. Crab Norfolk, a dish common in the Chesapeake Bay area, has become part of the South's culinary heritage. The dish is a simple sauté of lump crabmeat, butter, salt, pepper, Tabasco, and lemon juice or vinegar. Crab Imperial, or devilled crab—crabmeat flavored with hot seasonings then bound with egg and bread-crumbs—is packed into clean crab or scallop shells or ramekins then baked. Soups, pies, soufflés, omelettes, mousses, stuffings, and of course, crab cakes are but a few of the ways that early Southerners found to prepare the abundant blue crab.

This crab cake recipe is a variation on one created by my Baltimore friend, Lorraine Eppler, who knows that the best crab cakes are mostly crab with only enough egg and breadcrumbs added to bind the mixture. I like to serve these elegant, savory cakes with a thin slice of Smithfield ham and crisp lettuce leaves on soft, homemade cornmeal buns. The Lemon-Caper Mayonnaise adds a zesty, elegant touch. You can make the crab cakes smaller and serve them without buns for a first course.

LEMON-CAPER MAYONNAISE

2 egg yolks, room temperature
Pinch each of salt and freshly ground
    black pepper
1 tablespoon lemon juice, room tem-
    perature

1½ cups vegetable oil
½ cup light olive oil
2 to 4 tablespoons drained capers

CRAB CAKES

1 egg
2 tablespoons water
¼ cup chopped fresh parsley
3 to 4 tablespoons mayonnaise (use
    prepared mayonnaise or some of
    the Lemon-Caper Mayonnaise
    without the capers)

3 to 4 tablespoons unseasoned fine,
    dry breadcrumbs
1 pound backfin crabmeat, picked
    over
2 to 4 tablespoons butter (or use
    light olive oil or vegetable oil)

6 *Soft Cornmeal Buns (page 38), or*
   other soft buns, split and lightly
   toasted
2 *ounces very thinly sliced dry-cured*
   country ham, such as Smithfield

(for mail-order source, see page
   481)
1 *cup thinly shredded iceberg or ro-*
   maine lettuce
Lemon wedges

1. To make the mayonnaise: In a blender or food processor, combine egg yolks, salt and pepper, and lemon juice and process until well combined. With the machine running, add the oils very slowly. Turn the mixture into a bowl and fold in the capers. Adjust seasonings; set aside. Makes about 2 cups.

2. To make the crab cakes: In a medium-large bowl, beat together the egg and the water. Beat in parsley, 3 tablespoons of the mayonnaise and 3 table-spoons of the breadcrumbs until well combined. Add crab and toss very gently to mix, taking care not to break up the crab chunks. The mixture should just barely hold together; if it does not, add a little more of the breadcrumbs and mayonnaise.

3. Form the mixture into 6 patties about 1 inch thick and about 2½ to 3 inches in diameter.

4. In a large nonstick skillet, heat 2 tablespoons of the butter over medium-low heat. (Use 4 tablespoons butter if not using a nonstick skillet.) Add the crab cakes and cook about 4 to 5 minutes on each side or until golden-brown on the outside and warmed through on the inside.

5. Spread the buns lightly with the Lemon-Caper Mayonnaise. Place the ham slices on the bottom halves of the buns. Top each slice of ham with a crab cake, then with lettuce. Serve open-faced or top with remaining bun halves. Pass lemon wedges and extra mayonnaise at the table.

Serves 6 as a light lunch or supper, or 3 as a more filling main course.

Brown Rice and Scallop Pilau
with Wild Mushrooms and Bacon
• • •

TWO TYPES OF SCALLOPS can be found in the South: the small bay scallop (*Argopecten irradians*) found in shallow estuarine waters from Cape Hatteras down to Florida to the Gulf of Mexico, and the Calico scallop (*Argopecten gibbus*) which is common in deep waters off the east coast of Florida as well as waters near Carteret County, North Carolina. Sea scallops (*Placopecten magellanicus*), which are larger than the calico or bay scallops, are caught only in more northern waters, from Maine to New Jersey.

There are very few references to scallops in eighteenth- and nineteenth-century Southern American cookbooks, for three possible reasons. First, it may have been assumed that cooks knew how to open, clean, and cook these bivalves, thus eliminating the need for any sort of recipe. Second, because scallops, unlike other bivalves, cannot hold their shells firmly closed, they spoil quickly when out of water for too long. This was a problem before the days of refrigeration and it's possible that scallops simply were not known outside coastal areas. Finally, and perhaps most important, the popularity of oysters, shrimp, and crabs was such that other shellfish may have taken a back seat.

The scallops in this recipe are incorporated into a pilau. A basic Southern pilau might be described as a substantial rice dish usually containing bacon, onions, tomatoes, and either shellfish or vegetables. Recipes for pilaus appeared in the southeastern United States sometime after rice was first planted in South Carolina in the seventeenth century.

In Low Country patois, the dish is usually pronounced purlow, pilaw, or purloo, and is spelled pilau, perlew, or perlow. The word is thought to be of Turkish origin and a derivation of the Middle Eastern pilar or pilaf. One of the most common pilaus in the South is tomato and okra pilau (okra pilau is also sometimes known locally in South Carolina Low Country as "limpin' Susan," a cousin to the more popular, "hoppin' John").

Because Southerners usually insist on dry, flaky, separate-grained white rice, recipes calling for brown rice—which can be sticky—are few and far between in classic Southern cooking. Since whole brown rice is processed less (the outer hull is removed but the bran layers are retained) it's more healthful (higher in fiber, vitamins, protein, and minerals) and it tastes great. I love its deep, nutty flavor as a backdrop for the smoky bacon, woodsy mushrooms and sweet scallops in this recipe. I suggest serving this substantial dish as a main course. I am indebted to New York chef David Bouley of Bouley Restaurant for the scallop-cooking technique; the instant-blending flour seals in the juices for scallops that are beautifully golden-brown and lightly crisp on the outside and succulent on the inside.

6 ounces thick-sliced bacon (about 4
  slices), cut into 1-inch pieces
3 to 8 tablespoons unsalted butter
¾ pound shiitake mushrooms, or
  other wild or cultivated mushrooms, wiped clean, tough stems
  discarded, and caps cut into
  ½-inch-thick slices
¾ cup finely chopped onion
3 cups uncooked long-grain brown
  rice
5 cups water

1¼ teaspoon salt
4 tablespoons vegetable oil (or less if
  using a nonstick skillet)
¼ cup Wondra™ instant blending
  flour
1½ pounds bay scallops or sea scallops
⅓ cup dry white wine or vermouth
2 tablespoons chopped fresh parsley
1 tablespoon minced fresh chives or
  scallions (optional)

1. In a large skillet over medium-high heat, cook bacon until slightly crisp and fat is rendered. Remove with slotted spoon, drain on paper towels, and set aside. Discard fat.

2. In the same skillet, heat 3 tablespoons of the butter, add mushrooms and cook over medium heat 5 to 8 minutes or until tender but still firm. Remove with slotted spoon to plate or bowl and set aside.

3. Add onions to skillet and cook over medium-high heat 5 minutes or until softened, adding up to 2 tablespoons more butter if necessary. Add raw rice and toss until well coated with the butter and cooking juices. Remove from heat.

4. In a saucepan bring the water and salt to a boil. Add this to the rice in the skillet. Return to a boil, cover, and simmer 40 minutes or until all liquid is absorbed and rice is tender.

5. Ten minutes before serving, prepare scallops. In a large separate skillet, heat half the oil over medium-high heat. Pat scallops dry with paper towels. Dust scallops very lightly with flour, shaking off excess. Add half the scallops to the

skillet and cook 3 to 4 minutes, tossing once or twice, or until golden-brown and lightly crisp on outside, and opaque on inside. Do not overcook. Transfer scallops to a shallow dish and cover with foil to keep warm. Add remaining oil to the skillet and cook the second batch in the same manner. Add this batch to the first.

6. Add wine to skillet and boil, scraping up brown bits with a wooden spoon, until liquid is reduced to 2 tablespoons. Turn off heat, swirl in remaining 3 tablespoons butter. (Note: This final butter enrichment is optional.) Add mushrooms and any juices that have accumulated from the scallops (do not add the scallops) to the skillet and swirl to combine, reheating gently if necessary.

7. To serve, turn rice out onto large serving platter. Pour mushroom mixture evenly over rice; toss quickly to blend slightly. Top with scallops and reserved bacon, distributing evenly over rice. Sprinkle with parsley, and if desired, chives.

Serves 6 to 8 as a main course.

Poultry and Game

Poultry and Game

*C*HICKENS COULD SURVIVE ocean voyages with relative ease, so it comes as no surprise that eating domesticated poultry in North America probably dates as far back as Columbus. A little over a hundred years later, newcomers to the Jamestown settlement brought chickens with them. Because chickens are smaller than cows and pigs—the other preferred edible animals—and produced no storage or preservation problems (no need for curing or drying the meat since it could be eaten all at once), the keeping of barnyard fowl in the New World was common practice throughout the seventeenth century. In his book, *Virginia, the New Dominion,* Virginus Dabney quotes John Rolfe, who in 1616 described life in Virginia. Rolfe estimated that there were 351 English colonists, 144 cattle, 6 horses, 216 goats, "hoggs, wild and tame, not to be numbered. Poultry, great plenty."

Eighteenth- and nineteenth-century chicken recipes, for the most part, were simple and straightforward. Chicken was often boiled or steamed and served with drawn butter seasoned with parsley. Spit-cooked chickens (they were called "roasted" in very early Southern cookbooks) were commonly served with a sauce of melted butter thickened with mashed, hard-boiled egg yolks and seasoned with salt, pepper, and cayenne. Broiled birds were usually split, then placed on a gridiron set over hot coals or held before a brisk fire. They were often topped with melted butter, pepper, and sifted bread or cracker crumbs.

For special occasions, the more elaborate fricassees (which might be described as something between a stew and a sauté) were popular in the nineteenth century. (The usual accepted etymology of the word fricassee is the French *frire*—to fry—and *casser*—to cut up.) I suppose that the fricassee was a forerunner of smothered chicken and meat dishes prevalent in the South that usually consist of chops or chicken pieces to be browned, "smothered" with broth or pan gravy, then baked until tender.

Today, chicken is one of the South's favorite meats. This favored fowl is as versatile as it is popular, from Sunday-best platters of fried chicken served after

Poultry and Game

■

179

church to communal pots of "chicken bog" (a South Carolina concoction of chicken, sausage, and rice) ladled out to crowds gathered for fund-raisers, beach parties, or for just plain good eating. Barbecued chicken—usually with a tangy vinegar or tomato-based sauce—is another big-crowd pleaser. Chicken appears in such Southern classics as Brunswick stew, gumbo, and jambalaya; in pilaus, with dumplings, and spiced up with curry powder in Country Captain, a dish of English origin embraced by the South.

In recent years, consumption of chicken has increased from an estimated two pounds per capita to a whopping sixty pounds. Eight out of every ten broilers grown in the United States are produced in the South. Arkansas, Georgia, Alabama, and North Carolina are presently the top poultry-producing states. Mississippi and the states that comprise the Delmarva region (Delaware, Maryland, and Virginia) follow closely behind.

Fried Chicken

Kill the Chicken the night before, if you can, and lay on ice, or else kill early in the morning. When ready, wipe dry, flour it, add pepper and salt, and fry in a little lard.

—Marion Cabell Tyree, *Housekeeping in Old Virginia*

In her book, *North Carolina and Old Salem Cookery,* Tarheel author Elizabeth Sparks claims that fried chicken vies only with country ham and red-eye gravy as the most frequently eaten food in the South. While the consumption of ham may be down slightly due to health concerns about sodium, recent studies found that Southerners prefer their chicken fried to broiled, boiled, or even barbecued.

But it has been only in the last fifty years that fried chicken has become a year-round dish. In the 1940s and 1950s, farmers began raising chickens in temperature-controlled conditions so young broiler-fryers could be had year round. Prior to that time, most of the chickens consumed in the United States were those that were not specifically raised for their meat. These birds were surplus hens and roosters that were culled from egg-production blocks. Consequently, the birds tended to be old and tough. Tender young fryers were usually a spring-to-fall specialty. The reason is simple: hens would "set" on their eggs only during warm months. Although they would lay eggs all year round, maternal instinct told them that newly hatched chicks could survive only in warm weather when there was plenty of food to be had. Baby chicks would hatch after twenty-one days and be allowed to grow and roam free for several weeks. Tender, young fryers would then be enjoyed from mid-May through September. "Seasonal" chicken is virtually a thing of the past.

There are probably as many ways to fry chickens as there are Southern cooks. Some marinate the bird in milk or salt water. Others may discard the skin before dredging. Chicken pieces can be dusted in seasoned flour (once *or* twice) or dipped in batter. Lard, shortening, oil, bacon fat, or butter—or a combination of two or more—can be used as the cooking medium. Some cooks swear by cast-iron skillets, others (including myself) feel that any good, heavy skillet will suffice.

Pan gravy is frequently served with fried chicken. When I was growing up, gravy was strictly for ladling onto the accompanying boiled white rice. We never poured it over our chicken because that would have made the delicious crunchy coating soggy. Many Southern cooks—including my paternal grandmother—add chopped, hard-boiled eggs to gravy, to flavor and thicken it.

Although few cookbooks say so, it was—and still is—common practice to fry the livers, hearts, and gizzards along with the chicken pieces. They are delicious cooked this way. (And if you don't like innards, cook them anyway and give them to the cat.)

My fried chicken recipe is a bit more time-consuming than most, but the results are worth it. Marinating the chicken in a spicy buttermilk mixture both tenderizes and flavors the meat. Two dustings in seasoned flour ensures a crisp coating. I prefer vegetable oil to shortening or lard because to me it has a lighter taste—and it's healthier, too.

For special dinners, I like to use boneless breasts. They're more elegant, cook faster, and are easier to eat with knife and fork (I find that the uninitiated tend to feel strange picking up chicken with their fingers—something second nature to Southerners).

Early Southern cookbooks show that it was common practice to serve fried chicken with corn batter cakes, fried cornmeal mush, or "chicken biscuits"—

biscuits fried in the pan drippings instead of baked in the oven. I suggest serving Cornmeal Dropped Scones (my own updated version of "chicken biscuits," page 48), Dirty Brown Rice with Chives (page 260), Sautéed Green Beans with Country Ham (page 324), or a green salad of arugula, watercress, radicchio, leaf lettuce, and Belgian endive. If it is a company meal, you could begin with Mini Corn Puddings with Chive Cream (page 73), Spoon Bread Soufflé with Fresh Corn Sauce (page 66), Jerusalem Artichoke Soup (page 92), or Swirled Succotash Soup (page 87). For dessert, I like to serve something fairly basic and homey like Blackberry Roll (page 378), Peaches and Cream Shortbread Tart (page 370), or Bittersweet Chocolate Chunk–Pecan Pie (page 364). Any leftover chicken can be used to make Chicken Salad with Lemon-Chive "Boiled" Dressing (page 120).

Spicy Fried Chicken

• • •

INSPIRED BY FRIED CHICKEN prepared by two great cooks/friends: Detroit-born Miriam Rubin and South Carolinian Sadie Spratley.

2 cups buttermilk, preferably salt free
4 to 6 medium cloves garlic, smashed with flat side of a knife
1/8 teaspoon salt
1/4 to 1/2 teaspoon freshly ground black pepper
1/4 teaspoon ground red pepper (cayenne)
1 3-pound fryer, cut into eighths (or substitute 2 pounds boneless chicken breasts, skin intact)

1 1/4 cups unbleached all-purpose flour
1 1/2 teaspoons salt
3/4 to 1 1/4 teaspoons freshly ground black pepper
3/4 to 1 1/4 teaspoons ground red pepper (cayenne)
Safflower oil, or other vegetable oil, for frying

1. In a shallow, nonaluminum dish, combine first 5 ingredients. Add chicken and toss once to coat. Cover and chill 8 hours or overnight, turning once or twice.

2. Place pieces on rack to drain slightly but do not pat dry.

3. In a shallow dish, combine flour, salt, black pepper, and red pepper. Toss chicken in flour mixture and place on a clean rack or a baking sheet. Toss each piece again, shake off excess flour, and set aside at cool room temperature 30 minutes to 1 hour.

4. In 2 large, heavy skillets or 1 electric skillet, heat enough oil to reach a depth of ½ inch to 350° to 360° F. Add chicken pieces to the hot oil one by one. (Note: Adding too many pieces at once lowers the temperature of the oil and the chicken will not brown properly.) Adjust temperature so oil remains between 300° and 320° F. Cook, turning once with tongs, 10 to 12 minutes per side (4 to 5 minutes for boneless breasts) or until juices run clear when pierced in the thickest part. (Thicker pieces may require more cooking time.) Transfer pieces as they are done to paper towels to drain. Serve hot or warm.

Serves 4.

Grandmother's Roast Lemon Chicken

• • •

ROAST CHICKEN, a favorite dish throughout the Western world, is no less loved by Southerners. It cooks faster unstuffed and even faster if it is split, as in the recipe here, a variation on my grandmother's recipe. Lemon seasoning for chicken has always been a Southern favorite, a combination that goes back centuries to old English recipes for capons and boiled fowl flavored with lemon peel.

We had this dish once a week growing up. I loved it—and still do. It's thrifty, easy, light, and simple. It goes well with just about any side dish or first course and is satisfying any time of year. It is plain and comforting and appeals to all ages and appetites.

1 small (3-pound) frying chicken
20 sprigs fresh parsley
4 stalks celery, cut into thirds
1 medium-sized yellow onion, halved
Salt and freshly ground black pepper,
   to taste
¼ teaspoon ground paprika

2 tablespoons butter (or less, if desired)
2 cups chicken broth (preferably unsalted, homemade)
Juice of ½ lemon
¼ cup dry white wine
1 tablespoon cornstarch

1. Preheat oven to 375° F.

2. Place the chicken on its breast on a flat work surface. Using poultry shears, cut along the entire length of the backbone. Spread the chicken open and rinse with cold water. Dry with paper towels. Cut off excess fat at neck and tail and discard.

3. Open the bird out as much as possible. Use the heel of your hand and strike the breast firmly to break the breast bone, collarbones, rib cage, and wishbone. Place the parsley, celery, and onion in a 10- to 12-inch ovenproof skillet (or baking dish) and lay the chicken breast-side-up on top, arranging the bird so that it rests neatly in the skillet. Sprinkle chicken with salt, pepper, and paprika and dot with butter.

4. Roast uncovered for 35 minutes or until chicken has begun to brown. In a 2-cup measuring cup, combine broth, lemon juice, and wine. Reserve ¼ cup of the liquid and add the rest to the skillet. Baste the chicken and continue to roast uncovered, basting every 15 minutes, for 50 to 60 minutes longer or until skin is deep golden-brown and juices run clear when chicken is pierced in thickest part of the thigh and internal temperature registers 180° F.

5. Transfer chicken to a warm platter or grooved carving board and keep warm by covering with a tent of foil. Discard vegetables. Tilt the skillet and spoon off the fat (or, use a grease-separating cup). Strain the defatted cooking juices if desired and return juices to the skillet.

6. Stir the cornstarch into the reserved ¼ cup broth-wine mixture. Add the dissolved cornstarch mixture to the broth in the skillet. Bring to a simmer and stir frequently until thickened. Serve gravy alongside chicken.

Serves 2 very hungry people or 3 to 4 with side dishes, salad, and dessert.

Double Corn and Chicken Pie

• • •

CHICKEN PIES have been popular in the South at least since the mid-eighteenth century and they are, thankfully, still enjoyed today when there's time for real cooking.

The basic Southern chicken pie consists of a deep baking dish lined with pastry filled with cooked chicken parts, plus hard-boiled eggs, onions, herbs, and sometimes corn and bacon. Heavy cream or thickened broth moistens the mixture, which is then covered with a top layer of pastry, and baked. Variations include layering pastry and chicken in lasagne-like fashion, or topping the filling with a batter instead of pastry to make what some call "chicken pudding." Southern cooks have also used rice (or a mixture of rice, butter, milk, and eggs) instead of pastry to line the baking dish.

My recipe is based on a family favorite. The moist cornmeal topping is my own addition; you can substitute your favorite pie pastry if you prefer. The resulting dish is rich and comforting, yet rather simple, clean, and unadorned. My greatest compliment on this pie was from my friend, Danielle Delpeuch, who was President Mitterrand's personal chef for several years in Paris. Danielle hails from southwestern France and she once ate three *very large* helpings of this simple old American dish! It reminded her of the rich, homey favorites from her own region.

Serve with a light, simple green vegetable such as Sautéed Watercress and Radicchio with Pepper Vinegar (page 304), or a mixed green salad. For dessert, try Sweet Potato Ice Cream (page 416) with Rye and Indian Stars with Cinnamon Sugar (page 427), Brown Sugar Peanut Butter Shortbread (page 435), or Bittersweet Chocolate Chunk Pecan Pie (page 364).

FILLING AND SAUCE

½ cup dry white wine

2 large carrots, peeled and coarsely chopped

1 medium yellow onion, peeled and coarsely chopped

1 herb bouquet, tied in cheesecloth, consisting of:

2 sprigs fresh parsley

1 sprig fresh thyme (or ¼ teaspoon dried)

(ingredients continued)

½ imported bay leaf
6 whole black peppercorns
½ teaspoon salt
8 skinless, boneless chicken breast halves (about 1¼ pounds)
¼ pound bacon, cut crosswise into ½-inch-wide strips
6 scallions, finely chopped

2 cups fresh whole corn kernels, parboiled (or substitute a 10-ounce package frozen whole corn kernels, thawed)
3 tablespoons chopped fresh parsley
¼ teaspoon freshly ground black pepper
2 cups heavy cream
Generous pinch of ground red pepper (cayenne)

TOPPING

1 cup yellow cornmeal
1 cup unbleached all-purpose flour
1 teaspoon baking powder
1 teaspoon salt

2 eggs
1 cup milk
¼ cup vegetable oil

1. To make the filling: In a large skillet bring 1 quart water and the wine, carrots, onion, and herb bouquet to a simmer. Add salt and chicken, cover, and simmer very gently 15 to 20 minutes or until no longer pink inside. Cool in poaching liquid. Drain, reserving poaching liquid. Discard vegetables and herb bouquet. Chop chicken into 1-inch pieces. Set aside.

2. In a 10-inch skillet, cook bacon over medium heat, stirring frequently, for 10 minutes or until fat is rendered and bacon is lightly browned and crisp. Remove with slotted spoon and drain on paper towels. Discard all but 2 tablespoons of the drippings. Add scallions to the drippings and cook over medium heat 5 minutes or until softened. Off the heat, add corn, chicken pieces, bacon, chopped parsley, and black pepper and toss lightly. Turn the mixture into a buttered 10-inch deep-dish pie pan or quiche pan or a 6-cup gratin dish. Set aside.

3. To make the sauce: Return the poaching liquid to the skillet and boil uncovered to reduce to 1 cup. Add heavy cream and reduce to 2½ cups. Stir in red pepper. Pour ¾ cup of the sauce over the chicken mixture and toss lightly to coat. Set aside the remaining 1¾ cups sauce. (Note: May be made 2 days in advance at this point.)

4. Preheat oven to 400° F.

5. To make the topping: In medium bowl, mix together cornmeal, flour, baking powder, and salt. In a separate bowl, beat eggs well, then beat in milk and oil. Add to the dry ingredients and mix until just blended. Pour over chicken mixture and distribute evenly. Bake 25 minutes or until topping is golden-brown, cooked through, and beginning to crack on top.

6. Reheat sauce if necessary. Cut pie into wedges and pour hot sauce over each wedge. Can be served hot or at room temperature.

Serves 4 as a main dinner course; serves 6 as a lunch course.

Chicken and Dumplings

. . .

RECIPES FOR chicken and dumplings are virtually nonexistent in the earliest Southern cookbooks. The dish did, however, eventually become somewhat of a mainstay in the Southern diet, particularly in rural areas. Often the broth (which sometimes has milk added) is thickened with flour. Although some cooks may use chicken backs or other parts exclusively, most recipes call for a whole bird that is simmered in water, usually with the addition of aromatic vegetables. For simple family meals, the cooked meat might be left on the bones and served in pieces: leg, thigh, breast, etc. If company was coming, the meat might be removed from the bones and returned to the broth for a more refined presentation.

Southern dumplings can be made of flour, cornmeal, or potatoes either made into a loose, wet batter or into a firmer, biscuit-like dough rolled thinly and cut into strips. Whatever their form and texture, dumplings are always cooked in a simmering broth. (Dumplings are colloquially referred to as "slicks" or "slickums" by some, due to their rather slippery—but not unappetizing—texture.)

I love comforting dishes, but sometimes they can be too heavy. How many of us, after all, can work off thousands of calories in the fields after lunch? The very word "dumplings" seems to conjure up images of hefty fare, so I intentionally created this dish to be clean and light, both on the palate and the digestive system. The result is a tasty, familiar dish that won't make you feel like a force-fed goose. The cornmeal dumplings are light and airy—and not at all fattening. I call for an old fowl as its full-flavored flesh stands up to the long cooking time required to produce a succulent broth—the foundation, in my opinion, of a proper chicken and dumplings recipe. Although this dish is very easy, it does take time. Prepare it on a chilly, grey Sunday afternoon: its welcoming fragrance can soothe and comfort any mid-winter blues. (If you have two cooking vessels, it makes sense to double the recipe; leftovers reheat beautifully!) The dumpling dough may be prepared several hours in advance, cut into shapes (I like diamonds and squares but try stars, hearts, and half-moons for fun), then covered and chilled until ready to cook.

I've seasoned my broth with a light hand using fresh oregano, parsley, and cumin instead of the proverbial parsley-bay-thyme trio. Don't be put off by the idea of cumin. It adds a very mild, earthy tone. In fact it is barely recognizable, adding depth of flavor without taking center stage.

Serve chicken and dumplings as a main course with additional bread such as Crusty Cornmeal Yeast Bread (page 36), if desired. Follow with a mixed green salad, a perfectly ripe cheddar, Monterey Jack, or Dry Jack, and a rich red wine. For dessert, try Bourbon-Poached Pears with Pistachios and Cream (page 401), Bittersweet Chocolate Chunk–Pecan Pie (page 364), Gingered Honey Persimmon Fool (page 412), Frozen Banana Syllabub with Sauternes (page 410) and Homemade Vanilla Wafers (page 428), or Banana Soufflé with Bourbon-Butterscotch Sauce (page 418).

CHICKEN AND BROTH

1 4- to 5-pound stewing chicken
2 large carrots, peeled and cut into 1-inch chunks
2 medium yellow onions, peeled and quartered
4 slices bacon, preferably double-smoked

1 herb bouquet, tied in cheesecloth, consisting of:
  10 to 15 sprigs fresh parsley
  1 tablespoon chopped fresh oregano, or 1 teaspoon dried
  6 whole black peppercorns
2 teaspoons ground cumin
3/4 cup dry white wine
1 teaspoon salt

DUMPLINGS

¾ *cup unbleached all-purpose flour*
¼ *cup yellow cornmeal*
Generous pinch of salt
1 rounded teaspoon baking powder

1 tablespoon cold butter
⅓ *cup milk*
2 tablespoons minced fresh cilantro
(optional)

1. To prepare the chicken and the broth: Place chicken, carrots, onions, and bacon in a large Dutch oven. Add herb bouquet, cumin, wine, and salt and enough water to just cover the chicken, about 8 to 9 cups. Cover and bring to a boil. Reduce heat and simmer about 2 hours or until meat is very tender and falling off the bones.

2. Remove the Dutch oven from the heat and let the mixture cool uncovered for 30 minutes. Strain, and reserve the liquid. Skim off any fat from the surface. Discard vegetables, bacon, and the herb bouquet. Remove as much meat as possible from bones and cut meat into 1-inch pieces. Discard bones and skin. You will have about 1½ pounds skinless, boneless chicken. Set aside.

3. To make the dumplings: In a bowl combine flour, cornmeal, salt, and baking powder. Cut in the butter with a pastry blender or your fingertips. Add milk and cilantro and stir until just blended. Do not overmix or dumplings will be tough. Roll out on a lightly floured surface to a ¼-inch thickness. Using shaped cutters, cut into 1-inch diamonds, circles, hearts, or stars.

4. In a large, deep skillet heat 3 cups of the broth to a simmer. Drop in dumplings, cover tightly and simmer 20 minutes or until puffed and tender. Return chicken to remaining broth and heat through. To serve, ladle broth and chicken into bowls and top with some of the dumplings. Serve immediately.

Serves 4 to 6.

Chicken Maquechoux on Ham Biscuits

• • •

ACCORDING TO Rima and Richard Collin in their *The New Orleans Cookbook*, "Maquechoux" is a Cajun word meaning a smothered dish made with fresh corn. The following recipe is a variation on their chicken maquechoux in which browned chicken pieces are simmered in onion, fresh tomatoes, corn, cream, and herbs, then served in the cooking liquid almost like a stew or gumbo. This version is good for entertaining since the chicken, biscuits, and sauce can all be made in advance; reheat and serve when you are ready.

I like to prepare this in summer for a light supper, when corn and tomatoes are at their finest. Since the corn and tomatoes that make the sauce are naturally sweet, serve this dish with something that offers a certain amount of natural acidity or saltiness. Start with a simple green salad or "Pot Likker" Soup (page 90) then serve with Sautéed Watercress and Radicchio with Pepper Vinegar (page 304), Sautéed Green Beans with Country Ham (page 324), or Sautéed Zucchini "Ribbons" with Bacon and Basil (page 322). For dessert, I suggest Sweet Potato Ice Cream (page 416) and Cornmeal Sugar Cookies (page 425), or "Praline" Blondies (page 434) with Pineapple-Lime Sorbet with Vodka (page 405).

CHICKEN

1 large carrot, peeled and chopped
1 large stalk celery, chopped
1 large yellow onion, peeled and chopped
1 herb bouquet, tied in cheesecloth, consisting of:
  2 to 3 sprigs fresh basil
  4 to 6 sprigs fresh parsley
  2 to 3 sprigs fresh thyme

Generous pinch dried pepper flakes
2 cups unsalted or very lightly salted chicken broth, preferably home-made
1 cup dry white wine
1 pound boneless, skinless chicken breasts

MAQUECHOUX SAUCE

2 to 4 tablespoons unsalted butter
1 medium-sized yellow onion, chopped

3 large, fresh ripe tomatoes, peeled, seeded, and chopped

2 cups cooked whole corn kernels, preferably fresh
1 cup heavy cream
1 herb bouquet, tied in cheesecloth, consisting of:
  2 to 3 sprigs fresh thyme
  2 to 3 sprigs fresh basil
  10 sprigs fresh parsley
  Pinch dried red pepper flakes
Generous pinch salt, or to taste
¼ teaspoon freshly ground black pepper, or to taste
Generous pinch of ground red pepper (cayenne)

3 tablespoons tomato paste, or more to taste
Tabasco sauce, to taste
8 large, hot, homemade Basic Biscuits (See recipe, page 23. Prepare dough as recipe directs, then roll out to ½-inch thickness. Cut dough into 3-inch rounds and bake 12 to 15 minutes or until golden-brown.)
8 thin slices dry-cured country ham
3 tablespoons chopped fresh parsley, to garnish
Freshly ground black pepper to taste

1. To prepare the chicken: In a large skillet, combine carrot, celery, onion, herb bouquet, broth, and wine. Bring to a boil. Add chicken and lower heat. Cover and simmer very gently 20 minutes or until juices run clear when chicken is pierced in the thickest part. Cool chicken uncovered in the poaching liquid for 1 hour.

2. Remove chicken from broth (reserve broth) and shred or cut chicken into bite-sized pieces. You should have about 2½ to 3 cups chicken. Set chicken aside. Strain broth and set aside, discarding herb bouquet and vegetables.

3. To make the Maquechoux sauce: In a large skillet, heat 2 tablespoons of the butter over medium heat. Add onion and cook, stirring frequently, 5 minutes or until softened. Add tomatoes, 1 cup of the corn, cream, and herb bouquet. Add the reserved broth to the corn mixture. Cover and simmer 15 minutes. Uncover and simmer 5 to 10 minutes more or until reduced to about 2½ cups, stirring occasionally. Discard herb bouquet.

4. Purée the sauce mixture in a food processor or blender. Press through a conical sieve set over a saucepan; discard solids. (Note: Straining the sauce is for presentation purposes only, making for a sauce that is visually more refined. Purists may want to leave the sauce chunky. I happen to find that unstrained, the sauce is unappetizing to the eye.) Add reserved chicken, salt, black pepper, red pepper, tomato paste, and remaining corn to the strained sauce and heat through.

Poultry and Game

Taste, adding more salt, pepper, tomato paste, or Tabasco to taste. Mixture should be well seasoned.

5. To serve, split the biscuits and toast them lightly. Top each biscuit bottom with a slice of ham. Ladle ⅓ to ½ cup chicken mixture over ham. Sprinkle with chopped parsley and top with biscuit tops.

Serves 4 as a main course.

Peanut and Ham–Stuffed Chicken with Cider Sauce
· · ·

THIS DISH PAYS HOMAGE to my native Virginia, where some of the finest ham, peanuts, and apples are produced. Peanut stuffings for poultry were common in the nineteenth-century South—particularly Charleston—and are usually composed of peanuts, breadcrumbs, and butter. Ham and peanuts are a logical combination, since they not only taste good together—the salty, smoky ham is a nice foil to the rich nuts—but originally peanuts were one of the main foods fed to hogs destined to be Smithfield hams. The sweet-tart sauce—a mixture of puréed vegetables and a reduction of cider and cider vinegar—provides a counterpoint that is rich and deeply flavored.

The presentation of this dish is very pretty indeed. And, since the chicken can be stuffed and rolled in advance, it is a good choice for entertaining. Leftovers reheat well and may be served with warm, leftover sauce, or at room temperature on lettuce leaves drizzled with a vinaigrette made of cold pressed peanut oil, and good-quality apple cider vinegar. To begin, serve "Pot Likker" Soup (page 90). Try Sautéed Watercress and Radicchio with Pepper Vinegar (page 304) as a side dish. For dessert, Sweet Potato Cheesecake (page 391) or Sweet Potato Ice Cream (page 416) are my choices.

STUFFING

½ cup roasted, unsalted peanuts
1 tablespoon unsalted butter, room
   temperature

¼ cup heavy cream
¼ cup unseasoned breadcrumbs

¼ teaspoon salt

⅛ teaspoon freshly ground black
  pepper

⅛ teaspoon ground nutmeg

⅛ teaspoon ground red pepper (cayenne)

CHICKEN AND SAUCE

8 boneless chicken breast halves,
  skinned

⅛ pound very thinly sliced Smithfield
  ham (see page 481 for mail-order
  source)

2 medium yellow onions, peeled and
  coarsely chopped

1 large carrot, peeled and coarsely
  chopped

1 large, tart, firm apple, peeled, cored
  and coarsely chopped

5 tablespoons unsalted butter

1½ cups fresh, unfiltered apple cider

3 tablespoons cider vinegar

APPLE GARNISH

3 tablespoons unsalted butter

1 medium-sized, tart, unpeeled apple,
  cored and sliced to ¼-inch thickness

2 to 3 tablespoons sugar

1. Preheat oven to 375° F.

2. To make the stuffing: Process the nuts in a food processor or blender until they are finely ground. Add the butter and process until smooth. Add the cream, breadcrumbs, salt, pepper, nutmeg, and red pepper and process until well combined.

3. To prepare the chicken: Place each breast half between sheets of waxed paper and flatten with a mallet, the flat side of a cleaver, or a rolling pin to a thickness of about half an inch. Place the breasts smooth-side-down on a work surface and discard waxed paper. Lay one slice of ham on each breast half. Spread approximately 3 teaspoons of stuffing on top of the ham. Beginning with the narrowest end of the breast, roll up into a neat, plump shape, tucking the edges in. Secure with toothpicks.

4. Distribute the onions, carrots, and apple in a baking dish that's just large enough for the rolled breasts to fit in snugly, and place the breasts on top of the apple and vegetables.

5. In a saucepan, melt 4 tablespoons of the butter and brush some of it on the breasts. Bake breasts uncovered for 10 minutes. Baste with butter and bake 10 minutes more. Turn the breasts over, baste, and cook another 10 minutes.

6. While the chicken cooks, boil the cider and vinegar in a saucepan over high heat until reduced to 6 tablespoons. Set aside. Transfer the chicken breasts to a warm platter and cover to keep warm.

7. Transfer the onions, carrot, apple and any juices from the baking pan to a blender or food processor. Add the cider reduction and purée until smooth. Press through a sieve set over a medium saucepan, reheat over low heat, and whisk in remaining tablespoon of butter. Keep warm.

8. To prepare the garnish: Heat the butter in a large, heavy skillet. Dredge one side of each apple slice in sugar and place sugared-side-down in the hot butter. Cook over medium-high heat for 4 to 5 minutes or until deep golden-brown. Sprinkle the remaining sugar on the apples, turn over, and brown the other side.

9. Add any juices that have collected from the chicken to the sauce; reheat the sauce if necessary. To serve, cut each chicken breast crosswise into ¼- to ⅓-inch slices; discard toothpicks. Divide the sauce evenly among 4 plates, place slices on top of sauce in an overlapping pattern and garnish with 2 or 3 apple slices. Pass remaining sauce on side.

Serves 4.

Grilled Chicken Paillard with Peach Salsa

■ ■ ■

NOTHING'S BETTER in summer than a dead-ripe peach from Georgia or the Carolinas.

Serve this dish in summer, when peaches are at their peak and the grill is at the ready. (If it's winter, or there's no grill, chicken may be broiled.) This recipe lends itself particularly well to entertaining, since everything can be made in advance. The jalapeño butter and peach salsa were inspired by recipes from Jeremiah Tower, chef of Stars Restaurant in San Francisco, who creates innovative and delicious variations on classic sauces and condiments. Serve this dish with hot rice.

CHICKEN AND MARINADE

8 skinless, boneless chicken breast
  halves
½ cup light olive oil

2 cloves garlic, slivered
3 tablespoons freshly squeezed lime
  juice

PEACH SALSA

¼ cup minced red onion
3 large fresh ripe peaches
2 tablespoons light olive oil
2 to 3 tablespoons freshly squeezed

lime juice
2 tablespoons chopped fresh cilantro
  or mint

JALAPEÑO BUTTER
(OPTIONAL, BUT HIGHLY RECOMMENDED)

1 fresh jalapeño pepper, roasted,
  peeled, and seeded (or substitute 2
  tablespoons canned chopped green
  chiles, drained, or 2 tablespoons
  chopped pickled jalapeño peppers,

drained, or 1 tablespoon chile
  powder)
8 tablespoons (1 stick) unsalted butter, room temperature
Salt and freshly ground black pepper,
  to taste

1. To marinate the chicken: Place breasts between sheets of waxed paper and pound with a mallet, the flat side of a cleaver, or a rolling pin to a thickness of ¼ inch. Place in a shallow nonaluminum pan or dish and cover with oil, garlic, and lime juice. Cover and marinate at room temperature 1 hour, or marinate 4 to 8 hours in refrigerator.

2. Meanwhile, to prepare salsa: In a nonaluminum bowl combine salsa ingredients, mashing lightly with a fork so the mixture is still chunky. Cover and set aside at least 1 hour to blend flavors.

3. To make jalapeño butter: In a blender or a food processor with the machine running, drop in the prepared pepper and process to purée. Add butter and process until blended. Add salt and pepper to taste. Scrape the butter onto a sheet of waxed paper and form it into a cylinder that is about 1 inch in diameter. Place in freezer 30 minutes (or in refrigerator 1 hour or longer) or until firm.

*Poultry
and
Game*

4. To cook the chicken: Remove chicken from marinade and place on a lightly oiled grill set over hot coals. Cook about 2 minutes per side or until juices run clear and flesh shows no traces of pink when thickest part of chicken is pierced. Do not overcook or chicken will be tough and dry. (Note: If you don't have a grill or weather prohibits outdoor cooking, place chicken on lightly oiled broiling rack 4 inches from preheated broiler and cook as directed.) Serve hot topped with a pat of jalapeño butter and salsa on the side.

Serves 4.

Roast Turkey
with Herbed Cornbread Dressing
• • •

. . . [Christmas] supper was very fine—turkey, oysters, sangaree, marmalade ice cream, cake, . . . and all things nice. We danced, played games & had a fine time.

—Agnes Lee, from *Growing Up in the 1850's: The Journal of Agnes Lee,*
edited by Mary Custis Lee deButts

TURKEY HAS BEEN a festive Southern dish for well over a century. And on special occasions, it is often accompanied by oysters, just as in Agnes Lee's day. Cookbooks show that turkeys in the nineteenth century were boiled and stewed (in water, wine, and/or gravy) as well as roasted, and they were nearly always stuffed, usually with a forcemeat of sausage or veal.

Wild turkeys are native to America, and were plentiful during the seventeenth, eighteenth, and nineteenth centuries. Today, few people have even tasted wild turkey, which is darker and leaner than the domesticated bird. Organically raised turkeys are becoming more widely available, and I buy them whenever possible because I find them moister and with a more pronounced "turkey" flavor. They usually cost more than the supermarket variety, but I think they are worth the price.

Presently, North Carolina is the number-one turkey producing state in the nation, with Arkansas, Virginia, Georgia, and the Carolinas close behind.

Our holiday bird (we had turkey on Christmas as well as Thanksgiving) was always served with dressing—not stuffing—cooked outside the turkey in a baking dish, and served as a farinaceous accompaniment. We loved the crisp, buttery topping and wouldn't have traded our dressing for soggy, cooked-in-the-bird stuffing for all the oysters in the Gulf. There is another good reason not to cook the stuffing inside the turkey: Unstuffed birds roast faster—a plus at holiday time when there are sweet potatoes, rolls, pies, and side dishes to be baked.

The dressing here is an adaptation of my grandmother's recipe. It is composed of crumbled cornbread—to which celery, onions, herbs, and spices have been added—and whole wheat bread pieces tossed with broth and butter. That's it. No sausage, no oysters, and no pecans, all popular stuffing additions in the South. I welcome the simplicity of this meatless, oysterless dressing since the holiday menu tends to have so many other complex textures, flavors, and seasonings.

I begin roasting the turkey breast-side-down at a high temperature. This guarantees that the turkey back is just as golden-brown and crisp as the breast. Cooking the bird breast down for part of the time also helps keep the breast from drying out. The high temperature shortens the cooking time and ensures juiciness.

It is best to bake the Herbed Cornbread for the dressing a day in advance (there's enough to do on Thanksgiving day anyway) so that flavors marry and so the cornbread will be dry enough to maintain the texture when mixed with the other dressing ingredients. (If it is freshly made, it tends to become mushy.) Once the turkey is in the oven, you can prepare the broth for the gravy and complete the dressing.

Start your feast with Jerusalem Artichoke Soup (page 92), Sweet Potato Soup with Pine Nut Butter (page 94), Oysters and Leeks on Corn Pancakes (page 161), or Turnip, Rutabaga, and Beet Salad with Black Walnut Vinaigrette (page 122). For side dishes, serve Sautéed Green Beans with Country Ham (page 324), Louisiana Rice with Mushrooms and Hazelnuts (page 258), Spiced Winter Squash (page 317), Buttermilk Angel Biscuits (page 26), or brussels sprouts. For dessert, try Gingered Honey Persimmon Fool (page 412), Sweet Potato Ice Cream (page 416) with black walnuts, Pistachio-Apricot Fruitcake (page 382), "Double Decker" Citron Cranberry Pie (page 375), Bittersweet Chocolate Chunk–Pecan Pie (page 364), or White Chocolate Chess Tartlet with Pecan

Crust (page 367). I love Champagne or sparkling wine with turkey, but you can also pour a Beaujolais Nouveau, a mature Virginia or California Chardonnay, a French Chablis, or other white Burgundy.

HERBED CORNBREAD DRESSING

1 recipe Herbed Buttermilk Corn-
*   bread (recipe follows)*
4 large eggs
1½ cups cooled chicken broth
1½ cups (3 sticks) butter, melted and
*   cooled*

1 pound good-quality stale whole
*   wheat bread, torn or diced into*
*   ¼-inch pieces (you should have*
*   about 4 cups total)*

1. Prepare herbed cornbread as directed. (Note: If cornbread is freshly made, dry it out before tossing with the other ingredients; otherwise dressing will lack texture. To do this, simply crumble the cornbread into ¼-inch pieces and spread out on a large baking sheet. Place in a preheated 300° F oven until dry but not crisp, about 10 to 15 minutes.)

2. Preheat oven to 350° F.

3. In a large bowl, beat eggs thoroughly. Add broth and butter and beat well. Add whole wheat bread and cornbread and toss to combine. Turn the mixture into a shallow 2-quart buttered baking dish and bake 30 to 45 minutes or until hot throughout and crisp golden-brown on top. Leftover dressing reheats well and freezes beautifully.

Serves 10 to 12.

Herbed Buttermilk Cornbread

• • •

THIS IS BEST MADE at least twenty-four hours in advance.

1 cup unbleached all-purpose flour
1 cup cornmeal
4 teaspoons baking powder
1 teaspoon salt
½ teaspoon baking soda

1 tablespoon fresh thyme leaves (or 1
*   teaspoon dried)*
1 teaspoon fresh crumbled rosemary
*   leaves (or scant ½ teaspoon dried)*
1 tablespoon minced fresh sage leaves
*   (or 1 teaspoon dried)*

¼ cup finely chopped fresh parsley
½ teaspoon freshly ground black pepper
½ teaspoon ground red pepper (cayenne)

1 large egg
1½ cups buttermilk
4 tablespoons (½ stick) butter, melted and cooled
2 large stalks celery, diced
1 large yellow onion, diced

1. Preheat oven to 425° F.

2. In a large bowl, mix flour, cornmeal, baking powder, salt, and baking soda. Stir in herbs and spices.

3. In a separate bowl, beat egg. Beat in buttermilk and butter. Add to dry ingredients and stir until blended, about 20 to 30 strokes. Fold in celery and onion. Turn batter into a buttered 9-inch by 9-inch baking pan and bake 25 to 30 minutes or until top is golden-brown and toothpick comes out dry when tested in center. Let cornbread cool in the pan 5 minutes. Run a knife around the edges of the pan and turn cornbread out onto a rack to cool completely.

Note This is highly seasoned and not meant to be eaten as a bread. When mixed with the other dressing ingredients, the seasoning is appropriate.

Roast Turkey and Gravy

FIGURE 1 POUND OF TURKEY per person, 1¼ to 1½ pounds per person if you want leftovers. So, a 12-pound turkey will serve 8 people with leftovers.

TURKEY

12- to 15-pound turkey, room temperature
Salt and freshly ground black pepper, to taste
3 stalks celery
2 large carrots

2 medium yellow onions
15 to 20 sprigs fresh parsley
10 to 12 sprigs fresh thyme (or ½ teaspoon dried)
8 tablespoons (1 stick) unsalted butter, softened

(ingredients continued)

Turkey neck, wing tips, and giblets
2 large carrots, chopped
2 stalks celery, chopped
2 medium yellow onions, chopped
10 sprigs fresh parsley and 1 sprig
　　fresh thyme (optional) tied with
　　kitchen twine

Generous pinch of salt
1/2 cup dry white wine
1/4 cup cornstarch
Salt and freshly ground black pepper,
　　to taste

1. Preheat oven to 450° F.

2. To roast the turkey: Cut off the wing tips at the first joint and reserve for broth. Remove neck and giblets and reserve for stock and gravy. Rinse turkey under cold running water and thoroughly pat dry with paper towels. Sprinkle turkey cavity with salt and pepper.

3. Place 1 stalk celery, 1 carrot, 1 onion, the parsley, and fresh thyme inside the turkey cavity. Truss, and rub turkey all over with half the softened butter. Place breast-side-down on a roasting rack in a roasting pan. Place in oven and roast 35 to 45 minutes or until turkey back is golden-brown. Remove turkey from oven and turn breast-side-up. (To turn bird over, insert handle end of wooden spoon into cavity and hold neck end with pot holder or several thicknesses of paper towels.)

4. Rub bird with remaining butter. Chop the remaining vegetables and strew them in the pan around the bird, lower temperature to 350° F, and return bird to oven. Roast 12 to 15 minutes per pound (for birds up to 15 pounds), basting every 20 minutes, or until meat thermometer registers 180° F in the thickest part of the inner thigh. (If bird weighs over 15 pounds and/or is stuffed, roast 20 to 25 minutes per pound or until thigh registers 180° F and interior stuffing registers at least 165° F).

5. To make the broth: Chop neck and wing tip coarsely with a cleaver or crush with a mallet. Place in large saucepot along with giblets (use gizzard and heart only; the liver is strong in flavor and should be reserved for another use), carrots, celery, onions, parsley, thyme, and salt. Cover with 2 quarts cold water and bring to a boil, skimming occasionally. Lower heat and simmer partially covered 1 hour, skimming from time to time. Strain; discard solids, reserving giblets to add to the gravy if desired.

6. Return broth to saucepot and boil to reduce to 2½ cups. (If broth has reduced to less than 2½ cups, add enough water to measure that amount.) Cool; discard fat. You will have about 2¼ cups degreased broth.

7. Make gravy when the turkey comes out of the oven. Transfer the turkey to a grooved cutting board and cover with a tent of foil to keep warm.

8. Set a sieve over a bowl or a 4-cup grease separator. Pour all the pan juices and the roasting vegetables into the sieve. Press down on vegetables to extract aromatic juices, and then discard vegetables.

9. Pour wine into the roasting pan and boil 30 seconds as you scrape up the brown bits with a wooden spoon. Strain this deglazing liquid into the pan juices. If using a 4-cup grease separator, pour off fat. Otherwise, chill to congeal fat, then lift off fat and discard.

10. In a saucepan, combine degreased pan juices and all but ¼ of the cooled, degreased broth and bring to a simmer over medium heat.

11. In a small bowl, mix cornstarch with the reserved ¼ cup cooled stock to make a paste. Add this paste to the warm broth and simmer, stirring frequently, until thickened and heated through. Add any juices that have collected on the platter from the turkey to the gravy. Add salt and pepper to taste. Serve in a gravy boat alongside the turkey.

Makes about 3 cups gravy.

Game

SOUTHERNERS have always been great hunters. Although today hunting is more about sport than feeding the family, game is important in Southern culinary history. The seventeeth- and eighteenth-century American diet relied heavily upon game. It was eaten throughout the year, but especially in fall and winter when poultry and eggs were in short supply. During the 1800s, many furred and feathered species became scarce partially because of the indiscriminate and unrestricted killing for retail sale by market hunters. Their actions were curtailed in the early 1900s and, thanks to conservation and game restrictions, these animals have, to a certain degree, been replenished by nature.

According to my hunter friend and fellow Virginian, Thomas King, the most popular game birds (this does not include waterfowl) in the South are quail, dove, wild turkey (prized for its dark, moist, rather sweet flesh), and, to a lesser extent, snipe, pheasant, grouse, partridge, and woodcock. In the home, most of these birds are prepared much like they were hundreds of years ago: roasted, "smothered," grilled, fried, braised, stewed, potted, or baked in pies.

Waterfowl are also a favorite of the Southern hunter. The most common ducks currently found in Southern waters are known collectively as "puddle ducks" and include mallards, black ducks, wood ducks, teal, and widgeon. Coot and rail are hunted to a lesser extent and are not usually as flavorful as the other species. In the early nineteenth century, the canvasback duck, which fed on wild celery along the Chesapeake Bay, was highly prized for its fine flavor and was shipped to all principal American cities as well as to Europe. Recipes for the canvasback appear in the private recipe collections of many great Southern plantations, which instruct that the bird was to be served rare with head intact as proof of identity. Today, canvasback hunting is restricted, and they are not as flavorful as in the past because of the scarcity of wild celery.

Geese are generally more highly prized than ducks for eating and according to my friend, Georgia hunter Frank Hendryx, tender young swans (which may be taken legally in North Carolina where thousands end their migration every year) are preferred over geese.

Bear and deer are the only large furred animals taken for the table in the South. (Bear, in fact, was the favorite meat of William Byrd II, although he said that after eating it, "one is sure to dream of a woman, of the devil, or both.") The white deer—the only species hunted in the South—is quite abundant and if shot and handled with care, can be delicious. At one time, buffalo frequented the valley of Virginia, but they were ruthlessly hunted. The last buffalo reported seen in Virginia was in 1797.

Small furred animals hunted for the Southern table include opossum, raccoon, beaver, squirrel, muskrat, nutria, and rabbit, with all but the last consumed primarily in rural, wooded, or mountainous areas. As plebeian as the squirrel may seem, it was relished by Virginia's greatest gastronome, Thomas Jefferson, and even today it is considered by many to be flavorful. Rabbit are plentiful and popular throughout the South and are more versatile in the kitchen than other small game. Of all these little creatures there are probably more recipes for the opossum—a Southern native that can now be found as far north as New York State—than all the others. Opossums feed chiefly on wild berries and persimmons and were at one time considered to be a Virginia delicacy, consumed by Native Americans, white men, and slaves alike. Like rabbit and squirrel, opossums were popular game for servants and slaves since they usually did not possess firearms and these animals could be snared or caught with dogs. Opossums are usually roasted (parboiled first, if old and tough) and traditionally served with sweet potatoes for a classic combo known locally as, 'possum and sweets.

A Word about Exotic Game

Until recently, frogs' legs, turtle, and alligator were a fairly common part of the Southern game bag. They are still hunted, but are more restricted and therefore more costly to the purveyor and consumer. Frogs' legs are usually sautéed or deep fried; turtle is generally found in soups and stews; in Cajun country, alligator is popular served with a piquant sauce (roux plus tomatoes and spices) over rice.

Roast Duck
with a Light Lime and Molasses Sauce
• • •

UNLESS THERE is a hunter in your family, wild ducks can be rather hard to come by. Some specialty stores and butcher shops carry them, but they can cost two to four times more than domestic ducklings, which are less gamey in flavor and tend to have a wider appeal. While wild ducks can be delicious—especially if they have fed off corn for several days before being killed—they can also be dry, tough, stringy, and fishy tasting. For this reason, I call for domestic duck in the recipe below.

Cookbook author Paula Wolfert inspired the technique that I use here for cooking the breasts and legs separately. Since the legs need about 35 to 50

*Poultry
and
Game*

■

minutes more cooking time than the breasts, the method results in meat that is cooked just to the right degree of doneness.

Although it wasn't always so, Southerners usually now serve wild duck with a sweet sauce, chutney, preserve, or relish. (Early recipes show duck with more savory accompaniments: smothered with onion sauce, stuffed with onion and sage, and served with gravy seasoned with herbs, gizzards, pine nuts, mace, or anchovies.) The sauce here is my own creation and combines the fruity tang of Florida limes, to cut the richness of the duck, and a mere hint of earthy-sweet molasses. Homemade duck stock and a final swirl of butter add depth of flavor and richness to this light sauce. The resulting faintly tart-sweet sauce is a welcome foil to the richly flavored meat. Black peppercorns add a savory note. Serve with a well-chilled Johannisburg Riesling, iced tea, or lemonade. Start this game dinner with Mini Corn Puddings with Chive Cream (page 73), Spoon Bread Soufflé with Fresh Corn Sauce (page 66), or a fruit salad. Serve with Dirty Brown Rice with Chives (page 260), and Buttermilk Angel Biscuits (page 26).

DUCK AND STOCK

2 4- to 5-pound domestic ducklings (such as Long Island), thawed if frozen

1 large yellow onion, peeled and quartered

2 medium carrots, peeled and coarsely chopped

20 to 30 sprigs fresh parsley, tied with kitchen twine

8 whole black peppercorns, tied in cheesecloth

Pinch of salt, or to taste

Freshly ground black pepper, to taste

4 tablespoons rendered duck fat (see note), or 2 tablespoons butter plus 2 tablespoons vegetable oil

SAUCE

2 large limes

¼ cup unsulphured molasses (or substitute sorghum syrup)

2 cups reduced, concentrated duck stock (instructions given below)

2 to 4 tablespoons unsalted butter, room temperature (optional)

Salt and freshly ground black pepper, to taste

1. To cut up the ducks: Working with 1 duck at a time, lay duck breast-side-down on a flat work surface. Cut off the excess neck skin and discard. Remove excess fat from the body cavity and render (see note), if desired. (Duck fat is excellent for cooking potatoes, mushrooms, etc.) Turn duck over and remove wishbone. Cut off wings at the body and reserve for stock. Slice down along center of breast, through the skin and flesh, down to the breast bone. Separate breast meat from rib cage, lift off, and set aside. Remove skin from breasts and reserve. Pull the thigh-leg piece away from the carcass and detach with a knife. Trim the carcass of excess fat and skin and render the fat, if desired, or discard. Repeat with second duck.

2. To make the stock: Place carcasses in a stockpot along with wishbones, wings, necks, onion, carrots, parsley, peppercorns, and salt. Add enough cold water to the stockpot to cover the carcass mixture. Bring to a boil, skimming the surface as necessary. Lower heat and simmer partially covered for 1 hour. Strain, discard solids and set aside. (Note: If you are in a hurry, you can skip this step and use prepared chicken broth, omitting the pinch of salt if the chicken broth is already salted. The resulting sauce, however, will not be as richly flavored as if duck stock were used.) Pour stock into a large saucepan and bring to a boil. Boil rapidly until reduced by one-half. You should have about 2 cups of reduced stock; add water or reduce further to yield 2 cups.

3. To roast the duck: Preheat oven to 375° F. Using a fork or the point of a sharp knife, prick the legs and thighs all over every ¼ inch. Sprinkle the legs and thighs with salt and pepper. Heat 2 tablespoons of the rendered duck fat (or 1 tablespoon butter plus 1 tablespoon vegetable oil) in a large skillet. Add legs and thighs and cook over medium-high heat 2 minutes on each side or until golden-brown. (Note: Do this in 2 batches if necessary using the remaining rendered duck fat; skillet should not be crowded.) Drain the duck legs and thighs on paper towels. Place them in a roasting pan and roast uncovered in the oven for 35 to 40 minutes.

4. Add the uncooked, skinned breasts to the roaster with the thighs and legs and cook 5 to 7 minutes more or until breasts are medium-rare and rosy pink at the thickest point.

5. Remove duck pieces from roasting pan and keep warm. Pour off excess fat from roasting pan. Add 1 cup stock and boil to deglaze. Set aside.

6. For the sauce, remove the zest from the limes using a vegetable peeler (reserve limes). Cut the zest strips into fine julienne strips and drop into a small

saucepan of boiling water. Let water return to a boil, then drain and refresh zest under cold running water. Repeat this process 2 times more to extract bitterness. Finally, drain well and set zest aside.

7. Squeeze juice from the reserved limes. In a medium-sized nonaluminum saucepan combine lime juice, molasses, the reserved deglazed pan juices, and the remaining 1 cup duck stock. Bring to a boil and cook rapidly about 1 minute or until sauce has thickened slightly. Remove from heat and swirl in the optional butter enrichment. Add the lime zest; season to taste with salt and pepper.

8. To serve, carve each breast on the diagonal into ⅓-inch-thick slices. Pour a pool of sauce on one side of each of 4 warm dinner plates. Top with fanned-out breast slices and 1 leg or thigh. (Note: For small appetites, you may want to serve just the breast meat, and reheat the thighs and legs for another meal.)

Serves 4 to 6.

Note To render duck fat, chop the fat into thin (½-inch-wide) strips and cook in a skillet over medium heat until fat has been rendered and the resulting "cracklings" are deep golden-brown and crisp. Either discard the cracklings or drain them on paper towels and sprinkle over rice, potatoes, or other side dish. Set the rendered fat aside. Use rendered fat for cooking potatoes or mushrooms.

Goose with Damson-Port Sauce

■ ■ ■

LIKE WILD DUCK, wild goose can be delicious but it is not readily available and when you *can* find it, it tends to be quite expensive. Most Southern cooks presented with a wild goose stuff it with onions and apples, roast it like duck, and serve it with pan gravy. This stuffed, roast goose is usually accompanied by a sweet sauce or relish of some sort, often made with damson plums, those intensely flavored little plums beloved in the South that are used primarily in making preserves and jams.

Like my duck recipe, I've adapted cookbook author Paula Wolfert's technique for cutting up the bird, which to my mind is now the only way to cook waterfowl. The thighs need greater cooking time, so they go into the oven first.

The breasts cook in a mere 10 minutes—so they emerge rosy pink and bursting with juices. Once you try a goose in this manner, there is no going back to dry, tough, stringy whole roast goose. This technique, plus the fact that the goose is not stuffed, makes this a relatively quick dish. The only time-consuming step is the stock, which can be made ahead of time. So if you are short on time, I suggest cutting up the bird and making the stock a day in advance. The stock is reduced and concentrated, then flavored with port and damson preserves for a rich, meaty sauce that complements the dark, earthy meat beautifully. Serve with a Virginia Beau Noir, a Volnay, or other red Burgundy or a Pinot Noir from California or Oregon. Leftover goose makes a fine addition to salads: combine with red leaf and oak leaf lettuces and dress with a hazlenut or walnut vinaigrette and sprinkle with corresponding nuts. (To make nut vinaigrettes, in a jar combine 1 teaspoon Dijon-style mustard, pinch each of salt and pepper, 2 tablespoons wine vinegar, and ½ cup walnut oil or hazelnut oil and shake well to combine. Adjust seasonings.)

GOOSE AND STOCK

1 goose, about 10 to 12 pounds (thawed if frozen)
2 medium carrots, peeled and coarsely chopped
1 large yellow onion, peeled and quartered
1 stalk celery, coarsely chopped
8 whole black peppercorns, tied in cheesecloth

Pinch of salt, or to taste
Freshly ground black pepper, to taste
4 tablespoons rendered goose fat (see note), or substitute 2 tablespoons butter plus 2 tablespoons vegetable oil

SAUCE

1 cup Port (or substitute Madeira)
½ cup good-quality damson plum preserves (or substitute other plum preserves if damson is not available)

1½ cups reduced, concentrated goose stock (instructions given below)
2 to 4 tablespoons unsalted, softened butter
Salt and freshly ground black pepper, to taste

1. To cut up the goose: Follow the same procedure as for duck in step 1, page 205.

2. To make the stock: Remove skin from breasts and render fat (see note) if desired. Trim fat and skin from carcass and wings. Place carcass in a large stockpot. Add carrots, onion, and celery. Cover with water, bring to a boil. Add peppercorns and a pinch of salt. Reduce heat and simmer, partially covered, for 1½ to 2 hours, skimming as needed. Strain and discard solids. Set stock aside.

3. To roast the goose: Preheat oven to 375° F. Using a fork or the point of a sharp knife, prick the legs and thighs all over, every ¼ inch. Sprinkle the legs with salt and pepper. Heat 2 tablespoons of the rendered goose fat in a large skillet. Add legs and thighs and cook over medium-high heat 2 minutes on each side or until golden-brown. (Note: Do this in 2 batches if necessary, adding the remaining rendered goose fat; skillet should not be crowded.) Drain the duck legs and thighs on paper towels. Place them in a roasting pan and roast uncovered 50 minutes to 1 hour, or until tender. Add the uncooked, skinned goose breasts to the pan with the legs and thighs and roast 10 minutes longer or until medium rare and rosy pink in the center.

4. Pour off excess fat from roasting pan and discard. Add port and boil 1 minute while scraping up brown bits stuck to bottom of pan. Strain into a saucepan and add the preserves. Over high heat boil mixture until reduced by one-half. Add the stock, reduce by half again, or until slightly thickened and syrupy. Off the heat, swirl in the softened butter. Season with salt and pepper to taste. To serve, carve breasts on the diagonal into ⅓-inch-thick slices and place on a pool of sauce on each plate. (One goose breast will serve 2 people.) Carve meat from legs and thighs and serve alongside the breast as desired.

Serves 6 to 8.

Note To render goose fat, chop the fat into thin (½-inch-wide) strips and cook in a skillet over medium heat until fat has rendered and the resulting "cracklings" are deep golden-brown and crisp. Either discard the "cracklings" or drain them on paper towels and sprinkle over rice, potatoes, or other side dish. Set the rendered fat aside. Use rendered fat for cooking potatoes or mushrooms.

Grilled (or Broiled) Quail
with Herb Butter
• • •

Breakfast in the old dining room is a meal of quail, grits, beaten biscuits, fried apple rings, and . . . bowl-sized cups of chicoried coffee. I don't know whether Lucy or the uncle or Carrie Bon cooked it. The uncle is proud of the quail—they're his, he's got a freezerful—half a dozen hot little heart-shaped morsels per plate, six tender-spicy, gamey-gladdening mouthfuls.

—Walker Percy, *The Thanatos Syndrome*

QUAIL ARE MY FAVORITE of all small game birds. In the South, they are usually fried (often served for a special breakfast with grits), roasted, or stuffed with oysters, deep-fried, or smothered. Quail are elegant little creatures with all white meat, and are good for those who aren't fond of a gamey taste since they taste just a tad bit stronger than chicken. Quail (also called Bobwhite) are usually hunted from November to February. Now, thanks to quail farms such as Manchester Farms in South Carolina, quail are available all year round, even to city dwellers with no hunters in the family. Wild doves and pigeons are traditionally cooked in a similar manner, but they are even harder to come by for the average cook. This and the other quail recipes may be used for cooking doves and pigeons. The herb butter is stuffed under the skin so it keeps the bird moist. Serve the birds with rice of any kind (I like Wild Pecan Rice™, Louisiana popcorn rice, or brown basmati rice with this dish). Grilled vegetables such as bell peppers, zucchini, or mushrooms, or steamed brussels sprouts, green beans, or broccoli are also tasty accompaniments.

2 medium-sized garlic cloves, minced

12 tablespoons (1½ sticks) unsalted butter

Grated zest of 1 lemon

1 cup coarsely chopped parsley

3 ounces Smithfield ham (or use other dry-cured country ham), finely chopped (see page 481 for mail-order source)

12 quail, partially boned (have the butcher bone them for you), thawed if frozen (see page 481 for mail-order source)

Pinch of freshly ground black pepper

1. Light the coals or preheat the broiler.

2. In a blender or food processor, with the machine running, drop the garlic into the machine until finely chopped. Add butter, lemon zest, and parsley. Process until well mixed, about 10 seconds. Transfer to a bowl. Stir in the ham and the pepper until well blended.

3. Working with one quail at a time, gently lift the skin at the neck and, using the index finger, pry the skin loose from the body, being careful not to tear it. Go as far as the finger can extend, even loosening the skin from the legs if possible.

4. Using about 1 tablespoon of the herb butter for each quail, force the butter with your finger over as much of the surface of the flesh as possible. (Note: This is a rather delicate procedure; although the skin is quite sturdy, be careful because any tears will cause the butter to escape during cooking.)

5. Lightly brush a clean grill with oil (or line a broiler pan with aluminum foil and butter the foil lightly). Place quail on the grill (grill should be 5 to 6 inches from the coals), breast-side-down, and grill 10 to 15 minutes or until golden-brown. Gently turn quail over and grill 5 minutes or until golden-brown and juices run clear when flesh is pierced in the thickest part. Do not overcook or quail will be dry. (To broil, place quail breast-side-up on prepared pan and broil 5 to 6 inches from heat source for 15 minutes or until golden-brown. Turn quail over and broil 5 minutes more.

Serves 4 to 6.

Quail Roasted on a Bed of Aromatic Vegetables

• • •

THIS GLORIOUS DISH was created by my Georgia friend, Charles Pierce. Simplicity is a hallmark of Southern cooking, and this dish is about as straightforward and unpretentious as it gets. The simplest flavors set off the quail beautifully. Serve with rice of any kind or Fried Garlic Grits (page 267), Whole Wheat Cornsticks (page 35), and Sautéed Green Beans with Country Ham (page 324).

12 *partially boned quail (have the butcher bone them for you), thawed if frozen (see page 481 for mail-order source)*

Salt and freshly ground black pepper, to taste

5 *tablespoons unsalted butter (or less, if using a nonstick skillet)*

2 *tablespoons vegetable oil (or less, if using a nonstick skillet)*

¼ *cup dry white wine*

2 *medium carrots, peeled and julienned*

1 *medium yellow onion, julienned*

2 *medium stalks celery, julienned*

½ *pound wild or domestic mushrooms, wiped clean, tough stems trimmed*

Juice of ½ lemon

Chopped parsley or parsley sprigs, to garnish

1. Preheat oven to 450° F.

2. Season the quail with salt and pepper. Heat two tablespoons of the butter with the oil in a large, ovenproof skillet over medium-high heat. Add the birds and cook 2 minutes on each side or until deep golden-brown. Drain on paper towels. Discard the excess fat. Return the skillet to the heat. Add the white wine and boil over high heat for 1 to 2 minutes while stirring constantly to reduce slightly. Return the browned birds to the skillet, cover, and cook in the preheated oven for 10 minutes.

3. Melt the remaining 3 tablespoons of butter in a large, heavy saucepan. Add the carrots, onion, celery, mushrooms, and lemon juice. Cook over medium heat until vegetables are crisp-tender, about 5 to 10 minutes, stirring often to prevent scorching.

4. After the birds have cooked for 10 minutes, uncover the skillet and top birds with the vegetables. Cover and cook for 20 to 25 minutes more or until birds are tender.

5. To serve, arrange the cooked birds on a platter. Remove the vegetables with a slotted spoon and scatter over the quail. Pour over the cooking juices and garnish with parsley.

Serves 4 to 6.

Quail with Cornbread Stuffing

· · ·

THREE SOUTHERN CLASSICS are in this recipe: bacon, pecans, and cornbread. They complement the gentle flavor of the quail, which is a good dinner-party choice since it can be stuffed a day in advance. I like to serve this in autumn, and I usually begin the meal with Sweet Potato Soup (omit the pine nut butter) (page 94), or Jerusalem Artichoke Soup (page 92).

4 tablespoons unsalted butter (or less, if using a nonstick skillet)
2 medium yellow onions, finely chopped
1 stalk celery, finely chopped
4 cups crumbled, day-old cornbread (see recipe for Rich Buttermilk Cornbread, page 34)
1 cup finely chopped pecans

¼ to ½ cup chicken broth
Salt and freshly ground black pepper, to taste
12 quail, partially boned (have the butcher bone them for you), thawed if frozen (see page 481 for mail-order source)
12 strips of lean bacon

1. Preheat oven to 475° F.

2. Melt 2 tablespoons of the butter in a large, heavy saucepan or skillet. Add the onions and celery. Cook over low heat until translucent and soft, about 10 minutes. Stir frequently to prevent the onions from browning.

3. Add the cornbread, pecans, and remaining 2 tablespoons of butter. Increase heat and continue cooking for about 2 minutes or until the additional butter has melted and all ingredients are well mixed. Remove from heat and add just enough chicken broth to make a mixture that is moist but not soggy or mushy. Add more liquid if stuffing seems too dry. Season well with salt and pepper to taste. Let cool completely.

4. Working with 1 quail at a time, place the quail breast-side-up on a work surface. Season inside and out with salt and pepper. Using a small spoon, fill the cavity at the tail end with about 2 tablespoons of the stuffing. Truss or use small metal skewers or sturdy wooden toothpicks to secure both openings of the cavity. (Secure tightly to prevent stuffing from spilling out.) Spoon leftover stuffing into a shallow buttered ovenproof dish.

5. Wrap 1 piece of bacon around each quail, covering as much of the surface of the breast as possible to prevent drying out during roasting.

6. Place quail breast-side-up in a buttered baking dish large enough to hold quail snugly. Sprinkle with salt and pepper. Cook for 30 to 35 minutes or until juices run clear, not pink, when pierced at the thickest part and stuffing inside the bird registers at least 165° F. Place the baking dish of leftover stuffing in the oven during the last 15 minutes of cooking.

7. To serve, spoon the hot leftover stuffing in the center of a large serving platter. Remove toothpicks and strings from quail. Arrange the birds attractively around stuffing. Serve hot.

Serves 4 to 6.

Meat

Pork

FROM ITS SNOUT to its tail, there is little of the pig that has not found its way into some dish that's become a Southern standard. Fresh or cured, pork is more than just a food that Southerners happen to be fond of—it's almost a religion. It all began with the first pigs that the Spanish brought to America in 1539. In 1608 the English also brought pigs—three sows and a boar—to the Jamestown settlement. Within eighteen months, these porcine had multiplied to sixty. By 1705, historian Robert Beverley, writing in his *History and Present State of Virginia,* observed that "hogs swarm like Vermine upon the Earth, and are often accounted as such."

Pigs thrived in conditions that other livestock could not. Pigs could be left spring, summer, and fall to forage for roots, nuts, and berries— food that also happened to make their flesh flavorful. (Some of these animals turned wild, becoming thin, long-legged, and sharp-snouted "razorbacks.") Pigs were also more efficient than other animals at converting grain into flesh. And a pig that was born in the spring was generally ready for slaughter by fall—meaning that the animal would not have to be carried through the winter, and therefore feed would not need to be stored. When game grew scarce, the colonists naturally turned to pork as a primary source of meat.

Cured Pork

It was a time of great joy and celebration for the children. We played games and ran . . . and screamed and brought wood to the boiler and thought of that night, when we would have fresh fried pork and stew made from lungs and liver and heart in an enormous pot that covered half the stove.

—Harry Crews, from "A Childhood: The Biography of a Place,"
A Modern Southern Reader, B. Jorkner and S. J. Samway, editors

Although suckling pigs might be roasted at any time of the year, older pigs were usually slaughtered after the first frost, some time around Thanksgiving. A shoat (young hog) or gilt (young female pig) would generally be shot or stunned. The dead animal was then bathed in scalding water, and the hair scraped from the skin. Next the animal was suspended by its hind legs and bled, and then butchered. The shoulders yielded fresh roasts; the hind quarters, ham; and the center, sides of bacon, chops, ribs, and an ample supply of fatback. The head, feet, and ears were boiled and made into head cheese. Scraps of meat were made into sausage and the fat was rendered into lard for baking and frying. The feet were usually always pickled, and any other parts that weren't intended to be consumed fresh were pickled or dried, or salt-cured and smoked.

Pork remained the most popular meat in America up until the Civil War. In fact, the word "meat" was nearly synonymous with "pork." And salted pork, it seems, was preferred to fresh. It was not only eaten as a meat, but also used to flavor many dishes such as vegetables and legumes. Salt pork was sometimes dipped in cornmeal and then fried, and served with greens.

Breakfast for the poor and the wealthy alike regularly included sausage and bacon. And according to Richard J. Hooker in his *Food and Drink in America: A History,* in the polite circles of eighteenth-century Williamsburg, it was noticed that "it is the custom to have a plate of cold ham on the table, and there is scarcely a Virginian lady who breakfasts without it." Because they considered pork to be nutritionally superior to all other meats, planters generally also provided slaves with pork, usually fatback. At hog-butchering time, slaves might be given fresh spare ribs, backbone, jowl, feet, liver, and chitterlings as well.

During the Civil War, Union forces took the Southern saltworks, and a lack of salt and manpower eventually resulted in a widespread shortage of pork. After the war, the growing use of refrigeration led to the popularity of fresh meat. And although Northerners began to favor beef, Southerners continued to be fond of pork.

Today Americans eat twice as much beef as they do pork. But Southerners still eat more pork than is eaten in any other region of the country (even though most of the nation's hogs are raised in the Midwest). Overall, however, our appetite for meat has diminished somewhat in the last twenty years partly because we've grown more concerned with salt, fat, and cholesterol levels, as well as the presence of nitrites in meat.

The pork industry has begun to respond to these concerns by breeding leaner hogs, cutting back the salt in processed meats, and, in some cases, reducing the level of nitrites. Today, trichinosis has become a medical rarity. Some pork producers have begun marketing pork that is labeled "trichina-tested." Trichinae are killed at 137° F after long cooking and at 144° after brief cooking. They are also killed if pork is frozen for 20 days at 0° F.

Today's leaner pork (it has less than half the fat that it had twenty years ago) has less saturated fat than some cuts of beef. Certain pork cuts—like the loin and chops—should therefore be cooked quickly to avoid drying out.

Lean pork has only about 200 calories per three-ounce serving (a three-ounce serving of skinless chicken breast has about 9 grams of fat, with about a third of it saturated, and approximately 76 milligrams, or one-quarter of the American Heart Association's recommended daily maximum of cholesterol—plus generous quantities of vitamins B-6 and B-12, niacin, riboflavin, iron, zinc, and, according to the National Pork Producers Council, 42 percent of the recommended daily allowance of thiamine. So, believe it or not, pork can be a nice change from chicken if you're trying to keep calories down.

Quick Pork Chops
with Orange-Molasses Glaze
• • •

PORK CHOPS have been known to inspire memories of childhood dinners in a way that few other foods manage to. In the rural South, in particular, they are popular home-cooked fare, and thin chops (about ½ inch thick) are more common than thick ones. Thin chops are usually pan-fried and served with brown onions, pan gravy, and applesauce.

This dish brings together the light citrusy taste of oranges and the earthy flavor of molasses. Fruit and pork have been a longstanding combination in Southern cooking. And molasses, the mineral-rich syrup that's left over when sugar-cane extract is boiled to produce sugar, has traditionally been a favorite of Southern cooks for glazing hams and making barbecue sauces. The method here—adapted from a similar technique by Corby Kummer, a senior editor at *The Atlantic Monthly,* is timed to produce a juicy but thoroughly cooked chop.

4 teaspoons vegetable oil
8 thin (about ½-inch-thick) center-cut pork loin chops (about 2½ pounds) (Note: Do not use thick chops)
1 cup chicken broth
½ cup orange juice
3 tablespoons bourbon

1 tablespoon molasses
1 teaspoon Dijon mustard
1 teaspoon cornstarch combined with 1 tablespoon cold broth or water (optional)
Salt and freshly ground black pepper, to taste

1. Preheat oven to 200° F.

2. In 2 large skillets heat 2 teaspoons oil (in each) over medium-high heat. Add 4 chops to each skillet and cook 5 minutes on each side or until deep golden-brown. Transfer chops to an ovenproof baking dish, cover with foil, and place in oven to finish cooking (about 10 minutes) while you make the sauce.

3. Discard any excess fat from skillets. In a bowl, combine broth, orange juice, and bourbon. Add half to each skillet and boil 1 minute, while scraping up brown bits.

4. Consolidate sauce into 1 skillet. Lower heat so mixture simmers.

5. In a small bowl combine molasses and mustard. Add this to the sauce and simmer until lightly thickened, about 5 minutes.

6. Remove chops from the oven and add any juices that have collected in the baking dish to the sauce. If you prefer a thicker sauce, add the optional cornstarch mixture and simmer sauce for 1 minute. Season to taste with salt and pepper. Serve chops topped with sauce.

Serves 4.

Pork Chops Smothered with Fennel and Garlic

▪ ▪ ▪

SMOTHERED DISHES are down-home Southern classics. The term "smothered" probably grew out of the Cajun use of the word, *etouffée*, which, according to Cajun cookbook author and chef Paul Prudhomme, literally means "smothered." In his part of the country, it means covering with a liquid or a roux-based sauce. Where I come from, smothered usually refers to meats that are blanketed with a simple pan gravy, usually one with cooked onions. Here I use slivered fennel and garlic instead of the usual onions, for a fragrant, savory sauce. Serve this dish with rice or mashed potatoes.

As in the previous recipe, I have borrowed Corby Kummer's method of cooking pork chops. This technique results in moist, juicy chops and is the best method I have found for today's leaner pork.

2 teaspoons vegetable oil
4 center-cut loin pork chops, 1 inch thick
4 to 8 cloves garlic, peeled and slivered
1¼ cups chicken broth

⅔ cup dry white wine
2 fennel bulbs, trimmed, quartered, and cut into very thin slices
2 teaspoons cornstarch
Salt and freshly ground black pepper, to taste

1. Preheat oven to 200° F.
2. Heat oil in a large skillet over medium-high heat. Pat chops dry and add

to skillet. Cook 5 to 6 minutes on each side or until deep golden-brown. Discard fat.

3. Remove skillet from heat (leave pork chops in skillet) and add garlic. Cook 1 minute in the hot skillet.

4. Return skillet to heat and add 1 cup broth, wine, and fennel, and bring to a boil. Lower heat and simmer, covered, 5 minutes.

5. Remove only the chops to a pie plate or other ovenproof dish and cover lightly with foil. Place in the oven and let them continue cooking 10 to 15 minutes or until an instant-read meat thermometer registers 160° F when placed near the bone.

6. Meanwhile, simmer the sauce 5 minutes or until reduced slightly.

7. In a small cup or bowl mix remaining ¼ cup broth (it should be cold or at room temperature) with the cornstarch. Add this mixture to the sauce and boil 1 minute or until lightly thickened. Taste, adding salt and pepper as necessary. Serve chops "smothered" with sauce.

Serves 4.

Roast Loin of Pork with Pears

■ ■ ■

She did magic things with pork and changed the way I looked at the flesh of pigs forever.

—Pat Conroy, *The Prince of Tides*

EGGS AND BRAINS. Pigtails and rice. Fried hog maw and chitlins. Pork has certainly provided a modest sustenance for many, but it has appeared in its Sunday best just as often. The parades of Maryland stuffed hams, crown roasts of pork, and roasted whole young pigs at festive gatherings are all testimony to that. Here pork meets pears in an elegant dish that's easy, flavorful, and perfect for company. Serve with rice of any kind, or Spoon Bread Soufflé with Fresh Corn Sauce (page 66).

2½- to 3-pound boneless pork loin,
 tied
Vegetable oil, for brushing
⅓ cup pear brandy (preferably Poire
 Williams from France or Williams
 Pear from St. George Spirits in
 California), or substitute pear juice
 or pear cider, available from
 health-food stores

1½ cups chicken broth
1½ cups heavy cream
Salt and freshly ground black pepper,
 to taste
2 firm, ripe, unblemished pears
2 tablespoons unsalted butter
1 tablespoon sugar

1. Preheat oven to 425° F.

2. Place pork on a rack in a roasting pan and brush lightly with oil. Roast for 1 hour or until a meat thermometer in the center reaches 160° F. Transfer to a grooved meat board or platter, cover with foil, and keep warm while you make the sauce.

3. Pour off all but 1 tablespoon fat from roasting pan. Add brandy and boil 30 seconds while scraping up brown bits stuck to the bottom of the pan. Pour pan liquid into a saucepan. Add broth and cream to the saucepan and boil over high heat until mixture thickens and coats the back of a spoon lightly, about 15 minutes. Add any juices that may have collected from the roast. Season to taste with salt and pepper.

4. Meanwhile, peel and core pears and cut into eighths. In a large clean skillet heat the butter over medium heat. Add pears and sprinkle with sugar. Cook, tossing or turning constantly, until golden-brown. Set aside and keep warm.

5. Remove strings from pork. Carve into ⅓-inch-thick slices and place in pool of sauce on dinner plates (pass extra sauce separately). Garnish with pears.

Serves 6.

Medallions of Pork
with Apple-Thyme Sauce

• • •

PORK AND APPLES have been paired together in American cooking at least since the Cherokees stuffed pigs with nuts and apples and roasted them over open fires. It's a combination not unfamiliar to me (Mom *always* served pork chops with applesauce), and one that works well with the more luxurious medallions in this recipe. This dish was inspired by a similar recipe created by my apple-loving friend, Connecticut native Amanda Hewell. The herbs in this dish cut the natural sweetness of the apples, and the result is actually more savory than sweet. Serve with steamed rice or new potatoes.

PORK AND MARINADE

1½- to 1¾-pound boneless pork loin
4 cups dry white wine or vermouth
2 tablespoons vegetable oil
1 tablespoon fresh thyme leaves (or 1 teaspoon dried)

Grated zest of 1 lemon
1 teaspoon freshly ground black pepper

APPLE-THYME SAUCE

⅔ cup sugar
4 cups water
2 sprigs fresh thyme (or 1 teaspoon dried thyme)
16 whole black peppercorns
6 tablespoons cider vinegar
4 medium-sized firm, tart apples, peeled, cored, and quartered

1 to 2 tablespoons butter
1 to 2 tablespoons vegetable oil
⅓ cup dry white wine
Salt and freshly ground black pepper, to taste
4 sprigs fresh thyme, for garnish (optional)

1. To prepare pork and marinade: Trim pork and cut into 1-inch-thick slices. Pat dry.

2. In a shallow, nonaluminum dish large enough to hold slices snugly in 1 layer, combine the wine, oil, thyme leaves, half the lemon zest and the ground

black pepper. Add pork to the marinade, cover and marinate at cool room temperature 2 hours (or up to 8 hours in refrigerator), turning once.

3. To make the sauce: In a medium saucepan, dissolve the sugar in the water over low heat. Add thyme sprigs, peppercorns, remaining lemon zest, and vinegar and simmer uncovered 10 minutes. Add apples and simmer uncovered 10 to 12 minutes or until very tender but not mushy. Remove apples with slotted spoon (reserve poaching liquid). Purée apples in a blender or food processor until smooth. Press through a sieve set over a bowl and set aside. (You will have 1 to 1½ cups purée.)

4. Boil the poaching liquid (with herbs and peppercorns) until reduced to 1 cup. Strain; discard solids. Add this syrup to the apple purée and set aside.

5. In a large skillet, heat 1 tablespoon each butter and oil over medium-high heat. Remove pork from marinade and dry with paper towels. Add pork to the skillet. (Do not crowd the skillet; cook pork in batches if necessary.) Cook 4 to 5 minutes on each side or until no pink remains in center. Do not overcook or pork will be dry. Transfer to a warm platter; cover with foil to keep warm. If you are cooking pork in batches, add additional butter and oil if needed.

6. Discard fat in the skillet. Add wine and boil 30 seconds while scraping up brown bits stuck to the bottom of the pan. Reduce liquid to 2 tablespoons, then lower heat, add apple purée mixture and heat through. Add any juices that have collected from the pork to the sauce, and season with salt and pepper to taste. To serve, ladle about ¼ to ½ cup sauce onto each of 4 warm plates. Top with pork medallions and garnish with thyme sprig.

Serves 4.

Country Ham It's hard to find a Southern state that does not claim to produce a ham that rivals those of Smithfield, Virginia. This tiny town on the James River is perhaps more famous for ham than any town in the South, or indeed in the country. The distinguishing feature of a Smithfield ham used to be that the hog from which it came had spent at least part of its life eating peanuts. Today the hogs are usually corn fed and are raised on farms all over the South. By law, though, all Smithfield hams must still be cured within the corporate limits of the town of Smithfield, Virginia.

Long, lean and mahogany colored, a Smithfield ham has a firm texture and a complex salty, smoky, sweet, and spicy flavor. The flavor of any country ham depends, of course, not only on what the hog ate, but also on what the ham was cured with, how long it was aged, and, finally, whether it was smoked—and if so, what type of wood was used. Processing a dry-cured ham involves rubbing the meat with a mixture of granular or flaked salt, sodium nitrate (saltpeter) or nitrite, and sometimes sugar or other spices. The ham is then allowed to age for several days or weeks. Each ingredient has a certain function. The salt penetrates through to the bone, drawing moisture out and thereby creating an environment less hospitable to bacteria (which is why country hams keep well). The nitrate or nitrite guards against botulinum bacteria and gives the ham a deep pink color. (Colonists originally cured hams with sea salt because they found it had superior preserving properties—properties that were later attributed to the presence of nitrite in the sea salt.) And the sugar keeps the ham tender. A country ham, by definition, must be cured, aged, and dried at least seventy days. After the ham is aged, it may then be smoked for several weeks over a low-burning oak, hickory, apple, or other hardwood fire.

Most processed hams available at the supermarket are not dry-cured but wet-cured. That is, they are soaked in or injected with a brine solution. Boned, rolled, canned, and "water added" hams are all wet-cured.

A whole ham—which is the hind quarter of a pig, including the leg—usually weighs 12 to 18 pounds, but you can buy various cuts: a ham shank half (the lower half of a whole ham with the center slices removed); the center slices, (the meaty, oval-shaped cuts from the center of the ham); or a ham rump half (the hip, or upper half of a whole ham). A picnic ham is not a true ham. It's the shoulder, and may contain more fat and connective tissue than a true ham. Any of these cuts may be fresh—in other words, pork roasts—and still be called "ham," but most hams are processed.

Regardless of whether the ham is wet-cured or dry-cured, check to see whether it is labeled "fully cooked" (or "ready to eat") versus "cook before eating." "Cook before eating" hams must be heated to an internal temperature of 160° F before being consumed. "Ready to eat" hams may, of course, be eaten as they are, but you might want to heat them to about 140° F to bring out the flavor.

Country Ham
with a Tupelo Honey Glaze
. . .

She's as sweet as Tupelo honey,
She's an angel of the first degree,
She's as sweet as Tupelo honey,
Just like honey, baby, from the bee. . . .

—Van Morrison, "Tupelo Honey," on the album *Tupelo Honey*

SINCE COUNTRY HAMS can be quite salty, you should soak them before cooking. Here I am recommending that you soak the ham in water (many old recipes specify milk) for up to four days, changing the water each day to get rid of excess salt. The ham will still be salty, mind you, but not as salty as in those old-time recipes that call for only a day of soaking.

The glaze provides a sweet counterpoint to the savory saltiness of the ham. Country hams traditionally have been glazed with any combination of brown sugar, maple syrup, molasses, or honey and vinegar, ginger ale, apple cider, and mustard. Here the glaze is simple: Tupelo honey, which owes its distinctive taste to the blossoms of the water Tupelo, a tree (locally known as a sour gum) that grows along the Coastal Plain from southeastern Virginia to north Florida, to southeastern Texas, and north in the Mississippi Valley (including Tupelo, Mississippi) to western Tennessee and southern Illinois. Another distinctive honey from the Southeast to try is Sourwood honey, the source of which is a small-to medium-sized tree that is common in the southern part of the Appalachian mountains from West Virginia and southern Pennsylvania to northern Georgia.

10- to 14-pound dry-cured, uncooked country ham such as Smithfield (see page 481 for mail-order source)

1 cup Tupelo honey (or other honey)
2 tablespoons Dijon mustard

1. Scrub ham thoroughly. Rinse well, then place in large stockpot or deep covered roasting pan. Cover with water and soak at cool room temperature 48 hours to up to 4 days, changing the water every 12 hours. (Note: The longer the soaking time, the less salty the ham will be.)

2. Drain the ham, and change water a final time. Bring to a boil, lower heat, and simmer 20 minutes per pound.

3. Cool the ham in the liquid until it can be handled easily. Reserve ¼ cup of the cooking liquid. Remove the rind, leaving ¼ to ½ inch of the fat.

4. Preheat oven to 450° F. In a small saucepan over low heat, melt the honey with the reserved poaching liquid. Off the heat, stir in mustard.

5. Place the ham in a heavy roasting pan. Pour the glaze over the ham and place in center of oven. Cook 10 minutes, baste, and cook 10 minutes longer or until shiny and lightly browned.

6. Cool completely. Remove the aitchbone and carve into paper-thin slices with a very sharp knife.

Makes about 250 ham biscuits.

Hickory Pit Pork Barbecue on Cornmeal Buns (or in Cornmeal Crêpes) with Hot Sauce

■ ■ ■

MENTION THE WORD "BARBECUE" anywhere other than the South in this country, and people are likely to equate the term with a backyard event, or anything cooked over an open fire. But to any Southerner, "barbecue" conjures visions of a messy-good sandwich of hickory-smoked pork drenched with a tangy sauce and served with coleslaw. All over the South, you'll find roadside stands and restaurants that offer some version of barbecue, each pronouncing its method of cooking "distinctive." But whether it's wet (basted with sauce during the cooking) or dry (simply seasoned before it's placed over the coals, then smoke-cooked and basted afterward), barbecue is one of the few foods that somehow just doesn't taste as good cooked at home. It's hard to duplicate the flavor that long, slow cooking over a hickory fire imparts.

Traditionally, it's made from pork shoulder, which is placed over a pit of smoldering, white-hot hickory coals for eight to ten hours. (At a pig pickin', however, usually the whole pig is roasted.) The meat is sometimes basted with a vinegar–hot pepper sauce during the cooking; usually, though, the pork is basted after it has been removed from the grill and shredded or "pulled," sliced, or diced. The crisp skin is removed and either put back on the grill or deep-fried to crispen it further. The resulting cracklin's are often served, if you request them, with your take-out order.

Of course, whether the pork is shredded, sliced, or diced and the matter of which type of sauce should accompany it are divisive questions among Southerners—and ones that are regularly put to test at the multitude of barbecue cookoff contests held throughout the South each year. Perhaps no other food— save for chili—inspires the kind of good-natured dissension that barbecue does.

And then there is the question of which sauce is best. Some—like those in eastern North Carolina—favor a vinegar-based sauce for "Down East" barbecue. Others like a mustardy sauce, and still others prefer a sauce based on tomatoes.

As I said, I don't think good barbecue can be made at home by conventional methods, so I do not include a recipe here. Leave the cooking to the experts and buy it by the pound for the freezer. (For mail-order source, see page 481.) I *never* return from a trip to the South without several quart containers of real pit-cooked, hickory-smoked barbecue! Serve it on Soft Cornmeal Buns (page 38) with whatever hot sauce comes with your take-out order. Or roll it up in Cornmeal Crêpes (page 340); you will need one crêpe recipe per ½ pound of barbecue) and dunk them into the sauce. It's quick, it's special enough for company, and it is sheer hog heaven!

Beef

THE SPANISH are said to have brought cattle to Florida in 1550. In 1624, the English followed suit, bringing their own breeds to Plymouth colony. Bulls and cows were brought to the Southern colonies soon after, for in 1656, John Hammond, author of *Leah and Rachel, or, the Two Fruitful Sisters, Virginia and Maryland,* praised the abundance in Virginia: "Cattle and hogs are everywhere, which yield beef, veal, milk, butter, cheese, and other made dishes . . ." But seventeenth-century British observers noted that Southerners raised their cattle "like swine," allowing them to forage in fields and woods. (Open-range grazing, however, was common in the British Isles and other parts of Western Europe up until as late as the nineteenth century.) After a harsh winter fending for themselves, these bovine were lean and tough and their flesh never acquired the flavor and tenderness of English beef, even though the Southern breeds were of English descent. One reason may be that the open range in Europe was watched over by herders who more carefully tended their herds.

Because game and fish were in great abundance in the New World and pork was preferred over beef, these early cattle were valued more for their milk, butter, and hides and their capacity for work rather than for their flesh. Over the years, cattlemen learned to produce animals with more tender flesh, and by the 1860s, cattle were being bred specifically for meat. Grains—especially corn—were in abundance and used to fatten cattle before slaughter. This final grain feeding also gave the beef a better taste. (Wild onions and grasses eaten in pastureland makes beef taste strong and herbaceous.) With the first refrigerated train cars in 1867, good-tasting, lower-cost beef became more widely available. Further breeding experiments resulted in tasty, tender beef. Slowly but surely, beef became America's preferred meat.

In the seventeenth and eighteenth centuries the Southern colonies were major cattle producers because there was a great deal of unclaimed land between scattered land grants. The availability of public grazing land thus encouraged a cattle frontier in the Piedmont and across the Appalachians. Another reason that cattle herding developed in the Southeast—particularly the Carolinas—was that many of the African-born slaves were expert herders. Colonial herds multiplied rapidly. Four decades after it was settled, South Carolina was described thusly: "abounds with black cattle, to a Degree much beyond any other English Colony; which is chiefly owing to the mildness of the Winters, whereby the Planters are freed from the Charge and Trouble of providing for their cattle." Besides mild winters, grassy savannahs, pine barrens, and cane-filled marshes provided forage in the South.

Prior to the mid-eighteenth century, South Carolina, it seems, was the leading English colony for cattle raising. The Revolutionary War caused the demise of South Carolina's cattle industry. Cattle herding then spread into neighboring Georgia, then to Florida, southern Alabama, southeast Mississippi, and eastern Louisiana. It wasn't feasible for the pioneers to fence the land, so animals ran loose and unattended on the open range.

Beef Preservation and Cooking Although the ice box was patented in 1803, it was not widely used until the late 1820s when there were new methods of ice cutting. Before refrigeration, cattle—like other large animals—had to be eaten immediately or preserved; fresh meat was available only at butchering time. It has been noted that Southerners were more likely to eat beef in summer when the supply of cured pork had been exhausted. (Pigs were traditionally slaughtered in the fall.) Beef was preserved by several methods. Sometimes a cow was slaughtered in early spring to "dry" for summer eating. In this "drying" method, beef was cured in brine for three weeks. It was then wiped dry, rubbed with bran, then hung in a cool dark place. When cattle were slaughtered in midsummer, parts might be preserved for more immediate use by corning. In old Southern cookbooks we see recipes titled "To corn beef in hot weather" in which beef soaks in brine that sometimes had molasses added. One source claims that the origin of the word "corned" comes from the corns of gunpowder, which contained saltpeter (it was also known as "powdered beef").

Beef could also be preserved without salt. On the frontier, settlers took preserving tips from the Native Americans, who cut beef into thin strips or steaks and dried them on a gridiron over a slow fire.

Cooked, fresh beef could be kept for longer periods of time by potting it. It was beaten to a paste, and pressed into a pot or crock where it was then sealed with clarified butter and stored in a cool, dry place.

Cooking Beef—Early Recipes Eighteenth- and nineteenth-century recipes for beef show the cook's efforts to tenderize it and sometimes mask its taste. Several recipes of the era treated beef like venison, which, according to Karen Hess in her notes on Mary Randolph's 1824 book *The Virginia House-wife,* seems to have been preferred to beef by many.

During this time, beef rump was broiled or baked. Steaks were larded then stewed in water, vinegar, herbs, and served on "sippets" (toasts). Roasts were cooked on a spit and served with horseradish; flanks were marinated in saltwater, seasoned with herbs, "collared" (rolled up in a tight cylinder and tied with twine), then boiled. More involved preparations include "made dishes," such as daubes, fricassees, stews, beef à la mode, stuffed briskets, beef "olives," fricando, spiced beef—also known as hunter's beef or *boeuf de chasse*—(for more about spiced beef, see below), and recipes for beefsteaks, which were sometimes hashed or baked in puffed pastry. As the century progressed, cookbooks gave more recipes for roast beef and for steaks, perhaps reflecting beef's improved tenderness.

In the twentieth century, the quality of beef improved drastically, resulting not only in simpler recipes, but also increased consumption.

When I was growing up, beef appeared on the dinner table four to five nights a week. It was usually steak on Saturday nights, and roast beef about twice a month. The other "beef nights" featured hamburger, pot roast, stew (Mom called it "chuck wagon stew"), sloppy Joes, meatloaf, and country-style steak (swiss steak). I eat less beef now, because I enjoy a variety of meats. But about once a week, nothing seems to do it for me like beef.

Spiced Beef with Two Sauces

■ ■ ■

BEEF CURED in a solution of sugar, salt, and spices has probably been popular in the South since the first bovine was slaughtered and eaten. The method has its origins in British cookery, and is also known as hunter's or hunting beef (or the French, *boeuf de chasse*), or Christmas spiced beef, since it used to be a regular holiday dish in parts of England. It was to become a Christmas tradition in the New World, too.

In her *Spices, Salt and Aromatics in the English Kitchen,* author Elizabeth David says that various forms of the recipe have been known in England for at least 300 years. The formation of the British East India Company in 1600 may have contributed to the development of spiced beef in Great Britain since trading resulted in the ready availability of spices and sugar. The purpose of adding spices in English cooking, according to Mrs. David, was to add zip to a rather monotonous diet of salt meat and boiled fish, and also because the English have a penchant for highly seasoned food.

The English settlers in the New World brought this affection for spices with them, and found them to be a good addition to their own meat curing.

What sets spiced beef apart from corned beef is, as the name suggests, spices. While corned beef sometimes has a sweetener, such as molasses or brown sugar added to the brine (usually composed of salt and saltpeter), it does not traditionally have any other seasoning added. Spiced beef, on the other hand, is flavored with salt, sugar, and spices (such as cloves, ginger, nutmeg, mace, allspice, juniper, cayenne, and cinnamon) and sometimes herbs, garlic, and onions or shallots. Spiced beef is frequently larded, and usually cures for two to three weeks. It is then rinsed, simmered, drained, and sometimes weighted as it cools. It is generally thinly sliced and served at room temperature or lightly chilled. To eighteenth- and nineteenth-century Southern cooks, spiced beef was a sensible treatment for their tough, less-than-flavorful beef. The curing process not only preserved the meat, but tenderized it and masked any unwanted flavors.

Closely related to spiced beef are other Southern recipes that go one step further. In addition to the salt and spices, an acidic ingredient—such as lemon juice, wine, or vinegar—is added. The resulting dishes are similar to sauerbraten, which, by the way, was especially popular in nineteenth-century Kentucky due to a large German population. Many nineteenth-century recipes for beef à la mode, daubes, collared beef, and pot roast employ salty, sweet, spicy, and tangy ingredients.

My recipe for spiced beef is a somewhat simplified version of the old Southern classics. The beef cures in five days—rather than the usual fourteen to twenty-one—and is not larded, which I find a time-consuming chore to be eliminated if at all possible. A covering of bacon slices keeps beef moist while it simmers, and since it is sliced thinly I find larding unnecessary. This is a very, very easy make-ahead dish that is good for buffets or picnics or simply when you tire of ham, pastrami, or other cured meats. Thinly sliced and served on pumpernickel or rye with either of the two sauces here makes a tasty sandwich or canapé.

BEEF AND MARINADE

1 cup light brown sugar
1 cup kosher salt
2 teaspoons freshly ground black pepper
2 teaspoons ground allspice
1 teaspoon freshly ground nutmeg
½ imported bay leaf, crumbled

5- to 6-pound beef eye of round
1 large yellow onion, coarsely chopped
2 carrots, peeled and coarsely chopped
6 slices bacon

(ingredients continued)

MUSTARD MAYONNAISE

⅔ cup mayonnaise

2 tablespoons Creole mustard or

other whole-grain mustard, or to
taste

HORSERADISH CREAM

⅔ cup sour cream

1 tablespoon grated fresh or drained
  bottled horseradish

Salt and freshly ground black pepper,
  to taste

1. In a medium bowl, mix sugar, salt, pepper, allspice, nutmeg, and bay leaf.

2. Place the beef in a nonaluminum dish that will hold beef snugly and rub well with the seasoning mixture. Distribute onion and carrots around beef. Cover and refrigerate 5 days, turning beef twice a day and coating with pan juices as you turn.

3. Bring the beef to room temperature and preheat oven to 275° F.

4. Place beef in a Dutch oven and add the onions, carrots, marinating liquid, and 1 cup of water. Lay bacon strips on top to keep beef moist. Cover and cook 2½ to 3 hours or until very tender.

5. Remove beef from cooking liquid and discard the liquid and vegetables. (Beef and liquid will seem very salty at this point. Do not worry; the saltiness will mellow when beef cools.) Cool the beef to room temperature, then chill the beef thoroughly in the refrigerator. Store covered in refrigerator up to 1 week or freeze up to 3 months. Slice very thinly and serve chilled or at room temperature with either of the sauces.

6. To make the sauces: In a bowl combine mayonnaise and mustard. In another bowl, combine sour cream, horseradish, salt, and pepper.

Makes enough for about 75 canapé-sized sandwiches.

Steak with
Bourbon-Ginger Sauce

. . .

TO MANY SOUTHERNERS (or Americans in general, for that matter), ask "What's your favorite food?" or "What would you like to have for your birthday dinner?" and the answer is likely to be "A really good steak." But it has only been recently that steaks were so tender, juicy, well marbled, and properly aged so as to necessitate only a quick flop on the grill or a few minutes under a hot broiler. Beef used to be tough and sinewy and had to be tenderized before cooking. Nineteenth-century recipes for steak show this. Mary Randolph's 1824 recipe for broiled steak, served with mushrooms, catsup, and horseradish (three flavorings that continue to accompany our steaks today), is pounded before cooking. Another Virginia recipe dated 1879 calls for marinating the steak in vinegar before frying it. In a third recipe, the author says to season with pepper vinegar and mustard "to give the taste of venison," which suggests that beef was still second to venison as a preferred meat.

Other nineteenth-century treatments for steak include those for beefsteak pie (1824), beefsteak pudding (1871), and stuffed steak (stuffed with greens, mushrooms, vegetables, or breadcrumbs). Recipes combining beef and oysters are also common. In New Orleans cookbooks, we find exotic, involved recipes for steak such as grilled fillets topped with stuffed artichoke hearts and béarnaise sauce or smoked tenderloins with crawfish sauce—a kind of Creole surf 'n' turf.

Today's tender, aged beef is so flavorful it doesn't need much enhancement. The marinade here (a mixture of bourbon and ginger) adds just a whisper of flavor. This steak is good broiled, but I prefer to grill it, so the deep, smoky flavors act as a foil to the faintly sweet marinade. In winter, serve with baked or boiled potatoes. In summer, try corn on the cob and Green Bean Salad with Sesame Seed Dressing (page 113).

MARINADE

¼ cup bourbon
2 tablespoons firmly packed light
   brown sugar

¼ cup vegetable oil
3 tablespoons minced fresh
   gingerroot

(ingredients continued)

Meat

∎

3 tablespoons Balsamic vinegar

2 tablespoons red wine vinegar

½ teaspoon whole black peppercorns

¼ teaspoon salt

STEAK AND SAUCE

2½ to 3 pounds flank steak or top
   round sirloin steak, 1¾-inch to
   2-inch thickness

1 cup beef broth

2 tablespoons red wine vinegar

1 tablespoon bourbon

Salt and freshly ground black pepper,
   to taste

1. To make the marinade: In a saucepan combine bourbon, brown sugar, oil, gingerroot, vinegars, peppercorns, and salt. Stir over low heat until sugar dissolves. Remove from heat; cool to room temperature.

2. Pat steak dry with paper towels and place in nonaluminum dish. Pour marinade over steak. Cover and marinate 1 to 2 hours at cool room temperature or 4 to 6 hours refrigerated. Remove from refrigerator 1 hour before cooking.

3. Heat coals or preheat broiler. Reserving the marinade, place steak on lightly oiled grill or broiler pan. Grill steak about 5 to 10 minutes on each side, or to desired doneness. (Timing will depend on thickness of steak and how rare you like it.) To broil, place on broiling rack 4 to 6 inches from broiler and cook 5 to 10 minutes on each side or to desired doneness.

4. While steak is cooking, prepare sauce: Strain reserved marinade into small saucepan. Add broth and red wine vinegar and boil rapidly until reduced to about ¾ cup, about 5 to 10 minutes. Add bourbon and boil 30 seconds more. Season with salt and pepper to taste, cover and keep warm until ready to serve. Let steak stand on carving board 5 to 10 minutes, covered with a tent of foil.

5. Slice steak thinly and serve with sauce.

Serves 6.

Spiced Shepherd's Pie, Southern Style

· · ·

WHILE SHEPHERD'S PIES are not technically pies in that they have neither a lower nor upper crust, shepherd's pies are nonetheless considered a relative of the pie family, which includes those with "crusts" made of rice, cornbread, and bread dough. This version of shepherd's pie, created with my colleague, friend, and fellow Southerner Charles Pierce, combines a Southern staple, the sweet potato, and that mainstay of the American diet, ground beef.

In colonial America, one of the most common uses of finely chopped or shredded beef—both cooked and uncooked—was in mincemeat pies that also contained suet, apples, dried fruits, and spices. By the nineteenth century mince-meat pies only occasionally contained meat.

Nineteenth-century Southern cooks used ground beef in the making of forcemeat balls, sausages, beef cakes, and patties (both made by mixing chopped fat with barely cooked shredded beef, salt, pepper, and onion). Later recipes featuring ground beef include hash and Natchitoches meat pies, which hail from a town in Louisiana of the same name. (Natchitoches meat pies are like Cornish pastries or empanadas, except they are fried, not baked.)

The dish here is hearty, comforting, and good for a hungry crowd on a cold day. It's easy to make, freezes well, and reheats beautifully. A suggestion of cinnamon makes this dish special. The spiciness is suggestive of piccadillo, a spicy, chili-like meat dish eaten in Texas. Serve with a salad of mixed greens (such as romaine, curly endive, arugula, and red leaf lettuce) with a mustard vinaigrette, and serve Spiced Apple Stack Cakes with Cider Butter and Cream (page 389) for dessert.

MEAT FILLING

2 to 4 tablespoons bacon drippings
   or vegetable oil
1 medium-sized onion, finely
   chopped
1 pound ground beef
½ pound ground pork

1 tablespoon tomato paste
½ cup beef broth
1 teaspoon ground cinnamon
Salt and freshly ground black pepper,
   to taste

(ingredients continued)

Meat

■

POTATO TOPPING

4 pounds sweet potatoes (about 5 to
  6 medium-sized potatoes)
2 to 4 tablespoons unsalted butter
  (optional)

1 teaspoon Dijon mustard
2 to 4 teaspoons brown sugar
Salt and freshly ground black pepper,
  to taste

1. To make the filling: Heat oil or drippings in a large skillet over medium heat. Add onions and cook, stirring frequently, until translucent, about 5 minutes.

2. Add beef and pork and increase heat to medium-high. Stir constantly until meat has lost all pink color, about 10 minutes. Add tomato paste, beef broth, cinnamon, and salt and pepper. Continue cooking over high heat 5 minutes longer until some of the liquid has evaporated. Correct seasoning and transfer to a deep, lightly buttered 9-inch by 13-inch baking dish. Cool slightly.

3. Preheat oven to 350° F.

4. To prepare topping: Peel and rinse the potatoes. Cut into 1-inch pieces and place in a large saucepan. Cover with lightly salted cold water and bring to a boil over medium-high heat. Lower heat and simmer until potatoes are tender, about 20 minutes. Drain thoroughly.

5. Purée potatoes with the butter in food processor or blender (do this in batches if necessary). Add mustard and brown sugar to taste. Season with salt and pepper to taste. Topping may be prepared up to one day in advance up to this point.

6. Spread the potato purée over the beef in a thin, even layer. Bake 15 to 20 minutes or until hot in the center. Serve immediately.

Serves 6 to 8.

Veal

IN THE COLONIAL SOUTH, particularly in Virginia, veal was usually prepared according to recipes in favorite English cookbooks. Since beef at this time was exceedingly tough, one can assume that veal, being younger and therefore more tender, may have been preferable to beef.

For the next 200 years, veal was prepared in a variety of ways. Like beef, veal was often collared—long strips and flat cuts were rolled into cylinders and tied. Collops—thin slices—were dipped in egg and breadcrumbs and then fried; knuckles were boiled, breasts were stewed. Large joints were roasted, fillets were stuffed and rolled. Leftovers were turned into hash or potted. Jelly was made from the feet and used for aspics and desserts. The stomach was boiled for rennet and pâtés, pies, forcemeat, and croquettes made use of minced bits. A favorite "made" dish was calf's head, which was boned, stuffed, tied, and served with an array of sauces and garnishes. Mock turtle soup of calf's head (also called veal terrapin) was popular. Early Southerners also enjoyed calves' brains, sweetbreads, and liver and kidneys.

Today, the South raises about ¼ of the total U.S. production of veal. Some progressive operations such as Summerfield Farm outside Charlottesville, Virginia are producing veal from calves humanely nourished on fresh eggs and fresh whole cow's milk. This iron-rich diet results in veal that is pinker and more full-flavored than most commercially produced products, which often come from anemic calves, hurriedly fattened on medicated, ironless powdered-milk formula. Even though the label might say "milk-fed veal," it often refers to a milk-replacement formula.

Breast of Veal
with Herbed Rice Stuffing

∎ ∎ ∎

RECIPES FOR VEAL BREAST appear in eighteenth- and nineteenth-century Southern cookbooks with relative frequency. The breast was often stuffed with forcemeat and served with sweetbreads or forcemeat balls.

A well-trimmed, gently braised breast of veal is a wonderfully comforting, old-fashioned dish. Here, it has a light stuffing of Wild Pecan Rice™, parsley, Smithfield ham, and toasted pecans. Although this dish takes a long time to cook, it is easy to prepare. The deep, rich flavors—those that only happen with long, slow cooking—are a welcome change to the quick meals (hamburgers, chicken breasts, pasta) that make up most of our day-to-day diets. Try this recipe some wintery day. It will make you feel good all over.

3 tablespoons unsalted butter

2 medium-sized yellow onions: 1 finely chopped, 1 coarsely chopped

2 boxes (7 ounces each) Wild Pecan Rice™ (1¼ cups dry rice) or substitute white rice

4 cups chicken broth

2 eggs

½ cup minced fresh parsley

Pinch each of salt and freshly ground black pepper

¾ cup coarsely chopped, lightly toasted pecans

8- to -9-pound breast of veal, boned and very well trimmed; bones and trimmings reserved (Note: An 8-pound breast of veal yields about 4½ to 5 pounds boned)

6 ounces very thinly sliced Smithfield ham (see page 481 for mail-order source) or other dry-cured country ham (brine-cured ham, such as sandwich-type ham, may be substituted if Smithfield ham is unavailable)

2 large carrots, peeled and coarsely chopped

1. To make the stuffing: heat butter in large saucepan over medium heat. Add finely chopped onion and cook, stirring frequently, 5 to 10 minutes or until softened.

2. Add rice and toss to coat with butter. Add broth and bring to a boil. Cover, lower heat, and simmer 15 to 20 minutes or until liquid has been absorbed. Remove from heat, uncover, and cool completely.

3. In large bowl, beat eggs with parsley, salt, and pepper. Add rice, toss gently; stir in pecans. Set aside.

4. Preheat oven to 400° F.

5. Lay veal breast, boned-side-up, on work surface. Lay ham slices on top of veal, then spoon about ⅓ of the stuffing on the ham, leaving a 1-inch border along edges. Beginning with the short end, roll up (like a jelly roll) into a neat cylinder, tucking in edges. Truss or secure with skewers. (Note: Do not skewer

too tightly as stuffing will expand as it cooks.) Place remaining stuffing in a 9-inch buttered baking dish and cook alongside veal for last 20 minutes of cooking time.

6. Place veal in a heavy roasting pan, distribute coarsely chopped onions, the carrots, and the veal bones and scraps around the stuffed breast. Cover lightly with foil and cook 30 minutes. Add 3 cups water, lower heat to 350° F, recover tightly with foil, and cook, basting or turning frequently, 4 hours, or until veal is very tender, adding more liquid if necessary.

7. Place veal on a grooved carving board (reserve juices and vegetables), cover with foil and let stand 15 minutes before slicing.

8. To make the sauce: strain reserved pan juices and vegetables. Skim the fat off the top of the juices. Purée the reserved vegetables, and add to the defatted juices to thicken.

9. Remove string from veal and discard. Cut veal into ¾-inch slices and serve with the thickened broth and a selection of mustards such as Creole, Dijon, and green peppercorn mustard.

Serves 8.

Veal Chops
with Savory Sweet Potato Sauce

• • •

RECIPES FOR VEAL CHOPS do not appear with great frequency in old Southern cookbooks. I adore them especially when I'm in the mood for meat but beef seems too rich and chicken, too boring.

This easy recipe was inspired by one in *Housekeeping in Old Virginia* (1879) for roast veal that has a gravy thickened with mashed Irish potatoes. I've used sweet potatoes instead, and the resulting sauce is a suave, pumpkin-colored purée made savory by wine and rich, meaty juices. Try it. It isn't as weird as it sounds, and it's very easy to make. Serve with Sautéed Green Beans with Country Ham (page 324), Sautéed Watercress and Radicchio with Pepper Vinegar (page 304), or steamed mustard, turnip, or collard greens.

2 tablespoons butter (or slightly less,
  if using a nonstick skillet)
2 tablespoons vegetable oil (or
  slightly less, if using a nonstick
  skillet)
4 veal chops, ¾ to 1 inch thick
  (about ½ pound each, bone-in
  weight)
Salt and freshly ground black pepper,
  to taste

¼ cup dry white wine
1 cup chicken broth
½ cup puréed cooked sweet potato
  (1 large potato, cooked, peeled,
  puréed)
¼ cup golden raisins plumped in
  boiling water for 10 minutes,
  drained (optional)

1. Heat butter and oil in very large skillet over medium-high heat.

2. Pat chops dry with paper towels. Add chops to the hot fat and cook 5 minutes on each side or until well browned. Sprinkle with salt and pepper, cover tightly, lower heat and simmer 20 to 25 minutes or until tender, turning once. Remove chops to a platter and cover to keep warm.

3. Pour off the fat. Add wine and boil over high heat until liquid is reduced to about 2 tablespoons. Add broth and boil 1 minute. Whisk in sweet potato purée and simmer to desired consistency (it should be nicely thickened in about 3 minutes). Add raisins, if desired; remove from heat. To serve, place 1 chop on each plate and serve sauce on the side.

Serves 4.

Veal Scallops with Cider Cream, Onion Confit, and Glazed Apples

• • •

RECIPES FOR VEAL COLLOPS are common in eighteenth- and nineteenth-century Southern cookbooks. The English term "collop" gradually gave way to the use of the French *escalope,* the Italian *scallopini,* and the American scallop or cutlet. Technically, a scallop is a cutlet (a thin slice cut from the leg) that has only one muscle running through it.

The early recipes for collops usually called for beating or pounding the meat, then frying it. Collops were also used in making veal "birds" or were often spread with forcemeat and rolled. In Louisiana, natives cook thin slices of veal round (called grillades) and serve them with grits.

Onions, apples, and cider add a natural sweetness to this dish. If you live in the Shenandoah Valley or another apple region, this dish is a must in autumn when apples are at their most flavorful and cider is widely available. If hard cider is unavailable (some specialty food stores and some wine and liquor shops carry it), try a fruity Riesling or a combination of apple juice and apple cider instead. Serve with parslied rice or new potatoes and steamed green beans.

2 cups very thinly sliced sweet on-
ions, such as Vidalias, Walla
Walla, Maui, or Bermuda onions
(yellow onions may be used but
the confit will not be as naturally
sweet)
6 tablespoons unsalted butter (or
less, if using a nonstick skillet)
2 medium-sized firm, tart apples

1½ pounds veal scallops
Salt and freshly ground black pepper,
to taste
1 cup bottled hard cider (or substi-
tute a fruity Riesling wine or ¾
cup apple juice plus ¼ cup cider
vinegar)
1 cup heavy cream

1. To make the confit: In a heavy, medium-sized saucepan, cook onions and 2 tablespoons of the butter, covered, over very low heat, stirring frequently 1 hour or until very soft. Set aside.

2. Leaving apples whole, peel them (if desired), then remove cores using a long, metal corer. Slice apples crosswise into ¼-inch-thick rings. (Note: If you do not have a corer, halve the apples through the stem end then core and slice.)

3. Heat 1 tablespoon of the butter in a large, heavy skillet. Add half the apples and cook over medium heat 2 to 4 minutes per side or until lightly glazed and golden-brown. Transfer to a platter and cover with foil to keep warm. Add 1 tablespoon butter to the same skillet and repeat with second batch of apples. Add first batch of apples to the second batch and keep warm.

4. Pat veal scallops dry with paper towels; place between 2 sheets of waxed paper and flatten with a rolling pin, mallet, or the broad side of a cleaver to about ¼ inch thick. Season lightly with salt and pepper.

5. Heat 1 tablespoon of the butter in a large skillet over medium-high heat. Add half the veal to skillet and cook 1 minute on each side or until no pink

Meat

■

243

remains on inside and scallops begin to turn golden-brown on the outside. Set veal aside on a warm platter, cover with foil, and keep warm.

6. Add last tablespoon of the butter to the skillet and repeat with second batch of veal. Add second batch of veal to the first batch on the platter. Cover to keep warm.

7. Add cider to the skillet and boil until the liquid has reduced to about 3 tablespoons. Add the cream and reduce until lightly thickened. Add the onion confit and warm through. Season to taste with salt and pepper. To serve, place veal on warm plates. Nap with sauce and garnish with apples.

Serves 4.

Lamb

ENGLISH SHEEP accompanied the settlers to Jamestown in 1609. Although sheep were also raised in the Carolinas and Georgia in the seventeenth century, it was Virginia—with Washington, Jefferson, and Madison as active supporters—that led the way in the early stages of Southern sheep production. Virginia continues today to be the leading sheep producer in the Southeast. In some parts of the New World—in the North as well as the South—sheep did not thrive, since they were easy prey for wolves and wild dogs. Where they did survive, sheep provided the settlers with wool as well as meat. But because of the rather temperate Southern climate, wool was not of as much commercial importance in the South as it was in the North. So generally, Southern sheep tended to be raised only where mutton was in demand.

It was tough, old mutton—not young lamb—that was prepared for the early Southern table. Lamb is six to twelve months old; mutton is one to five years old. In the eighteenth- and nineteenth-century South, mutton saddles and shoulders were roasted, legs were boned and stuffed, necks were broiled, and ribs were stewed. Mutton chops were fried, breasts were grilled, and hash was made from mutton leftovers. Mutton was served at special dinners in Virginia and South Carolina, and in Mississippi, transplanted Virginus Dabney was said to have "fattened sheep until some of them suffocated" for his table. However, according to Dabney, "the sacrifice was worth it to assure the quality of the remaining mutton."

The Civil War caused a decline in sheep production throughout the South. When it revved up again in the late nineteenth century, interest in so-called "native" ewes was prominent. These sheep were survivors; they were hardy despite the meager diet provided by scrubby-grassed woodlands, and could contend with predators. Farmers in Tennessee and Kentucky were particularly interested in these hardy, native sheep, as well as in raising imported varieties such as merinos, Southdowns, Leicesters, and Costwolds.

In 1775, Colonel Richard Callow brought sheep to Booneseboro, Kentucky and ever since, the animal has played an important role in that state's agriculture. (Kentucky burgoo is generally made with lamb.) It was Kentucky, in fact, that became the active producer of spring lamb (as opposed to mutton) in this century. Ewes were shipped into Kentucky from the West, and were bought by local farmers and bred to top-grade Southdown rams for tender, elegant chops and roasts.

It was not until this century that in cookbooks lamb is mentioned more often than mutton. Most Americans today do not care for mutton, which has a stronger, richer flavor and tends to be tougher than lamb. Different breeds of sheep yield different grades of wool, but all sheep yield edible meat. It is primarily age that determines taste and tenderness. Mutton is difficult to find today, although some specialty butchers can order it for you.

Quick Lamb Scallops
with Herbed Egg Sauce
• • •

MUTTON OR LAMB SCALLOPS (then called collops) were fairly common on the early Southern table. This cut was popular because no matter how old and tough the animal, scallops—thin slices cut from the leg and usually pounded— were generally more tender than larger, more sinewy cuts.

In the 1800s, it was not uncommon to add chopped, hard-boiled eggs (or sometimes just the yolk) to gravy to accompany veal or lamb. At times, eggs might have been easier to procure than butter or cream, so they were a good choice for adding texture to a sauce.

The sauce here is a mélange of rich pan juices, white wine, shallots and herbs with butter, and hard-boiled egg for richness. This dish is easy and fast, a good choice for a special after-work supper. Fresh parsley may be substituted if tarragon and chives are not available. Serve with roasted new potatoes, steamed green peas, sugar snap peas or snow peas or braised baby carrots.

1½ pounds well-trimmed lean lamb scallops cut from the leg, about ¼ to ½ inch thick (or substitute veal scallops)

Salt and freshly ground black pepper, to taste

6 tablespoons unsalted butter (or less, if using a nonstick skillet and omitting the final butter enrichment)

2 tablespoons vegetable oil

½ cup dry white wine

2 finely minced shallots

2 tablespoons finely chopped fresh parsley

1 tablespoon finely chopped mixed fresh herbs (such as basil, tarragon, thyme, chives)

1 hard-boiled egg, finely chopped

1. Pat lamb dry with paper towels. Place lamb in 1 layer between sheets of waxed paper and flatten to ⅛ inch thick with a mallet, rolling pin, or the broad side of a cleaver. Pat dry again. Lightly season on both sides with salt and pepper.

2. Heat 1 tablespoon butter and 1 tablespoon oil in a large skillet and cook lamb in 2 batches, to avoid crowding, over medium-high heat.

3. Cook about 2 minutes on each side or until well browned on the outside but still pink on the inside. Transfer to a platter and cover to keep warm. Repeat procedure with remaining lamb and add additional 1 tablespoon each butter and oil as needed.

4. Discard drippings from skillet. Add ¼ cup wine to skillet and boil for 30 seconds while scraping up browned bits stuck to the bottom of the skillet. Transfer liquid from the skillet to a small saucepan. Add shallots to the wine reduction and simmer 2 to 3 minutes or until shallots are tender. Off the heat, whisk in the remaining 4 tablespoons butter, 1 tablespoon at a time. (Note: This butter enrichment can be omitted, but the sauce will be thinner.) Season to taste with salt and pepper. Stir in herbs and egg. Add any juices that have collected from the lamb to the sauce. Divide on 4 dinner plates, pour sauce on top, and serve immediately.

Serves 4.

Easy Lamb Patties with Spring Greens
and Creole Mustard Sauce

• • •

GROUND LAMB is often overlooked in this country where beef is the preferred meat for patties, meatballs, and meatloaf. I find lamb patties a welcome change from the ubiquitous hamburger. Here, lamb's mild, gamey flavor is balanced by lemon zest, the sprightly tang of young greens, and the assertive zing of Creole mustard. This easy dish is rich and hearty, but it can be lightened by substituting yogurt for the sour cream, steaming the greens rather than sautéeing them, and by using a nonstick skillet to cook the lamb patties. Serve with steamed rice or new potatoes, or baked or mashed sweet potatoes.

1½ pounds lean ground lamb
¼ cup fine, dry breadcrumbs
1 medium yellow onion, very finely minced
3 large cloves garlic, minced
1½ teaspoon salt
1 teaspoon grated lemon zest
Heaping ¼ teaspoon pepper
1 egg, beaten
4 tablespoons butter (or less, if using a nonstick skillet)

2 pounds very young, tender mixed greens, well washed and drained (I like to use ⅓ sorrel, ⅓ dandelion greens, and ⅓ Swiss chard, but you can substitute spinach, kale, and/or watercress.)
½ cup dry white wine
¾ cup sour cream (or substitute part plain yogurt)
1 tablespoon Creole mustard (or substitute whole-grain mustard)

1. In a bowl combine the lamb, breadcrumbs, onion, garlic, salt, pepper, and lemon zest until well mixed. Add egg and mix well. Form into 6 patties, 3 inches thick.

2. Heat 2 tablespoons of the butter in a large skillet over medium heat. Add patties and cook about 6 minutes on each side or until well browned on the outside but still juicy and pink on the inside. Transfer to a warm platter and cover with foil to keep warm. Reserve pan drippings.

3. While patties cook, heat the remaining 2 tablespoons butter in a separate large skillet. Add chard (and kale, if you are using it), cover and cook 3 to 4 minutes or until almost tender, tossing once or twice. Add sorrel, dandelion (and

watercress or spinach if you are using them), toss, cover and cook 2 to 3 minutes more or until just tender. Keep warm while you finish the sauce.

4. Add wine to the skillet with the reserved lamb drippings and boil 1 minute while scraping up brown bits stuck to the bottom of the pan. Remove from heat. Add sour cream and heat through but do not boil. (Note: If using yogurt, do not overheat or sauce may break.) Stir in mustard.

5. To serve, place patties on a bed of greens on each plate. Top with sauce or pass sauce separately.

Serves 3 to 6; hearty appetites will want 2 patties; serve 1 per person for a lighter meal.

Lamb Chops
with Vidalia-Mint Butter

■ ■ ■

OF ALL THE FLAVORS we associate with lamb, mint is probably the most popular. The mint-flavored apple jelly found on supermarket shelves, however, is a far cry from the original English "mint sauce" made of fresh mint leaves, sugar, and vinegar that the eighteenth- and nineteenth-century American Southern cooks prepared. When the English settlers found wild mint growing in the New World (the Native Americans are said to have used it to relieve flatulence) they were familiar with it and incorporated it into their new diet with ease.

Although lamb chops are one of the most popular cuts of lamb today, they do not appear with great frequency in Southern cookbooks until the middle of the twentieth century.

I adore mint, but like rosemary and sage, the flavor it imparts can be overwhelming and the herb should be used judiciously. The mint butter here is mild and delicately flavored; the natural freshness of the mint is mellowed by the onions, which add a gentle savory note. This dish is good all year round, but is particularly flavorful when spring lamb, Vidalia onions, and the first mint of the season coincide. If the weather permits, why not grill the chops instead? Serve with steamed baby carrots, roasted new potatoes, or mashed potatoes, sugar snap peas, or English peas.

VIDALIA-MINT BUTTER

⅓ cup loosely packed fresh, clean, dry mint leaves (*if mint is not available, substitute 3 tablespoons fresh rosemary leaves, lightly bruised in mortar and pestle*)

¼ cup coarsely chopped Vidalia onions (*or substitute Walla Walla, Maui, Bermuda, Texas 10-15 Su-persweets or other mild, sweet onions, or 2 tablespoons chopped shallots*)

Pinch of salt

Pinch of freshly ground white pepper

½ cup (1 stick) unsalted butter, room temperature

LAMB

2 tablespoons unsalted butter (*or less, if using a nonstick skillet*)

1 tablespoon vegetable oil

12 rib lamb chops (*about 2½ pounds*)

Salt and freshly ground black pepper, to taste

1. To make the Vidalia mint butter: In a food processor or blender, process mint, onions, salt, and pepper until finely chopped. Add butter and process until well combined. Form the mixture into a log shape on a sheet of waxed paper. Roll the butter up in the waxed paper and chill 1 hour or freeze 15 minutes.

2. To cook the lamb: Add half of the butter and half of the oil to a large skillet and place over medium-high heat. Pat chops dry with paper towels and add 6 chops to the skillet. (Cooking the chops in batches prevents overcrowding, or use 2 skillets if you wish.) Cook 3 minutes, sprinkle with salt and pepper to taste, then turn and cook on the other side 2 to 3 minutes longer or until rosy pink inside and nicely browned on the outside. Repeat with second batch of chops. (Note: Grill or broil chops if you prefer.) Transfer chops to warm plates and top each with a thin slice (about 1 teaspoon) of the mint butter. Serve immediately.

Serves 4.

Grits, Grains, and Beans

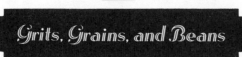

Rice

A Charlestonian is like a Chinaman; he eats rice and worships his ancestors.

—Anonymous

WHILE A GREAT DEAL of rice is indeed eaten in South Carolina (it ranks fourth in per capita consumption behind Florida, Louisiana, and Arkansas) it was in Virginia in 1647 that the the first rice seeds were sown in the New World. Old Dominion governor William Berkely reaped fifteen bushels from his crop—which subsequently failed. However, around 1685, rice was brought from Madagascar to Charleston (then known as Charles Towne) by Captain James Thurber who gave it to Henry Woodward, now known as one of the founding fathers of the Carolinas. The grain flourished, and was to become so important to that state's economy that in the eighteenth century South Carolinians used it for currency and called it "Carolina Gold."

During the American Revolution, tragedy struck when the British captured Charleston and shipped the entire harvest to England, leaving no seed behind to plant the next crop. But in 1787, Thomas Jefferson—Ambassador to France at the time—smuggled rice out of Europe and brought it to South Carolina, thus reviving the rice industry, and by 1840, South Carolina was producing 60 percent of all the rice grown in the New World with North Carolina and Georgia as her chief competitors. Rice continued to be grown in North Carolina until 1932 but it was rice from the South Carolina and Georgia swamplands that accounted for 90 percent of the rice produced in this country until 1865.

In South Carolina, land erosion plus the Civil War and the abolition of slavery, began the downfall of the state's rice production. In 1911 a hurricane that caused great destruction in the South Carolina rice fields, followed by a series of heavy rains (called freshets) twenty years later, contributed to the eventual end of South Carolina's rice industry. Rice production moved westward into Louisiana, Mississippi, Texas, and Arkansas. (Arkansas is presently the largest rice-producing state in the United States.)

So, for about 200 years, rice was the most important crop from Cape Fear River in North Carolina to St. John's River in Florida—a stretch of land also known as the Low Country. In 1978, rice was planted near Charleston at Twinbridge Plantation by Richard and Patricia Price to attract waterfowl. According to John Martin Taylor in an article in *The New York Times*, the grain grew successfully, so the Prices began experimenting with Carolina Gold seeds procured from a seed bank. This firm-textured, unpolished rice is available by mail order (see page 481).

Rice in the Kitchen From a parsimonious platter of hoppin' John to a sophisticated seafood pilau, rice has been an inspiration to Southern cooks of every social strata. In the deep South, rice served the same farinaceous purpose as did the Irish potato in the upper South, the North, and the West. Rice was not only plentiful and cheap, it was versatile and a good accompaniment to meats, shellfish, sauces, gravies, soups, and stews. Rice soup (boiled until tender, sieved, and enriched with egg yolks or cream) made a brief, fashionable appearance (it was served at the White House in 1802), but it is the pilaus, croquettes, breads, and griddle cakes that have survived the years. Rice flour, the residue that results from pounding rice from its outer shell, was used in the nineteenth-century South in breads, griddle cakes, waffles, and biscuits. Today, it is used primarily in food processing and nonallergenic baking.

Nineteenth-century cookbooks give detailed explanations of how to wash rice, a procedure that to the modern cook sounds like quite a tedious process. The many changes of water not only eliminated grit and dirt, but made the rice whiter and kept the grains separate—qualities that remain the hallmarks of properly cooked rice in the South. Low-Country cooks still prefer long-grain white rice to any other variety since it cooks up dry, fluffy, and separate.

In the early 1900s, rice recipes flourished. In South Carolina, these included all of those popular in the previous century—pilaus, croquettes, breads, and griddle cakes—plus combination dishes such as red rice, jambalaya, gumbos, Creole shrimp, and rice pies (cooked rice mixed with egg makes the "crust"). During the same time in Virginia, where rice was not grown, recipes for the grain are limited to rice waffles, breads, and puddings. And in Louisiana, red beans and rice became a traditional Monday (wash day) meal.

Double-Red Rice

. . .

LATE NINETEENTH- and early twentieth-century Southern cookbooks include recipes for green or emerald rice (rice with green vegetables added), yellow rice (flavored with saffron), brown rice (dry, raw rice toasted in a skillet before cooking), dirty rice (cooked rice combined with minced, cooked giblets, onions, and seasonings), and red rice (seasoned with tomatoes, bacon, onions, and lots of black pepper).

Basic red rice, also called Spanish rice by many Southerners (including my mother), has many variations and permutations and can be served hot or cold, either as a main course or side dish. Sometimes the rice is cooked separately from the flavorings, sometimes it is combined raw with other ingredients. Red rice is similar to tomato pilau in technique and flavor, although red rice is often flavored with tomato paste instead of whole tomatoes, which are de rigueur in pilaus. Some cooks add smoked pork sausage to their red rice for a heartier dish.

In this recipe I used a combination of red pepper purée and tomato paste to color and flavor the rice. Garlic, extra-virgin olive oil, and sun-dried tomatoes add a gutsy Mediterranean twist. Serve hot or at room temperature as a side dish to accompany grilled or broiled poultry, pork, veal, beef (it's great with kabobs or burgers), or with full-flavored fish such as swordfish.

RED PEPPER SAUCE

1 medium clove garlic
2 tablespoons roasted red pepper
    purée (purée drained pimientos or
    roasted, peeled red bell peppers in
    food processor or blender)

1 tablespoon tomato paste
¼ teaspoon salt, or to taste
3 tablespoons light olive oil
2 tablespoons extra-virgin olive oil

RICE AND SEASONINGS

2 cups water
¼ teaspoon salt
1 cup uncooked long-grain white rice
Salt and freshly ground black pepper,
    to taste

2 to 4 tablespoons drained, minced,
    sun-dried tomatoes

1. To make the sauce: With the machine running, drop the garlic into a blender or food processor until finely chopped. Add red pepper purée, tomato paste, and salt and process to blend. With machine still running, slowly pour in the oils. Set aside.

2. To prepare the rice and seasonings: In a medium saucepan, bring the water and salt to a boil. Add rice and return to a boil. Lower heat, cover tightly, and simmer for 15 minutes. Remove from heat and let stand 5 minutes covered to "steam."

3. Add the Red Pepper Sauce to the rice and toss with a fork until just blended. Season to taste with salt and pepper and sprinkle with sun-dried tomatoes. Serve warm, room temperature, or lightly chilled. Makes 2 cups.

Serves 4 as a side dish.

Green Risotto

• • •

SOUTHERN "GREEN" RICE or emerald rice is usually colored and flavored with cooked spinach and/or herbs. Here, I use short-grained Italian Arborio rice, fresh herbs, spinach, and seasonings to make a rich side dish or comforting supper. In the South, long-grain rice is the preferred type and when it is properly prepared, each grain is light, fluffy, and separate from the next. This Italian-inspired dish, on the other hand, is prepared so that a creamy, starchy mass results. If you like the comforting quality of grits, chances are you'll love risotto.

4 tablespoons unsalted butter
½ cup finely chopped onion
2 cups uncooked Arborio (short-grain) rice (available in supermarkets or specialty food stores)
6 cups chicken broth, preferably very lightly salted homemade broth
¼ cup dry white wine

½ 10-ounce package frozen chopped spinach, thawed, drained, and wrung dry in cheesecloth
2 tablespoons finely minced fresh parsley
2 tablespoons minced fresh chives
4 medium-large fresh basil leaves
Freshly grated Parmesan cheese, to taste
Freshly ground black pepper, to taste

1. In a medium saucepan heat butter over medium heat. Add onions and cook, stirring occasionally, 5 minutes or until softened but not browned. Add rice and toss to coat. Cook 2 minutes stirring constantly until all grains are well-coated with butter. Remove from heat.

2. In a separate saucepan, bring broth and wine to simmer. Add ½ cup broth mixture to the rice over medium heat and stir until liquid is absorbed. Continue cooking and stirring, adding only ⅓ cup of warm broth at a time— letting the liquid become absorbed before adding more—until rice is al dente (tender, but not mushy) and liquid is absorbed. (Note: If all the liquid is used and rice seems undercooked, add ½ cup hot water and continue to cook until tender.)

3. In a food processor or blender purée spinach and herbs until very fine. Stir the spinach-herb mixture into the risotto just before serving. Sprinkle generously with Parmesan cheese and freshly ground black pepper to taste and serve immediately.

Makes about 5 cups; serves 6 as a side dish, 4 as a first course, and 3 as a main course.

Rice Carbonara
(Rice with Eggs and Bacon)

■ ■ ■

A RECIPE in an old South Carolina cookbook for egg pilau was the springboard for this recipe. But the name "carbonara" comes from the classic Italian dish, spaghetti alla carbonara, in which hot spaghetti is tossed with beaten raw eggs. Like the spaghetti in the original dish, the heat from the rice in this recipe cooks the egg, forming a kind of sauce. I've added bacon (vegetarians may omit this), onion, and Parmesan cheese for a hearty, comforting dish that is very easy to make. Serve as a winter lunch or Sunday-night supper with a green salad or steamed vegetables vinaigrette, and fresh fruit for dessert.

6 slices bacon, cut into 1-inch pieces
½ cup finely chopped yellow onion
½ cup rice
1½ cups water
1½ cups chicken broth, preferably
    homemade

1 egg, room temperature
2 tablespoons butter, optional
Freshly grated Parmesan cheese, to
    taste
Freshly ground black pepper, to taste

1. In a large, heavy skillet, cook bacon over medium heat until crisp. Remove bacon with a slotted spoon and drain on paper towels. Discard all but 3 tablespoons of the drippings in the skillet. Add onion to the skillet and cook, stirring occasionally, 5 minutes or until softened. Add rice and toss to coat. Add water and broth; cover and simmer 15 minutes. Remove from heat and let stand tightly covered 5 minutes.

2. In a large, room-temperature serving bowl, beat the egg. Immediately add the hot rice and toss to coat. (Note: The rice should be hot enough to cook the egg. If it is not, heat the mixture in a microwave oven at medium power for 30 seconds, or until egg is cooked, or return to the warm skillet and toss lightly.) Serve hot with butter, if desired, Parmesan cheese, and freshly ground black pepper.

Serves 3 to 4 as a main course or 5 to 6 as a side dish.

*Louisiana Rice
with Mushrooms and Hazelnuts*

. . .

THIS LUSTY SIDE DISH combines the earthiness of wild mushrooms with toasty hazelnuts and the faint, natural sweetness of exotic-tasting Wild Pecan Rice™. Serve this dish alongside Goose with Damson-Port Sauce (page 206), Roast Turkey with Herbed Cornbread Dressing (page 196), Grandmother's Roast Lemon Chicken (page 183), or other simply prepared poultry or game.

RICE AND SEASONINGS

3 tablespoons unsalted butter

¼ pound shiitake or other wild
mushrooms, stems removed, caps
wiped clean and sliced into ¼-inch
strips

¼ cup finely minced yellow onion

1 cup Wild Pecan Rice™ (1 7-ounce
box) or substitute white rice

1 cup chicken broth, preferably
homemade

¾ cup water

HAZELNUT BUTTER

⅔ cup toasted, skinned hazelnuts
(Toast 3 to 3½ minutes in a microwave oven, stirring after 2 minutes, or 10 minutes in a preheated
370°F oven. Stirring frequently.

While nuts are still warm, place on
a clean tea towel and keep together
to loosen skins.)

Pinch of salt

4 tablespoons unsalted butter

1. To prepare the rice: In a saucepan heat butter over medium-low heat.
Add mushrooms and onions and cook, stirring frequently, 5 minutes or until
softened. Add rice and cook 1 minute, tossing once or twice. Add broth and
water. Cover and simmer 20 minutes. Remove from heat and let stand tightly
covered for 10 minutes.

2. To make the hazelnut butter: Place toasted, skinned nuts and salt in a
food processor and process until finely ground. Add butter and process until
smooth and well blended.

3. To serve, add 4 tablespoons of the hazelnut butter to the rice and toss,
adding more hazelnut butter if desired. (Cover and chill remaining butter to
dress steamed green beans or carrots, or to spread on muffins, waffles, French
toast, or scones.)

Serves 4 to 6.

*Grits,
Grains,
and
Beans*

■

Dirty Brown Rice with Chives

. . .

THIS CAJUN FAVORITE gets its name from the giblets that color the rice. The orange zest and chives are my own addition to this dish, which can be served as a side dish or as a simple, economical supper.

4 cups chicken broth
1 cup whole-grain brown rice
2 tablespoons butter
1 large stalk celery, minced
1 small yellow onion, minced
¾ pound chicken livers (or mixed livers and giblets)

1 teaspoon freshly ground black pepper
1 teaspoon grated orange zest
½ teaspoon salt, or to taste
1 tablespoon chopped fresh chives

1. Bring broth to a boil in a large saucepan. Add rice and return to a boil. Lower heat and simmer partially covered 40 to 50 minutes or until all liquid is absorbed and rice is tender.

2. Meanwhile, in a medium skillet heat butter over low heat. Add celery and onion and cook, stirring frequently, 5 minutes or until softened.

3. In a food processor or blender, purée uncooked livers (or mince very finely by hand). Add liver purée to skillet and cook until livers have lost all traces of redness. Add pepper, orange zest, and salt; toss to mix. Add cooked rice and chives, toss to mix. Serve hot.

Serves 4 as a side dish or 2 as a main course.

Cornmeal, Hominy, and Grits

Men usually shelled corn, threshed peas, and cut potatoes for planting and platted shucks. Grinding corn into meal or hominy was woman's work . . .

—Deborah Gray White, *Aren't I a Woman?*
Female Slaves in the Plantation South

CORN, as basic as it may seem, can be confusing. Sweet corn (so-called because of its high sugar content) is eaten as corn on the cob, and considered a farinaceous vegetable (for more information, see "Vegetables" page 311). Dried field corn (also called feed corn, grinding corn, or maize) on the other hand, is thought of as a grain. Besides being used as fodder for animals, field corn—at one time the principal crop and most important food of the Native Americans of the Southeast—is processed to make cornmeal, corn flour, hominy, and grits.

There are two main types of corn used to make cornmeal: flint corn, which has a hard kernel and grows well in northern climates, and dent corn, a popular Southern corn that is soft on the top so it "dents" when the kernel dries. Flour corn, which contains soft starch and can be ground into corn flour, which is finer than cornmeal and is used in the processing of commercial breakfast cereals. Dent is the type that usually is made into hominy, while both dent and flint can be ground into cornmeal. Popcorn, by the way, although it is not used to make cornmeal, has the hardest kernels of all.

Cornmeal In making cornmeal, most commercial milling processes proceed as follows: dried field corn kernels are cleaned, then steamed to loosen the hull. The kernel is then split, which removes the hull and the germ—which are used to make corn bran, used in cereals—leaving only the endosperm. (Cornmeal that has the hull and germ removed is called degerminated cornmeal.) The endosperm is passed through heavy rollers that break it up into granules of various sizes—fine, medium, and coarse. These granules are separated by a screening process, then graded.

Cornmeal can also be ground between two stones. In stone-ground cornmeal, the hull and germ will remain intact, differentiating it from degerminated cornmeal. Cornmeal that has the germ and endosperm intact, but is sifted so that a portion of the hull (or bran) is removed, is called bolted cornmeal. Bolted cornmeal is lower in fiber than unbolted cornmeal, but other nutrients remain the same. (Up until the 1890s with the introduction of the roller mill, all grains were ground on millstones.) In stone-ground meal, the natural oils which are inside the germ, are distributed throughout the flour. Stone-ground meal is more flavorful than the mechanically ground type and is more nutritious since the high heat produced by the rollers destroys vitamins and enzymes. (Rhode Islanders have always insisted on stone-ground white cornmeal for their Johnny cakes.)

Stone-grinding mills are sprinkled throughout much of the South and their grains and flours can be purchased in specialty food stores and many supermarkets nationwide. (See mail-order source, page 481.)

Hominy In the South, whole hominy—which is about the size of a fresh corn kernel— is sometimes referred to as "big hominy," "whole hominy," or "great hominy," and grits are often called "small hominy." Hominy—the word probably comes from an Algonquin term, *rockahominy,* meaning hulled corn, or *tackhummin,* which refers to grinding—can both be made from either white or yellow field corn. In the North where hominy was also eaten during the New World's beginnings, yellow hominy was called "hulled corn" while white hominy was sometimes called samp from the Narragansett *suamp,* meaning coarsely ground corn or cornmeal porridge. Yellow and white hominy are virtually the same in flavor. Originally, hominy eaten by the Native Americans may have been reconstituted, cooked, or parched corn of any kind. But hominy later came to refer only to processed kernels.

Hominy is made by soaking whole, dried field corn kernels in a caustic alkali solution (such as lye or ground limestone and water), which loosens the tough outer hull (the bran) from the softer edible center. It is this lye or lime that changes the flavor of the corn and gives hominy and grits their unique taste. (According to the author in his book *Bill Neal's Southern Cooking,* Native Americans of the east coast used hardwood ashes from hickory and oak to obtain lye, whereas Native Americans further west used lime from limestone to make hominy.) The kernels are then winnowed, the husks are discarded, and the kernels can be cooked in water like dried beans. When hominy is dried and coarsely cracked, the result is cracked hominy, which cooks in less time than whole hominy. (Cracked hominy is edible in two to three hours; whole hominy requires up to six hours cooking time.) Whole and cracked hominy are available in specialty food stores. Finely ground hominy is called *masa harina,* and is used in Southwestern and Mexican cooking, particularly for tortilla making.

From the eighteenth through the early twentieth century, corn remained king of the grains in America and whole hominy was eaten daily by many Southerners. It was usually served at breakfast with butter, gravy, or pan juices from ham or sausage and, because of its rather neutral flavor, was a natural accompaniment to salty cured pork. There was often hominy left over from breakfast and early Southern cooks found many uses for it. Cold, cooked hominy was often fried in a skillet and served as a hot side dish with ham, shellfish, or game. Sometimes it was added to biscuits, waffles, pancake batter, or used to make corn journey (a variation on the Johnny cake) or croquettes. Some cooks added leftover hominy to cornmeal batter to make awendaw bread. According to Richard Hooker in his *Food and Drink in America: A History,* in Virginia and Maryland, hominy was often boiled with dried beans and milk until it became a solid mass eaten hot or cold with bacon or other meat.

In the 1900s, whole hominy was canned for the Southern market, and while canned hominy lacks some of the firmness of freshly cooked dried hominy, it tastes very good and the time saved is well worth it.

Grits When dried hominy is ground more finely than cracked hominy but not as fine as *masa harina,* the result is grits, also known as hominy grits. The word has been used since colonial times and probably comes from the Old English, *grytt,* meaning bran, or *greot,* meaning ground. Grits are also called grist or pearl hominy in some older cookbooks, probably because they were ground at what was known as a grist mill.

Up until the early twentieth century, grits were purchased in bulk and could be procured in fine, medium, or coarse grind. These early grits had to be washed in several changes of water, soaked overnight or for several hours, then boiled until tender. Today, grits are added directly to boiling, salted water, and cooked in a much shorter time. Regular grits cook in about thirty minutes. More finely ground grits, so-called "quick grits," are ready in about five minutes. Instant grits are ready to eat as soon as they are stirred with boiling water. Like cornmeal, the best-tasting grits—whether white or yellow—are stone-ground because the germ is intact.

Grits are still daily fare for much of the South (they were on the breakfast table every day of my childhood) and remain one of the region's most characteristic foods. Grits are usually served as a breakfast side dish, often with a pool of red-eye gravy in the center. In South Carolina and Georgia, grits are often served for supper to accompany shrimp. Like hominy, grits left over from breakfast were often added to a batter and baked on a griddle. In *The Virginia House-wife* (1824), there is a Johnny cake recipe calling for "small hominy" (grits) as well as one for "an excellent and cheap pudding." This so-called pudding is actually a griddle cake of cooked grits, cornmeal, eggs, milk, and butter. They were baked on a hot griddle and eaten with butter and molasses.

Fontina Grits

. . .

RECIPES FOR combining cheese and grits are common throughout the South. Most "Cheese Grits" recipes call for cheddar cheese mixed into cooked grits for a dish that is served immediately or poured into a buttered casserole and baked. In experimenting with various cheeses, I found Italian fontina to be a welcome change from the predictable cheddar. Fontina's mild, nutty taste complements the subtle flavor of grits very nicely. Serve this as a breakfast side dish to accompany eggs, bacon, or sausage. Or serve instead of rice or potatoes along-side grilled or roasted poultry or game. Fontina grits are also terrific by them-selves: have a bowl of it in bed while you watch the Sunday night movie or as a comforting supper in front of the fire.

3 cups water
Scant teaspoon salt
¾ cup uncooked regular grits, prefer-ably stone-ground
3 tablespoons unsalted butter (or more to taste)

¼ pound Italian fontina cheese, grated (about ½ cup)
Salt and freshly ground white pepper to taste

1. Bring water and salt to a boil in a heavy saucepan. Add grits slowly while stirring constantly. Cover and simmer 18 to 20 minutes or until water has been absorbed.

2. Stir in butter and cheese until they melt. Season to taste with salt and white pepper. Serve hot.

Serves 4 to 6.

Garlic Cornmeal Mush

. . .

HOT, COOKED CORNMEAL (often called porridge or mush) was common breakfast fare in both the North and South. Leftover breakfast mush was often sliced and fried in hot fat and served at supper or the next morning. Molasses, maple syrup, sugar, or red-eye gravy are the usual accompaniments.

Here, hot, cooked cornmeal is fragrant with garlic butter. Serve it instead of potatoes as a side dish to game or poultry. (Mush differs from polenta—Italian-style cooked cornmeal—in that polenta is made with coarsely ground cornmeal and requires less liquid than the standard size grind of American cornmeal. If you prefer polenta, add 1 cup *coarsely ground* cornmeal to 3¼ cups boiling, salted water, then proceed with directions below.) For a cozy supper, serve Garlic Cornmeal Mush alongside Italian or German sausages. For a tasty variation, add fontina cheese to the mush (see note).

4 cups water
Scant teaspoon salt
1 cup yellow cornmeal, preferably
   stone-ground

2 large cloves garlic, minced
4 tablespoons unsalted butter, or
   more to taste

1. In a large, heavy saucepan, bring water and salt to a boil. Add cornmeal very slowly while whisking vigorously to avoid lumps. Cook 18 to 20 minutes uncovered over low heat (mixture should bubble gently) whisking or stirring constantly (or at least every 3 to 4 minutes). Mush is done when it pulls away from the sides of the pot as you stir.

2. Meanwhile, prepare garlic butter. In a small skillet or saucepan cook garlic in butter over very low heat 3 to 4 minutes or until garlic just releases its fragrance and is a pale golden (do not overcook or garlic will be bitter). Remove from heat and let stand until cornmeal is done.

3. Stir garlic butter into cornmeal and serve piping hot with game, chicken, or sausages.

Serves 4 to 6.

Note To make cornmeal mush with fontina, follow directions for garlic mush but omit garlic butter. When cornmeal is cooked, stir in 3 tablespoons unsalted butter and ¼ pound grated fontina cheese.

Ham and Grits Custards
with Cheddar Cream

• • •

THESE ELEGANT little custards take grits to gastronomic heights. Ham-lined soufflé cups filled with a grits-and-cheese mixture lightened with beaten eggs are baked, unmolded, and served with a suave cheese sauce. It makes an attractive and comforting side dish for a special breakfast. (Calorie watchers can make the custards with milk instead of cream, substitute low-fat cheddar cheese, and omit the cheddar cream. The resulting dish will not be as rich and elegant as the original version, but will, nevertheless, be tasty.) Serve with fresh fruit compote or melon, and hot biscuits with peach preserves. (They can also be served for supper with scrambled or poached eggs and a mixed green salad.) Custards can be made a day in advance, brought to room temperature, then baked as directed.

CUSTARDS

2 to 3 tablespoons butter, room temperature (or substitute vegetable oil)

1 pound smoked, brine-cured ham, very thinly sliced (Note: Dry-cured ham may be used, but it may be too strong in flavor for some tastes)

5 cups cooked grits, cooled slightly

4 large eggs, beaten

1 1/2 cups grated medium-sharp cheddar cheese

Fresh ground white or black pepper, to taste

Ground red pepper (cayenne), to taste

3/4 cup heavy cream (or milk), scalded

CHEDDAR CREAM

2 cups heavy cream

1/2 teaspoon Dijon mustard

2 tablespoons unsalted butter, to enrich sauce (optional)

1 1/2 cups grated, Parmesan cheese, cheddar cheese, or aged Monterey Jack cheese

Strained juice from timbales

Ground red pepper (cayenne), to taste

Grits,
Grains,
and
Beans

■

266

1. Preheat oven to 350° F.

2. Use the room-temperature butter to grease the insides of 8 8-ounce soufflé or custard cups. Line the bottoms of the cups with rounds of buttered parchment paper. Line bottoms and sides of the cups with ham slices to cover completely. Set aside.

3. In a bowl, combine cooked grits, eggs, cheese, white or black pepper, red pepper, and cream. Mix until well combined. Divide evenly among lined cups.

4. Place cups in a roasting pan or baking pan large enough to hold them easily and pour in enough boiling water to come halfway up the sides of the cups. Bake for 30 minutes, or until set.

5. Unmold custards onto a warm platter. Cover with foil and tilt platter slightly. Let stand for 3 to 5 minutes so that juices from ham collect at one end of platter. Reserve juices for the cheddar cream.

6. To make the cheddar cream: Gently boil cream in a saucepan over medium-high heat until reduced to 1½ cups, or until it coats the back of a spoon, about 10 to 15 minutes.

7. Remove from heat and whisk in mustard and the optional butter. Add cheese and stir until cheese melts; return to low heat if necessary, but do not boil. Add strained juices from timbales and taste for seasoning. Add ground red pepper to taste.

8. Place each custard on a warm plate and pour a ribbon of cheese sauce over or around it.

Serves 8.

Fried Garlic Grits

. ■ .

At night they might eat fried steak, hot squares of grits fried in egg and butter, pork-chops, fish, young fried chicken.

—Thomas Wolfe, *Look Homeward, Angel*

DON'T THROW OUT leftover grits! Southern cooks often slice and fry it. Crunchy on the outside and creamy in the center, fried grits are a delicious accompaniment to eggs and bacon, or with simply prepared poultry or shrimp for supper.

Grits, Grains, and Beans

■

Here, I add garlic butter to the grits as they cook for a rich, savory flavor. The egg-and-breadcrumb coating keeps slices from breaking up and results in a fabulously crunchy crust.

1½ cups water
Scant ½ teaspoon salt
6 tablespoons uncooked regular grits,
    preferably stone-ground (see note
    in step 1)
4 tablespoons unsalted butter (or
    less, if using a nonstick skillet)
1 large clove garlic, minced

6 tablespoons unbleached all-purpose
    flour
1 large egg beaten with 2 tablespoons
    milk
½ cup unseasoned dry breadcrumbs
2 tablespoons vegetable oil (or less, if
    using a nonstick skillet)

1. In a small, heavy saucepan, bring water and salt to boil. Add grits slowly while stirring constantly to prevent lumping. Lower heat, cover, and simmer 20 to 25 minutes or until all liquid is absorbed. (Note: If using quick grits or instant grits, follow package directions.)

2. Meanwhile, in a small skillet or saucepan heat 2 tablespoons butter over medium heat. Add garlic and cook over very low heat, stirring once or twice, about 3 to 4 minutes or until garlic just releases its fragrance. (Note: Do not let garlic brown or it will be bitter.) Set aside.

3. When grits are done, stir in garlic butter. Spread grits quickly but evenly into a buttered 9-inch pie plate. Let cool to room temperature, cover, and chill 1 to 2 hours or until cold and firm.

4. In 3 deep plates or shallow bowls, pour flour into one, egg mixture into another, and breadcrumbs into the third.

5. Heat oil and remaining butter in a large skillet over medium-high heat.

6. Cut grits into 8 wedges. Carefully remove each wedge with a narrow flexible spatula. Dip wedges 1 at a time first into the flour, then into the egg mixture, then into the breadcrumbs.

7. Fry grits wedges in hot fat 2 to 3 minutes on each side or until golden-brown and crisp on the outside. Drain briefly on paper towels and serve hot.

Serves 4 as a side dish.

Beans

THE BEANS I discuss here refer to the edible seeds of leguminous plants that grow in the South. Such beans are also referred to as "shelling beans" or, more colloquially, "shelly beans" or "shellies" because they are grown primarily for the edible seed inside (the pod is usually tough and stringy) and one has to shell them to release the seed. Information on green or snap beans appears in "Vegetables" (page 323).

Long before the first settlers arrived in the New World, beans were second only to corn as a vital part of the Native American diet. They taught the colonists how to grow and prepare native beans, and since the newcomers were already familiar with the European broad bean, they readily accepted the New World species.

In spite of their humble character, beans have always been an important component of the American diet, especially now as most of us try to eat less meat and more complex carbohydrates as a source of protein. Some of our nation's finest beans grow prolifically in the South, and over the centuries good cooks—talented, frugal, or just plain hungry—have created a variety of bean dishes.

Beans from the *Phaseolus vulgaris* family include several celebrated Southern varieties. Pinto beans (*pinto* is Spanish for paint, a word describing this kidney-shaped bean's dappled appearance) taste much like kidney beans and are usually cooked with salted or smoked pork and served warm as a side dish, sometimes sprinkled with chopped white onions or scallions and a splash of vinegar. A bowl of beans prepared in this manner—served with cornbread and iced tea—often constitutes a simple meal in some rural and mountainous areas of the South. Navy beans—sometimes called small white beans or pea beans—are often cooked and served like pintos. Or, they might be simmered with brown sugar and spices for Memphis-style "barbecue beans." Cranberry beans—so called because of their cranberry-colored "netting" on the pod and shell—are favored in some parts of the South, particularly Kentucky and West Virginia. Small red beans (which resemble kidney beans but are smaller and deeper red in color) can be used instead of kidney beans as the base for that celebrated New Orleans specialty, red beans and rice. In Florida, "Moors and Christians"—black beans served over rice—is the regional version of the classic beans-and-rice combination. Lima or butter beans originated in Peru. They were introduced to the New World at an early date and, by Jefferson's day, at least, they were widely grown in Virginia. These are sometimes cooked with salt pork or smoked meats like other legumes but they are also frequently simply stewed with butter and/or cream and salt and pepper. Lima beans range in size from about ⅛ inch to nearly 1 inch long. Young fresh limas are sweet and tender, becoming starchier as they mature. Speckled butter beans are a variety that, when fresh, are covered with light and dark brown spots that all but disappear when cooked. Soy beans are widely grown in the South, but are primarily used as fodder for cattle. Perhaps as tofu and other soy products increase in popularity throughout the country, some of the harvest will be converted into high-protein soy products for human consumption. At this writing, tofu is presently being made in Washington, D.C., and it may just be a matter of time before this low-fat, low-calorie, cholesterol-free, economical source of protein is more widely known in the South.

Southern Peas It is the so-called Southern peas that are truly a regional specialty. Also called cowpeas, this group of legumes includes the familiar black-eyed pea, which grows in a green or white pod, has a distinct eye, and is rather earthy in flavor. The purple-hull pea, a tender, light-colored bean, is smaller and firmer than the black-eyed pea, has a definite eye, and an elongated shape and comes from purple pods, hence its name. Crowder peas differ from the black-eyed and purple-hull varieties in their slightly spherical shape and lack of a definite eye. Crowder peas are identifiable by their warm reddish-brown color. Field peas range in color from a soft gray to a rich, warm brown. (The term "field pea" often designates one of the older varieties such as Dixie Lee and Whip-pur-will, from which modern peas were bred. They are small and slightly elongated with a very slight eye or none at all.) Field peas generally have a firmer texture than black-eyed and purple-hull and are therefore preferred by those who find larger beans too mealy. Cream peas and White Acre peas—the two smallest of the field-pea family—are slightly elongated and have no eye. They are identifiable by their pale color (they resemble white hominy). Because of their scarcity, these mild-flavored peas—sometimes called Lady peas—can be difficult to find outside the South in fresh form. Southern peas are canned by Bush Brothers and Co. in Dandridge, Tennessee, and can be found in many supermarkets around the country.

Herbed Hoppin' John
with Country Ham

· · ·

"Tell me. Is it just us who call this hopping-john? Or is it known by that name through all the country? It seems a strange name somehow . . ."

"Well, I have heard it called peas and rice. Or rice and peas and pot-liquor. Or hopping-john. You can vary and take your pick."

"But I'm not talking about this town," F. Jasmine said. "I mean in other places. I mean through all the world. I wonder what the French call it."

—Carson McCullers, *The Member of the Wedding*

ACCORDING TO WAVERLEY ROOT in *Food*, this characteristically Southern dish is also called Hoppin' Jack. Although it is best known for its magical qualities—eating it on New Year's Day is said to bring the eater good luck for the rest of the year—it is eaten all year in the South. According to culinary historian, Jessica Harris, Hoppin' John is similar to a West African dish, *chiebou niebe*.

It is believed that black-eyed peas originated in India then traveled to the West Indies. From there, they were an important source of food on slave-trading ships. They were said to have been introduced to Florida in the early eighteenth century, after which they gradually made their way further north. Since black-eyed peas don't grow well in Northern climates, they remained a Southern food. Thomas Jefferson grew them and Mrs. Randolph's recipe in *The Virginia House-wife* (1824) appears to be among the earliest ones recorded.

Hoppin' John varies through the South but it is generally always a simple dish, usually calling for no herbs, butter, and only limited spices. Some cook the rice and peas all in one pot, first cooking the peas until tender, then adding the rice (and sometimes bacon drippings). Others cook the rice separately in the pea-cooking liquid. Some cooks add chopped tomato and onion to the peas as they cook, others may add a bay leaf or parsley. Old Creole books often call for serving bacon or sausages on the side, a tasty combination indeed.

Here, I've taken the classic dish—which may seem plain and unadorned to the non-Southern palate— and spiced it up a bit. Fresh herbs add flavor to the peas as they cook and a garlic-flavored herbed vinaigrette is tossed with the peas while they are still warm so they will absorb flavors. I use the pea-cooking liquid

*Grits,
Grains,
and
Beans*

■

to cook the rice, therefore enriching the rice with an earthy flavor. Serve this as a main course with a salad of tomatoes and young bitter greens (such as arugula, watercress, dandelion, and radicchio) or warm-cooked broccoli rabe, escarole, kale, collards, turnip, or mustard greens. Or, serve as a side dish to Spicy Fried Chicken (page 182), or grilled meats or poultry. It's also great on picnics to accompany grilled hamburgers or sausages. Since legumes and rice comprise a complete protein, the ham is not necessary for nutritional value, but as a flavoring element, and may be omitted if a meatless dish is desired.

BLACK-EYED PEAS

½ pound (2 cups) dried black-eyed peas, washed, picked over, and soaked overnight in cold water (Or, quick-soak the peas: Bring water and peas to a boil, then boil for 2 minutes. Cover, and set aside off the heat for 1 hour. Drain thoroughly.)

6 cups water

4 large cloves garlic, peeled

1 herb bouquet, tied in cheesecloth, consisting of:
3 fresh thyme sprigs (or 1½ teaspoons crushed, dried thyme)
6 fresh parsley sprigs
3 fresh sage leaves (or ¾ teaspoon dried rubbed sage)

1 large, meaty ham hock, rinsed (Note: If omitting ham hock, add 1 teaspoon salt)

DRESSING AND RICE

3 tablespoons Red Pepper Vinegar (see recipe, page 304) or substitute red wine vinegar

2 tablespoons chopped fresh parsley

4 teaspoons fresh thyme leaves (or 1½ teaspoons dried)

2 large cloves garlic, minced

½ cup light olive oil

½ teaspoon salt

1½ cups uncooked regular or popcorn rice

3 to 6 ounces thinly sliced Smithfield ham, julienned (see page 481 for mail-order source) optional

Fresh thyme sprigs, to garnish

Tabasco sauce, to taste

1. Drain the soaked peas and place in a large, clean saucepan with water. Add garlic, herb bouquet, and ham hock. Bring to boil; lower heat, and simmer, covered, 45 minutes to 1 hour or until tender but not mushy.

2. Meanwhile, in small bowl, combine vinegar, herbs, and garlic; whisk in oil and salt. Set aside.

3. Drain peas, reserving liquid. Discard garlic, herb bouquet, and ham hock. While still warm, toss peas with the dressing. Cover to keep warm and set aside.

4. In a large saucepan, bring 2¼ cups pea-cooking liquid and the salt to boil. Add rice, return to boil. Lower heat and simmer, covered, 15 minutes or until all liquid is absorbed and rice is tender.

5. To serve, reheat peas if necessary. Divide rice evenly among 4 dinner plates then distribute peas evenly on top of rice. Sprinkle each serving with 2 to 3 tablespoons ham and garnish with thyme sprigs; pass Tabasco sauce separately.

Makes 4 main-course servings.

Note Peas and rice may be prepared up to 2 days in advance. Serve room temperature or hot. Also, because the rice cooks in the pre-cooking liquid, it will not be white. If you prefer plain, white rice, prepare rice according to package directions.

Lima Beans with Capers and Garlic

• • •

GARLIC AND CAPERS add a lively Mediterranean touch to mild, sweet limas without overwhelming them. Serve as a warm side dish to grilled or roasted lamb, chicken, or pork or with steamed shrimp. Or serve at room temperature on lettuce leaves as a salad.

2 tablespoons light olive oil
1 medium-sized clove garlic, crushed
2 cups cooked fresh or frozen baby lima beans
1 to 2 teaspoons drained capers

Salt and freshly ground black pepper, to taste
Nasturtium blossoms, to garnish (optional)

1. In a medium saucepan heat oil over medium-low heat. Add garlic and cook 3 to 4 minutes or just until garlic releases its fragrance. Add beans and toss to coat. Cover and cook until beans are warmed through, about 1 to 2 minutes, stirring once or twice.

2. Remove from heat and add capers; toss to mix. Season to taste with salt and pepper; garnish with nasturtium blossoms, if desired. Serve warm.

Serves 4 as a side dish.

Lima Beans in Fresh Tarragon Cream

▪ ▪ ▪

RICH, SILKY CREAM and fresh, licorice-y tarragon adds grace to humble limas. Serve as a side dish to simply prepared fish, poultry, or meat.

2 teaspoons unsalted butter	*Salt and freshly ground black pepper,*
½ cup heavy cream	*to taste*
1 to 1½ teaspoons chopped fresh	*2 cups cooked fresh or frozen baby*
tarragon	*lima beans, kept warm*

In a medium saucepan, heat butter, cream, and tarragon over medium heat. Cover and simmer gently 1 minute. Uncover, simmer until cream has reduced to 3 tablespoons. Add warm, cooked limas and toss to coat. Season with salt and pepper to taste. Serve warm.

Serves 4 as a side dish.

Field Peas with Caviar and Chives

▪ ▪ ▪

A VARIATION on the Italian combination of cannellini beans and caviar, firm-textured little Southern peas are a lusty match to caviar. The earthy flavor of the beans works with the caviar in a similar way to that of buckwheat blini: the contrasting earthy and salty flavors seem to meld in perfect harmony. I don't suggest beluga for this dish (that's best for eating right out of the spoon). Choose instead a moderately priced caviar such as American sturgeon.

2 tablespoons light olive oil

2 teaspoons freshly squeezed lemon juice

2 teaspoons (or more) caviar

2 teaspoons chopped fresh chives

2 cups cooked, drained field peas (cook fresh peas with ham hock in water to cover 20 minutes or until tender), or substitute canned field peas, drained of all but 1 tablespoon of their juices

In a large bowl, combine olive oil, lemon juice, caviar, and chives. Add peas and toss gently to blend. Serve lightly chilled or at cool room temperature on Bibb lettuce leaves.

Serves 4 as a first course.

Smoky Maple Pinto Beans

Almost as popular as fried chicken is that universal favorite, barbecue. Wherever one goes, he isn't far from the smell of some restaurant or back yard grill slowly cooking pork, beef, or chicken in a highly seasoned barbecue sauce. Many restaurants specialize in nothing but barbecue, evidence of the popularity of barbecued meat. There are so many commercial barbecue sauces for the homecook that no one sauce has claimed the number one spot among loyal enthusiasts. The only requirement is that the bottle's label show that the barbecue sauce, like hot sauce, is manufactured somewhere in the south; otherwise, true barbecue connoisseurs won't trust it.

—Michael Andrew Grissom, *Southern by the Grace of God*

THERE ARE MANY great barbecue joints in the South, and Charlie Vergos' Rendezvous in Memphis is certainly one of them. The Rendezvous is famous for its "dry" ribs, which are tender and highly seasoned with a mixture of dried herbs and spices. Memphis' other famous rib joint, Gridley's, offers the more traditional "wet" barbecued ribs. I love both rib styles, as well as the sweet and spicy barbecue beans served with them. John Vergos, the owner's son, wouldn't reveal the Rendezvous recipe, but I detected cumin, onions, molasses, and a little tomato and vinegar for sharpness. In this version, I use maple syrup instead of molasses for interest. I've also added fresh ginger, a pleasant counterpoint to the cumin. Serve warm as a side dish to hamburgers or sausages, or, as they do in Memphis, to accompany barbecued ribs, or a pork barbecue sandwich. These beans keep one week in the refrigerator or they may be frozen for several months.

1 pound (2 cups) dried pinto beans, picked over, washed, and soaked overnight in cold water (Or use quick-soak method: Bring water and beans to a boil, then boil for 2 minutes. Cover, and set aside off the heat for 1 hour. Drain thoroughly.)

1 ham hock (or substitute ½ pound slab bacon or lean salt pork or fatback)

1 large yellow onion, chopped

½-inch piece fresh ginger, peeled and halved

1 herb bouquet, tied in cheesecloth, consisting of:
  2 large cloves garlic, peeled

8 whole black peppercorns

¼ to ½ teaspoon dried red pepper flakes

4 whole cloves

1½ teaspoons cumin seed, crushed coarsely in mortar and pestle

3 to 4 tablespoons cider vinegar

4 to 6 tablespoons maple syrup (or substitute 3 to 4 tablespoons molasses)

2 tablespoons prepared spicy brown mustard

½ to 1 teaspoon salt

Crumbled bacon, to garnish (optional)

Chopped parsley, to garnish (optional)

1. Transfer the drained, soaked beans to a 3- to 4-quart heavy saucepan. Add ham hock, onion, and ginger and enough water to cover by 2 inches.

2. Add herb bouquet to the beans and bring to a boil. Boil for 10 minutes. Lower heat and simmer uncovered 45 minutes, skimming as needed and adding more water if necessary. (Beans should be covered at all times by at least 1 inch of water.)

3. After 45 minutes cooking time, add 1 tablespoon vinegar, 4 tablespoons

syrup (or 3 tablespoons molasses), 1 tablespoon of the mustard, and ½ teaspoon salt. Stir to blend, then simmer 45 minutes to 1½ hours longer or until beans are tender and cooking liquid is creamy. Taste for seasoning, adding remaining vinegar, syrup, mustard, or salt, if desired. Serve hot, topped with crumbled bacon and chopped parsley if desired.

Serves 6 to 8 as a side dish.

Pasta

IN 1789 after eight years in France as a diplomat, Thomas Jefferson returned to the United States to be George Washington's secretary of state. It is said that at this time Jefferson brought back a noodle recipe to be served "like macaroni" and that it was he who introduced pasta to this country.

But it was in the late nineteenth century with the large immigration of Italians that pasta became widespread, and it went from being an upper-class "luxury" food to one with a more democratic status.

The Carolina Housewife (1847) by Sarah Rutledge gives a recipe for Macaroni à la Sauce Blanche (a baked pasta layered with a Parmesan-flavored béchamel sauce). In the same book, there is a recipe for macaroni boiled in milk as well as one for Macaroni à la Napolitana (a meaty tomato sauce). Several old Carolina cookbooks have recipes for macaroni pie, more familiarly known as macaroni and cheese. Aside from a scattering of Italian restaurants serving spaghetti with tomato sauce and meatballs, pasta seems to have been given short shrift in the South until the early 1980s. Indeed, rice, legumes, and maize and its derivatives—grits, hominy, and cornmeal—have played a more important role in the South than pasta. However pasta is nonetheless noteworthy, not only because Southern ingredients—like shrimp, country sausage, and bitter greens— go so well with it, but also because it has recently become one of America's favorite foods, and cooks across the South have incorporated it into their repertoire. Today, innovative chefs throughout the South are creating pasta dishes utilizing indigenous Southern ingredients, and home cooks from Virginia through New Orleans and back north through Tennessee, Kentucky, and West

Virginia are discovering classic pasta dishes such as pasta primavera and fettuccine Alfredo.

Many of the pasta recipes here call for heavy cream. Cream marries well with Southern flavors, which are the point of this book. Broth can be used instead of cream in most of these recipes, but please know that the resulting dish will not be as rich as the original.

Ziti with Country Sausage and Sun-Dried Tomato Sauce

• • •

OLD-FASHIONED GROUND COUNTRY SAUSAGE—the kind Southerners form into patties and fry for breakfast—adds a spicy touch to this zesty, meaty sauce; sun-dried tomatoes add a pungent, sweet-tangy note. Serve in cool weather when appetites are hearty along with an arugula and radicchio salad.

½ pound spicy ground country pork sausage (do not use link sausage)

½ pound uncooked pasta (I like to use ziti or medium-sized shells)

6 to 8 scallions, finely chopped (about ½ cup)

1 large clove garlic, peeled and slivered

½ cup slivered, drained, oil-packed sun-dried tomatoes

⅛ teaspoon ground red pepper (cayenne)

⅛ teaspoon dried red pepper flakes

Freshly ground black pepper, to taste

½ cup dry white wine

2 to 4 tablespoons butter (optional)

Grated Parmesan cheese

Grits, Grains, and Beans

■

1. Crumble sausage into a large skillet and cook over medium heat, stirring frequently, about 5 to 10 minutes or until no traces of pink remain and meat is beginning to turn golden-brown and lightly crisped.

2. Meanwhile, bring a kettle of lightly salted water to a boil and cook pasta according to package directions.

3. With a slotted spoon, transfer sausage to a bowl. Pour off all but 2 tablespoons fat. Add scallions to the skillet and cook, stirring frequently over medium heat about 3 to 5 minutes or until beginning to soften. Do not brown. Add garlic and cook 1 minute or until fragrant.

4. Off heat, add tomatoes, ground red pepper, red pepper flakes, and black pepper; toss to mix. Add to sausage mixture.

5. Add wine to skillet and boil 3 to 5 minutes, scraping brown bits from bottom of the pan, until liquid is reduced to 2 to 3 tablespoons. Whisk in butter, if desired.

6. Return sausage mixture to skillet and heat through. Add cooked pasta and toss to mix. Sprinkle with cheese and serve hot.

Serves 3 to 4 as a main course or 6 as a first course.

Sweet Potato Pasta with Pepper and Nutmeg

• • •

THESE SALMON-COLORED NOODLES accompany roast chicken, turkey, or game beautifully. Nutmeg is a natural with sweet potatoes; freshly ground black pepper is a savory, pungent counterpoint. To serve them as a main course dish, combine with butter plus blanched, peeled julienned red bell peppers or chopped blanched turnip greens, diced Smithfield ham, or toasted pecans. Sweet potato pasta is also a good vehicle for Alfredo sauce.

1 medium-large sweet potato, scrubbed
2 large egg yolks
1 teaspoon salt
2¼ to 2½ cups unbleached all-purpose flour

4 to 8 tablespoons unsalted butter, to taste
Freshly grated nutmeg, to taste
Freshly ground black pepper, to taste

1. Prick sweet potato in several places with a fork. Wrap in a paper towel (to absorb excess moisture) and cook in microwave oven on high 5 to 8 minutes, turning once, until tender. Peel potato, then purée in food processor or blender until smooth. You should have about ¾ cup purée. (Or, prick potato and bake in a preheated 350° F oven 1 to 1½ hours or until tender. Peel, then purée.)

2. In food processor or mixer, combine ¾ cup potato purée, egg yolks, and salt. Add 2¼ cups flour in 3 additions, blending well after each addition. Turn dough out onto lightly floured board and knead 5 minutes or until smooth, adding up to ¼ cup more flour as needed. Wrap in waxed paper; let rest 15 minutes.

3. Divide into 2 equal portions. Working with 1 portion at a time, roll dough through pasta machine according to manufacturer's directions. Cut into fettuccine noodles. Let dry for later use, or cook in 4 quarts boiling salted water until al dente, about 3 minutes. Drain thoroughly. To serve, toss with butter and sprinkle with nutmeg and pepper. Serve immediately.

Serves 4 as a main course or 6 to 8 as a first course or side dish.

Buckwheat Pasta
with Kale and Goat Cheese

▪ ▪ ▪

KALE IS ONE of the South's favorite greens. Although it is usually cooked with ham hocks and served as a vegetable side dish—along with its flavorful pot likker—it is also good with pasta. The assertive flavor of buckwheat noodles stands up to the hearty kale. A mild, to medium-mild goat cheese mellows out the sauce, while a hint of Smithfield ham adds a smoky, savory note. If you are watching your weight, omit the cream and use 1 cup (or more) homemade chicken broth to moisten the pasta.

*1½ pounds (untrimmed weight) kale
   (or substitute collard greens),
   tough stems removed
2 tablespoons butter*

*¼ cup minced shallots
2 ounces very thinly sliced Smithfield
   ham or other dry-cured country
   ham trimmed of fat and cut into
   ¾-inch squares*

1¾ cups heavy cream
4 ounces mild goat cheese, such as Montrachet or Bûcheron, lightly crumbled
½ to ¾ cup grated Parmesan cheese

1 pound buckwheat pasta (pizzocheri, available at specialty food stores), or substitute whole wheat fettuccine, cut or broken into 3-inch lengths.
Freshly ground black pepper, to taste

1. Wash the greens well. Stack the leaves and cut into ⅓-inch-wide ribbons.

2. Blanch the kale in a large pot of boiling salted water for 2 minutes or until just tender. Drain thoroughly; squeeze dry.

3. In a large skillet, heat the butter over low heat. Add the shallots and cook, stirring frequently, for 2 minutes. Add the ham and cook, stirring frequently, for 2 to 3 minutes more or until shallots are tender. Remove from heat, stir in 1 cup of the cream, and set aside.

4. In a small bowl mash half the goat cheese with the remaining ¾ cup cream until smooth. Stir into the contents of skillet along with ¼ cup Parmesan cheese and the greens.

5. Cook the pasta according to package directions. Drain thoroughly.

6. Return skillet to heat and simmer the sauce, stirring frequently, for 1 to 2 minutes or until very lightly thickened. (Do not cook too long or cream will reduce too much and sauce will be cloying.) Toss the pasta with the sauce. Sprinkle with freshly ground black pepper and the remaining goat cheese and Parmesan to taste.

Serves 4 as a light lunch or supper or 6 as a first course.

Whole Wheat Spaghetti with Bel Paese, Cream, and Pecans

• • •

THIS CREAMY DISH featuring Southern pecans is an elegant first course. Yes, it's rich. But it's no worse than letting guests fill up on cheese, nuts, or other heavy hors d'oeuvres. Skip the hors d'oeuvres and sit right down to dinner after a quick glass of wine. Keep the main course light—and no one will get up from the table feeling stuffed.

1 pound whole wheat spaghetti
4 tablespoons unsalted butter
1 cup heavy cream
½ pound Bel Paese cheese, grated
½ cup toasted pecan halves

½ cup toasted pecans, coarsely
   chopped
Freshly ground black pepper, to taste
1 cup freshly grated Parmesan cheese

1. Bring a large pot of lightly salted water to a boil and cook spaghetti according to package directions.

2. Meanwhile, heat butter and cream in a large skillet to a simmer. Add Bel Paese by handfuls, stirring until smooth after each addition. Remove from heat when cheese has melted.

3. Drain pasta thoroughly and toss with sauce in skillet. Serve on warm plates and top each serving with pecans and pepper. Serve immediately and pass Parmesan cheese separately.

Serves 4 as a main course; 6 as a first course.

Pasta with Shrimp, Fennel, and Basil

■ ■ ■

GULF SHRIMP and country bacon are a common duo in the South, particularly South Carolina, Georgia, and Alabama. I love the combination with the addition of fresh fennel, tomatoes, and spices in this dish.

Serve as a main course with a mixed green salad or as a first course to precede grilled lamb, beef, veal, or chicken.

4 slices bacon
1 tablespoon unsalted butter
1 large clove garlic, slivered
3 to 4 shallots, minced (or substitute
   4 scallions, finely sliced)

1 fresh fennel bulb, trimmed and
   chopped
¼ cup homemade fish broth or bottled clam juice
2 tablespoons dry white wine

6 plum tomatoes, peeled, seeded and
   puréed (about 1 cup purée)
½ teaspoon fennel seeds
¼ teaspoon ground red pepper (cayenne)
½ teaspoon freshly ground black
   pepper

Pinch of salt
½ pound medium-sized pasta (such
   as shells or corkscrews)
¾ pound medium or large shrimp,
   shelled and deveined

1. In a medium-large skillet, cook bacon over medium heat until crisp. Remove bacon from skillet with a slotted spoon and drain on paper towels; set aside. Pour off all but 2 tablespoons of the drippings in the skillet.

2. Add butter to drippings; over medium heat, add garlic and cook 1 to 2 minutes until it is golden and releases its fragrance. Remove garlic with slotted spoon and discard.

3. Add shallots and cook 2 to 3 minutes or until softened. Add fennel and cook 1 minute. Add broth or clam juice, wine, tomatoes, fennel seeds, red pepper, black pepper, and salt. Simmer uncovered 8 minutes or until fennel is crisp-tender.

4. Meanwhile, cook pasta according to package directions.

5. Add shrimp to the skillet, cover, and simmer 2 to 4 minutes longer or until shrimp are cooked through. Add cooked, drained pasta, and toss to blend. Crumble bacon and sprinkle on top.

Serves 2 as a main course or 4 as a first course.

Pasta with Chicken and Chicken Liver, Bacon, and Fresh Sage

■ ■ ■

FRIED CHICKEN LIVERS are a Southern specialty. Bacon and fresh sage add to the earthy richness of this dish. Diet watchers can omit the cream, and use ½ to ¾ cup homemade chicken broth to moisten the pasta. Serve as a main course with a mixed green salad or sliced tomatoes.

*Grits,
Grains,
and
Beans*

■

12 *fresh sage leaves, cut in half
lengthwise if large (or substitute 1
tablespoon dried crumbled sage
leaves)*
6 *slices bacon, cut in half lengthwise*
12 *medium-sized chicken livers,
washed, dried, and trimmed of
connective tissue*
6 *boneless, skinless chicken breast
halves, cut into 1-inch chunks*
2 to 3 *tablespoons light olive oil*
*Salt and freshly ground black pepper,
to taste*

1 *pound large pasta (such as ziti or
rigatoni*
1½ *tablespoons unsalted butter (or
less, if using a nonstick skillet)*
4 *medium shallots, minced*
2 *cloves garlic, minced*
1 *cup heavy cream*
½ *teaspoon salt*
¼ *teaspoon freshly ground black
pepper*

1. Wrap 1 sage leaf and ½ slice bacon around each liver. (Note: If using dried sage, add it later.) Spear wrapped livers onto long-bamboo skewers. Spear the chicken onto separate skewers.

2. Place livers and chicken on a heavy-duty foil-lined broiler pan or roasting pan that has been lightly brushed with olive oil. Brush livers and chicken with olive oil and sprinkle lightly with salt and pepper.

3. Broil 6 inches from heat source for 5 minutes. Turn skewers and broil 5 minutes longer or until livers are cooked through but still slightly pink inside, and chicken is cooked through and juices run clear when pierced through the center. Cover with foil to keep warm. (Note: For an earthy flavor, grill livers and chicken over medium-hot coals.)

4. Cook pasta according to package directions.

5. Meanwhile, heat butter in a large skillet over medium-low heat. Add shallots and cook until softened, about 3 minutes. Add garlic and cook until it just releases its fragrance, about 1 minute. Add cream and heat through. Stir in salt. (Note: If using dried sage, add at this point.)

6. Drain pasta and toss with sauce. Remove livers and chicken from skewers, add to pasta, and toss to mix. Season to taste with pepper. Serve hot with sliced tomatoes and a green salad.

Serves 6 to 8 as a first course; 4 as a main course.

Fettuccine with Asparagus, Country Ham, and Red-Eye Sauce

• • •

IN FRENCH COOKING, ham and asparagus are a classic combination. It's a marriage that fares well in the South, too, where ham is an obsession. Here the ham creates a sauce that is a rich variation on the most Southern of all sauces, red-eye gravy. Serve as a main course with a simple green salad, or as a starter to precede grilled salmon or chicken.

2 pounds asparagus, trimmed

2 tablespoons butter (or less, if using a nonstick skillet)

½ pound Smithfield ham (or other dry-cured country ham), cut into ¼-inch cubes (for mail-order source, see page 481)

½ cup dry white wine

1 cup chicken or beef broth, preferably homemade

2 cups heavy cream (use only 1 cup for a lighter dish)

1 pound fettuccine (or substitute corkscrews or other pasta of choice)

Salt and freshly ground black pepper, to taste

¼ cup minced fresh parsley

1. Using a vegetable peeler, peel asparagus stalks if they are tough. Drop asparagus into a skillet of lightly salted boiling water and simmer until just tender (timing will depend on the thickness of stalks). Drain, refresh under cold running water to stop the cooking, and drain again. Cut into 1½-inch pieces; set aside.

2. In a large skillet melt butter over medium-high heat. Add ham and sauté 4 to 5 minutes until ham just begins to turn crisp. Remove with slotted spoon and set aside. Pour off excess fat out of skillet and discard.

3. Add wine to skillet and boil until it is reduced to a glaze. Add broth and boil over high heat 5 minutes. Add cream and boil until sauce is thickened and coats the back of a spoon. (Do not reduce too much or sauce will be unpleasantly thick.) You should have about 1¾ cups sauce. Cover to keep warm.

4. Cook pasta according to package directions. Drain well, add to sauce in the skillet along with asparagus and ham. Toss to coat; season to taste with salt and pepper. Sprinkle with parsley.

Serves 4 to 6 as a main course; 6 to 8 as a first course.

Grits, Grains, and Beans

■

Angel Hair Pasta
with Vidalia Sauce and American Caviar

• • •

THIS ELEGANT PASTA DISH features a gently flavored onion sauce made with broth, cream, and mild, sweet Vidalia onions. Any sweet, mild onion can be used for this dish, but I prefer the variety grown in Vidalia, Georgia. These onions—hybrids of the yellow Granex variety—are milder than regular onions because of the soil and mild climate in this particular region. Georgia's early spring allows for early harvesting (Vidalia season extends from early May through July), so this onion does not have a chance to develop the "bite" of regular onions. Vidalias have a high water content and do not store well. I find they will keep about one month if wrapped individually in foil and refrigerated. Vidalias are available in many supermarkets, and in specialty food stores or by mail order (page 481).

Caviar makes this dish special. I like to use American caviar from the Mississippi River (for more about caviar, see page 75), but use whatever type you prefer. Serve as a first course to precede simply prepared roasts, chops, etc. Or serve as the main course along with Bibb Salad with My Favorite Vinaigrette (page 112) for a simple, elegant supper for two.

6 tablespoons butter (less if using a nonstick skillet)

1½ cups very finely diced Vidalia onions (or substitute Spanish onions or other mild onions such as Maui, Texas 10-15 supersweet, or Walla Walla)

½ cup dry white wine

2 cups homemade fish stock or bottled clam juice

¾ cup créme fraîche or sour cream (or use less, to taste)

½ pound angel hair pasta

4 ounces (or more) salmon roe or caviar (for American caviar mail-order source, see page 481)

Salt and freshly ground black pepper, to taste

Fresh dill sprigs, to garnish

1. In a large skillet melt 3 tablespoons of the butter over medium heat. Add onions and cook, stirring frequently, until soft, but not browned, about 15 minutes.

2. Add wine and boil 1 minute. Add stock and boil until reduced to 1 cup, about 8 to 10 minutes.

3. Add ½ cup crème fraîche and boil 1 minute. Keep warm.

4. Cook pasta in a large saucepot of salted water until al dente, about 5 minutes. Drain well.

5. Add 2 to 3 tablespoons caviar and the remaining butter (if desired) to the sauce. Add pasta and toss well to mix.

6. To serve, twirl some of the pasta on each plate to make a "nest." Top each serving with 1 tablespoon crème fraîche and 1 tablespoon caviar. Garnish with dill.

Serves 4 as a first course or 2 to 3 as a light supper dish.

Pasta Primavera
with Green Beans, Peas, and Herbs
• • •

GREEN BEANS are a staple in the Southern kitchen, but instead of boiling them for hours with ham hocks, here they're cooked until just tender. For a lighter dish, omit the cream and increase broth to three cups. Serve as a first course to precede grilled salmon steaks, shrimp, or chicken, or Lamb Chops with Vidalia-Mint Butter (page 248).

1½ cups shelled fresh green peas (1½ pounds in the shell)

¾ pound tender young green beans, washed, trimmed, and cut in half crosswise on the diagonal

½ pound snow peas, washed, trimmed, and cut in half crosswise on the diagonal

4 tablespoons butter (omit for a lighter sauce)

½ cup dry white wine

2 cups chicken broth, preferably homemade (use 3 cups if omitting cream)

1½ cups heavy cream (omit for a lighter sauce)

Salt and freshly ground black pepper, to taste

2 tablespoons minced fresh chives

2 tablespoons minced fresh chervil or parsley

1 tablespoon minced fresh tarragon

1 pound pasta (I like to use corkscrews or thin spaghetti)

Grated Parmesan cheese, to taste

Grits,
Grains,
and
Beans

■

287

1. Bring 2 vessels—a saucepot for the pasta and a large saucepan for the vegetables—of lightly salted water to a boil. Add peas to the saucepan and boil 3 minutes. Add beans and boil 3 minutes more. Add snow peas and boil 2 minutes more or until all vegetables are crisp-tender. Drain well, cover to keep warm, and set aside.

2. In a large skillet, melt butter over medium heat. Add wine and boil 1 minute. Add broth and cream and boil until reduced to about 1½ cups. (Note: This will take about 7 to 10 minutes. Mixture should lightly coat the back of a spoon.) Add salt and pepper and half the herbs and stir to mix.

3. Cook the pasta according to package directions; drain thoroughly.

4. Add vegetables to sauce and heat through if necessary. Add pasta and toss to coat. Sprinkle with remaining herbs, more black pepper, to taste, and Parmesan cheese. Serve hot.

Serves 4 to 6 as a main course or 6 to 8 as a first course.

Cold Buckwheat Noodles with Cucumbers and Spicy Virginia Peanut Sauce

. . .

IN RECENT YEARS oriental buckwheat noodles bathed in a spicy sesame or peanut sauce have become an American favorite. In this interpretation, I use Virginia peanuts, fiery Southern pepper vinegar, spices, and cool cucumbers for a dish that's perfect for hot summer nights.

PASTA AND VEGETABLES

2 medium cucumbers (about ¾ pound), peeled, halved lengthwise, seeded, and sliced about ¼ inch thick

1 large red, yellow, or green bell pepper, quartered, seeded, and cut into ¼-inch-wide strips

½ pound Japanese buckwheat noodles (or substitute whole wheat spaghetti)

2 tablespoons dark oriental sesame oil

SAUCE

1½ cups roasted, skinless unsalted peanuts (preferably Virginia peanuts, (see page 481 for mail-order source)

2½ teaspoons sugar

¾ teaspoon salt, or to taste

½ cup peanut butter, preferably unsalted

3 tablespoons Red Pepper Vinegar (see recipe, page 304) or substitute rice wine vinegar or red wine vinegar

½ cup peanut oil, preferably cold pressed (available at health-food stores), or substitute vegetable oil

1 tablespoon dark oriental sesame oil (optional)

Pinch of ground red pepper (cayenne)

¼ teaspoon Tabasco sauce, optional

Freshly ground black pepper, to taste

Soy sauce or tamari, to taste

1. In a large bowl, combine cucumbers and bell pepper; set aside.

2. In a large saucepan, bring lightly salted water to boil and cook noodles according to the package directions. Drain thoroughly. Toss in a medium bowl with the 2 tablespoons sesame oil. Set aside to cool to room temperature.

3. Meanwhile, to make the sauce: In a blender or food processor, chop peanuts with sugar and salt just until very coarsely ground. Put this mixture in a medium bowl and set aside.

4. In a blender or food processor, process peanut butter and vinegar until well blended. With the machine running, add peanut oil and sesame oil. Add red pepper, Tabasco, and black pepper to taste. (Mixture should be spicy.) Add to the reserved chopped nut mixture and mix well with a wooden spoon.

5. Add cooked, drained noodles to cucumbers and peppers. Pour sauce on top; toss to blend. Let stand 1 to 2 hours to blend flavors. Taste; add more salt, black pepper, red pepper, Tabasco, or soy sauce, if desired. Serve very lightly chilled or at cool room temperature. (Do not serve cold, as peanut butter will harden and sauce will be unpleasantly stiff.) Can be made 1 day in advance.

Serves 2 as a main course or 4 to 5 as a first course.

Grits,
Grains,
and
Beans

■

Pasta Roll
with Country Ham and Three Cheeses
. . .

THOUGH A BIT TIME CONSUMING, this elegant dish is a good first course for a special party since it can be made in advance and served warm or at room temperature. It calls for homemade pasta sprinkled with sliced ham and a lush mixture of cheese. It is rolled like a jelly roll, poached, and sliced.

Serve as a first course to precede any simply prepared meat, fish, or poultry, or as a main course with sautéed escarole, Fennel, Orange Pomegranate Salad with Raspberry Vinaigrette (page 109), or lightly dressed, mixed green salad.

PASTA ROLL

2 tablespoons butter

4 scallions, minced

½ cup (2 ounces) country dry-cured ham, finely diced

8 ounces cream cheese, room temperature

½ cup ricotta cheese

1 egg

¼ cup grated Parmesan cheese

½ teaspoon freshly ground black pepper

¾ to 1 pound fresh pasta dough, preferably spinach pasta (Note: Fresh pasta is available at specialty food shops. Or make it following a standard recipe using about 1½ to 2 cups flour, 2 eggs, 1 tablespoon olive oil, salt, and ½ pound raw spinach, cooked, well drained, and puréed or very finely chopped.)

½ pound country dry-cured ham, sliced ⅙ inch thick

BASIC TOMATO SAUCE

16-ounce can Italian plum tomatoes

¼ cup chopped fresh parsley

2 large cloves garlic, halved

2 tablespoons minced fresh basil (or 1 teaspoon dried basil)

3 tablespoons unsalted butter

1. To prepare pasta roll: In a skillet, melt butter over low heat. Add scallions, and cook until softened, 1 to 2 minutes. Add diced ham and cook over medium heat for an additional 1 to 2 minutes. Set aside.

2. In a bowl beat cream cheese and ricotta together until smooth. Add egg and beat well. Stir in Parmesan cheese, ham mixture, and pepper; mix well. Cover and refrigerate.

3. Divide pasta dough in half. Working with ½ of the dough, roll out on a lightly floured surface to a 12- by 8-inch rectangle ¼ inch thick.

4. Spread half the filling on the sheet of pasta, leaving a ½-inch border all the way around. Place a layer of sliced ham over the cheese mixture to cover.

5. Beginning at one of the short ends, roll up the pasta, jelly-roll style. (Do not roll too loosely or the water may seep in as it poaches.) Repeat the entire procedure with the remaining pasta, making 2 complete rolls. Wrap each roll in a double thickness of washed cheesecloth and tie each end securely with string.

6. Fill a large, deep oval casserole, Dutch oven, sauté pan, or fish poacher with water and 1 tablespoon salt. Bring to a boil and add pasta rolls. Reduce heat to a simmer and cook gently, turning occasionally, for 20 minutes.

7. To prepare sauce: In a saucepan, simmer all ingredients except butter, uncovered, until reduced by ⅓, about 40 minutes. The sauce should be thick and strongly flavored.

8. Strain over another saucepan, pressing out the liquid. Discard solids. Add butter; reheat until butter melts. Makes about 1½ cups.

9. Drain pasta rolls; cool until easy to handle. Remove cheesecloth and string.

10. Cut each roll into ½-inch-thick slices. Pour a pool of sauce on each plate and top with the pasta slices. Serve warm or at room temperature.

Serves 6 as a first course, 4 as a main course.

Vegetables

Vegetables

. . .

It was the time of early afternoon when in the old days a sweet band would be playing. Now with the radio turned off, the kitchen was solemn and silent and there were sounds from far away. A colored voice called from the sidewalk, calling names of vegetables in a dark, slurred tone, a long, unwinding hollering in which there were no words.

—Carson McCullers, *The Member of the Wedding*

*T*ODAY, THERE IS STILL A "VEGETABLE MAN" in many parts of the suburban South. But instead of a cart or a wagon, he—and perhaps his son or wife—will hawk his wares from a slow-moving farm truck. Just-picked eggplant, corn, and tomatoes might be among the offerings, along with green beans, yellow squash, cucumbers, peaches, and canteloupes. Throughout the South, farm stands and open-air markets are where you'll find the freshest vegetables (aside from your own garden) as well as homemade jams, and warm, salty boiled peanuts to snack on while you examine the produce.

Vegetables are a dieter's best friend and a primary staple of a vegetarian's larder. Vegetables are also the "cure" for many dietary deficiencies, from carrots for beta carotene to potatoes for potassium. But this food group was not always so popular in our country. From the sixteenth century to the early 1900s, many vegetables were believed to be unwholesome or poisonous, especially when raw or undercooked. They were often linked to illnesses and death, when more than likely it was the polluted waters in which they were washed, or the fact that they were eaten during epidemics, that were to blame. The excessive boiling of vegetables probably rose out of these fears and remains a practice that continues today in most of the South.

In the seventeenth century, "vegetables" to those living in the Southern colonies meant potatoes, pumpkin, cabbage, and a few root crops. For the next 100 years, vegetables, unlike grains and meats, did not play a large role in the American diet, partially because of plant diseases and poor gardening practices. Vegetables were especially limited in winter, when potatoes were often the only vegetable available.

In the nineteenth century, some wealthy planters had extensive gardens, but for most Southerners, vegetables were limited to sweet potatoes, cabbage, okra, turnips, collards, pumpkins, cowpeas, and, in the spring, wild dandelion and pokeweed. During the Civil War, vegetables were scarce in Southern cities, so herbs and edible flowers—when they could be gotten—were consumed instead.

Following the war, there was an increase in vegetable production in the South (notably tomatoes, radishes, cucumbers, spinach, cauliflower, eggplant, and salad greens) for Northern markets. Then, from 1900 to 1930 there was a substantial rise in vegetable consumption in some regions of the South. They were still well cooked, however, since partially cooked vegetables were believed to transmit cholera. During this same time in rural areas, many Southerners still subsisted on pork, cornbread, greens, and coffee—a limited diet that faded out as the Depression receded. After World War I, the consumption of fresh vegetables across the country dropped, while that of canned and frozen vegetables rose. Large conglomerates were processing food on a massive scale and savvy public relations departments persuaded the homemaker that these "new" vegetables were a more modern approach to cooking.

In the 1960s and 1970s, an interest in nutrition, ecology, and Eastern religions (many which espouse vegetarianism) led to a slight increase in fresh vegetable consumption. But it was not until the next decade, the '80s, when nutritional findings made by medical experts revealed the health benefits of vegetables, that a significant increase in vegetables (fresh, frozen, and canned) resulted.

Today, Southern supermarkets offer an ever-growing array of produce. Green markets are popular all over the country (there are numerous open-air markets in New York City where farmers from as far south as North Carolina sell their wares) offering the cook just-picked produce that is usually more flavorful, less adulterated, and less costly than the supermarket equivalent. Gourmet food stores have sprung up across the country and carry specialty produce—such as fresh fennel and haricots verts—that were once nearly impossible to procure outside major metropolitan areas. They also often carry produce found in the wilds such as ramps from the West Virginia mountains. Thanks to these shops, a New Yorker can buy Vidalia onions from Georgia and a Southerner can buy fiddlehead ferns from New England.

Presently, the South provides the rest of the country with fresh corn, tomatoes, squash, cabbage, eggplant, bell peppers, and sweet potatoes. Southern snap beans, cucumbers, corn, and peas are commercially processed and sold nation-wide. No matter where you live in the United States, that frozen corn and that canned sauerkraut on your pantry shelf are most likely from the South.

Southern vegetables have the unfortunate reputation of being mushy, greasy, overcooked, and lacking in nutrition. It is not uncommon in rural areas for the cook to put the vegetables on to boil right after breakfast, then cook them—often with a piece of smoked pork—until the noon meal. They emerge deliciously rich in flavor yet often lacking in texture. (Southerners aren't alone in their penchant for overcooked vegetables. Fannie Farmer, for example, in her 1906 edition of *The Boston Cooking School Cookbook,* says to boil string beans up to three hours, and vegetables in general "until soft.") Green beans and other vegetables simply blanched for two minutes retain more crunch and nutrition than those boiled for two hours. But most die-hard Southerners—from the farmer to the banker—are passionate about the long-simmered, deeply flavored, pork-enhanced vegetables that they grew up with. I love cooked-all-morning vegetables too, but I usually don't prepare them that way. It's too time consuming and too many vitamins are lost in the process. Texture is one of the delights of the vegetable, so unless it is to be puréed to make a soup or sauce, it seems a crime to cook it to mush. I remember as a five-year-old being forced to "take just one bite" of stewed summer squash. I knew that this warm, lumpy mass, still with its slippery seeds, was not fit to eat. That must have been the beginning of my campaign to cook most vegetables only until crisp-tender.

Vegetable Side Dishes I feel that for most everyday home-cooked meals it is best to let only one dish be the star. If the main course is rich and highly seasoned, keep the accompanying vegetables simple and light. On the other hand, if the main course is relatively unadorned (roast chicken, broiled steak, grilled fish, or sautéed tofu—enhanced with not much more than salt and pepper and pan juices) then vegetable side dishes can be more complex in flavor and richer in ingredients.

In the Southern tradition, many of the vegetables here are flavored with cured pork. If you are on a sodium-free or meatless diet, in most cases the pork may be omitted. In nearly every recipe, the amount of butter or oil can be reduced to suit your taste or dietary needs, and yogurt may be substituted for sour cream or heavy cream in some recipes. The resulting dish will not be as rich or full flavored, but you will save calories and minimize your sodium intake.

Greens

Portia opened a paper sack she had placed on the kitchen table.

"I done brought a nice mess of collard greens and I thought maybe we have supper together. I done brought a piece of side meat, too. These here greens need to be seasoned with that."

—Carson McCullers, *The Heart Is a Lonely Hunter*

IN OTHER PARTS of the United States, the term "greens" is often used rather loosely, referring to lettuces or to green vegetables in general. But in the South, the term refers specifically to the leaves or shoots of certain vegetables or herbs (the kind that are often descriptively called "potherbs") that are cooked in water with pork or pork drippings. A "mess of greens" can include cultivated varieties like kale, collards, turnip, and mustard greens, and, to a lesser extent, rapeweed (which resembles turnip greens but has an oilier, more bitter taste), plus certain wild species such as pokeweed, dandelion, purslane, and the wild cresses. Chickweed, lamb's-quarters, dock, and amaranth are also gathered and eaten in the traditional Southern manner, but to a lesser degree. Greens range in assertiveness from mild—such as kale—to the more moderate watercress and dandelion, to mustard greens, the most pungent of all. Young, tender greens can be eaten raw, while older, stronger-tasting greens must be cooked to eliminate their tough texture and bitterness. I find that greens have released most of their bitterness after about 10 minutes of cooking in boiling water. Longer cooking creates a richer tasting "pot likker," but it also destroys fiber and vitamins.

Greens must be harvested at their peak then carefully washed and picked over. Then they are usually simmered with smoked pork—either ham hock, fatback, salt pork, or slab bacon and often a hot pepper pod—long enough to yield "pot likker." Sometimes they are simply wilted with warm pork drippings, either in the skillet or in the salad bowl. Greens have held an important place on the Southern table—from Tara to Graceland—for well over a century, and there is perhaps no other vegetable that is quite so unique to the region.

Since cultivated greens are easier to be had—most grocery stores and farmers' markets carry at least one or two kinds—they are more widely consumed. Wild greens, on the other hand, can be enjoyed only when in season. Pokeweed, for example, tastes best in spring, before summer's heat turns its leaves tough and bitter. The same goes for dandelion, a popular spring "tonic."

Prepared in the traditional manner, a bowl of greens with "pot likker" is not exactly tea-party fare. We're talking earthy aromas and strong, eye-opening flavors. This is a dish for body and soul, one that originated in an era when sodium was not a health issue, but something you cured ham with.

Collards and their like have strong personalities, important in a region where, like Provence, heat and humidity often dull the palate, which demands shouting flavors and a contrast of textures. They nevertheless marry well with an array of foods, their natural bitterness acting as a welcome foil to other items on the traditional Southern plate. A hearty, old-fashioned noontime meal, for example, might include something salty (ham or bacon), something sweet (syrupy iced tea and candied sweet potatoes), something starchy (black-eyed peas or rice) and something rich (fried pork chops or fried chicken—definitely fried something). And it goes without saying that there would be plenty of cornbread or hot biscuits for sponging up gravy and "pot likker."

Frozen greens, by the way, are just as nutritious as fresh—perhaps even more so since they are processed immediately after picking. You can substitute frozen greens in all the recipes here except for the salads. Perhaps frozen greens' biggest asset is that they are already washed and trimmed; they need only be thawed (the microwave oven does this beautifully) and drained and they're ready to use. Since frozen greens are precooked, cooking times should be reduced so that the greens do not become mushy.

Mustard Greens
with Warm Walnut Vinaigrette
• • •

THE MOST COMMON VARIETY of mustard greens in our markets has bright green, fuzzy oval leaves with ruffled edges. Collards or turnip tops—or a mixture of various strong-flavored greens may be used instead. Quick blanching eliminates excessive bitterness; the warm, nutty dressing adds a rich, mellow note.

Like a crisp, white wine, greens can have an astringent, rather cleansing effect in the mouth and can cut right through many rich, unctuous foods. I've found that greens not only pair up well with fried chicken and gravy, but also with cream, buttery cheeses, nuts and nut oils, and rich-tasting meats and fish, like calves liver, foie gras, sweetbreads, pâté, grilled salmon, and shad roe.

Use half the amount of oil and nuts if you are watching your fat intake. Serve as a side dish with Veal Chops with Savory Sweet Potato Sauce (page 241); Quick Pork Chops with Orange-Molasses Glaze (page 220); or Quick Lamb Scallops with Herbed Egg Sauce (page 245). This dish is also good with broiled, grilled, or pan-cooked pork, veal, or lamb chops or scallops; grilled or broiled chicken, game, or beef.

1 pound fresh mustard greens (or substitute collards or turnip greens), washed and drained
2 tablespoons walnut oil
1 teaspoon vegetable oil

2 teaspoons red wine vinegar
Pinch of salt
Freshly ground black pepper, to taste
½ cup chopped walnuts, lightly toasted

1. Drop greens into a large pot of boiling, salted water and cook uncovered 5 to 10 minutes, or until bitterness is gone but greens still have a mild "bite" (timing will depend on size, age, and variety of greens).

2. Drain well in a colander or sieve and press with the back of a wooden spoon to release water. Chop greens coarsely and set aside.

3. In a small saucepan, heat walnut oil and vegetable oil over low heat until warm but not hot. Whisk in vinegar, salt, and pepper. In a bowl, toss greens with warm vinaigrette and walnuts and serve immediately.

Serves 4.

Sautéed Collard Greens
with Dijon Mustard and Sour Cream
. . .

Eagerness came into Dr. Copland's face. He crumbled his hoecake into the collard juice on his plate and began to eat with a new appetite.

—Carson McCullers, *The Heart Is a Lonely Hunter*

COLLARD GREENS came to America from Africa and have been a popular staple in the South ever since. In the late 1800s collard greens were, in fact, often the only green vegetable available throughout the winter months. They have a mild, cabbage-y flavor.

In this quick and easy recipe, sour cream and mustard add a pleasant tang that complements the greens' natural bitterness. Cut the amount of butter and sour cream in half if you are dieting, or substitute plain yogurt for the sour cream, taking care not to overheat the mixture or the yogurt may curdle.

This rather homey side dish is good with Spicy Fried Chicken (page 182); Veal Chops with Savory Sweet Potato Sauce (page 241); Pork Chops Smothered with Fennel and Garlic (page 221), or grilled or broiled veal scallops, pork chops, steak, swordfish, tuna, grouper, halibut, or cod.

1 to 1 ¼ pounds collard greens (or substitute turnip, mustard, or beet greens)
3 tablespoons butter
1 medium-sized yellow onion, very finely diced

¼ cup sour cream
1 tablespoon Dijon mustard
Pinch of ground red pepper (cayenne)
Salt and freshly ground black pepper, to taste

1. Remove coarse stems from greens and discard. Wash leaves thoroughly and drain well. Stack leaves and cut crosswise, then cut lengthwise into 1-inch pieces.

2. Drop the greens into a large pot of lightly salted boiling water. Cook uncovered 5 to 10 minutes, or until just tender. Timing will depend on age and size of greens; very young greens will need only 1 minute. Drain thoroughly.

Vegetables
■

3. Meanwhile, in a large, nonaluminum skillet, melt butter over medium heat. Add onion, cover, and cook, stirring frequently, 5 minutes or until softened. Add drained greens and toss to coat.

4. In a small bowl combine sour cream, mustard, and red pepper with a fork. Add to greens and cook, stirring frequently, 3 to 5 minutes or until liquid has almost evaporated. Season with salt and pepper and serve warm.

Serves 4.

Turnips and Turnip Greens with Ginger and Garlic

∎ ∎ ∎

She was the kind of cook who would heap up your plate with such as ham hock, greens, black-eyed peas, fried fish, cabbage, sweet potatoes, grits and gravy, and cornbread. And the more you put away, the better she felt. I worked out at Ella's kitchen table like there was no tomorrow.

—Malcolm X, *The Autobiography of Malcolm X*

TURNIP GREENS, also known as turnip tops and turnip salad, are available year-round, peaking November through March. Greens from baby turnips can be used in summer when mature turnip tops—often quite bitter at this time of year—are hard to find.

Neither Scarlett nor Elvis would have been served turnip greens with garlic and ginger, but one only has to look to the Far East to know that bitter greens stand up beautifully to aggressive seasonings. Cured pork is the classic Southern accompaniment to greens, but here I've used soy sauce as a saline substitute. Serve this dish as a side dish to fried shrimp or oysters, smoked or grilled pork chops, pork-fried rice from your favorite Chinese take-out restaurant, roast chicken, or barbecued ribs. Or, spoon over rice and sprinkle with julienned country ham for a simple supper accompanied by a cold beer.

Some Southern cooks always cook the turnips along with their greens, but some varieties of turnip greens don't even produce a turnip root. In the ingredients list I call for the greens and turnips separately as they are usually not sold together, and when they are, the weights of leaves and roots will vary with type and maturity of the vegetable. If you use baby turnips, your dish will have a more refined contemporary look, but larger, more mature turnips, will offer more flavor.

½ pound turnips (about 4 2-inch turnips), trimmed, peeled, and diced into ½-inch cubes (or substitute whole, unpeeled baby turnips, trimmed)

2 tablespoons vegetable oil or cold-pressed light sesame oil

3 medium-large cloves garlic, minced

1 tablespoon minced, peeled fresh gingerroot (about ¾-inch piece gingerroot)

¼ cup water

1½ pounds trimmed turnip greens (because greens vary in size and maturity, you will probably need about 2½ pounds untrimmed turnip greens), washed well, drained, and chopped into 1-inch pieces

2½ teaspoons sugar

2 tablespoons soy sauce or tamari

1. In a vegetable steamer set over boiling water steam the turnips, covered, 2 to 3 minutes or until crisp-tender. Do not overcook. Set aside.

2. In a large skillet heat the oil over low heat. Add garlic and ginger and cook, stirring frequently, until garlic just releases its fragrance, about 1 minute.

3. Add water and raise heat so mixture simmers gently. Add the turnip greens by handfuls, letting them wilt slightly before adding the next handful as the skillet becomes full. Cook uncovered, stirring frequently, 5 minutes or until greens are wilted and crisp-tender. (Do not raise heat or garlic may burn and will taste bitter.)

4. While greens cook, in a small cup or bowl combine sugar and soy sauce. Add to greens and toss to mix. Simmer uncovered 2 minutes. Add turnips, toss to coat, and continue to simmer uncovered until most of the liquid has evaporated and turnips are lightly glazed, about 3 minutes.

Serves 4.

Note If serving with Spicy Fried Chicken, unless you're a real garlic lover you may want to reduce or eliminate garlic in the chicken marinade.

Sautéed Watercress and Radicchio
with Pepper Vinegar

• • •

IN RURAL AREAS, wild watercress (also called creasies, field cress, pepper grass, "cressies," or "creasy greens") are found along slow-moving streams and rivers and around the edges of lakes or in bottomland. Wild watercress is available year-round, although leaves are milder during cooler months. Upland cress is one wild variety; other kinds are native varieties hybridized with cultivated varieties that had escaped to the wild. Cultivated watercress is milder in flavor, is widely available in markets, and is highly nutritious. Mildly bitter and very tender, it can be eaten raw or cooked. Here, it's sautéed with radicchio and served warm, sprinkled with homemade pepper vinegar, a milder version of the fiery Dixie condiment of vinegar infused with Tabasco peppers. (The pepper vinegar should be made in advance. If you forget to make it, simply mix distilled white vinegar and Tabasco sauce to taste.) Serve with Peanut and Ham–Stuffed Chicken with Cider Sauce (page 192); Spicy Fried Chicken (page 182); Veal Scallops with Cider Cream, Onion Confit, and Glazed Apples (page 242); Veal Chops with Savory Sweet Potato Sauce (page 241); or Quick Pork Chops with Orange-Molasses Glaze (page 220).

½ cup distilled white vinegar

1 small whole dried red pepper (or 2 teaspoons dried red pepper flakes)

4 tablespoons butter

¾ pound watercress, trimmed of very tough stems, washed well and dried

1 medium-small head radicchio, washed well, dried and leaves separated

Salt and freshly ground black pepper, to taste

1. To make the pepper vinegar: In a cup or small bowl, combine the vinegar with the pepper or red pepper flakes. Cover and let stand at least 8 hours. Strain into a clean bottle and cap tightly.

2. In a large skillet heat butter over medium-low heat. Add watercress and radicchio and toss to coat with butter. Cover and cook, tossing once or twice,

for 4 or 5 minutes or until wilted but crisp-tender. Serve hot, letting each guest sprinkle pepper vinegar and salt and pepper over his or her serving.

Serves 4.

Julienned Beets
and Beet Greens with Ham

■ ■ ■

BEET GREENS are not as popular in the South as collards, turnip tops, or mustard greens, a fact that has always surprised me since they share similar texture and flavor. The South commercially produces a limited quantity of beets, but consumption is growing. Some Southerners still view beets as poor-man's fare, but with increased knowledge of nutrition and health, more Southerners are eating their beets.

The earthy, slightly sweet flavor of both beet roots and greens is a pleasant foil to the salty, smoky ham. Since the beets are julienned, they cook quickly. Serve with Spicy Fried Chicken (page 182); Quick Lamb Scallops with Herbed Egg Sauce (page 245); or Breast of Veal with Herbed Rice Stuffing (page 239).

2 pounds beets (about 2 inches in diameter), with greens
5 tablespoons unsalted butter (or less, if using a nonstick skillet)
3 ounces Smithfield ham (or other dry-cured country ham), minced or

julienned (for mail-order source, see page 481)
¼ cup sour cream or crème fraîche (optional)
Freshly ground black pepper, to taste

1. Trim beets and peel with a vegetable peeler. Cut into julienne strips or grate coarsely. Set aside.

2. Remove and discard tough stems from the greens. Wash well, drain, then chop greens into 1-inch pieces. Set aside.

3. In a skillet, heat 1 tablespoon butter over medium-low heat. Add ham and cook, stirring frequently, 1 minute, or until pale golden-brown. Drain on paper towels and set aside.

Vegetables

■

4. Heat 2 tablespoons butter in the same skillet, and remaining 2 tablespoons butter in an additional 10- to 12-inch skillet over medium heat. Add beets to one skillet, the greens to another. Toss to coat, then cover and cook each 5 minutes, stirring once or twice, until crisp-tender. Off the heat, stir the sour cream into the beets. Stir half the ham into the greens. Serve a mound of beets on top of or alongside a mound of greens and sprinkle remaining ham over all. Season with freshly ground pepper.

Serves 4.

Note To serve as a room-temperature vegetable for a buffet or picnic, substitute olive oil mixed with vegetable oil for the butter.

Broccoli Rabe
with Anchovy–Red Pepper Butter
∎ ∎ ∎

ALTHOUGH BROCCOLI RABE is related to the turnip and shares its pungency, it is actually a kind of broccoli, which it closely resembles. Broccoli rabe is too bitter and tough to eat raw, but requires very little cooking to extract its bitterness. Here, it is dressed with a pungent, make-ahead red pepper butter that is redolent with garlic and has a hint of anchovy paste to counterbalance the sweetness of the peppers. (Anchovies were a popular seasoning in eighteenth- and nineteenth-century Southern cooking.) Serve warm as a side dish to grilled pork or veal chops, roast chicken, or broiled steak.

2 medium-sized red bell peppers
2 medium cloves garlic
6 tablespoons unsalted butter, room temperature
1 tablespoon tomato paste, room temperature

1 teaspoon anchovy paste, room temperature
1½ pounds broccoli rabe, trimmed of tough ends, well washed and drained

1. To prepare the red peppers: Place peppers on a lightly oiled foil-lined broiler pan. Broil 2 inches from preheated broiler until black and blistered all

over. Place peppers in a brown paper bag and let cool to room temperature. Peel the peppers and discard seeds and core. Purée in a food processor or blender. Set purée aside; wash and dry food processor. (Or, purée drained pimientos from a 4-ounce jar.)

2. To prepare red pepper butter: In the clean blender or food processor, with the machine running, drop in garlic cloves and process until well chopped. Add the butter, red pepper purée, tomato paste, and anchovy paste and process until well blended. (Note: Anchovy–red pepper butter may be made up to 1 week in advance.) Scrape the flavored butter onto a sheet of waxed paper and form it into a 1-inch-thick cylinder. Wrap and chill until firm; slice when ready to serve.

3. Drop broccoli rabe into large pot of boiling water and cook 5 minutes or until crisp-tender. (Or steam 8 to 9 minutes.)

4. Drain broccoli rabe and serve hot with a thin slice (about 2 teaspoons) of red pepper butter.

Serves 4.

Note Use any remaining anchovy–red pepper butter to dress other vegetables such as green beans, broccoli, or greens.

Broccoli with Sesame Seed Sauce

∙ ∙ ∙

BROCCOLI MADE AN APPEARANCE in the New World as early as 1720 and by 1775 John Randolph of Williamsburg wrote of it in *A Treatise on Gardening by a Citizen of Virginia,* "The stems will eat like asparagus and the heads like cauliflower."

Thomas Jefferson planted broccoli in his Monticello garden and by the mid-1800s broccoli was a vegetable enjoyed in both Virginia and South Carolina where it was usually boiled and served with butter. Broccoli disappeared from the American table briefly, but was reintroduced in the twentieth century by Italian immigrants who served it with garlic and olive oil. In the South, butter or hollandaise sauce appears to have been preferred. In our house, hollandaise was the sauce my mother and grandmother always served with this vegetable on special occasions; for family suppers, it was dressed with butter.

Until recently, fresh broccoli consumed in the Southeast was either grown in California or in local backyard gardens. In 1985, however, Virginia and North Carolina began growing broccoli commercially as a result of research, by those states' departments of agriculture, to find supplementary crops for tobacco farmers. When the tobacco harvest is over, the first broccoli comes in and continues until Christmas, unless autumn is unusually cold. In Louisiana farmers growing soybean, sugar cane, and corn are also looking to broccoli as a possible secondary crop.

Now that Southerners have fresher broccoli, plus the fact that its rich nutritional properties are becoming widely known, they are eating more of it than ever before. The leading Southern varieties are green comet and green duke.

Broccoli can be prepared in many ways, but I particularly like it simmered in chicken broth and white wine. In this recipe I add minced onions to the cooking liquid, which is then reduced and whisked into a mixture of sesame oil, sesame paste, and red wine vinegar. (Sesame seeds—also known as benne seeds—were a symbol of good luck in the South.) The resulting sauce is rich, but less fattening—and healthier since it has no cholesterol—than the proverbial hollandaise. Serve as a side dish with Veal Chops with Savory Sweet Potato Sauce (page 241); Steak with Bourbon-Ginger Sauce (page 235); or grilled or broiled fish, chicken, chops, or sautéed tofu or tempeh.

BROCCOLI

1 pound broccoli
2 teaspoons dark oriental sesame oil (available in oriental markets and specialty food stores)
2 teaspoons vegetable oil
1 small, yellow onion, chopped

2 cups unsalted chicken broth, preferably homemade (Note: If using canned broth seek out broth without salt or the resulting sauce will be too salty)
¼ cup dry white wine

SAUCE

2 tablespoons tahini (Middle Eastern sesame paste; available in health-food stores or specialty food stores)

2 teaspoons dark oriental sesame oil
2 teaspoons red wine vinegar
Salt and freshly ground white pepper, to taste

1. Wash the broccoli. Trim stalks with a sharp paring knife or vegetable peeler and cut stalks into ½-inch pieces. Cut heads into small florets.

2. In a large skillet, heat 2 teaspoons sesame oil with 2 teaspoons vegetable oil over medium heat. Add onions and cook 2 minutes. Add broccoli and cook, stirring frequently, 1 minute. Add broth and wine and simmer uncovered 3 to 4 minutes or until crisp-tender, stirring frequently. With slotted spoon, remove broccoli to warmed serving platter and keep warm. Boil the cooking liquid in the skillet until it is reduced to ¼ cup.

3. While the liquid reduces, in a bowl whisk together the sauce ingredients until smooth. Slowly add the reduced broth to the sauce, whisking constantly. Pour sauce over broccoli and serve hot.

Serves 4.

Fresh Pea Purée

. . .

IN THE SOUTH, green peas are also known as English peas or, less frequently, May peas (a term distinguishing them from the so-called "Southern peas"; for more about Southern peas, see page 270). Green peas were one of the many plants imported to the New World that fared better on American soil than it did Europe. Peas were a favorite of Thomas Jefferson, who cultivated over thirty varieties. Throughout the New World, peas were a spring delicacy after a long winter limited to root vegetables, cabbage, and collards. Neighbors often competed to have the first peas, and it is said that Thomas Jefferson won the local "contest" so regularly that one year he told his daughter to let a neighbor believe that he had won.

Perhaps it is because of their delicate flavor and fleeting freshness that peas have always been prepared rather simply. In Sarah Rutledge's *The Carolina Housewife* (1847), "Green Peas à la bourgeoise" calls for stewing peas with butter, sugar, and cabbage, then thickening the cooking liquid with egg yolks and cream. In *The Virginia House-wife* (1824), the author, Mary Randolph, instructs: "To have them [peas] in perfection, they must be quite young, gathered early in the morning, kept in a cool place, and not shelled until they are to be dressed; put salt in the water, and when it boils, put in the peas; boil them quick twenty or thirty minutes, according to their age; just before they are taken up, add a little mint chopped very fine, drain all the water from the peas, put in a bit of butter, and serve them up quite hot." In the same book, mint also flavors a soup of dried green peas.

Other old Southern recipes of the same era call for simmering fresh peas with lettuce, in the classic French manner, or combining them with salt pork and tiny new potatoes for a heartier dish. English peas are grown commercially in Maryland and Virginia and in home gardens throughout the South.

The recipe below is a nod to Mary Randolph's combination of mint and peas—a successful marriage that seems to capture the freshness and the very essence of spring. If you are watching your fat intake, use only 2 tablespoons butter and cream. Serve with Easy Lamb Patties with Spring Greens and Creole Mustard Sauce (page 247); Broiled Soft-Shell Crabs with Vidalia-Butter Sauce (page 168); substitute orange zest for the mint and serve with Lamb Chops with Vidalia-Mint Butter (page 248); or use any of the seasonings and serve with simply prepared lamb, chicken, or fish.

4 cups shelled fresh peas (4 pounds in the shell)
4 tablespoons (or less, to taste) butter, room temperature
3 to 4 tablespoons heavy cream
1/4 to 1/2 teaspoon salt

Flavorings (choose one of the seasonings below):
1 to 2 teaspoons minced fresh mint
1 1/2 tablespoons minced fresh basil
1 1/2 tablespoons minced fresh chives
1/2 to 1 teaspoon curry powder
1/2 to 1 teaspoon minced fresh dill
1/2 teaspoon orange zest

1. In a small saucepan, cook peas in lightly salted boiling water to cover for 6 to 10 minutes, until tender. Drain.

2. Purée cooked peas in food processor or blender until smooth. Press through a sieve into saucepan and discard skins. Place over medium-low heat and stir in butter and enough cream to produce a smooth—but not loose—consistency. Add salt, to taste, and *one* of the flavorings.

Serves 4.

Corn

THE WORD MAIZE refers to all types of corn, but it has commonly come to mean the decorative Indian flint corn that adorns front doors from September through Thanksgiving. Maize was one of the first foods introduced to the Jamestown settlers by the Indians in 1607. It was the staff of life for the Native Americans and perhaps their greatest culinary contribution to the North American diet. Sweet corn (also called sugar corn) is the type we most often eat fresh as a vegetable: as corn on the cob, in corn puddings, etc. It has a greater proportion of sugar to starch than any other type of corn. (For more about corn, see page 261)

Sweet corn was found along the Susquehanna River, which flows into the Chesapeake Bay in Maryland, as early as 1779. But it would be another forty years before farmers paid much attention to it, and another twenty years before it made a frequent appearance on the table as a vegetable. Up until about 1920, corn eaten as a fresh vegetable was actually "green" corn, the immature ears of any corn species. In the South "green" corn was stewed, creamed, fried in pork drippings, roasted, eaten on the cob, or used in making custards, puddings, and succotash. Fresh corn was often preserved by canning, drying (dried corn was reconstituted and boiled before serving), or packed in brine, like sauerkraut.

Sweet corn is grown in the South for both the fresh market and for processing, with the Silver Queen variety being one of the most popular. Some states are growing varieties called Super Sweets. Fresh Southern sweet corn is shipped across the country. Corn is second only to potatoes as a leading crop in Alabama; and is one of Florida's most important commercially produced vegetables.

Quick Corn, Tomato, and Bacon Sauté

■ ■ ■

IT IS QUITE COMMON in the South to serve cooked corn off the cob. Here, it is combined with sweet, ripe tomatoes, smoky bacon, and a subtle hint of garlic. This quick, easy dish has a easy, down-home appeal that makes it a good accompaniment to Grandmother's Roast Lemon Chicken (page 183); Grilled Catfish with Two Sauces (page 154), or any simply prepared chicken, chops, hamburgers, or steaks. To serve at room temperature as part of a buffet or for a picnic, use olive oil instead of bacon drippings (bacon drippings solidify if not kept warm).

6 slices bacon
2 cups fresh whole corn kernels (or substitute 1 10-ounce package frozen corn kernels, thawed)
2 large cloves garlic, finely chopped
2 medium-sized firm, ripe tomatoes, chopped (or substitute 8 to 10 cherry tomatoes, washed, stemmed, and cut into eighths)
Salt and freshly ground black pepper, to taste

1. In a large skillet, cook bacon over medium heat until golden-brown and crisp. Set aside on paper towels to drain. Pour off all but 2 tablespoons of the pan drippings.

2. Add corn to the skillet. Add just enough water to cover kernels. (Omit water if using thawed, frozen corn.) Simmer until crisp-tender and water has evaporated. (For thawed frozen corn, stir-fry until heated through.)

3. Add garlic and cook, stirring frequently, 1 minute or until garlic releases its fragrance. (Do not cook over high heat or garlic may burn and taste bitter.)

4. Add tomatoes and toss to mix. Warm through over low heat about 2 minutes. Season with salt and pepper to taste. Crumble bacon on top and serve hot.

Serves 4.

Tomatoes

THIS SOUTH AMERICAN VEGETABLE was not cultivated in the New World until the eighteenth century. At this time, most of the few Americans who had heard of the tomato held on to an age-old myth that it was poisonous. The tomato is a member of the so-called "nightshade" family of vegetables, which also includes eggplant and potatoes. Indeed, some part of each nightshade plant contains naturally occurring toxins. The edible part of the potato, for example, is harmless but all other parts of the plant—roots, vines, etc.—contain poisonous substances that can, in extremely large amounts, be harmful. In the case of the tomato, unripe specimens contain the naturally occurring poison solanine, but it is in such very small quantities that the green tomato is harmless.

By 1770, tomatoes were being grown in home gardens in Charleston and in 1781 at Monticello by Thomas Jefferson. Other Virginians were growing tomatoes for their own tables at this time as well.

Even through much of the nineteenth century, Americans remained wary of the "tomata," as it was often called. Most Southern recipes call for cooking the fruit, sometimes for up to four hours—a practice that may have been a cautionary measure to destroy suspected toxins as well as to mellow the tomato's natural acidity. Sugar was frequently added to cooked tomatoes, which may have been another way to balance an otherwise naturally acrid taste. In *The Carolina Housewife* (1847), Sarah Rutledge instructs: "The art of cooking tomatoes lies mostly in cooking them enough. In whatever way prepared, they should be put on some hours before dinner. This vegetable is good in all soups and stews where such a decided flavoring is wanted." Mrs. Rutledge would not be pleased with our insatiable appetites for fresh, raw, sliced summer tomatoes!

Stewed tomatoes were very popular on the nineteenth-century Southern table. They were usually sliced and cooked gently with butter and sometimes breadcrumbs, then eaten as a side dish or added to omelettes. Another popular dish was baked tomatoes. Whole tomatoes were scooped out, then filled with a mixture of buttered breadcrumbs and the mashed, strained tomato flesh taken from the cavity. Creole cooks often added minced ham or veal to the filling. Tomatoes were also "scalloped"—peeled, covered with breadcrumbs, salt, pepper, and butter, then baked. Green tomatoes—and sometimes ripe red ones—were often floured, fried, and served with pan gravy. Tomatoes were preserved by sun-drying them or by turning them into tomato paste or catsup.

By 1900, Southern farmers began propagating tomatoes on a widespread basis, and by 1929 Americans were eating thirty-six pounds of tomatoes per capita annually. Cooked tomatoes continued to be popular in the early part of the twentieth century. They were simmered with okra to make gumbos or pilaus, added to rice to make red rice (see my recipe Double-Red Rice, page 255), and in Louisiana, Creoles made soup with fresh tomatoes. Recipes for tomato pudding (sometimes called tomato pie) appear frequently in early to mid-twentieth-century cookbooks. Tomato pudding is similar to scalloped tomatoes, but often included large amounts of brown or granulated sugar. Sugar was also added to stewed tomatoes and stuffed, baked tomatoes.

Sautéed Green Tomatoes with Rosemary-Browned Butter

■ ■ ■

THIS VERSION of fried green tomatoes is lighter than the classic dish. Despite the browned butter topping, which *is* rich, the tomatoes here lack the traditional thick batter coating and lard. The rosemary-flavored butter adds a herbaceous, yet mellow, note. Serve with Grandmother's Roast Lemon Chicken (page 183) or with any grilled or broiled chicken, pork chops, veal chops, lamb chops, or fish. Serve with plenty of Crusty Cornmeal Yeast Bread (page 36) or French bread for savoring every last bit of the brown butter.

5 to 6 tablespoons clarified butter (To make clarified butter, heat 8 tablespoons unsalted butter in a small saucepan until foamy. Carefully skim off and discard foam. Carefully pour off and reserve the clear yellow liquid, which is the clarified butter. Discard the milky white solids in the bottom of saucepan.)

3 large or 4 medium-large firm, green tomatoes, sliced ¼ inch to ⅓ inch thick (about 5 slices from each tomato)

1½ teaspoons dried rosemary (or 1½ tablespoons fresh rosemary), crumbled

Salt and freshly ground black pepper, to taste

1. Preheat oven to 200° F.

2. Heat half the clarified butter in each of 2 large skillets over medium-high heat. Add tomatoes and cook about 2 to 3 minutes on each side or until golden-brown and slightly crisp. (Note: Watch carefully; the butter should be nutty brown, not burned.) Remove tomatoes with slotted spatula or spoon to an ovenproof platter and keep warm in the oven.

3. Pour the butter from one skillet to the other to consolidate. Add rosemary and warm through, about 30 seconds. Pour the butter over the warm tomatoes and season to taste with salt and pepper. Serve hot.

Serves 4 to 6 as a side dish.

Okra

Okra can be boiled, but I've never seen a kid yet that would eat it.

—Michael Andrew Grissom, *Southern by the Grace of God*

AUTHORITIES ARE DIVIDED on okra's birthplace. Some say it is from the Nile Valley, but most believe it originated in northeast India or Africa. It was via African slaves that okra, a member of the mallow family, reached North America. The vegetable flourished in the temperate Southern climate and even Thomas Jefferson was growing okra by 1781. Although it was an important part of the Southern diet by the nineteenth century, recipes were somewhat limited. Because sliced okra becomes mucilaginous when cooked in liquids, okra was often used specifically *for* its thickening abilities in smothered dishes and gumbos. Okra was also fried in lard or boiled whole and served as a side dish.

Today, although okra is usually associated with Louisiana and gumbo, it is the state of Georgia that leads the South in okra production, with Louisiana running in second place. Okra is commercially grown throughout the South. The demand has increased in some areas partially because of the popularity of Cajun cooking and salad bars, where pickled okra frequently appears.

Because of its somewhat slimy quality, okra is really a love-it or loathe-it vegetable. However, when whole okra is fried, pickled, sautéed, or eaten raw,

Vegetables
■

this unique characteristic is virtually nonexistent. It is okra's seedy interior that seems to be behind slime production. Slice the pods and subject them to moisture—be it water, tomatoes, or other liquid—and the okra will become mucilaginous. Dry-heat cooking methods—such as frying and sautéeing—don't seem to have the same slime-producing effect.

Sautéed Okra
with Garlic, Red Pepper, and Herbs
• • •

IN THIS RECIPE, I trim away only the tiny stem, so that the seedy, goo-producing interior remains intact. The pods are then quickly tossed in olive oil flavored with garlic, red pepper, and herbs. Okra is relatively bland and can stand the seasoning. Serve hot or at room temperature. They're even better made several days in advance since they take on the seasoning with time. Serve with Shad Roe with Balsamic Vinegar and Capers (page 146), Fried Oysters (or Clams) with Green Tomato Salsa (page 162), or Grilled Catfish with Two Sauces (page 154). Also good with fish, shrimp, chicken, pork, or veal chops.

1 pound fresh okra, preferably very young and small (about 1½ inches long)

3 tablespoons olive oil

3 large cloves garlic, finely chopped

1 teaspoon dried red pepper flakes

½ teaspoon dried thyme (or 1½ teaspoons fresh thyme)

½ teaspoon dried basil (or 1½ teaspoons chopped fresh basil)

Salt and freshly ground black pepper, to taste

1. Wash okra and pat dry. Trim away stems only, leaving the "cap" intact.
2. Heat 1 tablespoon oil in a large skillet over medium-high heat. Add half the okra (or use 2 skillets if you want to cook all at once) and sauté 3 to 5 minutes or until crisp-tender (timing will depend on size of okra). With slotted

spoon, remove okra to a warm serving platter or bowl. Cover to keep warm. Repeat with second batch of okra, using another tablespoon olive oil as needed, and remove to warm platter.

3. Add remaining tablespoon of oil to the skillet over very low heat. Add garlic, red pepper flakes, thyme, and basil and cook 30 seconds or just until garlic releases its fragrance. Do not overcook or use high heat or garlic may burn and taste bitter. Pour flavored oil over okra and season to taste with salt and pepper.

Serves 4.

Spiced Winter Squash

• • •

THE WORD SQUASH comes from the Narragansett word, *asquatasquash*, meaning "that which is eaten green" or "eaten raw." Most likely the word originally referred to cucumbers and summer squash, members of the *Cucurbitaeeae* family. Squash were being grown by the Native Americans in Virginia as early as 1585. Pumpkins—referred to as "pompions" in early English diaries—were probably the most abundant of the winter squashes and a staple throughout North America. The Native Americans showed the colonists in the North and Southeast how to grow and prepare this native vegetable.

In the seventeenth and eighteenth centuries, pumpkins were cooked whole in hot ashes, stewed, mashed, or baked, often seasoned with brown sugar or smoked meat. Pumpkin blossoms were battered and fried. Pumpkins kept well—but not indefinitely—so savvy cooks peeled, sliced, and hung pieces of pumpkin flesh in front of the fire—or some other dry place—to dry. As time moved on, other winter squashes made their appearance on the Southern table.

Cookbooks from the late nineteenth to early twentieth century include recipes for butternut squash as well as pumpkin; the latter remains in great use in the Northeast. Southern recipes for butternut squash show that it was boiled, mashed, baked, candied, or used in a pie like sweet potatoes or pumpkin.

Today it seems many cooks shy away from winter squash (the most common varieties are pumpkin, butternut, and acorn squash) because they take so

Vegetables

■

long to cook. Even in a microwave oven they can require more time than most other vegetables.

In this recipe squash is peeled and thinly sliced so it cooks quickly. Cinnamon, cloves, ginger, and nutmeg add spiciness; the small amount of honey renders this dish much less sweet than most common winter squash preparations. This savory dish is an ideal accompaniment to Quail Roasted on a Bed of Aromatic Vegetables (page 210); Grandmother's Roast Lemon Chicken (page 183); Easy Lamb Patties with Spring Greens and Creole Mustard Sauce (page 247); Quick Pork Chops with Orange-Molasses Glaze (page 220); Roast Turkey with Herbed Cornbread Dressing (page 196); or any sautéed, roasted, or grilled game or chops.

2¼- to 2½-pound butternut squash
3 tablespoons unsalted butter (or slightly less, if using a nonstick skillet)
1 tablespoon plus 2 teaspoons honey
¼ cup water
2 tablespoons bourbon
⅛ teaspoon ground cinnamon
⅛ teaspoon ground ginger
Pinch of ground cloves
2 teaspoons freshly squeezed lemon juice (or more to taste)
½ teaspoon grated lemon zest
Salt, to taste

1. Trim off the blossom end from the squash and cut the squash in half lengthwise. Cut off the bulbous end and reserve for another use (I like to scoop out the seeds and bake it like acorn squash).

2. Cut each half of the "neck" in half lengthwise and remove peel with a sturdy, sharp paring knife or a good-quality swivel-edged vegetable peeler. Cut each long squash quarter into ¼-inch slices.

3. In 2 10- to 12-inch skillets (or use 1 skillet and cook in 2 batches) melt butter over medium heat. Add squash and cook uncovered 5 minutes, stirring occasionally. Remove from heat.

4. Meanwhile, in a small saucepan, heat honey with water, bourbon, cinnamon, ginger, and cloves until honey dissolves, about 1 minute. Remove from heat and stir in juice and lemon zest.

5. Add half the honey mixture to each skillet and cook uncovered, stirring occasionally, 2 to 5 minutes, or until squash is tender but not mushy and liquid has evaporated to a glaze. Do not overcook. Season to taste with salt, and add more lemon juice if desired.

Serves 4.

Summer Squash

SOUTHERN RECIPES FOR SUMMER SQUASH—specifically yellow crook-neck and straight-neck squash as well as cymlings and mirlitons—are even more plentiful than those for the winter variety.

Yellow straightneck and crookneck squash grow throughout the South and are the most abundant and the most popular of the summer varieties. They have always been prepared rather simply. They are stewed with butter or cream; sliced, coated with cornmeal, and fried; or cooked then mashed with onions, pepper (and sometimes eggs, milk, and bacon) then baked. In some areas, squash cakes—boiled, mashed, floured, and fried patties—are a common side dish.

Cymlings—also known as petticoat or patty pan squash—were recorded in 1705. According to Bill Neal, author of *Bill Neal's Southern Cooking,* the word is from the English "simnel," an English currant cake, the round shape of which the squash is said to resemble. Like yellow squash, cymlings were commonly stewed, mashed, or fried. In her *The Virginia House-wife* (1824), Mary Randolph said that ". . . the most delicate way of preparing squashes" was to peel, seed, boil, and strain them, then cook the purée with butter and cream "until dry." In specialty food stores, you can now find tender, young baby cymlings (about 1½ inches in diameter), which can be sautéed or parboiled whole, then dressed with butter, salt and pepper.

Mirlitons (also known as chayote or vegetable pear) are a subtly flavored pale green squash, native to Central America and the Caribbean. Mirlitons flourish in Louisiana, where they are candied, baked, pickled, or stuffed with ham or seafood mixtures.

Grilled Squash
with Parsley Vinaigrette

...

YELLOW SQUASH has a fresh, slightly sweet, but very mild flavor that I find is enhanced by grilling then dressing with a vinaigrette flavored with scallions and fresh parsley. If yellow squash is unavailable, use zucchini. If you don't have a grill, broil them instead. This easy, fresh-tasting side dish is a good accompaniment to hamburgers, Grandmother's Roast Lemon Chicken (page 183); Poached Red Snapper with Double Tomato Bouillon (page 156); or any grilled poultry, veal, or fish.

½ cup light olive oil

4 tablespoons vegetable oil

2 tablespoons white wine vinegar or red wine vinegar

1 teaspoon Dijon mustard

¼ cup minced scallions or red onions

¼ cup minced fresh parsley

Pinch of salt

Pinch of freshly ground black pepper

6 4- to 5-inch-long yellow squashes or zucchini, halved lengthwise

Olive oil, for brushing

    1. In a bowl, whisk together oils, vinegar, mustard, scallions, parsley, salt and pepper and set aside.

    2. Lightly brush squash all over with olive oil. Place cut-side-down on a grill 4 to 6 inches from medium-hot coals. (Or broil 4 to 6 inches from heat source.) Cook 2 to 5 minutes until golden-brown and lightly crisped, turn and cook 2 to 5 minutes on the other side or until tender. Serve warm or at room temperature drizzled with vinaigrette to taste.

Serves 6.

Baked Yellow Squash
with Chèvre and Corn Stuffing
• • •

STUFFED SQUASH has been a popular dish in the South for years but I object to many of the traditional stuffings (which usually consist of watery boiled squash pulp, breadcrumbs, eggs, and milk), as they can be bland and mushy. Here, I discard the seedy inner flesh, and fill the squash cavities with a mixture of fresh corn kernels, mild goat cheese, and minced scallions. This dish may be prepared partially in advance, so it's good for entertaining. Serve with grilled chicken, fish, roasts, or chops. Or serve as a first course with thinly sliced toasted Whole Wheat Lemon Sally Lunn Bread (page 45), or toasted buttered Basic Biscuits (page 23).

6 small (about 4 inches long) yellow crookneck or straightneck squash

2 ounces mild goat cheese, such as Montrachet or Bûcheron, room temperature (for Southern goat cheese mail-order source, see page 481)

¼ cup chopped scallions

1 cup cooked fresh whole corn kernels (from about 2 ears corn) or substitute thawed, frozen corn kernels

Salt and freshly ground black pepper, to taste

1. In a large saucepot, parboil whole squashes 5 minutes or until barely tender. Cool until easy to handle. Trim ends, cut in half lengthwise, then scoop out and discard seeds, leaving ¼ inch flesh.

2. Preheat oven to 350° F.

3. In a medium bowl, mash the cheese with the scallions. Fold in corn. Divide mixture evenly among hollowed-out squash halves. Place stuffed-side-up in a buttered 9-by-15-inch baking dish. Cover with foil and bake in the upper half of the oven for 15 to 20 minutes or until filling is hot. Sprinkle with salt and pepper to taste and serve hot.

Serves 6.

Sautéed Zucchini "Ribbons" with Bacon and Basil

• • •

IT SEEMS ONLY in recent years that the green squash—zucchini—has been available on a large scale in Southern markets. (I never even *saw* a zucchini until I spent a summer in Rome—at age twenty!) Although many Southern states have grown zucchini for years, most are seeing an increase in demand for this prolific crop. Southerners tend to prepare zucchini as they do other summer squashes— fried or stuffed. In this recipe I cut them lengthwise into paper-thin slices. These "ribbons" are quite pretty and cook in virtually no time at all. Like yellow squash, zucchini is a rather subtle-tasting vegetable, so I like to team it with smoky bacon and aromatic basil. Serve with Shrimp (or Crawfish) with Spicy Chile-Saffron Sauce and Cucumber-Melon Relish (page 166); Fried Oysters (or Clams) with Green Tomato Salsa (page 162); Grilled Catfish with Two Sauces (page 154); or grilled or roasted poultry, lamb, veal, or fish.

1 pound young, tender zucchini (about 6 4-inch zucchini), washed and trimmed

6 slices bacon, cut into 1-inch-wide pieces

2 tablespoons unsalted butter (or less if using a nonstick skillet)

4 teaspoons minced fresh basil (or substitute fresh tarragon, chives, or thyme)

Freshly ground black pepper, to taste

1. Using a vegetable peeler, cut zucchini into very thin lengthwise strips.

2. In a large skillet, cook the bacon until crisp and drain on paper towels. Discard all but 1 tablespoon pan drippings.

3. Add butter and zucchini to skillet and cook over medium-low heat, stirring frequently, 3 to 5 minutes, or until crisp-tender. Add basil or other herb and toss to mix. Serve hot, sprinkled with bacon and pepper to taste.

Serves 4.

Green Beans

She remembered (as one remembers first the eyes of a loved person) the old blue water cooler on the back porch . . . among the round and square wooden tables always piled with snap beans . . .

—Eudora Welty, *Delta Wedding*

WHEN A NON-SOUTHERNER has his first real down-home Southern culinary experience, one of the first things he remarks upon usually are "those overcooked green beans." (That is, of course, unless that meal is breakfast, in which case he will talk about how loathesome grits are.) The fact is, Northerners are guilty of overcooking vegetables, too. Many old non-Southern cookbooks call for boiling beans "until soft."

Even though "snaps" or "string beans" simmered with smoked pork have been a classic component of the Southern meal for at least a century, they did not always play such an important role. Until the nineteenth century, snaps were frequently called French beans. According to cookbook author Madeleine Kamman, "to French" beans means to peel off the strings on both sides of the bean. Frozen "French-style" green beans are cut lengthwise into slivers; possibly in an effort to resemble the very slender, French green beans, haricots verts. In *The Virginia House-wife* (1824), a recipe for "French Beans" instructs the cook to trim, string, and boil the beans for fifteen to twenty minutes. They are then drained and served whole if young. The author adds that "when a little more grown, they must be cut across into two, after stringing; and for common vegetables [I assume this means more mature beans] they are split, and divided across; but those who are nice do not use them at such a growth to require splitting." This suggests that it was more elegant to serve very young, slender beans, but that if more mature beans must be offered, to split them lengthwise and crosswise to make them appear more delicate.

I love old-fashioned, richly flavored, simmered-for-hours beans. I remember as a child coming home from school and inhaling the aromas from "Lottie's beans"; our housekeeper had that extra-special touch that only comes from years of experience with the soul of Southern ingredients. But now that I do my own cooking, I rarely have the time to cook beans—or any vegetable—for an extended period of time.

Vegetables

■

Sautéed Green Beans
with Country Ham
● ● ●

HERE, I'VE TAKEN the revered combination of green beans and smoked pork to new gustatory heights by using tender haricots verts and that queen of all country hams, the Smithfield. This recipe is fast, and can be prepared partially ahead by parboiling the beans one to two hours in advance. Although you won't end up with any "pot likker," these beans retain more fiber and vitamins and can be ready in a moment's notice. Haricots verts are not commercially grown in the South, but may be found in specialty produce markets. Tender, young green beans may be substituted for haricots verts.

1 pound very young, tender green beans, preferably haricots verts, trimmed and washed

2 ounces Smithfield ham (or other dry-cured country ham), julienned (see page 481 for mail-order source)

2 to 3 tablespoons unsalted butter
Freshly ground black pepper, to taste

1. In a large saucepot of lightly salted boiling water, boil beans 1 to 5 minutes or until just crisp-tender. Drain and refresh with cold water. Drain again.

2. In a large skillet over medium heat, cook ham in 2 tablespoons butter, stirring frequently, until golden-brown, about 2 minutes. Reduce heat to medium-low, add beans, and toss to coat, adding more butter if necessary, and cook about 4 minutes or until heated through. Serve hot with freshly ground black pepper.

Serves 4.

Port-Braised
Red Cabbage
• • •

THE JAMESTOWN COLONISTS were growing cabbage at least by 1620 and it has been part of the Southern diet ever since. Cabbage could survive both cold weather and long-term storage so it was a staple during the winter months, adding nutrients to a meager diet based on cornmeal and salt pork. Cabbage was versatile, too, and in some areas of the South it was common for it to appear on the table every day, cooked, raw, or preserved in the form of sauerkraut. Cooked cabbage was usually boiled until very soft, then dressed with butter or pork drippings. More involved preparations included cabbage puddings (heads were stuffed with a spiced-meat mixture then simmered); creamed cabbage (a thickener such as flour or cornstarch was added to the cooking water); fried (chopped leaves were sautéed in bacon drippings); stewed and served with cream gravy; or au gratin (shredded, layered with cream sauce and cheese, and baked). In addition to mature heads, cabbage sprouts were common Southern fare. These small sprouts—resembling brussels sprouts—appear seven to ten days after the mature cabbage is harvested and were usually steamed or boiled then, like regular cabbage, dressed with butter or drippings.

Cabbage grows throughout the South, and is a particularly important commercial crop in Georgia, Louisiana, and Florida. While today green cabbage is more popular than red, many cabbage recipes in old Southern cookbooks specify the red. Red cabbage was usually combined with a sweetener—such as molasses or brown sugar—plus an acidic ingredient, such as vinegar, lemon juice, or red wine. Here, port adds sweetness and complexity while the red wine adds a gentle acidity. The result is a rich, mellow dish that makes a fine accompaniment to the Thanksgiving turkey or to roast chicken, game, pork, veal, or German-style sausages.

4 tablespoons unsalted butter (or slightly less, if using a nonstick skillet)

1 pound red cabbage (about ½ medium-large head), outer leaves and core removed, cut into wedges, and thinly shredded

⅓ cup port wine
⅓ cup dry red wine
⅛ teaspoon salt, or to taste

1. In a 10- to 12-inch skillet, heat butter over medium heat. Add cabbage and cook uncovered, stirring occasionally, 5 minutes or until it begins to soften.

2. Add port, red wine, and salt and cook uncovered over medium-low heat stirring occasionally, 15 minutes, or until cabbage is tender and braising liquid has reduced and thickened slightly. Serve warm.

Serves 4.

Sweet Potatoes

It was a good meal they had together on that night. Miss Amelia was rich and she did not grudge herself food . . . There was fried chicken . . . mashed rootabeggars [*sic*], collard greens and hot, pale golden sweet potatoes. Miss Amelia ate slowly, and with the relish of a farm hand.

—Carson McCullers, *The Ballad of the Sad Café and Other Stories*

SWEET POTATOES were being grown in the Southeast—particularly by the Cherokees, who were expert farmers—when the first settlers arrived in 1607. The sweet potato had been accepted in England (it was a favorite food of Henry VIII, who thought it was an aphrodisiac) so the colonists were already familiar with it. Jamestown cooks usually simply roasted sweet potatoes in ashes, as the Native Americans had taught them.

In the eighteenth century, sweet potatoes remained popular in the South, especially in Georgia, Tennessee, and the Carolinas. Since the sweet potato ripens late in the season when the weather is cool, it escapes mold or mildew and can be successfully stored for the winter. Some cooks liked to preserve sweet potatoes by drying slices in the sun.

In the 1800s, sweet potatoes were often baked (some old cookbooks say the potato is sweeter when baked slowly at a low temperature or when baked twice) or used in making pones and puddings. They were also fried, mashed, candied, boiled, or made into rustic soufflés. Sweet potatoes were the choice accompaniment for possum—the combo is referred to as "possum and sweets"—and they are frequently paired with pork, thereby creating a combination that balances salty and sweet. Ham and sweet potatoes might be considered the South's "meat and potatoes."

Yams versus Sweet Potatoes What most of the world recognizes as a sweet potato is *Ipomoea batatas,* a member of the morning glory family also sometimes known as a white sweet potato. It is actually yellowish in color, with rather dry, slightly sweet flesh. Sweet potatoes and yams are not the same; the term "yam" is actually a misnomer. The confusion between the two is a result of two things: First, when the slaves first arrived in the New World, they referred to the American sweet potato as "yam," a corruption of the Gullah word *nyam*— probably from the African *unyamo,* which means "to eat." (Slaves came to refer to the Irish potato as "buckra yam"; buckra in Gullah means "white man.") The second confusing factor is that in the 1930s a moist, orange-fleshed sweet potato from Puerto Rico was marketed as a Louisiana "yam" in an effort to distinguish it from other sweet potatoes that were somewhat drier and mealier. A Southerner who eats sweet potatoes in the North is likely to find them drier and starchier than those back home. Northern farmers tend to grow more of the drier Jersey varieties, such as Jersey Gold.

True yams, the *Dioscorea alata,* grow primarily in tropical and subtropical areas. The species most often found in American markets is a brownish, shaggy-coated tuber that may be shaped like a log or an elongated sweet potato. Its flesh is looser, coarser, and drier than the sweet potato. Yams are available in this country in Latin markets.

North Carolina is the number one state in sweet potato production, providing 30 to 40 percent of the national supply. The primary commercial growing area is from the Piedmont through the eastern part of the state. The principal type is the so-called "jewel." North Carolina sweet potatoes are sold to fresh markets nationwide. Louisiana ranks second in sweet potato production.

Julienned Sweet Potatoes with Bacon and Cayenne

• • •

MANY OLD SWEET POTATO RECIPES call for added sweeteners—brown sugar, molasses, maple syrup, or honey—which usually results in a rich, sometimes cloying dish that is too sweet for some tastes. Here is a very unsweet side dish combining sweet potatoes with pork—a classic marriage—plus dry white wine and spicy red pepper. The resulting dish is savory and full-flavored, with a balance between the natural sweetness of the potatoes, the saltiness of the bacon, the heat of the pepper, and a touch of acidity from the wine. Serve with Goose with Damson-Port Sauce (page 206); Steak with Bourbon-Ginger Sauce (page 235); Quick Pork Chops with Orange-Molasses Glaze (page 220); Grandmother's Roast Lemon Chicken (page 183); or any simply prepared poultry, game, or chops.

4 slices thick-sliced bacon (or 6 slices regular-sliced bacon)

2 tablespoons unsalted butter (or less, if using a nonstick skillet)

2 medium-large sweet potatoes (about 1 to 1¼ pounds) peeled and julienned or grated

3 tablespoons dry white wine

2 tablespoons water

Pinch of ground red pepper (cayenne)

1. Stack bacon slices and cut crosswise into ½-inch-wide strips. In a large skillet, cook bacon over medium heat, tossing frequently, 5 to 10 minutes, or until fat has been rendered and bacon is crisp. Drain on paper towels. Pour off all but 2 tablespoons of the pan drippings.

2. Add the butter to the skillet over medium heat. Add potatoes and toss to coat. Add wine and water and toss to mix. Cover and simmer 5 to 8 minutes, stirring 2 or 3 times, until just tender but not mushy. Sprinkle with red pepper and bacon.

Serves 4.

Double Potatoes Anna

• • •

THIS VERY COLORFUL DISH is easy and versatile. Concentric circles of sweet potatoes and unpeeled red-skinned boiling potatoes make a pretty presentation. Add the slices of Smithfield ham if the rest of the menu has little or no smoked or cured meats. Add as much or as little butter as your diet allows (yes, it's better with the maximum amount, but it's still good with less). Serve with Grand-mother's Roast Lemon Chicken (page 183); Steak with Bourbon-Ginger Sauce (page 235); or other simply prepared poultry, game, or chops.

¾ pound red-skinned new potatoes, scrubbed but not peeled, very thinly sliced
¾ pound sweet potatoes (about 2 medium) scrubbed but not peeled and sliced very thinly crosswise

6 tablespoons butter, melted
¼ pound Smithfield ham (or other dry-cured country ham), very thinly sliced (optional) (see page 481 for mail-order source)

1. Preheat oven to 375° F.

2. Arrange a layer of sweet potatoes on the bottom of a generously buttered 9-inch pie plate, overlapping slices to form neat concentric circles. Brush lightly with butter. Top with a layer of ham, if desired. Add a layer of the red potatoes, brush with butter, and top with ham. Repeat until all ingredients are used.

3. Place in center of oven and bake 40 minutes or until bubbling hot and potatoes are tender, lightly crisped, and golden-brown.

4. Place a large, flat plate on top of pie plate. Using pot holders, quickly invert to unmold. Let stand a few minutes, then cut into wedges.

Serves 6.

"Creamed" Potatoes
with Saffron and Garlic

■ ■ ■

IN 1674, ANTHONY ASHLEY COOPER, Earl of Shaftsbury, one of the eight
properties of the newly created colony, Carolina, ordered settlers on the Edistro
River to grow white potatoes. A decade later, white potatoes were being grown
in home gardens in South Carolina and Virginia, including Thomas Jefferson's.
Potatoes were met with much resistance, however, as they were thought to be
poisonous. And, in fact, if exposed to sunlight, potatoes will turn greenish and
those greenish parts can be very mildly toxic, but not enough to make you sick.
In addition, they were up against stiff competition: the other farinaceous staples
of the region—sweet potatoes, rice, and corn—were already well accepted.

By the nineteenth century, fears had subsided and potatoes were widely
accepted throughout the South, although they were frequently imported from
regions further north. Nineteenth-century Southern cooks prepared potatoes
simply. They were baked, boiled, roasted, mashed, scalloped, smothered (sliced
and fried with onions in pork drippings), used as a base for savory puddings,
soups or salads, or layered with cheese and béchamel sauce, then baked. Tiny
new potatoes were often simmered with green beans or collards, or with the first
green peas of the season.

All-purpose white potatoes, particularly the dual-purpose Kennebec, grow
throughout the South. Mississippi, Florida, and Kentucky grow potatoes for
commercial production, the other states grow them for the fresh market and
home use only.

In this recipe, richly flavored potatoes (the term "creamed" is common in
some regions of the South when referring to mashed potatoes) are the color of
a summer sunset. They are redolent with saffron—one of the exotic spices the
Jeffersons brought back to the New World—and a gentle hint of garlic. These
potatoes are rich and elegant. Serve with salmon, swordfish, steamed shrimp,
boiled lobster, roasted game, chicken, lamb chops, or steaks. They can be prepared up to a day in advance and reheated.

2 pounds mature (not "new") boiling
potatoes, peeled and diced into 1-
inch cubes

8 large garlic cloves, peeled but left
whole (Note: Since the garlic is
boiled, it becomes very mild)

½ cup heavy cream or milk
Large pinch of saffron threads
3 to 6 tablespoons unsalted butter, or
  to taste

Salt and freshly ground white pepper,
  to taste

1. Bring a large pot of lightly salted water to a boil. Add potatoes and garlic and boil 15 minutes or until potatoes are tender.

2. While potatoes are cooking, in a small saucepan bring cream and saffron just to the scalding point. Remove from heat, stir to mix, cover, and keep warm.

3. Drain potatoes and garlic and return to pot. Cover pot with a clean kitchen towel and then the pot lid, to absorb excess moisture. Let stand for 5 minutes.

4. While still hot, beat or mash potatoes and garlic, adding the hot saffron cream a bit at a time. Mash to desired consistency. Season to taste with butter, salt, and pepper and serve hot.

Serves 6.

Carrots and Parsnips with Orange Butter and Chervil

• • •

ACCORDING TO JAMES BEARD, no one recorded the appearance of the first carrot in the New World, but it is believed to have come within months of the first settlers. Carrots were not exceedingly popular as a side-dish vegetable even as late as the 1800s. They were, however, used in soups and stews. There are very few recipes for carrots even into the early twentieth century, and those that exist usually call for boiling or stewing them—sometimes with cream or a sweetener such as sugar or honey—until quite soft.

Late nineteenth- and early twentieth-century Southern cookbooks show that parsnips—those peppery, off-white carrot look-alikes—were frequently eaten in the South. They were stewed or mashed or beaten with milk then fried like potato pancakes.

Carrots are grown for processing in Maryland, and Florida grows them for the fresh market. At one time carrots were grown commercially in the Charleston area, but most of them were exported because no one ate them locally! Parsnips are grown only in small quantities in the South and only in home gardens. Always enamored with history, Virginia gardeners often grow old heirloom varieties.

When carrots and parsnips are simmered in orange juice, they take on a mild, tangy-sweet flavor. The cooking liquid—reduced to a glaze, then enriched with butter—becomes a kind of citrusy beurre blanc sauce. It is rich, elegant, and vibrant with orange flavor. Fresh chervil, an herb that is a member of the carrot family, heightens the carrot flavor. Serve with a simple main course such as Grandmother's Roast Lemon Chicken (page 183); Quick Lamb Scallops with Herbed Egg Sauce (page 245); Spiced Beef with Two Sauces (page 232); roast turkey; or grilled or broiled game or chops.

½ pound carrots, trimmed and peeled

1½ cups freshly squeezed orange juice, strained (Note: For a slightly tangier sauce, use 1 cup freshly squeezed orange juice and ½ cup freshly squeezed grapefruit juice)

½ pound parsnips, trimmed and peeled

3 tablespoons cold unsalted butter (or less, if desired), cut into small pieces

Salt and freshly ground black pepper, to taste

Fresh chervil sprigs, to garnish

1. Cut the carrots into 1½-inch pieces. Cut the larger pieces (those from nearer the stem end) *lengthwise* into sixths or eighths; cut smaller pieces lengthwise into fourths, leaving tips of carrots whole if carrots are slender. (The idea is to make sure all pieces are approximately the same length and width so they will cook evenly.)

2. In a medium saucepan bring the orange juice to boil. Add carrots, cover, and simmer 3 minutes. Meanwhile, peel parsnips and slice to the same size as carrots. Add parsnips to carrots and simmer covered 3 to 5 minutes or until vegetables are crisp-tender. With slotted spoon transfer vegetables to serving dish and cover tightly to keep warm.

3. Bring the orange juice to a boil over high heat and reduce to 3 tablespoons. Off the heat, tilt the pan and whisk in butter piece by piece, allowing each piece to become thoroughly incorporated before adding the next, returning pan to very low heat if the sauce becomes too cool. Season with salt and pepper. Pour the sauce over the vegetables, garnish with chervil sprigs, and serve immediately.

Serves 4.

Eggplant, Tomato, and Onion Papillotes
▪ ▪ ▪

FLORIDA is the country's number one producer of eggplant and it is an important commercial crop in Georgia and Kentucky as well. It grows throughout the rest of the South, and is particularly popular in Alabama, Mississippi, North Carolina, and Louisiana. Most Southern cooks batter and fry sliced eggplant, which is perhaps why it has a reputation for being fattening. Here, I combine this subtly-flavored vegetable with tomatoes, onions, and herbs and a mere two teaspoons of oil per serving. Light and fresh tasting, serve it with any fried, baked, or broiled meat or fish.

3 large firm, ripe tomatoes (about 1½ pounds cored, peeled—if desired—halved, and seeded)
3 medium eggplants (about 2½ pounds), peeled and cut into 1-inch cubes
¼ cup extra-virgin olive oil

2 medium yellow onions, sliced about ¼ inch thick
6 sprigs fresh thyme (or 1½ teaspoons dried)
Salt and freshly ground black pepper, to taste

1. Preheat oven to 350° F.
2. Cut 6 12-inch squares of aluminum foil. Brush each lightly with olive oil.
3. Cut tomatoes into 1-inch pieces and distribute evenly among foil squares.

4. Bring a large saucepan of lightly salted water to a boil. Add eggplant; return to a boil and let cook over high heat for 1 minute. Drain thoroughly; set aside on paper towels.

5. Heat all but 1 tablespoon of the olive oil in a large skillet. Add onions and cook over medium-high heat until soft and almost transparent, about 5 minutes. Drain well.

6. Add eggplant and onion to tomatoes, distributing vegetables evenly among foil squares. Season with thyme, salt, and freshly ground pepper. Drizzle remaining olive oil over each.

7. Seal each packet by bringing up 2 opposing corners to form a triangle. Crimp the open sides to seal tightly.

8. Bake 20 minutes. (Or, place directly over hot coals). Remove from oven, cut open with scissors, and carefully turn out onto plates.

Serves 6.

"What have you got for breakfast?" he said to Eliza.

"Why," she said, pursing her lips meditatively, "would you like some eggs?"

"Yes," said he, "with a few rashers of bacon and a couple of pork sausages."

—Thomas Wolfe, *Look Homeward, Angel*

EGGS FRIED IN BACON DRIPPINGS, escorted by country ham, hot biscuits, grits with butter and red-eye gravy, and a cup of coffee so hot that the less acquainted might term it "scalding"—these aren't merely the makings of a Southern breakfast, they're the substance of a Southern lifeblood.

Although there have been pockets of resistance—with parts of Louisiana, for example, contributing veal or beef grillades, beignets, pain perdu, and many French-inspired sauced egg dishes—pork and corn have been the staples of a true Southern breakfast for about 400 years. Southerners can probably thank the English for their skepticism toward "fancy" food in general and for the notion that breakfast isn't really breakfast unless it contains meat and grains—in quantity. The English colonists brought with them their preference for puddings, porridge, meat pies, beef, mutton, and pork. In fact, the appearance of country ham on the breakfast plates of Southerners can probably be traced to the first pigs that were carried from England to Jamestown, Virginia in 1608.

When the Virginia colonists arrived, corn was the principal crop grown on American soil. By the 1700s wheat was still scarce in the South, so simple cornbread—in various forms known as pone, johnny cake, corn dodger, hoecake, cornmeal mush, and couche-couche (fried crumbled cornbread) and big hominy were found on the breakfast tables of plantation owners and small farmers alike. (Colonial New Englanders were fond of corn, too, and breakfasted on hasty pudding, later to be called cornmeal mush.) But even after the Civil War, when many Southerners were attempting to modify their image and also their food, pork and pone continued to be inextricably bound together on many breakfast tables. Culinary minds of the late 1800s would undoubtedly have agreed with Mrs. Porter, writing in 1871 in *Mrs. Porter's New Southern Cookery Book,* that hominy was a "necessary accompaniment to pork."

The Southern breakfast saw its heyday during the plantation era of the eighteenth and nineteenth centuries—when breakfast was the first and most substantial meal of the day. As Southern lore has it, plantation owners generally would begin the day with a julep or brandy, then inspect the crops, and sit down to a large breakfast at ten A.M. Such breakfast might consist of ham, sausage, salted fish, creamed sweetbreads, a platter of fried eggs, fried green tomatoes, hominy grits, buckwheat cakes, waffles, biscuits, plus damson plum or peach preserves and boiled coffee. Toward the end of the nineteenth century, however, Americans became more sedentary and breakfast grew less elaborate: bacon, eggs, grits, and toast became standard fare.

Some Southerners have lamented that the Southern breakfast of the twentieth century has become little more than a gleam on the bottom of a well-greased but unused skillet—a hypothesis that seems to be at least partially borne out by a trend toward more healthful eating. Citrus fruit—which had become highly popular at breakfast in the late 1800s—began to be canned as juice around 1915. Frozen concentrated juice became available in the 1950s. And although lard and shortening are still the stuff of the most true-to-method Southern biscuits today, many Americans have eschewed the use of animal and hydrogenated fats in baking and frying. Over the last several years the South has also had one of the fastest-growing consumption rates of any region for yogurt. Today, it's not unusual for the morning repast to be yogurt and a piece of fruit. Yet, many Southerners couldn't go more than a week without a good, hot breakfast—and maybe that's why you'll still find heaping plates of grits, ham, and biscuits on the breakfast tables on Saturday and Sunday mornings.

When I was growing up, breakfast was the same ninety-nine days out of a hundred, consisting of eggs (poached, scrambled, or fried), bacon, grits, and toast. The occasional mornings that we savored pancakes, French toast, waffles, or Grandmother's coffee cake were special indeed. Oatmeal—because it rarely appeared on the table—was even considered a treat. Most Southerners eat oatmeal as they do grits—with salt, pepper, and butter. When I discovered that some people eat cream and brown sugar on their oatmeal, it seemed almost heretical if not downright nauseating.

Layered Brunch Torte of Sausage, Cheese, and Cornmeal Crêpes

• • •

"BRUNCH" AS A BREAKFAST CONCEPT is somewhat more elaborate than the Southern habit of collecting a few basic and singularly good foodstuffs and calling them breakfast. However, a late Sunday breakfast (following Church) has long been a Southern tradition in some areas. Big-name restaurants in New Orleans, in particular, are known for creations that bring together cheese, meat, eggs, and rich sauces. Some restaurants, like Brennan's, add live jazz and plenty of coffee with chicory to let the good times roll.

To be sure, the makings of an ineffably good omelette (not to mention Eggs Hussarde or Eggs Sardou) are abundant in the South. This region today produces more than a third of the nation's eggs. And although the South produces relatively little cheese in comparison to that made in Wisconsin, there are several small cheese producers throughout the South who still practice time-honored methods of cheese making. In Kentucky, for example, Trappist monks at Gethsemani Farms have been making Port du Salut-style cow's-milk cheese since 1848. (Port du Salut cheese is traditionally made by French Cistercian monks, the order to which Trappists belong.) There are also several family farms producing excellent goat cheeses: Fromagerie Belle Chèvre, in Ardmore, Alabama; Scuppernong Farm in Loganville, Georgia; Le Chèvrier Farms in Monroe, Tennessee; Brier Run Farm in Birch River, West Virginia; and Glen Crannoc Farm in Weaverville, North Carolina, to name a few. (See mail-order source, page 481.)

Some cheeses are made just for local consumption, as in Helvetia, West Virginia. There, the elderly daughters of the original Swiss immigrants (who settled in 1869) make a cheese that has the texture of a Danish Port du Salut and the flavor of a true Swiss raclette. It's made with unpasteurized milk and, like moonshine, it is not regulated by the government and can only be procured locally.

In this recipe, though, cheddar, which is still the number one favorite among Americans, is the star. It is combined with farmer cheese, eggs, and pork sausage layered with cornmeal to create a rich torte.

Because it can be made in advance, this dish is a good choice for a company brunch. (No last-minute details.) This dish is rich and hearty. It serves up to ten people, and it need be accompanied only by a fresh fruit compote (try Water-melon in Virginia Riesling, page 395), Bibb Salad with My Favorite Vinaigrette (page 112), coffee, tea, and juices. For a more bountiful spread, offer Whole Wheat Lemon Sally Lunn Bread (page 45) or Whole Wheat Raisin Pecan Biscuits (page 28), Maple Walnut Stickies (page 433), or any of the muffin recipes in the "Breads" chapter.

CORNMEAL CRÊPES

2 large eggs, beaten
1 teaspoon salt
⅛ teaspoon white pepper
2 tablespoons unsalted butter, melted
½ cup milk
½ cup water
½ cup unbleached all-purpose flour

½ cup yellow cornmeal, preferably stone-ground
2 tablespoons melted unsalted butter mixed with 2 tablespoons vegetable oil for brushing skillet (or use a nonstick skillet and vegetable spray)

FILLING

1 pound ground pork sausage (not links)
1 bunch of scallions, trimmed and thinly sliced
2 cups (8 ounces) shredded sharp cheddar cheese

2 tablespoons butter (or less, if using a nonstick skillet)
6 large eggs, beaten
⅛ teaspoon each salt and freshly ground black pepper
1 package (8 ounces) farmer cheese

1. To make the crêpes: In a medium bowl, whisk together eggs, salt, pepper, butter, milk, and water. Whisk in flour and cornmeal. Brush an 8-inch skillet with some of the butter-oil mixture and place over medium-high heat. (If using a nonstick skillet, you will need less butter-oil mixture.) Add ⅓ cup crêpe batter, tilt the pan so that batter coats bottom of pan, and cook 1 to 2 minutes or until firm. Flip the crêpe and cook 1 minute more on other side. Remove from pan and place on a waxed-paper-lined plate. Repeat with remaining batter, brushing skillet with more butter-oil mixture as needed. Makes 6 8-inch crêpes. (Note: Crêpes may be made up to 3 days in advance, layered between sheets of waxed paper, and refrigerated, or frozen for 1 month.)

2. To make the filling: In medium-large skillet, cook sausage over medium heat 5 to 8 minutes or until no pink remains. With a slotted spoon remove sausage to large bowl. Pour off all but 2 tablespoons of the drippings. Cook scallions in drippings over medium heat about 1 minute or until crisp-tender. Add scallions to sausage in bowl. Stir in cheddar cheese.

3. Melt butter in the same skillet. Over low heat, add eggs and scramble slowly until barely set, seasoning with salt and pepper. Do not overcook. Remove from heat and stir in farmer cheese.

4. Preheat oven to 425° F.

5. To assemble the dish: Line a buttered 8-inch-diameter, 2½-quart soufflé dish with buttered waxed paper. Place 1 crêpe on the bottom of the dish on top of the waxed paper. Spread on half of the egg mixture. Top with another crêpe. Spread on half of the sausage mixture. Top with another crêpe. Continue repeating layers, ending with a crêpe. (Can be made 1 day in advance up to this point.) Bring to room temperature before baking.

6. Bake 35 minutes or until heated through (insert knife into center to test). Let stand 5 minutes. Invert to unmold, peel off waxed paper; slice into wedges.

Serves 8 to 10.

Poached Eggs and Country Ham with Couscous

■ ■ ■

As for ham, Virginians are weaned on it. Very quickly they prefer it to their mother's milk.

—Virginia Moore, *Virginia Is a State of Mind*

COUSCOUS, which has grown increasingly popular in this country during the last few decades, has a mild flavor and a grainlike texture similar to that of grits. (North African in origin, couscous is actually a type of pasta made from a wheat flour dough that is pressed through a fine sieve.) Like the benign flavor of grits, couscous is a good foil for the richness of eggs and salty ham. The combination of flavors and textures here maintains the idea that a good Southern breakfast should be hot, comforting, filling fare. P.S.: If you love ham and eggs but can't bear the thought of grits, this dish is for you.

5 tablespoons unsalted butter (optional)
1¼ cups uncooked quick-cooking couscous
4 large eggs

4 center-cut slices (about 2 to 3 ounces each) Smithfield or other dry-cured country ham (see page 481 for mail-order source)
Freshly ground black pepper, to taste
Parsley, to garnish (optional)

1. In a medium skillet, bring water to a simmer for poaching the eggs.

2. In a medium saucepan, bring 1 cup plus 2 tablespoons water and 4 tablespoons of the butter (if using) to boil. Add couscous, stir once, cover, remove from heat, and let stand 5 minutes. Uncover and fluff with a fork to avoid lumping.

3. Carefully add the eggs to the skillet, 1 at a time, and poach over very low heat to desired doneness. High heat will make the egg whites tough.

4. In a separate large skillet, heat remaining 1 tablespoon butter over medium-high heat. (Omit butter if using a nonstick skillet.) Add ham and fry 2 minutes on each side. Remove to paper towels to drain; keep warm. Pour off all but 2½ tablespoons drippings.

5. Add couscous to the drippings and cook over medium heat, stirring occasionally until warmed through. (This step may be omitted if a less rich dish is desired.)

6. To serve, place 1 ham slice on each of 4 plates and top with couscous. Top with poached egg, season with pepper, and garnish with parsley, if desired. Serve immediately.

Serves 4 for breakfast, lunch, or supper.

Braised Artichoke Bottoms
with Eggs and Spinach

. . .

OUT OF THE FRENCH QUARTER of New Orleans have come numerous combinations of shirred or poached eggs, cream, and vegetables in elegant breakfast dishes. A classic example is Eggs Sardou, created in 1908 by Antoine Alciatore for French playwright Victorien Sardou. Sardou traveled throughout the United States, stopping in New Orleans, where he ate at Antoine's Restaurant. Although Sardou's satire on American life, "L'Oncle Sam," has largely been forgotten, the combination of eggs and spinach has stayed with us. There is some dispute as to whether artichokes or spinach were used in the original. Here, to solve the dilemma, artichoke bottoms are placed on a bed of gently cooked spinach, then topped with poached eggs. Eggs Sardou are classically cloaked in hollandaise sauce, which I think is too thick and assertive here. (Actually, I loathe hollandaise sauce.) The sauce here is lighter, piqued with a hint of Creole mustard. (It is still a rich dish, mind you, so go for a run in the park before cozying up to this elegant breakfast.) Serve with Champagne flavored with peach liqueur (such as Pêcher Mignon), Buttermilk Angel Biscuits (page 26), smoky bacon, and fresh melon.

4 large globe artichokes
1 whole lemon
¼ cup lemon juice mixed with 1½ cups water
2 tablespoons butter
1 small yellow onion, finely chopped
2 tablespoons dry white wine or vermouth

1 cup heavy cream
1 tablespoon Creole mustard or whole-grain mustard
Salt and freshly ground black pepper, to taste
¾ pound fresh spinach, washed and trimmed (about 4 cups)
4 eggs

1. Using a sharp knife, cut off artichoke stems and outer leaves and discard. Trim artichoke bottoms and remove fuzzy chokes from the inside. Rub stem ends and insides with a lemon half. Drop artichoke bottoms into bowl of lemon water to prevent discoloration.

2. In a large nonaluminum skillet, heat butter over low heat. Add onions and cook 5 minutes or until translucent, stirring occasionally.

3. Add wine and boil 30 seconds. Add artichokes and enough of the lemon water to cover artichokes by half. Cover and simmer 25 to 35 minutes or until tender, adding additional water if necessary. Remove artichokes and keep warm.

4. Boil the cooking liquid until it is reduced to 2 tablespoons, about 10 minutes. Add cream and boil 3 minutes or until very lightly thickened. Stir in mustard; season with salt and pepper. Add spinach and simmer until just tender. Cover and keep warm.

5. In a large skillet of simmering water, poach 4 eggs to desired doneness.

6. To serve, use a slotted spoon to distribute spinach evenly among 4 plates. Place an artichoke bottom on each bed of spinach; place an egg on top of each artichoke heart. Nap with sauce. Sprinkle with pepper and serve hot.

Serves 4.

Sautéed Hominy with Country Ham

■ ■ ■

FOR AS LONG AS PIGS have been rooting around on this continent, corn and pork have been served together at breakfast in the South, fried ham and boiled hominy probably being the most elementary pairing. (Along coastal areas of the South, hominy is often served with shrimp for breakfast.) According to traditional recipes, hominy (also called big hominy) should be simmered for several hours, after which cream and butter are often added. Few cooks today have time to honor the old-fashioned cooking method, opting instead for the canned variety. Although its popularity has declined somewhat, some households still serve hominy as part of a big breakfast. This fast, easy side dish offers all the flavor of a classic Southern breakfast in mere minutes. Serve with eggs and biscuits.

2 tablespoons unsalted butter (less if using a nonstick skillet)

⅓ cup diced or julienned uncooked Smithfield or other dry-cured country ham (I like to use the center-cut slices; see mail-order source, page 481)

1 can (15½ ounces) cooked hominy, drained (about 1¾ cups)

Freshly ground black pepper, to taste

1. In a medium skillet, melt 1 tablespoon butter over medium-high heat. Add ham and sauté 2 to 3 minutes or until ham edges are crisp and deep golden-brown. Push ham to one side of the skillet (or remove it and keep warm). Lower heat to medium.

2. Add remaining butter and the hominy to the skillet and toss hominy several times, scraping bottom of pan to loosen the flavorful ham bits. Cover and cook 1 minute or until heated through. Add ham and toss; serve hot, sprinkled with pepper.

Serves 2 to 3.

Sweet Potato Hash

. . .

"HASH," A WORD THAT COMES from the Old French word *hacher* or "to chop," supposedly found its way into the English language in the mid-1600s, but there are recipes for hash-type dishes dating at least as far back as the fourteenth century. An invention of necessity that has seen many variations, the dish generally combines leftover cooked meat—mutton, pork, beef, chicken, turkey—with potatoes and other vegetables, often onions and parsley. The traditional New England version, red flannel hash, for example, is generally made of the leftovers of a New England boiled dinner: corned beef, carrots, and potatoes. (Some authorities assert that the red color comes from the addition of beets.) Hash houses in the mid-nineteenth century gave the dish a bad name. The workers in these cheap establishments were known as "hash slingers." However, hash began to be popular again by the early twentieth century. And today it is

Breakfast

∎

as likely to be an item on a thoughtfully conceived menu of sophisticated new-American cooking as the "breakfast special" at a roadside diner. (The annual Kentucky Derby Breakfast, incidentally, regularly features turkey hash.) The version here blends the slight sweetness of sweet potatoes with the saltiness of ham and the bite of onion to produce a rich flavor more surprising, perhaps, than traditional hash. But it's as wholesome a hash as any!

2 tablespoons vegetable oil (less, if using a nonstick skillet)
2 tablespoons unsalted butter (less, if using a nonstick skillet)
1 pound sweet potatoes (about 2 medium), peeled and diced into ¼- to ⅓-inch cubes (approximately 3 cups)

1 large yellow onion, finely chopped
¼ pound Smithfield or other dry-cured country ham, diced into ¼-inch cubes (see mail-order source, page 481)

1. Heat oil and butter in a large, heavy skillet over medium heat. Add sweet potatoes and onion, toss to coat, then cover and cook over medium-low heat 5 to 7 minutes, stirring occasionally.

2. Increase heat to high, add ham and cook, tossing occasionally, 4 to 5 minutes, or until potatoes are golden-brown with some crisp edges. Serve hot, accompanied by fried or poached eggs.

Serves 4.

Country Ham with Red-Eye Cream

. . .

RED-EYE GRAVY served with ham and grits is arguably the most "Southern" of any Southern breakfast combination. The origin of the name of this gravy, however, is somewhat mythical. According to one theory, Andrew Jackson once asked a cook for gravy as red as the cook's eyes. Another source purports that the appearance of a "red eye" in the middle of a pan of a correctly made ham gravy reduction is what gives this sauce its name. The proper way to make it is perhaps equally contentious: some recipes (like my dad's) call for nothing more than ham drippings boiled with water, while others require the addition of a bit of strong, black coffee. (Some even call—heaven help us—for Coca Cola.) Here, the flavors of chicken stock and cream subtly enrich this upscale version of a Southern classic. (The saltiness of the ham is tempered by the cream.) Served on hot toasted cornbread, this makes a delightful breakfast.

½ pound uncooked, Smithfield or other dry-cured country ham (preferably the center slices), sliced about ⅛ inch thick (see page 481 for mail-order source)
½ cup unsalted chicken stock

¾ cup heavy cream
5 tablespoons unsalted butter (less, if using a nonstick skillet)
Rich Buttermilk Cornbread (page 34), split and toasted

1. In a skillet, fry ham in 3 tablespoons butter for about 2 minutes over medium-high heat on each side or until edges are lightly browned and crisp. Set aside and keep warm.

2. Pour excess drippings out of pan. Add stock and boil until it is reduced to 3 tablespoons, about 5 to 8 minutes. Add cream and reduce by half, or until it coats the back of a spoon, about 10 minutes.

3. Remove from heat and swirl in remaining 2 tablespoons butter. Place ham on toasted cornbread or other toast and nap with red-eye cream.

Serves 4.

Sweet Potato Galette

• • •

THERE IS A well-documented tradition of Southern dishes made with grated sweet potatoes baked with sugar, butter, and spices. Here, julienned potatoes are fried into a large cake—a Southern interpretation of the French straw-potato pancake, *paillasson de pommes de terre*, or *pomme paille*. The cake is quartered, and each quarter is graced by a gently poached egg.

5 eggs
1 egg white
½ teaspoon salt
½ teaspoon freshly ground black pepper
¾ pound sweet potatoes, peeled and julienned
2 tablespoons unbleached all-purpose flour

2 tablespoons unsalted butter (use 1 tablespoon if using a nonstick skillet)
2 tablespoons vegetable oil (use 1 tablespoon if using a nonstick skillet)
4 teaspoons minced fresh parsley

1. In a medium bowl, beat 1 egg and the egg white with salt and pepper. Add potatoes and toss to coat; add flour and toss to coat.

2. Heat butter and oil in a large skillet over medium-high heat. Tilt pan to swirl butter and oil up sides of skillet.

3. Add potato mixture to skillet, distributing it evenly. Press down lightly to form a neat round. Cover and cook 10 minutes or until deep golden-brown on bottom. Holding onto the lid, turn skillet upside down to flip the galette onto the lid, then slide the galette back into the skillet, cooked-side-up. Cook 10 minutes longer uncovered or until golden-brown on bottom.

4. Meanwhile, in a large skillet of simmering salted water, poach 4 eggs to desired doneness.

5. To serve, cut the galette into 4 wedges and place on serving plates. Top each wedge with a poached egg, sprinkle with additional pepper and the parsley. Serve hot.

Serves 4 as a main course, 6 (omitting eggs) as a vegetable side dish.

Sweet Potato and Ham "Pancake"
• • •

Here's another variation on the French *pomme paille*.

1 medium-sized sweet potato, peeled and coarsely grated (about 2 cups)
1 small green pepper, julienned and cut in ½-inch lengths
½ medium onion, minced
2 cups (about ½ pound) finely julienned Smithfield or other dry-
cured country ham (see page 481 for mail-order source)
1 beaten egg
2 tablespoons unbleached all-purpose flour
Freshly ground black pepper, to taste
4 tablespoons unsalted butter
4 tablespoons vegetable oil

1. In a large bowl, mix sweet potato, green pepper, onion, and ham. Add egg, flour, and black pepper, and toss to mix.

2. In an 8-inch skillet, heat 1 tablespoon each of butter and oil over medium-high heat. When butter and oil are hot, add half the potato mixture and press it into a pancake shape. Reduce heat to medium, cover, and cook about 10 minutes.

3. Invert a flat plate over the skillet and flip the pancake out onto it. Add another tablespoon each butter and oil to skillet and heat until very hot. Return the pancake to the skillet by sliding it in cooked-side-up, and cook over medium heat for an additional 10 minutes. Flip pancake onto a plate and keep warm. Repeat the procedure with remaining sweet potato mixture. Drain both pancakes briefly on a towel. Serve warm, each topped with a poached egg.

Serves 2.

Cornmeal Crêpes with Country Sausage
• • •

THIS RICH DISH has similar flavors to Layered Brunch Torte of Sausage, Cheese, and Cornmeal Crêpes (page 339), but in a simpler guise. It's a rib-sticking meal that's perfect before a day of cross-country skiing, skating, or a long walk through cold winter streets.

CRÊPES AND FILLING

1 recipe Cornmeal Crêpes, page 340
½ pound ground pork sausage (not link), crumbled
1 bunch scallions, finely chopped (about ½ to ¾ cup)
1 cup shredded medium-sharp cheddar cheese
3 tablespoons unsalted butter (or less, if using a nonstick skillet)

4 large eggs, beaten
8 ounces cottage cheese, puréed in food processor or blender until smooth
⅛ teaspoon salt
⅛ teaspoon freshly ground black pepper

CHEESE SAUCE

1 cup heavy cream
1 tablespoon dry white wine (optional)
1 large shallot, minced
¼ teaspoon Dijon mustard, or more to taste
Dash of ground red pepper (cayenne)

½ cup shredded medium-sharp cheddar cheese
Salt and freshly ground black pepper, to taste
Minced scallions for garnish (optional)

1. Make crêpes as directed, stacking crêpes on a plate as they're cooked.

2. To make filling: In a large skillet over medium-high heat, cook sausage, stirring frequently, until no pink remains, about 5 minutes. Transfer with slotted spoon to medium bowl; pour off all but 2 tablespoons drippings.

3. Add scallions to skillet and cook over medium-high heat until tender, about 5 minutes. Add scallions to sausage.

4. Stir cheddar cheese into sausage mixture. Set aside.

5. In a separate large skillet, melt 2 tablespoons of the butter over very low heat. Add eggs and cook slowly 5 to 8 minutes or until barely set (slow cooking is important so eggs don't toughen). Cool slightly. Stir cottage cheese into eggs. Fold egg mixture into sausage mixture. Season with salt and pepper.

6. Preheat oven to 350° F.

7. Place ⅓ cup filling down the center of each crêpe and roll up. Place

crêpes seam-side-down close together in buttered 9-inch by 9-inch baking dish. (Note: May be frozen for up to 1 month at this point.) Dot with remaining butter and cover with lid or aluminum foil. Cook 20 minutes or until heated through. (If frozen, this will require 45 minutes).

8. Meanwhile, to make the sauce: In a medium skillet, over medium-high heat, boil the cream, wine, if using, and shallots until reduced to ¾ cup or until sauce lightly coats the back of a spoon. Stir in mustard and tiny bit of red pepper. Stir in cheese until melted; season with salt and pepper. Keep warm.

9. To serve, place 2 hot crêpes on each of 4 warm plates and nap with 2 to 3 tablespoons sauce. Garnish with scallions, if desired.

Makes 8 crêpes; serves 4 hungry eaters, or 8 lighter eaters.

Skillet Breads and Waffles

AMERICA'S LOVE for hotcakes grew during the last half of the nineteenth century as bacon and eggs replaced steaks and pies for breakfast. Called flapjacks, slapjacks, and griddlecakes, they all referred to the same basic skillet bread made with flour, salt, milk, oil or butter, and eggs. Some were named for the liquid used: buttermilk cakes, sourmilk cakes, or cream cakes; and others for the grains or flour used: battercakes and flannelcakes (which contain wheat flour plus cornmeal), as well as buckwheat cakes, corncakes, hominy cakes, and rice cakes.

Waffles date from the late eighteenth century in this country when, according to John Mariani in his *The Dictionary of American Food and Drink*, "waffle parties" were quite popular. One hundred years later, he says, vendors on city streets sold waffles hot with butter and molasses or maple syrup. Thomas Jefferson served them at Monticello.

In the latter part of the eighteenth century, "waffle parties" became popular in America. And, like pancakes, they soon became an American breakfast favorite. In the South, waffles made with part cornmeal or rice flour were common because of the abundance of these grains, as was the practice of adding cooked hominy or rice to plain waffle batter. By the 1830s and 1840s, they were generally made with wheat flour rather than cornmeal.

My mother often recounts her girlhood memories of Sunday night "waffle suppers" in South Carolina. These feasts would begin with bacon waffles as the "first" course, proceed to plain, and end with cocoa-flavored waffles.

Whole Wheat–Bacon Waffles with a Selection of Flavored Butters

▪ ▪ ▪

WHEN I WAS GROWING UP, waffles were a special breakfast treat, prepared by my mother or grandmother on a lazy Saturday morning. The recipe here is an adaptation of my grandmother's bacon waffles. I've substituted whole wheat flour for part of the all-purpose flour, resulting in a heartier, healthier waffle. Vegetarians can, of course, omit the bacon.

Serve these waffles hot with one—or all four!—of the flavored butters that follow. Whole wheat–bacon waffles may be prepared in advance and frozen. Undercook them slightly and freeze up to four months, stacked between layers of waxed paper. To serve, do not thaw, but place on a baking pan and broil several minutes on each side. If omitting the bacon, simply pop the frozen waffles in a toaster to reheat.

1⅓ cups unbleached all-purpose flour
⅔ cup whole wheat flour
4 teaspoons baking powder
1 tablespoon light brown sugar
1 teaspoon salt
2 eggs, separated
1⅔ cups milk
½ cup (1 stick) unsalted butter, melted and cooled

Melted butter, for brushing waffle iron (use less if waffle iron has a nonstick coating)
16 slices bacon, slightly undercooked and cut into ¼-inch pieces
Flavored butters (see below)

1. Preheat the waffle iron.

2. In a large bowl, mix together flours, baking powder, sugar, and salt. Make a well in the center, add egg yolks and lightly beat them together with a fork. Add milk and butter to the yolks in the well and beat together, gradually incorporating dry ingredients until just blended. Do not overmix.

3. In a separate bowl, beat egg whites until stiff but not dry. Gently fold into batter.

4. Brush hot waffle iron with melted butter, and pour in ½ cup batter. Quickly sprinkle some of the bacon pieces on top. Cook waffles until as brown as desired. Serve immediately or stack and keep warm in low oven until all waffles are cooked.

Makes 6 to 7 6-inch waffles.

Flavored Butters

. . .

Molasses Butter

Blend 1 to 2 tablespoons molasses into 4 tablespoons unsalted butter.

Benne Seed (Sesame Seed) Butter

Blend 4 tablespoons tahini (Middle Eastern sesame seed paste) into 4 tablespoons unsalted butter and 2 tablespoons toasted sesame seeds.

Peanut Butter Butter

Blend 3 tablespoons peanut butter with 4 tablespoons unsalted butter.

Coconut Butter

Blend 4 tablespoons unsweetened shredded coconut with 4 tablespoons unsalted butter.

Carolina Rice Flour Pancakes

. . .

IN SOUTH CAROLINA and Georgia, griddlecakes made with rice and/or rice flour were common and were called by many names, including rice cakes, rice griddles, rice cookies, rice slapjacks, rice crumpets, rice wafers, rice spider bread, and rice drops. Whatever the name, they were no doubt a good solution for what to do with leftover rice. In some cases, however, rice was cooked for the sole purpose of making griddlecakes. I came across a recipe that instructs the cook to soak the rice overnight, boil it in the morning, then mix it with the other batter ingredients.

The recipe here contains cooked rice as well as rice flour. The rice flour adds a subtle, naturally sweet flavor to these unusual light little cakes. Serve them hot with butter and peach preserves or maple syrup for breakfast. Or, serve instead of rice or potatoes to accompany roast poultry, game, or shrimp. Cooked whole white hominy can be substituted for the rice.

½ cup unbleached all-purpose flour
½ cup rice flour
Scant ¾ teaspoon salt
Scant ¾ teaspoon baking powder
1 large egg
1 cup milk

4 tablespoons unsalted butter, melted and slightly cooled
½ cup cooked long-grain white rice (or substitute cooked whole white hominy)
2 tablespoons vegetable oil

1. In a medium bowl, combine flours, salt, and baking powder.

2. In a separate bowl, beat the egg, then add milk and 3 tablespoons of the butter. Add liquid ingredients to dry ingredients and stir until just blended. Fold in the rice; do not overmix.

3. Brush a griddle or skillet with some of the oil and remaining butter. Heat over medium-high heat, then drop batter by slightly rounded tablespoons. Cook about 1 minute or until small bubbles appear around edges and bottom is golden-brown. Turn cakes over and cook about 1 minute on the other side. Keep warm in an ovenproof dish lightly covered with foil in a warm oven while you make remaining pancakes.

Makes about 16 2-inch pancakes.

Note These may be made in advance and frozen. To reheat do not thaw but wrap in foil and place in center of preheated 350° F oven 10 minutes or until piping hot.

Cornmeal Pancakes

• • •

CORNMEAL PANCAKES are ideal for breakfast with butter and honey, sorghum, or maple syrup. For pancakes to serve as a base in the recipes Oysters and Leeks on Corn Pancakes (page 161), and Fresh Corn and Cornmeal Pancakes with Crème Fraîche and Caviar (page 75), I prefer a firmer pancake, made by adding ¼ cup more cornmeal.

½ cup plus 2 tablespoons unbleached all-purpose flour
½ cup cornmeal (use ¾ cup for a firmer pancake if making for "Oysters and Leeks" or "Crème Frâiche and Caviar" recipes)
¾ teaspoon sugar
¾ teaspoon salt

1 teaspoon baking powder
1 large egg, beaten
¾ cup milk
3 tablespoons melted butter
2 teaspoons vegetable oil mixed with 1 teaspoon melted butter

1. Preheat griddle or skillet. In a bowl, mix together flour, cornmeal, sugar, salt, and baking powder. Add egg, milk, and butter, stirring until just incorporated.

2. Brush hot griddle with oil and butter mixture. Drop batter by spoonfuls (about 2 tablespoons each, see note) and cook 1 to 2 minutes or until bubbles appear around the edges and bottom is lightly browned.

Makes 12 3-inch cakes; serves 4.

Note To make smaller, hors d'oeuvre-sized pancakes, use only 1 tablespoon batter per pancake. Makes about 24 1½-inch pancakes.

Desserts

Desserts

TO KNOW HOW TO CLARIFIE YOU SUGAR

Take a pinte of faire water & beat y^e white of an egg into it to a froth. then put a pound of sugar in to it, & let it boyle very fast, & there will rise a black scum on ye top of it. as it riseth, take it of till it is very clean, & then streyne it thorough A Jelly bagg or wet cloth, & soe use it as you plea[s]. to every pound of sugar as you clarefie, you must put a pinte of faire water, & ye white of an egg. ye white of one egge will clarefy 2 pound of sugar as well as one pound.

—from *Martha Washington's Booke of Cookery and Booke of Sweetmeats*

THROUGHOUT AMERICA, many traditional desserts and savories—from Pennsylvania Dutch shoofly pie to Boston baked beans—are undeniably sweet. But perhaps nowhere is the love of sugar more evident than in the South. Few other confections can match the sugary jolt of a New Orleans praline, or the syrupiness of pecan pie, sweets so intensely rich your teeth ache after the first bite. Sweeteners also find their way into Southern dishes other than desserts: pork barbecue is typically tangy-sweet, as are salad dressings and slaws. Even vegetables often get a hefty dose of sugar in the cooking water. In more complex vegetable mixtures, such as corn pudding and sweet potato pone, sugar, molasses, or marshmallows is added with such a generous hand that, to the modern palate, the final dish tastes more like a dessert than a side dish.

In addition to treasured recipes for puddings, pies, marchapane (marzipan), and other sweetmeats, the seventeenth-century settler brought along his sweet tooth to the New World. It was Mother England who had nurtured his undying love for sweets, which included those made with honey and treacle (molasses) as well as with the more costly cane sugar. Numerous Southern desserts are rooted in Great Britain's culinary history; bakewell pudding and treacle tart are but forerunners of our chess and pecan pies.

Sugar is so readily available and affordable today that it is hard to imagine that it was difficult to procure in the early New World. When they could get it, seventeenth-century settlers soothed their cravings with cane sugar that was imported, primarily from Holland, Madeira, or the West Indies.

The tropical reed itself is said to have been brought over by Spanish and Portuguese explorers to South Carolina where it was grown as early as 1650. A hundred years later, sugar cane was brought to Louisiana by Jesuits from French Saint Domingue. Records indicate, however, that cane sugar may not have been successfully refined in America until the end of the eighteenth century.

Sugar cane became an important crop because it was not only the source for sugar (which was used as a preservative and for medicinal purposes as well as a sweetener), but also for molasses and rum. Molasses was not only a staple in colonial pantries, it was a valuable trade commodity. It was so valuable that the founders of the Georgia colony sweetened the deal for the first settlers by offering sixty-four quarts of the thick, brown syrup to every man, woman, and child who endured a year there.

Refined cane sugar was costly and could be indulged in only by those who could afford it. However, molasses—the liquid by-product of sugar refining—was cheap and plentiful and became the common sweetener of the not-so-well-to-do in America. Once scorned by the elite because of its dark color and strong flavor, molasses eventually lost its social stigma. Like cornbread, which was considered coarse and plebeian, molasses became appreciated for its distinct character and was eventually enjoyed by all classes. During this same era, honeybees were imported from Europe and their golden elixir was used by the colonists to a certain extent. Maple sugar, however, seems to have been appreciated only by the Native Americans.

Another important Southern American sweetener is sorghum syrup. Sweet sorghum (*S. vulgare saccharagum*) is a grass that grows in corn-like stalks, which, like sugar cane, exudes a juice when pressed. (The nonsweet variety of sorghum is grown for fodder or used in making ethyl alcohol.) The juice is then boiled down to make a syrup, which is called sorghum syrup or sorghum "molasses," although, technically speaking, molasses is only made from sugar cane. Sorghum syrup closely resembles molasses in taste and appearance and they may be used interchangeably in cooking. Sweet sorghum is believed to have originated in China or Africa. In fact, it was sometimes called Chinese sugar cane. However, it was introduced to America via France in 1863 when a nursery man brought some seeds into the country.

Up until the end of the nineteenth century, sugar was sold in five- to thirty-five-pound conical loaves called "sugar loaves" that came in varying degrees of refinement. The expensive, precious white crystals were kept under lock and key.

Frugal households could make a ten-pound cone last an entire year, while wealthy planters might go through the same amount in three weeks. Molasses remained cheap and plentiful and grew in importance. Honey and maple sugar were beginning to be used more and more, but it was not until the Civil War that their usage grew out of necessity. In 1862, the cane-growing areas around New Orleans came under Union control. Sorghum was the most common replacement, but honey and maple sugar were also substituted.

After the Civil War, competition from the Caribbean and the Far East all but wiped out the domestic sugar cane industry, then concentrated in Louisiana, Alabama, Mississippi, Florida, and Georgia. Today, sugar cane continues to be cultivated in the United States. Florida leads in production followed by Louisiana, Texas, and Hawaii.

In the late nineteenth century, the sugar-refining process was modernized so that granulated sugar, which was easier to use, replaced loaf sugar. As a result, sugar consumption doubled between 1880 and 1915.

Despite concerns with health and fitness, Southerners—like the rest of the country—are still passionate about sweets. It is no coincidence that the dessert chapter is one of the largest in this book. It reflects all of the family reunions, funerals, and church suppers south of the Mason-Dixon line where the tables are laden with just as many desserts as savories. In many recipes, I have reduced the sugar from one-quarter to as much as one-half, since I don't think the modern palate cares as much for excessively sweet desserts. Mine are by no means diet recipes, but I have occasionally employed other ingredients—spices, spirits, dessert wines, fresh and dried fruits, crème fraîche, sour cream—in place of some of the sugar to give depth of flavor and interest. I just believe that a peach pie should taste more like peaches than sugar.

Pies and Pastries

IF A HUNDRED PEOPLE were asked to name one Southern dessert, my bet is that at least ninety would answer, "pecan pie." This all-American confection has become synonymous with Southern cooking, as it features the region's indigenous nut, and is a shining example of the South's love for sweets.

Southerners are great pie bakers. In my experience, there are often two pies for every cake at any given covered-dish supper. The basic single- and double-crust types are more common in the South than the cobblers, crisps, slumps, grunts, and the pie derivatives so popular in other regions. The Southern baker is particularly fond, however, of two pie variations: the turnover—which when fried is called a "fried pie" or when filled with fresh apple becomes an "apple-jack" (a name that also sometimes refers to apple dumplings)—and the roly-poly, a jam-filled roll made with pastry dough.

In the eighteenth and nineteenth centuries, many desserts called "puddings" were baked in a crust and are actually what today we'd call pies. Two examples are Transparent Pudding (the filling includes eggs, sugar, butter, and nutmeg) from Mary Randolph's *The Virginia House-wife* (1824) and Cocoa-nut [*sic*] Pudding, (grated coconut, sugar, eggs, and rosewater) in Sarah Rutledge's *The Carolina Housewife* (1847). Both are baked in puff pastry. These two "puddings" evolved into honest-to-goodness classic Southern pies. Coconut cream pie and chess pie (the latter has fundamentally the same ingredients as transparent pie) are a common offering at many home-style restaurants and church bazaars.

Like the rest of the country, in the rural South it was not uncommon to find pie—particularly fruit pie—on the breakfast table. Weight watching and cholesterol counting has all but eliminated this delicious tradition, which is actually not any worse calorically than the sugary doughnuts, nut-rich sticky buns, or even the two-eggs-bacon-grits-gravy-and-biscuits choice. Pies are most often served for dessert nowadays, and despite premade crusts and ghastly aerosol-type whipped "cream," there are still enough honest pie bakers in the South who keep the tradition alive and well.

I've used the classics—from spicy sweet potato to rich and sugary chess—as a springboard for the recipes that follow. Tarts—which technically have only a bottom crust—are not as common as pies in the South. Recipes for transparent tarts, sherry tarts, and bakewell tarts can be found in *Charleston Receipts,* but few others exist in old cookbooks. I love tarts and find that they can be very elegant and refined. If the meal calls for a finale that is dressier than a big, double-crust, deep-dish, country-style pie, a slim, glistening tart may be a better choice. I also offer tartlets for much the same reason; they are generally not as bulky as pies (although they can be just as caloric). A tiny tartlet is like eating a truffle after dinner; it is small, but intensely flavored, so it can often satisfy the craving for "something sweet."

Basic Pastry

. . .

2 cups unbleached all-purpose flour
¾ teaspoon salt
¼ teaspoon sugar
8 tablespoons (1 stick) cold, unsalted

butter, cut into small pieces
3 tablespoons cold shortening
5 to 6 tablespoons cold water

1. To make pastry by hand, mix flour, salt, and sugar in a large bowl. Cut in butter and shortening by using your fingertips, a pastry blender, or two knives until mixture looks like oatmeal or coarse cornmeal. Do not overblend or pastry will be tough. Add 5 tablespoons water and blend quickly until dough gathers into a mass. Sprinkle remaining water over any dry dough in bottom of bowl and add them to the mass. The dough should hold together, not sticky.

(Note: To make pastry with a food processor, mix flour, salt, and sugar in processor bowl by running the machine for several seconds. Add butter and shortening and pulse 8 to 10 times or until mixture looks like oatmeal or coarse cornmeal. Add 5 tablespoons water and pulse 5 or 6 times or until mixture holds together when pressed in a mass. Add an additional tablespoon water to any dry dough if needed.)

2. Turn the dough out onto a clean work surface. With the heel of your hand, quickly push small portions of the dough mass away from you. (This process—called the *frisage* in French—blends the flour and fat completely.) Gather dough back into a mass and pat into a flat cake. Wrap and chill 2 hours or freeze 1 hour.

3. On a lightly floured surface roll out dough to ¼-inch thickness (slightly less than ¼ inch if making tartlets).

4. To blind bake (prebake) the pie shell preheat oven to 425° F. Line the pie or tart pan or tartlet pans with dough and crimp the edges. Line the pastry shell with lightly buttered (buttered-side-down) foil, then fill with pie weights or dried beans, place on a baking sheet, and bake 10 minutes. Remove foil with beans or pie weights. Return pastry to oven and bake 10 to 15 minutes or until pale golden-brown and dry. Cool completely before filling.

Makes enough pastry for 1 single-crust 9- or 10-inch pie or tart, or 8 4-inch tartlets.

Bittersweet Chocolate
Chunk–Pecan Pie

· · ·

THOUGH PECANS probably originated in the area that is now Texas, they were introduced to the east coast by Thomas Jefferson and were also grown by George Washington at Mount Vernon. As their botanical name, *Carya illinoensis* ("Illinois hickory") indicates, pecans grow in Illinois, but are more common further south in the Carolinas, Alabama, Georgia, Mississippi, Louisiana, Missouri, Oklahoma, Texas, and New Mexico. Because of their rich, naturally toasty flavor, pecans are especially pleasing when baked in a dense, sweet pie filling.

The changes rung on the pecan pie theme are as numerous as the counties of the Southern states. Eked out with cornmeal, enriched with butter, spiked with bourbon, or plumped with raisins, these chess-pie cousins are found throughout pecan-growing territory. The sweetener varies with the baker as well. Some pecan pies are made with brown sugar, some with white, some with honey, maple syrup, molasses, or corn syrup. The makers of Karo corn syrup devoted a whole recipe folder in the 1940s to The Famous Karo Pecan Pie: "Crunchy, nut-brown and crisp on top . . . the goodness of slightly toasted pecans . . . a delicious pudding-like filling . . . a tender flaky crush—that's KARO PECAN PIE, a Southern favorite and the prize pie of many of our best cooks."

The inspiration for this version comes from Kentucky where "Derby Pie" combines chocolate chips with a classic pecan pie filling. I use less sugar than most recipes since I would rather taste nuts and chocolate than sugar.

1 recipe Basic Pastry (page 363)
1 ounce unsweetened chocolate, finely chopped
4 tablespoons unsalted butter
2 large eggs, room temperature
½ cup sugar
½ cup dark corn syrup
¼ cup heavy cream

¾ teaspoon vanilla extract
¼ teaspoon salt
1½ cups coarsely chopped pecans
6 ounces best-quality bittersweet chocolate (such as Lindt or Tobler), broken into ½-inch pieces

1. Prepare dough as directed. Roll out dough and fit into a 10-inch pie pan. Blind bake (prebake) the pastry as directed.

2. To make the filling: In the top of a double boiler (or in a cup in a microwave oven), melt the unsweetened chocolate and the butter. Set aside to cool.

3. Preheat oven to 350° F.

4. In a large bowl, beat the eggs until light and fluffy. Beat in sugar and corn syrup until well blended. Beat in cream, vanilla, and salt, then the cooled chocolate-butter mixture. Fold in nuts and chocolate chunks.

5. Pour filling into the cooled piecrust and place on a baking sheet. Bake in the center of the oven 35 to 40 minutes or until center still wiggles very slightly (it will set completely as it cools; do not overbake or filling will be dry). Cool slightly; cut into wedges and serve warm or chilled with unsweetened whipped cream if desired. Makes 1 10-inch pie.

Serves 6.

Blackest Bottom Pie

■ ■ ■

JOHN MARIANI'S *Dictionary of American Food and Drink* cites two possible derivations for "Black-Bottom Pie." Mariani suspects that the name comes from the "low-lying area inhabited by a coloured population." He also recalls the popular flapper-era dance of the same name. But there is also the more obvious explanation—that the pie was named for its dark chocolate bottom layer.

Black-bottom pie is traditionally made with a gingersnap or graham cracker crumb crust, then filled with chocolate-flavored egg custard. The custard is topped with meringue or another custard layer lightened with egg whites and sometimes flavored with rum. My Blackest Bottom Pie has a homemade brownie crust and chocolate-flavored meringue topping for a triple chocolate experience.

The American chilled custard pie is a fairly recent development, made possible by the invention of the icebox and then the refrigerator. The availability of easy-to-use powdered gelatin gave this type of recipe a boost as well. By 1934, icebox pies had become an American standby.

BROWNIE PIE CRUST

½ cup (1 stick) unsalted butter,
  room temperature
½ cup sugar
1 egg, room temperature
½ teaspoon vanilla

⅔ cup unsweetened cocoa
½ cup unbleached all-purpose flour
¼ teaspoon salt
⅓ cup chopped pecans or walnuts

FILLING AND TOPPING

1 cup sugar
1 tablespoon cornstarch
Pinch of salt
2 cups milk
4 large eggs, separated
1 package unflavored gelatin dissolved in ¼ cup cold water

2 ounces unsweetened chocolate
Pinch of cream of tartar
1 teaspoon vanilla
⅛ teaspoon unsweetened cocoa,
  sifted
1 ounce good-quality semisweet
  chocolate, grated

1. Preheat oven to 350° F.

2. To make the crust: In a bowl cream together the butter and sugar until light and fluffy. Beat in egg and vanilla.

3. In a separate bowl, sift together cocoa, flour, and salt. Stir into the butter-sugar mixture until just combined (do not overmix).

4. Fold in nuts and spread batter with a wet spatula (dipped in water), into a well-buttered 10-inch pie pan, spreading batter up the sides, but not on the rim. (Note: Batter will fall down sides significantly as it bakes but will still slope somewhat.) Bake 15 minutes. Cool completely on a wire rack.

5. To make the custard filling: In a medium saucepan, combine half the sugar, the cornstarch, and the salt. Whisk in milk until smooth. Stir constantly over medium-low heat 5 to 10 minutes until mixture is steaming and slightly thickened; do not boil.

6. In a medium bowl, beat yolks. Slowly add the steaming milk mixture while whisking constantly. Return the mixture to the saucepan and cook over medium heat stirring constantly 3 to 5 minutes, or until mixture coats the back of a spoon. Remove from heat; whisk in dissolved gelatin and strain into a bowl.

7. In a double boiler, melt unsweetened chocolate over low heat. Whisk in

all but 1 cup of the custard mixture, setting it aside for the topping. Pour the chocolate custard mixture into the cooled brownie pie shell and chill at least 1 hour.

8. When chocolate custard has chilled 1 hour, prepare topping. In a medium bowl, beat whites with cream of tartar until foamy. Beat in vanilla, then continue beating while adding the remaining ½ cup sugar slowly until stiff.

9. Sift the cocoa into the reserved 1 cup of custard and whisk vigorously until smooth and well-blended. Fold in the beaten egg-white mixture and spread on top of the chilled chocolate custard.

10. Chill at least 3 hours, preferably longer. Before serving, sprinkle top with grated chocolate. Let pie sit at room temperature about 20 minutes before slicing.

Serves 8.

White Chocolate Chess Tartlets

■ ■ ■

THE SOUTHERN CHESS PIE carries on an old—even ancient—tradition of puddings and pastries with the rich texture of cheese. "Chess" is probably derived from the word "cheese," although various other theories have arisen about the origin of the name. Elizabeth Hedgecock Sparks, author of *North Carolina and Old Salem Cookery,* says it is "an old, old tart which may have obtained its name from the town of Chester, England." Others believe that "chess" is a corruption of "chest" (as in pie chest) where pies were often kept. Then there is the story about the cook who was asked what she put in the pie, and she replied, "Anything in your chest." Or the one who was asked about the kind of pie. The answer was "Oh, jes' pie."

The cheese etymology seems the most likely one, because in old cookbooks, cheesecakes and pies that were sometimes made with cheese, sometimes without (referring to cheese in the textural sense—lemon card, for example, is often referred to as lemon cheese), are often included in a single category. A selection of cheeseless "cheese" pastries in *Housekeeping in Old Virginia* (1879) are made with egg yolks, sugar, butter, milk, and lemon juice—very much like chess pie filling. Something called "Cheesecake Pudding" (the filling is made of yolks, brown sugar, butter, nutmeg, and brandy or rum) is baked in a crust in small tins—like the little individual chess tarts here.

This firm fixture in the constellation of Southern desserts has been associated with several noted personalities. With recipes available today, we can replicate the chess pie Rebecca Boone made for Dan'l; President Tyler's Pudding Pie; James K. Polk's Vinegar Pie; and Andrew Jackson Pie, a simple chess pie made with white sugar.

In winter, when fresh fruit was not available, the chess pie was an obvious choice for the cook since it required little more than sugar, butter, flour, and eggs. Some chess pies are made with white sugar, some with brown—these may be called simply "sugar pie" or "brown sugar pie"—some with sorghum or molasses in place of sugar. An acidic ingredient such as buttermilk, lemon juice, or vinegar is often added. The fillings often include a small amount of biscuit or cracker crumbs, pounded almonds, cornmeal, or flour. The inclusion of raisins and chopped pecans gives us Osgood—or "Oh-so-good"—pie. Chess pie filling puffs, then sinks, and sometimes cracks as it bakes, so meringue is often used to mask it.

Chocolate chess pies are not as common as plain chess pies, and these white chocolate tartlets may be a first. The brown-sugar pecan crust is a variation on one created by my friend and colleague, cookbook author Susan Wyler. It is light, very tender, and not too sweet, and, to my mind, the perfect vessel for the filling, which is a good deal less sweet than traditional chess pies.

This filling works better as individual tartlets as opposed to one big pie. The longer cooking time that pies require results in a rather crusty, overly brown, hard-on-top filling. The tartlets require a mere twelve to fifteen minutes baking time so both crust and filling are light, delicate, and tender. Serve these warm or at room temperature with strong espresso or black coffee. Tartlets may be prepared completely in advance and refrigerated for up to 5 days.

BROWN SUGAR–PECAN CRUST

6 ounces pecan halves or pecan
    pieces
3 tablespoons firmly packed light
    brown sugar
1 3/4 cups all-purpose unbleached flour

1/2 teaspoon salt
12 tablespoons (1 1/2 sticks) unsalted
    chilled butter, finely diced
4 to 6 tablespoons milk

6 ounces good-quality white chocolate, such as Callebaut, chopped
5 tablespoons unsalted butter
¾ cup sugar
1 large egg, room temperature
3 egg yolks from large eggs, room
   temperature

¾ teaspoon vanilla
Heaping ¼ teaspoon salt
Fresh raspberries (optional)
Whipped cream or vanilla ice cream
   (optional)

1. To prepare the crust: In a food processor, process nuts and sugar until ground to a fine powder. Add flour and salt and process until well blended.

2. Add butter and pulse 10 to 12 times or until mixture is the consistency of coarse meal. Add 4 tablespoons of the milk and pulse 5 to 10 times or until mixture just holds together when pressed. Do not overprocess dough.

3. Turn dough out onto a clean work surface and sprinkle with remaining milk if dough seems too dry. With the heel of your hand, quickly push small portions of the dough mass away from you. (This process, called *frisage* in French, blends the fat and the flour completely.) Gather dough back into a mass. Divide dough into 2 equal portions and pat each into a neat, flat cake. Wrap each dough cake in waxed paper and chill at least 2 hours.

4. Preheat oven to 425° F.

5. Dust dough lightly with flour on both sides. Roll out between sheets of waxed paper to about ⅛ inch thick. Remove top sheet of waxed paper.

6. To make individual 3½-inch tartlets, cut out a cardboard circle 4½ inches in diameter to use as a stencil. With a sharp knife cut out dough circles and place in 3½-inch tartlet tins. With a sharp knife trim edges. Prick bottom and sides of dough with a fork.

7. Cut out rounds of aluminum foil to fit into each tartlet. Place foil circles on top of dough, then fill with pie weights or dried beans. Place tartlets on a jelly-roll pan and bake for 8 minutes. Remove foil and weights, return tartlets to oven, and bake 5 minutes longer or until dry and pale golden-brown. Cool completely on a rack. (To make bite-sized 2-inch tartlets, roll out dough as directed, remove top sheet of waxed paper, and roll the dough onto the rolling pin, peeling off the bottom sheet of waxed paper as you go.) Arrange tins 1 inch apart on a work surface and loosely drape the dough over the tins. Roll the

Desserts

■

rolling pin over the dough to cut it into dough circles. Lift off excess dough and reroll or discard. Lightly fit dough circles into the tins. Prick on bottom and sides with a fork and place on jelly-roll pan. Bake 8 minutes (you do not need pie weights for tiny tartlets) or until golden-brown. Cool completely on racks).

8. Lower oven temperature to 325° F.

9. To make the filling: In the top part of a double boiler—*over,* not in—hot water, heat the chocolate and butter together, stirring constantly until melted. Set aside to cool *briefly* to warm room temperature.

10. In a large bowl, beat sugar, egg, egg yolks, vanilla, and salt. Add the cooled chocolate mixture and beat until well blended. (Note: Do not let this mixture stand; proceed immediately to step 11.)

11. Pour about 2½ tablespoons filling into each cooled tartlet shell (use 1½ teaspoons per tiny 2-inch tartlet) and bake 12 to 14 minutes or until golden-brown on top and set in the center. Do not overcook; the filling will settle and solidify somewhat as it cools. Cool at least 20 minutes. Garnish with fresh raspberries and a tiny dollop of whipped cream, if desired.

Makes about 12 3½-inch tartlets or 24 2-inch tartlets.

Peaches and Cream Shortbread Tart
. . .

PEACHES, with their almost acid-free sweetness and lush texture, are perhaps the best-suited fruit to combine with cream. The combination has been popular for centuries. Nellie Custis Lewis, granddaughter of Martha Washington, made a dessert called a "fromage" of fruit and cream. Her "Peach Cheese" was made from poached peaches and peach kernels—the soft heart of the peachstone that carries an intense almond flavor. The puréed fruit was mixed with cream and a gelling agent called isinglass, and whipped over ice.

A recipe in *Housekeeping in Old Virginia* (1879) keeps the peaches and cream separate until serving, and presumably lets the kitchen maid do the combining: "While the first course is being served" the peaches are peeled, stoned and sprinkled with sugar. They are piled in a bowl lined with "handsome, glossy leaves" and served with cream. The *Picayune Creole Cook Book* (1900) styles a similar presentation.

Southern cooks were also fond of cooking fresh peaches with butter and brown sugar, then served with vanilla ice cream.

Fresh peach pies are undyingly popular in the South, despite the fact that heat and humidity can be problematic in pastry making. Whatever the weather or climate, a crumb crust, like the rich shortbread crust used here, solves the pastry problem: You simply combine crumbled cookies with melted butter (a technique made even easier if you use a blender or food processor). But before the days of crumb crusts—and food processors—cookbook authors inscribed dire warnings on the hazards of pastry making: "Never attempt this in warm weather unless you are supplied with ice"; "Keep cool"; "Set it upon ice," etc., then went ahead and offered recipes for peach pies, especially meringue-topped versions.

The filling here is even simpler than the crust. Simply blend crème fraîche with a little honey and vanilla, and top with poached peach slices.

PEACH FILLING

6 cups water

2 cups sugar

2 tablespoons good-quality peach liqueur (such as Pêcher Mignon or Liqueur de Pêche from Willm (optional)

1 large lemon

1½ to 1¾ pounds fresh, unblemished ripe peaches (about 4 large peaches), washed but not peeled

SHORTBREAD CRUST

4 tablespoons unsalted butter

12 ounces good quality shortbread cookies such as Pepperidge Farm™, broken into medium-sized pieces

CREAM FILLING

1 cup crème fraîche or sour cream

¼ teaspoon vanilla

2 tablespoons honey

1. To prepare peach filling: Place water, sugar and liqueur, if using, in a medium saucepan. Remove the peel in long strips from the lemon by using a vegetable peeler. Add lemon peel to the saucepan along with 1 tablespoon of lemon juice.

2. Heat over medium heat until sugar dissolves. Bring to a boil, add whole peaches, cover, and lower heat so peaches simmer gently. Cook 15 minutes or until just tender. Cool peaches in the syrup, then drain on a rack. Cut peaches in half, remove pits, and peel if desired. Reduce the syrup over high heat until thick and syrupy. Set aside.

3. Preheat oven to 375° F.

4. To make the crust: In a medium saucepan, melt butter and cool to room temperature. When cooled, process the butter with the shortbread in a food processor or blender until well combined. Press mixture into a lightly buttered 9-inch false-bottom tart pan. Bake 8 to 12 minutes or until pale golden-brown. Cool thoroughly.

5. To make the cream filling: In a bowl combine crème fraîche, vanilla, and honey until smooth and creamy. Spread evenly into the cooled crust.

6. Using a very sharp stainless-steel knife, cut peaches into thin, crosswise slices. Overlap peach slices closely together in concentric circles. Drizzle the reduced syrup evenly over peaches. Chill 1 hour before serving.

Serves 6.

Fig and Pecan Custard Tart

. . .

When the Raineys, after their barn got blown away in a big wind, had no more money to throw away on piano lessons, Miss Eckhart said she would teach Virgie free, because she must not stop learning. But later she made her pick the figs off the trees in the backyard in summer and the pecans off the ground in the front yard in winter, for her lessons. Virgie said Miss Eckhart never gave her a one. Yet she always had nuts in her pocket.

—Eudora Welty, *The Golden Apples*

MENTION THE WORD "FICUS" and most people will think of the graceful potted trees that adorn offices and homes today. But the fig tree is a species of the ficus genus and in the South the "real thing" can be seen growing in backyards, around old farmhouses, and espaliered against walls in town gardens. Figs were grown in the sixteenth century in St. Augustine, Florida, and Captain John Smith reported a good harvest of "excellent figges" at Jamestown in 1629.

A 1769 entry in *Thomas Jefferson's Garden Book* includes among his March plantings "In the Hollow" at Monticello "1. row of Pomegranates . . . [ditto] of figs." Jefferson eventually introduced several varieties of European figs to Virginia. In 1794 Jefferson wrote enthusiastically to his friend George Wythe of Williamsburg, "I ever wish to have opportunity of enjoying your society, knowing your fondness for figs, I have daily wished you could have partaken of ours this year. I never saw so great a crop, & they are still abundant. Of three kinds which I brought from France, there is one, of which I have a single bush, superior to any fig I ever tasted anywhere." This must have been the Marseilles fig, which he again extolls as "incomparably superior" in an 1809 letter to William Thornton.

Although truly hardy only in the lower South, fig trees can be grown in sunny, sheltered areas or as container plants elsewhere in the region. In most of the South, the fruit can be harvested twice, first in summer from year-old growth, then later, in the autumn, from the new branches that have grown over the summer. Today the most popular fig trees in the South are the Brown Turkey (also called Brown Naples or Blue Burgundy), a medium-large brownish-purple fig with red flesh, and the Celeste, a smaller, violet-purple fruit with white flesh. (Both varieties are the teardrop-shaped Mission, or Adriatic, type, different from the rounder Smyrna figs commonly grown commercially for drying.) Figs, especially those grown in humid climates, are extremely perishable, and they must either be eaten or preserved soon after picking. Southern cookbooks provide a bounty of ways to use and keep figs.

Nineteenth-century Southern cooks made fresh fig puddings, preserved figs whole in sugar syrup, and baked cakes with dried figs. Figs were also poached in syrup, then sprinkled with sugar and dried, then packed in boxes or jars with sugar sprinkled over each layer of figs. Later, fig ice cream, fig conserve, and candied figs were added to the roster of fig preparations.

I have always adored figs—fresh, dried, but especially preserved. Every year my grandmother would send a case of her best fig preserves to my father and me, the family fig freaks. After poaching, the dried figs in this recipe resemble my grandmother's preserves and offer a mellow counterpoint to bourbon-flavored pastry cream. The toasty flavor of pecans is a natural with figs, though they are often combined with almonds or walnuts in European recipes.

SWEET PIE PASTRY

2 cups unbleached all-purpose flour
1 tablespoon superfine or confectioners' sugar
1 teaspoon salt

12 tablespoons (1 ½ sticks) unsalted
butter, softened
1 egg
Cold water

POACHED FIG TOPPING

1½ cups dried figs
2 cups water
½ cup bourbon

3 tablespoons sugar
2 tablespoons lemon juice

BOURBON PASTRY CREAM

½ cup sugar
6 large egg yolks
½ cup unbleached all-purpose flour

Pinch of salt
2 cups milk
3 to 4 tablespoons bourbon
1 cup pecan halves, lightly toasted as
garnish

1. To make the sweet pie pastry: Sift flour with sugar and salt onto a work surface or into a large bowl. Make a well in the center and put butter and egg into it. Mix butter and egg together with your fingertips or fork until well blended. Gradually bring in flour and work mixture until it resembles coarse meal. Add just enough cold water to form a soft, not sticky dough. Wrap in waxed paper and refrigerate for 2 hours.

2. To make the topping: In a saucepan simmer figs, water, bourbon, sugar, and lemon juice for 10 minutes. Cool figs in the syrup to room temperature.

3. Drain figs thoroughly, reserving liquid. Cut figs in half and set aside. Reduce liquid to ¼ cup over medium heat, about 15 to 20 minutes. Set aside.

4. To make the bourbon pastry cream: In a bowl whisk sugar with egg yolks until thick and light. Gradually whisk in flour and salt.

5. In a heavy saucepan, bring milk to a boil. Stirring constantly, pour the hot milk into the egg mixture in a very thin stream. Return this mixture to the saucepan and cook over medium heat, stirring constantly, until it comes to a boil. Boil about 2 minutes, remove from heat, and cool to room temperature. Stir in bourbon, taste, and add another tablespoon or less if desired. Chill until ready to use.

6. Preheat oven to 400° F. On a lightly floured work surface, roll out chilled pastry dough to slightly less than ¼-inch thickness. Place in a 12-inch tart pan with a removable bottom. Line pastry with parchment or lightly buttered foil and pie weights and bake for 8 to 10 minutes. Remove weights and paper and reduce oven temperature to 375° F. Bake 12 to 15 minutes longer or until just golden-brown. When cool, brush inside of pastry with reduced fig poaching liquid. Spread with pastry cream and arrange figs and pecans in a pattern on top of pastry cream. Refrigerate until ready to serve.

Serves 10 to 12.

"Double Decker" Citron-Cranberry Pie

■ ■ ■

DOUBLE-DECKER PIES, hypocrite pies, two-story pies, or stacked pies come in several varieties. In so-called hypocrite pies, a layer of custard or chess filling covers (or hypocritically "hides") a fruit filling. A similar type of double-layered pie is composed of two separately baked pies stacked together. This classic variation has an open-faced damson-filled pie topped with an entire so-called "citron" pie that has been baked in a separate pan, and unmolded. Similar to chess pie, citron filling may have gotten its name because its color resembles that of the field melon called "citron." It may have been the citrus, i.e., lemon juice and zest, that inspired the name, although some citron filling recipes are made with vinegar instead of lemon.

As many as five layers went into the Kentucky stack pies (or cakes) recalled by Marion Flexner in her *Out of Kentucky Kitchens* (1949). One such pie tower, served as a wedding cake by a Louisville resident, consisted of five separately filled and baked chess pies. The cooked pies were carefully stacked and frosted with boiled white icing. A much simpler stack pie from Kentucky is Min-ell Mandeville's Transparent Pie (another name for chess pie), for which a baked pastry shell is spread with jelly, then topped with chess filling. Some call this creation an "amber pie," because of its amber hue. Stack pies are said to have originated at a time when a cook would take several pies to a church supper or family reunion. She would simply "stack" one on top of the other. Instead of separating the pies, they were presented as a tiered concoction, the layers sliced through.

In my version, a layer of "citron" filling is topped with a layer of homemade cranberry conserve. Damson preserves—a more traditional accompaniment to citron filling—may be substituted for the conserve.

The tart cranberry conserve that tops this pie provides a pleasant contrast to the rather intense sweetness of the chess-type filling. The cranberry is so often linked with New England and that New England–born holiday, Thanksgiving, that you might not expect to find cranberries used much in the South, but it does appear in many old Southern recipes. Cranberries grow wild in West Virginia and in northern North Carolina. In *North Carolina and Old Salem Cookery,* one "Aycock Brown of Manteo" asserts that "the quantity of cranberries which grows in the natural bogs in Dare County is sufficient to make wives hand their husband [*sic*] cranberry scoops and send them out to gather a mess of berries."

Although the provenance of the fruit is not specified, recipes for cranberry pies are found in *The Carolina Housewife* (1847), and *Mrs. Hill's New Cook Book* (1873) and one for cranberry jelly appears in *Housekeeping in Old Virginia* (1879). The *Picayune Creole Cook Book* (1900) lists several recipes for "airelles," or cranberries. In the sauce chapter, there are more lines devoted to Cranberry Sauce than to any other sauce, including that foundation of Creole cookery, the roux. A Compote d'Airelles, or Cranberry Syrup (to be served over ice) and a Cranberry Pie, filled with sauce as prepared below, are also included.

I love to make this pie for Thanksgiving dessert, but you can also make it into tartlets for a holiday tea or dessert party. I think these taste even better the second day.

1 recipe Basic Pastry (page 363) (2 recipes if making tartlets)

BUTTERMILK FILLING

1 cup sugar
2 tablespoons cornmeal
⅛ teaspoon salt
3 large eggs

¼ cup buttermilk
⅓ cup unsalted butter, melted and cooled
½ teaspoon vanilla

CRANBERRY TOPPING

2 cups fresh (or substitute thawed frozen) whole cranberries

½ cup sugar
¼ cup light corn syrup

1. Preheat oven to 425° F.

2. To make the pastry: Mix, roll (reserve dough scraps), and blind bake as recipe instructs. Roll out dough scraps and cut into stars, hearts, moons, or other shapes (these will later decorate the finished pie). Place cut-outs on ungreased baking sheet and sprinkle lightly with sugar. Bake 10 minutes or until pale golden-brown and crisp. Cool and set aside.

3. Lower oven to 350° F.

4. To make buttermilk filling: In a large bowl mix sugar, cornmeal, and salt. Beat in eggs one at a time, beating well after each addition. Beat in buttermilk, butter, and vanilla until well blended. Pour into prepared pie or tartlet shells (you will need about 2 tablespoons buttermilk filling for each 4-inch tartlet). Bake 30 to 35 minutes (or 15 to 20 minutes for tartlets) or until golden-brown and center is set. (Note: If crust is browning too quickly, cover with strips of aluminum foil.) Cool completely.

5. To make the topping: In a small, heavy saucepan over low heat combine cranberries and sugar. With a wooden spoon crush cranberries lightly against the side of pan. Stir in corn syrup. Simmer, uncovered, over medium-low heat, stirring frequently, 20 to 30 minutes or until most of the liquid has evaporated. Cool completely. Makes about 2 cups topping.

6. Spread cranberry filling over cooled buttermilk filling. (Use about 1 tablespoon cranberry topping for each 4-inch tartlet.) Decorate with baked cut-outs if desired. Serve at room temperature or chilled.

Makes 16 4-inch tartlets or 1 9-inch pie.

Blackberry Roll

• • •

[In April,] Dewberries and Blackberries are brought in by the Negroes in large quantities, and the cry fills the streets. [In June,] Blackberries . . . are everywhere in abundance.

—The *Picayune Creole Cook Book* (1900)

BLACKBERRY PIE (Tarte de Mures) and Blackberry Roll (*Bourrelet aux Mures*) were two New Orleansian delicacies that took advantage of the bountiful crop. The pie was baked "as . . . Apple Pie"; the Roll was encased in white muslin and boiled for two hours, like many old-fashioned fruit puddings. Similar desserts have been called Valise Pudding, Roly-Poly, Roley-Poley Pudding, Dolly in the Blanket, and in New Orleans, Bourrelet.

I did not know about blackberry rolls until several years ago when I asked my friend Frances King (a native Virginian and excellent cook) what childhood dessert she remembered most clearly. "Blackberry Roll" was her answer. Intrigued by the name, I was inspired to create my own version of this summer classic.

Blackberry desserts are especially precious because of the effort involved in picking the berries yourself. As children, my sister and I braved the thorns in late June each year, gathering enough blackberries to make two birthday pies: one for our mother, the other for our grandfather, "Daddy Jim."

Blackberries were not always highly prized; this country's first agricultural books gave instructions on how to destroy the plants. Both wild and cultivated blackberries grow well in the South, and are particularly bountiful in Arkansas and Maryland. Trailing blackberries—also known as dewberries—are also popular in the South, especially in North Carolina where they are grown commercially. (Dewberries, unlike blackberries, have canes that are not self-supporting.)

2 cups unbleached all-purpose flour
2 teaspoons baking powder
1 teaspoon salt
½ cup plus 2 tablespoons sugar
4 tablespoons butter
2 tablespoons shortening

½ cup milk
2 cups blackberries (or substitute dewberries, raspberries, or blueberries)
1 egg yolk beaten with 1 tablespoon water for glaze

1. Preheat oven to 350° F.

2. In a large bowl, combine flour, baking powder, salt, and 2 tablespoons sugar. With a pastry cutter or two knives, cut in 2 tablespoons of the butter and the shortening. Stir in milk until just blended (do not overmix).

3. On a lightly floured surface, roll out dough to a 12-inch by 18-inch rectangle, ⅛ inch thick. Distribute berries evenly on the dough, leaving a 1-inch border on all sides. Sprinkle with remaining sugar; dot with remaining butter. Roll up lengthwise like a jelly roll; pinch edges together to close. Place seam-side-down on buttered jelly-roll pan. Brush with egg glaze.

4. Bake 40 to 45 minutes or until juices are bubbling and dough is golden-brown. Cool at least 10 minutes before slicing. Slice and serve with lightly sweetened whipped cream or vanilla ice cream, if desired.

Serves 6 to 8.

Cakes

SOUTHERN CAKES are one of the region's most delectable, time-honored culinary traditions and any potluck supper or family reunion without at least a half-dozen or so is practically unthinkable. Cake baking was one of my favorite pastimes when I was young, and coconut was the cake dearest to my heart. On my tenth birthday, I tinted the entire celebratory confection robin's-egg blue— even the coconut frosting was the color of a crystal clear spring sky! I still have a weakness for coconut cake as do many dessert lovers in the South where, along with caramel and chocolate, it is one of the most popular layer cakes in the region.

Until recently, in many parts of the South (particularly rural areas), cakes were a special dessert. Pies were much more commonplace since they could be made from ingredients that were generally less costly and easier to obtain. The makings for the most basic pie—fruit, sugar, flour, and lard—were nearly always at hand, whereas butter and eggs (which were more plentiful in summer than in winter) might not be.

Festive occasions in the eighteenth-, nineteenth-, and early twentieth-century South might have included jam cakes, jelly rolls, tipsy cakes (containing spirits of some sort), scripture cakes, funeral cakes, and spice cakes (sometimes known as hermit cakes) or Dolly Varden. Then there were the cakes named according to their color: snow cake and silver cake—white cakes sometimes flavored with almonds, coconut, or bitter almond extract; black cake—deep and dark with spices, molasses, raisins, and currants; and gold cake—brightened with egg yolks, citrus juices, and zest. Nut-enriched cakes included those made with black walnuts, hickory nuts, and of course, pecans and peanuts. There were even cakes named after people, like Robert E. Lee, the region's favorite general. His favorite cake is said to have been a white cake—sometimes flavored with coconut—then filled with lemon curd or a citrusy frosting. A similar cake was named after its turn-of-the-century Alabama cook-inventor, Emma Rylander Lane. Lane Cake—a white cake layered with a raisin-, coconut- and pecan-enriched frosting and topped with a sweet white icing—has also become a Southern classic. Similar to Lee and Lane cakes is Lady Baltimore cake, said to have been created by Charleston belle Alicia Rhett Mayberry, for the novelist, Owen Wister. He titled his next book, *Lady Baltimore,* and a tea room called Lady Baltimore opened a short time later. Lady Baltimore Cake is an almond-flavored yellow or white cake frosted with a lemon-flavored meringue that has walnuts and raisins. One of the most popular cake-based desserts in nineteenth-century South Carolina was Charlotte Russe. To make it, plain sponge cake slices were used to line a charlotte mold, which was then filled with a rich, custard-like filling.

Perhaps the most charming cake names come from those used to attract a gentleman caller. Knowing that the way to a man's heart is through his stomach, what young maiden could resist trying her hand at such seductions as Introduction Cake, Acquaintanceship Cake, or Flirtation Cake? There were also Rival Cakes and Jealousy Puffs should she need to really prove herself. And if all went well, there were Engagement Cakes, Wedding Cakes, Brides' Cakes, and Bachelor's Cakes.

As much as I dearly love the idea of the old classics, some are too sweet for my taste. The meringues or boiled frostings depend almost entirely on sugar for flavor. I prefer rich, tangy ingredients to sweet ones, so I let other flavors—bourbon, coconut, pecans, molasses, dried fruit, and apple cider—shine forth.

None of the cakes here require any special ingredients or pastry bag acrobatics and all but the Apple Stack Cake can be frozen (and even that can be made well in advance), so they are perfect for entertaining.

Bourbon Tea Cakes

• • •

AS IT WAS IN MOTHER ENGLAND, afternoon tea in the old South was an occasion for gracious entertaining. In the nineteenth century, when "afternoon calls" might fill the better part of the day, the conscientious hostess was well supplied with a selection of toothsome little cakes and biscuits with which to sustain (and impress) her guests as they stopped on their appointed rounds.

The earliest treats were from a hearth-heated griddle. Crumpets, scones, and griddlecakes were served hot, slathered with butter and jam. Later, favorite tea dainties included cinnamon toast, muffins, and quickbreads, finger sandwiches and iced cakes.

Housekeeping in Old Virginia (1879) provides rules for making a proper tea (black, green, or iced) plus the following possibilities to accompany it: Nun's Puffs, cream puff shells baked in cups or tins and sprinkled with sugar while hot; Boston Cream Cakes, another puffy confection but this time baked in muffin rings and filled with pastry cream; Velvet Cakes, yeast raised and baked in muffin rings; Tea Cakes, which seem to be a kind of sour-cream sugar cookie; Delicate Tea Cakes, made with almonds and pulverized sugar; and Delicious Small Cakes, "the consistency of Shrewsbury cakes," made with egg yolks and iced with caramelized sugar glaze.

The torte-like, not-too-sweet, bourbon-flavored cakes here have ground almonds and breadcrumbs standing in for the flour. They are quickly mixed and baked; you can be ready to serve them to afternoon guests whether your teatime is a long-established tradition or a spur-of-the-moment gesture. Serve with sweet butter, Devonshire cream, or crème fraîche. Cakes may be made in advance, wrapped in plastic wrap, and frozen. To rewarm, remove plastic, then wrap cakes in paper towels and cook in microwave until slightly warm but not hot. Or heat through (do not thaw first) in a 350° F oven.

2 cups finely ground unblanched almonds (grind ½ pound whole, shelled almonds in a food processor or blender until powdery)

½ cup fine, dry unseasoned breadcrumbs

¾ cup golden raisins or currants

6 large eggs, separated

1 cup firmly packed light brown sugar

½ cup good-quality bourbon

Confectioners' sugar, for dusting

1. Preheat oven to 375° F.

2. In a bowl, mix almonds, breadcrumbs, and raisins together. In a separate bowl, beat egg yolks and ¾ cup brown sugar together until thick and light colored. In a third bowl, beat egg whites until foamy, gradually adding remaining ¼ cup brown sugar. Continue beating egg whites until soft peaks form.

3. Alternately fold egg whites and nut mixture into egg yolk mixture. Stir in bourbon until just combined.

4. Fill buttered or paper-lined 2-inch muffin tins ⅔ full with batter and bake 13 to 15 minutes or until toothpick comes out clean. Serve warm or cool, dusted lightly with sieved confectioners' sugar.

Makes 18 to 20 tea cakes.

Pistachio-Apricot Fruitcake

■ ■ ■

I am sending your Christmas herewith, a white fruitcake ... I have never understood why everybody loves it but they swear they do ...

—Reynolds Price, *Kate Vaiden*

THOSE BAD, OLD JOKES about fruitcake were no doubt inspired by a leaden, stygian loaf, booby-trapped with rubbery bits of green and yellow candied fruit. Picking the citron and green cherries out of a sodden cake was a Christmas ritual for me as well as unfortunate thousands. Because of my disdain, I created this coconut-almond cake, enriched with my favorite dried fruits—apricots, raisins, pears, pineapple—plus a full pound of pistachios, and a liberal dose of bourbon. As a result, it happily bears no resemblance to those benighted creations mentioned above.

This cake is the Southern "white" or "light" fruitcake derived from and similar to English cakes, and more delicately spiced than classic dark fruitcakes. The Southern white fruitcake usually contains coconut and candied, crystallized, or preserved pineapple. Almonds are also a sine qua non, and spirits, in the form of Madeira, brandy, or wine, are added to the batter and sometimes used to saturate the cake after baking. Occasionally the cake and fruit are layered, and sometimes the cake is filled and/or iced.

The 1⅔ cups of bourbon in this 8-inch cake has a subtle, but distinct presence. The whiskey used to macerate the fruit will lose its alcohol in baking, but the uncooked bourbon-apricot glaze will retain some of its kick. If you are making the cake ahead of time, brush it with bourbon, and wrap it tightly in plastic. It keeps in the refrigerator for up to two weeks, or in the freezer for up to six months. The day before serving, glaze and decorate the cake, then rewrap in plastic and let it stand for another twenty-four hours.

3 cups sugar

2 cups water

1 cup plus 6 tablespoons bourbon

2 cups chopped dried (not glacéed) apricots

1 cup golden raisins

1 cup chopped dried (not glacéed) pears

1 cup chopped dried (not glacéed) pineapple

1 cup shredded coconut

1½ cups (1 pound) shelled, skinned, unsalted natural pistachios, chopped

1 cup (¼ pound) finely ground, blanched almonds

1½ cups unbleached all-purpose flour

8 tablespoons (1 stick) unsalted butter, softened

1 tablespoon grated orange zest

4 large eggs, room temperature

1¼ teaspoons nutmeg

¼ teaspoon salt

¼ teaspoon baking soda

6 tablespoons buttermilk

¼ cup orange juice

¼ cup bourbon mixed with 2 tablespoons strained apricot preserves for glazing (Note: To prepare fruitcake 2 to 4 weeks in advance, increase bourbon to ½ cup)

Nuts and dried fruits for garnish (optional)

1. In a saucepan dissolve 2 cups of the sugar in 2 cups of water over low heat. Bring slowly to a boil, remove from heat, and cool to room temperature. Add 1 cup bourbon. Add the dried fruit, toss to mix, and let stand 2 hours.

2. Preheat oven to 275° F.

3. Drain fruit very well, discarding the liquid, then in a large bowl toss fruits, coconut, pistachios, and almonds with ¾ cup flour; set aside.

4. In a large bowl, beat butter, the remaining 1 cup sugar, and orange zest until fluffy. Add eggs one at a time, beating well after each addition.

5. In a medium bowl, combine remaining flour with nutmeg, salt, and baking soda. In a small bowl, combine remaining 6 tablespoons bourbon, buttermilk, and orange juice. Beat dry and liquid ingredients alternately into butter-sugar mixture, beginning and ending with the dry ingredients. Do not overbeat. Fold in fruits and nuts.

6. Pour into an 8-cup buttered tube pan that has been lined with buttered brown paper. Bake in center of oven 2 to 2½ hours or until skewer comes out clean.

7. Let cake stand in pan 15 minutes; then invert to unmold. Remove brown paper. While cake is still warm, brush with bourbon-apricot mixture. Garnish top with extra fruits and nuts, if desired. Cool completely, wrap well, and let stand at least 24 hours before slicing.

Makes about 20 slices.

Note If making cake 2 to 4 weeks prior to serving, store in refrigerator or a very cool, dark place.

Bourbon-Orange Pound Cake with Bourbon Glaze and Orange-Apricot Sauce

■ ■ ■

That afternoon was like the center of the cake that Berenice had baked last Monday, a cake which failed. . . . Frankie had been glad the cake had failed, not out of spite, but because she loved these fallen cakes the best. She enjoyed the damp, gummy richness near the center, and did not understand why grown people thought such cakes a failure. It was a loaf cake, that last Monday, with the edges risen and light and high and the middle moist and altogether fallen— after the bright high morning the afternoon was as dense and solid as the center of that cake.

—Carson McCullers, *The Member of the Wedding*

LIKE FRANKIE, I've always loved fallen cakes, as does my Georgia friend, Betsy Hunter, who, when she was young, adjusted the cooking time of her pound cakes making them "fall" on purpose so that the "sad streak"—that moist strata where the ingredients had cooked but not risen—promised to be there.

Pound cakes have been made throughout the country for centuries, and they continue to be especially popular in the South. American poundcakes, like their English forbears, were usually made with "a wineglassful of brandy" and flavored with nutmeg and/or mace. Sometimes rosewater was used, and a family recipe from Virginia even takes its subtle fragrance from rose-geranium leaves placed in the bottom of the pan.

One recipe in *Housekeeping in Old Virginia* (1879) allows for replacing the traditional brandy with a wineglass of "good whiskey flavored with nutmeg, or the grated rind of a lemon." Perhaps this was the cake that evolved into Kentucky's pecan bourbon cake. Marion Flexner includes the recipe in her *Out of Kentucky Kitchens* (1949), but reluctantly discloses its dubious provenance: Supposedly a Southern woman "coaxed" the recipe from "a famous New York maitre d'hotel" by "crossing his palm with a lot of silver." But in its defense, she continues, "if it wasn't born here, it has become a Kentuckian by adoption and certainly deserves a place in any collection of that State's most delicious dishes." Her version is made with ½ cup of bottled-in-bond Kentucky bourbon, which results in a batter that "looks and tastes a great deal like eggnog."

The pound cake here is also flavored with bourbon. Orange zest and juice add a subtle tang to the cake, glaze, and sauce. The cake may be baked and glazed, then stored at room temperature (tightly wrapped) for one week or frozen up to six months. It makes a special Christmas gift: prepare the sauce and pack in a French canning jar tied with a ribbon to accompany the cake.

CAKE

½ pound unsalted butter, room temperature
1 cup sugar
5 large eggs, separated
2½ cups self-rising cake flour (or substitute 2½ cups plain cake flour and 3½ teaspoons baking powder and 1¼ teaspoons salt)
Note: if using self-rising cake flour, it must be very fresh.
Grated zest of 2 oranges
¼ cup good-quality bourbon

(ingredients continued)

1½ cups apricot jam

*2 tablespoons freshly squeezed or-
ange juice (use the zested oranges
from the cake recipe)*

2 tablespoons good-quality bourbon

SAUCE

*1 cup strained apricot jam, reserved
from making glaze, above*

*2 to 3 tablespoons freshly squeezed
orange juice*

*1 to 2 tablespoons good-quality
bourbon*

1. Preheat oven to 350° F.

2. In a bowl cream butter and sugar until light and fluffy. In another bowl, beat egg yolks until thick and pale in color. Add to the butter mixture and mix well. Sift flour (or flour plus baking powder and salt) over the batter and stir it in along with orange zest and bourbon, taking care not to overmix.

3. In another bowl, beat egg whites until stiff but not dry and fold into batter. Butter a 9-inch by 5-inch loaf pan and line the bottom with parchment or waxed paper. Pour in the batter and bake 50 to 55 minutes or until cake tester inserted in the center comes out clean. Do not overbake.

4. Meanwhile, to make bourbon glaze: In a saucepan, heat jam until simmering. Simmer 1 minute and strain. Reserve 1 cup strained jam for the sauce. To remaining jam, add orange juice and bourbon and set aside to pour over cake just after baking.

5. To make sauce: In a bowl mix the 1 cup reserved strained jam with orange juice and bourbon. Taste, and add more juice or bourbon if desired.

6. As soon as the cake is removed from the oven, poke holes in the top with the tines of a fork. Pour half the glaze over the cake. Let stand 5 minutes and pour on remaining glaze. Let cool 10 minutes in the pan, then turn out onto rack to cool completely. Slice and serve on a pool of sauce or drizzle sauce over the cake.

Serves 12 to 14.

Peanut Layer Cake
with Whipped Cream Filling and
Caramel-Peanut Sauce

• • •

THE UNITED STATES is the largest producer of peanuts used as food (other countries where they are grown process most of their crops for oil), and most of our peanuts come from Georgia. The other Southern states that grow peanuts include Florida, Alabama, Virginia, and the Carolinas. Despite the availability of the nut (actually, the peanut is a legume) peanut dessert recipes are not common in Southern cookbooks. Some that do exist include *The Carolina Housewife*'s (1847) "An Excellent Receipt for Groundnut Candy" (peanut brittle made with molasses) and Ground Nut Cake, another candy (not a cake) made with pounded peanuts, brown sugar, and beaten egg whites. The book's Groundnut Cheese Cakes (unlike today's "cheesecakes") are made with blanched, beaten peanuts, brandy, sugar, and butter, then baked in puff pastry.

Many eighteenth- and nineteenth-century Southern cakes were made with ground almonds, like the peanut-sauced, whipped-cream layer cake recipe here.

Caramel cake, a longtime Southern favorite, also inspired this recipe. This cake may be made in advance and frozen; thaw, split, and fill up to twenty-four hours before serving. Whipped cream deflates with time, so if you prefer a higher cake, fill just before serving. The sauce may be made up to five days in advance.

CAKE

1 cup sugar
1/4 cup unsalted toasted peanuts
1/4 cup slivered almonds
3 large eggs

1/4 cup unbleached all-purpose flour
1/2 teaspoon baking powder
1/4 teaspoon salt
1/2 cup (1 stick) unsalted butter, melted and cooled slightly

CARAMEL-PEANUT SAUCE

1 cup sugar
1/2 cup water
1/2 cup chopped roasted unsalted peanuts

1 cup heavy cream

(ingredients continued)

FILLING

1 cup heavy cream   *Confectioners' sugar, for dusting*
¼ cup superfine sugar

1. Preheat oven to 300° F.

2. To make the cake: Butter a 9-inch-round cake pan and line it with parchment paper. Lightly butter and flour the paper.

3. In a food processor or blender, process ¼ cup of the sugar, the peanuts, and almonds until the mixture is almost paste-like. Add remaining sugar and process to blend. Transfer mixture to a large bowl.

4. Beat in eggs one at a time. Sift flour, baking powder, and salt over egg mixture and fold until just combined. Fold in melted butter; do not overmix.

5. Turn the batter into the prepared pan and bake for 25 to 30 minutes or until a toothpick comes out clean when inserted into the center. Cool cake in the pan for 5 minutes. Run a knife around the edges, then turn cake out onto a rack. Cool completely.

6. To make the caramel-peanut sauce: Heat the sugar and water in a heavy saucepan—without stirring—over medium-low heat until sugar is dissolved. Increase heat to high and continue to cook without stirring until bubbles are large and slow to burst. When syrup is almost beginning to turn golden, add the peanuts. Continue cooking until syrup is deep, golden-brown. Do not overcook or syrup will taste bitter.

7. Immediately remove from heat. Stand back and carefully add 1 cup cream while whisking constantly. Be careful because mixture may splatter. If mixture does not blend easily, return to heat for 1 to 2 minutes. Cool to room temperature, then chill several hours before serving.

8. To make the filling: Cut cake in half through the center with a long, serrated knife. In a bowl, whip the cream with superfine sugar until stiff. Spread whipped cream thickly on the bottom cake layer and cover with top cake layer. Dust with confectioners' sugar. Cut into wedges and serve with caramel-peanut sauce.

Serves 8.

Spiced Apple Stack Cakes
with Cider Butter and Cream

• • •

ARKANSAS BLACK. Buckingham. Black Twig. Horse Apple. Albemarle Pippin. Tar-Button. Yates. These are some of the apples of the old South. Most people think of the Northeast and Northwest as apple country, but many apple varieties were (and still are) grown in the South. The York Imperial and Stayman varieties are largely produced in Virginia and West Virginia, and the Golden Delicious, rated by many as America's best all-around apple, was discovered in Clay Country, West Virginia in 1914.

One of the most distinctive old-fashioned Southern apple desserts is the stack cake, which is sometimes attributed to Tennessee. However, stack cakes are enjoyed in the Carolinas, Kentucky, West Virginia, and Virginia as well.

There are many ways to make stack cake, but it is basically layers of cake (or pastry, biscuit, gingerbread, or cookie) alternating with layers of applesauce, cooked fresh apples, or reconstituted dried apples. Both stack pies and stack cakes may have been born out of convenience: It is far easier to carry a four-tiered cake or pie to a picnic or church supper than to transport four separate desserts.

The stack cake here uses fresh, unpeeled apples and cider butter, a tart spread composed of sweet butter and cider syrup. Cider syrup is made by boiling sweet apple cider until it is reduced to a thick syrup.

STACK CAKES

2 cups unbleached all-purpose flour
1½ teaspoons ground ginger
1 teaspoon baking powder
½ teaspoon baking soda
½ teaspoon salt
¼ teaspoon ground cinnamon
8 tablespoons (1 stick) unsalted butter, room temperature

¼ cup firmly packed light brown sugar
1 large egg, room temperature
1 tablespoon grated lemon zest
½ cup buttermilk, room temperature
½ cup molasses, room temperature

(ingredients continued)

Desserts

■

1½ to 1¾ pounds firm, tart cooking
  apples
1½ tablespoons lemon juice
4 tablespoons unsalted butter

3 tablespoons firmly packed light
  brown sugar

1 gallon fresh unfiltered apple cider
  (see note)
8 tablespoons (1 stick) unsalted butter, room temperature

2 teaspoons grated orange zest
Lightly sweetened whipped cream

1. To make stack cakes: In a medium bowl, sift together flour, ginger, baking powder, baking soda, salt, and cinnamon. Set aside.

2. In large separate bowl, cream butter and brown sugar and beat until light and fluffy. Add egg and zest and beat well. In separate bowl, whisk together buttermilk and molasses.

3. Add dry ingredients and molasses mixture alternately to butter mixture, beginning and ending with dry ingredients. Beat until just combined (do not overmix). Dough will be sticky. Cover and chill at least 2 hours.

4. Preheat oven to 350° F.

5. To make apple filling: Peel, core, and slice apples into rings ¼ inch thick. Toss apples in a bowl with lemon juice as you work to prevent discoloration. Heat butter in a 12-inch skillet over medium heat. When butter is hot, add apples and sugar and toss to coat. Cook uncovered, tossing gently 4 to 6 minutes or until just tender (do not overcook or apples will be mushy). Cool thoroughly. Set aside.

6. Line 3 buttered 8-inch-round cake pans with parchment or brown paper. Butter the paper. Divide dough into 3 equal portions. Working with lightly floured fingertips, pat 1 portion of dough into each prepared pan to make neat, even rounds. Place pans on baking sheet and bake 1 at a time in upper third of oven 20 minutes or until edges are golden-brown, the top is firm, and the center springs back when pressed lightly. Cool in the pans 10 minutes each. Run a knife around the edges, turn out onto racks. Remove paper and cool thoroughly. (Note: Cakes may be made ahead, wrapped, and frozen.)

7. To make cider butter: In large, nonaluminum pot, boil cider rapidly 30 to 45 minutes or until reduced to 2 cups. (This cider reduction is known as cider jelly.) In a medium bowl, beat the butter until light and fluffy. Beat in the cider jelly and the orange zest until well incorporated.

8. Assembly: Spread half the cider butter on top of 1 cake. Arrange half the apples on top in a radiating pattern. Top with a second stack cake, spread with remaining cider butter and apples. Top with remaining stack cake. Cover with plastic wrap and set aside at room temperature at least 2 hours and preferably 8 hours or overnight for flavors to blend. Cut into wedges and serve at room temperature with whipped cream.

Serves 8.

Note If fresh apple cider (for making the cider jelly for the cider butter) is unavailable or if time is limited, substitute apple butter or apple jelly. Cider jelly is available by mail order. See page 481 for source.

Sweet Potato Cheesecake

■ ■ ■

Take 6 quarts of stroakings or new milke & whey it with runnet as for an ordineary cheese, yn put it in a streyner & hang it on a pin or else press it with 2 pound weight. Yn break it very small with yr hands or run it through a sive, then put to it 7 or 8 eggs well beaten . . .

SO BEGAN the seventeenth-century formula for cheesecake in *Martha Washington's Booke of Cookery and Booke of Sweetmeats*. "Stroakings" refers to the rich milk (also called strippings) expressed at the end of milking. "Runnet" is, of course, rennet, which causes milk to curdle, the first step in making cheese. The homemade cheese in that recipe was mixed with butter, cream, sugar, currants, rosewater, nutmeg, and salt, and baked in "coffins of paste," or pre-baked pastry shells, to make what was a forerunner of the ever popular American dessert, cheesecake.

In dessert making, Southern cooks have used both fresh cheese and sweet potatoes, but not necessarily together. Another recipe in Martha Washington's book is one for a "Pie of Seuerall Things" which transcriber Karen Hess believes to have included sweet potatoes. The pie, also referred to as an "olio pie," is an amazing jumble of ingredients including cocks' combs, veal kidneys, "sheepes tonges," rabbits, "harty-choak bottoms," "orringes," mace, nutmeg, wine, and sugar. Hess points out that sweet potatoes were not grown in Britain (that country imported them from Spain) and that white potatoes were a mainstay of the poor, and as such were shunned by the well-to-do, who enjoyed sweet potatoes. Although the recipes in the book reflect Elizabethan and Jacobean England, many early Southern dishes were based on the English cuisine of this period, and such a pie could have been a forerunner of the classic Southern sweet potato pie.

But prior to pies made with sweet potatoes were the so-called puddings. In Mary Randolph's *The Virginia House-wife* (1824) the author clearly distinguishes between puddings made with sweet potatoes and those made with white potatoes. Her recipe for Sweet-potato Pudding—as mouthwatering today as it was when first written down—calls for sieved cooked potatoes combined with beaten eggs, sugar, butter, grated nutmeg, lemon peel, and brandy. It is baked in a crust and topped with sugar and citron. "Irish potato pudding is made in the same manner, but is not so good." The closest Mrs. Randolph comes to a cheesecake is in her Curd Pudding. It is made by boiling milk with white wine to curdle it, then straining the curds and pounding them with butter, sugar, rice flour, beaten eggs, and nutmeg. It is baked, garnished with citron, and napped with a mixture of melted butter, sugar, and wine.

Fifty years after Mary Randolph's book, Sarah Rutledge's *The Carolina Housewife* (1847) includes a cheesecake similar in ingredients to that in *Martha Washington's Booke of Cookery and Booke of Sweetmeats,* but the milk is mixed with beaten eggs and cooked until it curdles.

Next to pecan pie, sweet potato pie must surely be the most Southern of all pies. It's my Uncle Albert's favorite and, lucky for him, he lives in Tabor City, North Carolina where an abundance of sweet potatoes are grown. Like chess-type pies and pecan pies, sweet potato pie can be flavored in a variety of ways. Most cooks add spices (nutmeg, cloves, and cinnamon being the most common), some add coconut and/or pecans. Classic Southern sweet potato pie has an unsweetened piecrust and is served with a little whipped cream on the side.

In my opinion, sweet potato pie—like gumbo, jambalaya, and many other classics—can't really be improved upon. If you're searching for a basic pie recipe, I direct you to any of the classic Southern cookbooks listed in the bibliography. I do, however, adore sweet potato desserts, so I concocted this one—a Southern variation on the cheesecake.

CRUST

6 tablespoons unsalted butter, room temperature

3 tablespoons sugar

¾ cup unbleached all-purpose flour

1 large egg yolk

¼ cup finely ground pecans

¼ teaspoon ground nutmeg

FILLING

1 pound cream cheese, room temperature

¾ cup firmly packed light brown sugar

½ cup granulated sugar

1 large egg

1 egg yolk

1¼ cup sweet potato purée (about 2 medium-sized sweet potatoes, cooked, peeled, and puréed in a food processor or blender)

¾ teaspoon ground cinnamon

¼ teaspoon ground cloves

TOPPING

1 cup sour cream

1 tablespoon firmly packed light brown sugar

½ teaspoon vanilla

1. Preheat oven to 350° F.

2. To make the crust: In a bowl beat butter and sugar until light and fluffy. Add remaining crust ingredients and mix until just combined. Press into the bottom and sides of a 10-inch springform pan and bake for 15 to 20 minutes or until golden-brown; set aside. Lower oven temperature to 275° F.

3. To make the filling: In a bowl beat cream cheese, brown sugar, and granulated sugar until light and fluffy. Add egg and egg yolk and beat until thoroughly combined. Beat in sweet potato purée and spices.

4. Turn the filling mixture into the cooled crust and bake for 1½ hours or until set. Remove from oven. Increase oven heat to 350° F. Let cheesecake stand at room temperature for 5 minutes while you make the topping.

5. To make the topping: In a bowl beat together sour cream, sugar, and vanilla. Spread evenly on warm cheesecake and return to oven to bake for 10 minutes longer. Cool cake in the pan on a rack. Then chill at least 8 hours. Release spring and cut cake into wedges.

Serves 8.

Fruit Desserts

THINK SOUTHERN FRUIT and what probably comes to mind are peaches and watermelon. But this vast, temperate region, with its long growing season, also provides the rest of the country with blueberries, blackberries, strawberries, mangoes, starfruit, and a wealth of citrus fruits and melons. Perhaps because of the availability of fruit in the South, it has always been the basis for countless recipes, particularly desserts.

In the seventeenth and eighteenth centuries, fruit was put into puddings or pies either to be eaten right away or preserved for later use. Fruit was dried, pickled, candied, made into marmalades, conserves, and syrups, or cooked to a paste. Fruit was also used to flavor vinegars, and was made into wines and cordials.

In the eighteenth century, many Southern farmers planted apple, pear, cherry, and peach orchards. Wild fruits added to the array of naturally available food in the early Southern diet. Fruits from the wild included berries, persimmons, plums, and both purple and white grapes.

Tropical and semitropical fruits—including oranges, nectarines, and pomegranates—grew from South Carolina to Florida. The West Indies provided the colonies with additional oranges, lemons, limes, pineapples, and figs.

In the early nineteenth century, desserts made with fresh fruit (i.e., rather than cooked fruit desserts, such as pies and cobblers) were quite popular and, throughout the South, peaches became the favorite fruit. During this time, there was a slow but steady increase in the quantity of tropical fruits in American markets. However, many still feared raw fruit as a source of illness.

In the late nineteenth century, the consumption of uncooked fruit increased as health professionals began to praise its health value. The refrigerated train car, the cold-storage warehouse, the canneries, the better overall transportation by land and sea helped fruit growers reach markets throughout the United States.

Current concerns with health and nutrition have resulted in an overall national increase in fruit consumption and the creative use of fruits in desserts by chefs and home cooks alike.

Watermelon in Virginia Riesling
• • •

August 13–15, 1861
Ate water melon with Miss Sally Tompkins and Mrs. Carter.

—*The Private Mary Chestnut: The Unpublished Civil War Diaries*,
C. V. Woodward and Elisabeth Muhlenfeld, editors

NO DOUBT MARY CHESTNUT and her friends ate watermelon in a ladylike fashion, but it's hard not to think of that fruit as slurpy and sloppy—one that's most fun when its consumption results in the rather ungenteel pastime of seed spitting. At watermelon festivals such as the sixty-year-old event in Hope, Arkansas (home of the Guinness Book of World Records' champion melon), the watermelon-eating contest is a highlight. The image of frenzied contestants awash in slushy fruit is hardly a picture of refined dining.

But in the nineteenth-century South, watermelon also had a place on the gracious table. Simple sliced watermelons with their brilliant red flesh were considered showy and were frequently served for dessert. The recipe for watermelon ice that appears in *Housekeeping in Old Virginia* (1879) has a novel touch: "A few of the seeds interspersed will add greatly to the appearance," suggests the recipe's author. (Surely it never crossed her mind that an uncultured luncheon guest might be tempted to expectorate the decorative black accents on the carpet.) Watermelon rind was not wasted: it was cooked in sugar syrup and spices to make watermelon marmalade, preserves, or pickles.

If the thought of seed-spitters at your table makes you blanch, look for seedless watermelons. They're a bit pricier, but there's less waste.

Florida, Georgia, and California are the largest watermelon producers in the United States, with South Carolina not far behind.

2 pounds watermelon
½ cup sugar

½ cup dry Riesling wine (I use Virginia Riesling)
Mint sprigs, to garnish (optional)

1. Using a melon baller, carve balls from the watermelon, avoiding seedy parts. You will have about 3 to 4 cups balls. Chill.

2. In a small saucepan dissolve the sugar in the wine over low heat. Cool to room temperature, then chill thoroughly.

3. To serve, divide melon among 4 glass compotes or wine goblets. Pour 2 tablespoons of the Riesling syrup over each serving. Garnish with mint sprigs, if desired.

Serves 4.

Cornmeal Shortcakes with Peaches and Cream

• • •

July 19, 1861
Two Carolina regiments went by to day. The two Carolinas furnished men every day. So far no news today. Will Chestnut come up to the Congress—that is the question now to me. Mallory has sent to ask Mrs. Preston & me to go & see the Patrick Henry. We declined. He sent me two lovely peaches.

—The Private Mary Chestnut: The Unpublished Civil War Diaries,
C. V. Woodward and Elisabeth Muhlenfeld, editors

DIARIST MARY CHESTNUT would probably think today's peaches even more lovely than those given to her in 1861. Modern-day fruit has less fuzz than the old varieties, and most peaches today are the freestone type.

But peaches could be had long before Mary Chestnut's day. The English settlers found wild peach trees growing so profusely that early botanists thought them to be native. The Spaniards planted trees on their explorations, and the

Native Americans, including the Natchez, cultivated them, propagating the trees throughout their territory. In fact, some wild peach trees can still be found in the South. English settlers also brought their own peach varieties, and Thomas Jefferson loved peaches and planted the "Maddelena" peach, "Melon" peaches, and Italian Pesca *poppe de venere* (breast of Venus) peaches at Monticello in 1802. The climate could not have been more agreeable, and peaches have been grown commercially in the South since the early nineteenth century. Today South Carolina and Georgia hold second and third place behind California.

In this dessert, peaches and whipped cream top rich biscuits. The novel touch is the cornmeal in the biscuits. The long litany of Southern cornbreads does indeed include cornmeal biscuits; Mrs. Rutledge, author of *The Carolina Housewife* (1847), concocts rather formidable-sounding biscuits of hominy, cornmeal, lard, and milk. (Her Short Cake, incidentally, is a simple white-flour loaf cake, with no mention of fruit.)

Mrs. Rutledge did know her peaches, however. She cooked them down into marmalade; dried them; preserved them in brandy; and made peach leather. She told her readers how to pickle them with garlic and ginger (or with brown sugar, cinnamon, and cloves); and confected a dessert called "matrimony" by sugaring peach pieces, beating them into a quart of cream or rich custard, and then freezing them.

Whenever I indulge in a fresh peach, the kind so ripe and juicy you have to eat over the sink, my mind leaps back to summer mornings in my grandmother's kitchen where the scent from bowlfuls of the fruit permeated the entire room. The glorious simplicity of perfectly ripe peaches inspired this dessert, in which the peaches are merely sliced: no poaching, soaking, or macerating is necessary. Dead-ripe fruit—almost too soft to eat—is not too ripe for these shortcakes: the uncooked, unsweetened fruit stands on its own, so the sweeter and juicier it is, the better.

¾ cup unbleached all-purpose flour
¼ cup yellow cornmeal
1 teaspoon baking powder
¼ teaspoon salt
1 tablespoon sugar
3 tablespoons chilled butter
2 tablespoons chilled shortening

⅓ cup milk
2 ripe medium-sized peaches (peeled if desired), sliced
1 cup heavy cream, whipped (add ¼ teaspoon vanilla and 1 tablespoon sugar, if desired)

1. In a bowl sift flour, cornmeal, baking powder, salt, and sugar. With your fingertips, a pastry cutter, or two knives cut in butter and shortening until mixture resembles coarse meal. Make a well in the center and add all but 3 tablespoons of the milk. Mix until dough just holds together, adding additional milk if necessary. Knead only 2 to 3 times to blend, then pat out to a flat cake about 1 inch thick. Wrap in waxed paper and chill 1 hour.

2. Preheat oven to 375° F.

3. On a lightly floured surface, roll dough out to a thickness of ½ inch. Cut out 4 1½-inch circles with a floured biscuit cutter.

4. Place on ungreased baking sheet and bake in upper third of the oven for 12 to 15 minutes or until golden-brown on bottom. Cool briefly. Split through the center and sandwich with sliced peaches and whipped cream.

Serves 4.

Crisp Pecan "Shortcakes" with Strawberries and Rhubarb Sauce

■ ■ ■

May 4, 1861

Yesterday after dinner. Saw Mrs. Huger's maid come in with strawberries and cream—had eaten dinner, a meal I have abstained from so long it disagreed with me.

—*The Private Mary Chestnut: The Unpublished Civil War Diaries,*
C. V. Woodward and Elisabeth Muhlenfeld, editors

WHEN CAPTAIN JOHN SMITH tasted the native American strawberry (*Fragaria virginiana*) he pronounced it "foure times bigger and better than ours in England." A century later, William Byrd, founder of Richmond, Virginia, subtitled his account of his home colony the Newly Discovered Eden, and so it must have seemed, with an array of fruits including persimmons, pawpaws, pomegranates—and strawberries. Strawberries continue to grow profusely in the South. And although California leads in commercial production, Florida is number two, followed by North Carolina and Louisiana. Georgia, Tennessee, and Virginia also have substantial commercial harvests.

Although William Byrd enjoyed strawberries for supper, he ate rhubarb at breakfast. How unfortunate if the twain never met, for this is a seasonal marriage made in heaven, the tangy rhubarb contrasting with the sweet berries. Thomas Jefferson grew rhubarb—one row in 1809—and inexplicably records in *Thomas Jefferson's Garden Book* "the leaves excellent as Spinach." We can only wonder whether this was written from experience or hearsay (the entry is dated April 13, so he would not have picked the first leaf yet); rhubarb leaves contain oxalic acid and they should not be eaten.

Somewhere in history the berry and the tender pink "pie-plant" stalks did come together, and strawberry-and-rhubarb desserts have become a classic combination.

Strawberry shortcake—usually on a biscuit base—is a time–honored American institution. (My brother always requested it as his birthday "cake"; his early May birthdate coincided exactly with Virginia's first harvest.) Like lilacs, strawberries are a true sign that spring has finally come.

Cooks vary in shortcake protocol. The biscuits are often buttered, sometimes before and sometimes after baking. Some shortcake fanciers sweeten the cream, and crush the sugar with the berries while the biscuits bake; others, knowing the fruit is lushly ripe and not lacking in sweetness, simply slice the berries and pile them on the hot biscuits. The pleasure of eating shortcake makes heating the oven (and therefore the kitchen) worthwhile in warm berry season; some cooks make use of the lingering oven heat by returning the berry-filled cake to the oven for a moment to "ripen" the flavors.

In my adaptation, the shortcakes are crisp, cookie-like layers made with ground pecans, breadcrumbs, and brown sugar. The whipped cream is unsweetened, and the shortcakes are served with a tart-sweet rhubarb purée.

PECAN "SHORTCAKES"

2½ cups cake flour (do not use self-rising cake flour)
¼ teaspoon baking powder
⅛ teaspoon baking soda
½ teaspoon salt
3 ounces (about ¾ cup) pecans
⅔ cup firmly packed light brown sugar

6 tablespoons unsalted butter, room temperature
1 large egg, room temperature
⅛ teaspoon vanilla
¼ cup dry, unseasoned breadcrumbs

(ingredients continued)

Desserts

■

RHUBARB SAUCE

3 pounds fresh rhubarb   *⅔ cup sugar*
¾ cup water

STRAWBERRY FILLING

Whipped cream   *6 additional large or 12 medium*
1 pint (2 cups) strawberries, cleaned,   *fresh strawberries*
* hulled, and sliced*

1. To make the "shortcakes": Sift flour, baking powder, baking soda, and salt in a bowl. In a blender or food processor, process pecans with 2 tablespoons of the sugar until finely ground.

2. In a separate bowl, cream the butter and the remaining sugar until light and fluffy. Add egg and beat well to combine. Add vanilla, pecan mixture, and breadcrumbs, then fold into flour mixture until just combined. Pat into a flat cake; wrap in waxed paper and chill 2 hours.

3. Preheat oven to 375° F.

4. Roll the dough out on a lightly floured work surface to a thickness of ¼ inch. Cut into 3-inch rounds and bake on buttered baking sheet for 12 to 14 minutes or until firm and beginning to turn golden. Cool.

5. To make rhubarb sauce: Cut off ends of rhubarb and discard. Cut stalks into 1-inch pieces. Place in saucepan with water and sugar and boil 15 to 20 minutes, stirring frequently, until thickened. Press through a large sieve set over a bowl. Cover and chill.

6. Place 1 "shortcake" on each of 6 individual dessert plates. Top with a dollop of whipped cream, then a portion of the sliced berries (about 2 sliced berries for each portion). Top with another "shortcake," then another dollop of whipped cream in the center. Top with 1 large or 2 medium whole strawberries. Serve with rhubarb sauce on the side.

Serves 6.

Bourbon-Poached Pears
with Pistachios and Cream

. . .

Again she thought of a pear—not the everyday gritty kind that hung on the tree in the backyard, but the fine kind sold on trains and at high prices, each pear with a paper cone wrapping it alone—beautiful, symmetrical, clean pears with thin skins, with snow-white flesh so juicy and tender that to eat one baptized the whole face, and so delicate that while you urgently ate the first half, the second half was already beginning to turn brown. To all fruits, and especially to those fine pears, something happened—the process was so swift, you were never in time for them. It's not the flowers that are fleeting, Nina thought, it's the fruits—it's the time when things are ready that they don't stay. She even went through the rhyme, "Pear tree by the garden gate, how much longer must I wait?"—thinking it was the pears that asked it, not the picker.

—Eudora Welty, *The Golden Apples*

FIRM-TEXTURED POACHING and stewing pears, whether for immediate consumption or for preserving, are popular because this fruit is not always available at its peak ripeness. Today pears are invariably picked unripe for shipping (some varieties actually ripen best off the tree) and we are expected to hold them for a few days to allow them to develop their natural sweetness. But cooking them in a sweetened syrup makes them appetizing even if they are not fully ripe. That master gardener, Thomas Jefferson, planted several kinds of pear trees in his orchards. But Jefferson may have resorted to poaching even his own pears in sugar syrup, for though he thought American apples and peaches superior to French, he found French pears "infinitely beyond anything we possess."

With the exception of Virginia's Seckel pears and the "Warren" pear in Mississippi, smooth-fleshed "eating" pears are not commercially grown in the South, although some are grown in home gardens. More widely available in the Southern states are Kieffer pears, which—although edible raw—are rather hard, coarse, and gritty in texture and used mostly for making chutney, pickles, jams, preserves, and jelly. Every winter, my mother makes a ginger-flavored chutney with Kieffers—my all-time favorite accompaniment to ham and turkey.

These bourbon-poached pears are rubbed with lemon to preserve their color, and cooking them in a nonreactive pan assures that no untoward minerals will find their way into your dessert. Pears are classically poached in sugar-syrup or wine—either red or white—in French cooking, but I have found that a bourbon-flavored poaching syrup lends a wonderful taste to pears. The cooking time can vary by as much as twenty minutes, depending on the size and ripeness of the pears. Choose firm, ripe, unbruised fruit so it will hold its shape during cooking. Serve with Homemade Vanilla Wafers (page 428), or Cornmeal Sugar Cookies (page 425).

2 cups sugar

4 cups water

Peel of 1 lemon, removed in strips with paring knife

6 large, firm, ripe, unblemished pears, peeled and rubbed with lemon

2½ cups good-quality bourbon (or more, to taste)

Chopped pistachios, for garnish (optional)

1 cup heavy cream, whipped

1. Combine the sugar, water, and lemon peel in a nonaluminum saucepan large enough to hold the pears. Bring to a boil over medium heat, reduce to a simmer, and gently add pears to the syrup with a large spoon. Cut a round of waxed paper the circumference of the saucepan and place it directly on top of the fruit.

2. Reduce heat to medium-low. Weigh down the pears with a heatproof plate small enough to fit inside the saucepan and keep the pears submerged in liquid, and simmer partially covered until the pears are tender but not mushy, 10 to 30 minutes (timing will depend on size, type, and ripeness of pears). Add bourbon to the poaching liquid and remove the saucepan from the heat for 5 minutes.

3. With a slotted spoon, transfer pears to a heatproof (preferably clear glass) serving bowl. Boil the bourbon syrup until reduced by half. (This may take as long as 15 minutes.) Strain the reduced bourbon syrup over the fruit and cool completely. Chill, or serve at room temperature. Taste for seasoning, adding additional bourbon for a more pronounced flavor, if desired. Serve pears in bowls and spoon some of the poaching liquid over each. Sprinkle with pistachios, if desired. Pass the whipped cream separately.

Serves 6.

Carolina Blueberries
in Black Muscat Wine

· · ·

BLUEBERRIES are one of three native American fruits (cranberries and concord grapes are the other two). Called whortleberries by some New Englanders, blueberries grew so profusely in the New World that little was done to cultivate them. Wild blueberries—which are up to four times smaller than cultivated ones—can still be found in some parts of the United States. Of the fifty species of blueberries, about twenty varieties grow east of the Plain States.

The first commercial berries of the season (about mid-May) come from North Carolina. Small commercial plantings in the South can be found in Maryland, Florida, and Georgia. Blueberries can also be found in the deep South along the Gulf States and Florida.

This simple dessert combines the native blueberry with sweet black Muscat wine. (I like to use Elysium, made by Quady winery in California. If Elysium is not available, use a ruby port or crème de cassis, a black currant liqueur. The resulting dessert will be sweeter, but still delicious.) Serve cold for a refreshing finish to any meal.

4 cups (2 pints) blueberries, rinsed and well drained
1 cup black Muscat wine, such as Elysium (or enough to cover), or

substitute ruby Port or crème de cassis
Fresh mint sprigs, to garnish (optional)

Combine ingredients and let stand in a shallow bowl in refrigerator 1 hour or up to 4 hours. Serve chilled in goblets and garnish with mint leaf if desired.

Serves 4.

Raspberries and Plums
in Virginia Cabernet

...

THE AMERICAN PLUM (*Prunus americana*) grows throughout the Southeast except Mississippi and Louisiana. Its fruit is orange-red with a bright yellow flesh. It is used to make jams, jellies, preserves, and pies. Flatwood plums (*Prunus umbellata*) grow from southern North Carolina through South Carolina, Georgia, Alabama, Mississippi, Louisiana, and Florida. The fruits mature from June to September, are round and covered with a dark red skin. The tart flesh is used for jams, jellies, and preserves. These native species, although employed by the home cook, are not grown commercially. The most common commercially grown Southern plums are the Stanley varieties, which are a cross between Japanese and American plums.

Damson plums are grown in home orchards in the mid-Atlantic states, but do not fare well in the hotter, more humid deep South. Damsons can be eaten fresh, but are used mostly in making jellies, jams, and marmalades.

Raspberries grow in some isolated areas in the South, but generally they cannot withstand the hot climate, with the exception of wild black raspberries, particularly the Red Heritage and Dorman varieties. Jefferson planted black raspberries at Monticello.

It is interesting to note that in old Southern cookbooks one finds recipes for "Plumb Pudding" and "Plumb Gruel" and "Plumb Porridge" but they do not contain plums—or even prunes. Raisins seem to be the ingredient referred to. Mary Randolph in *The Virginia House-wife* (1824) calls for preserved damsons as an alternative to preserved cherries in a pudding recipe. She also provides a recipe for preserving greengage plums in brandy. As for raspberry recipes, she offers one each for raspberry cordial, ice cream, jam, vinegar, and raspberry cream (raspberry marmalade stirred into cream, strained, then poured into glasses).

I like to make this easy dessert with red or purple plums so that the final dish is a glistening mélange of garnet and ruby. Serve on hot summer nights with Whole Wheat Sesame Seed Cookies (page 421), Brown Sugar–Peanut Butter Shortbread (page 435), or Cornmeal Sugar Cookies (page 425).

½ pound (about 2 cups) raspberries
½ pound (about 4 medium) ripe
   black friar plums (or substitute
   other sweet eating plums of
   choice), cut into eighths or fourths,
   depending on size of plum

¼ cup sugar
1 cup Cabernet Sauvignon wine
   (preferably from Virginia)

In a large nonaluminum bowl, combine all ingredients. Cover and refrigerate 30 minutes or up to 3 hours. Serve in goblets or compotes.

Serves 4.

Pineapple-Lime Sorbet with Vodka

• • •

THE NATIVES of the West Indies placed fresh pineapples at their doors to signal welcome, and this symbol of hospitality was adopted by the Spanish settlers and later by the English colonists: pineapples of wood and plaster appear in Early American architecture, furniture, and decor. When George Washington tasted a pineapple in Barbados in 1751, he preferred it to the other native fruits, but it was not until the end of the nineteenth century, when commercial pineapple production was established in Hawaii, that the fresh and canned fruit was widely available in this country. (It was commercially grown in Florida until the 1940s.)

Washington's stepgrandaughter, Nellie Custis Lewis, was apparently able to secure a pineapple on at least one occasion: her *Housekeeping Book* includes a Fromage of Pineapple among other Fromage recipes. This seems to have been a sort of gelatin mold; the pineapple version is made with puréed fruit, sugar, and isinglass, a jelling agent made from fish. The mold is surrounded with ice and salt to stiffen the fruit mixture.

Sherbets, ices, and frozen creams of many sorts are found in old Southern cookbooks. The *Picayune Creole Cook Book* (1900) rhapsodizes: "Sherbets are among the most pleasant of the Creole summer desserts; they are also extensively served of a hot summer evening . . . and are grateful and refreshing of-ferings, both for the family and guests, who may drop in for a social half hour." The proposed sherbets were made from apples, apricots, bananas, cherries, currants, grapes, lemons, oranges, peaches, pineapple, pomegranates, raspber-ries, strawberries, and watermelon. Other frozen desserts from nineteenth-century Southern cookbooks include *The Virginia House-wife*'s (1824) Lemonade Iced and Citron Cream ("Pine apples [*sic*] may be used in the same way").

This pineapple sorbet is simple to make and exceedingly refreshing to eat. Serve with Coconut Tuiles (page 429), Homemade Vanilla Wafers (page 428), or Cornmeal Sugar Cookies (page 425).

1 cup sugar

1 cup water

1 large, perfectly ripe pineapple

4 to 10 tablespoons lime juice

4 to 10 tablespoons lemon juice

Vodka, to serve

1. Make a simple syrup by melting the sugar and water in a heavy saucepan over medium heat. Bring to a boil, remove from heat, and cool completely.

2. Remove skin, stem, core, and "eyes" from pineapple. Cut flesh into chunks (you will have about 4 cups pineapple chunks). Purée in food processor or blender until smooth and frothy. Add syrup and lemon and lime juices. (Note: the amount of citrus juices you need will depend on the ripeness and acidity of the pineapple. Add citrus juices by the tablespoonful, taste, and continue adding until mixture is very tangy.)

3. Turn the mixture into the bowl of an ice-cream maker and freeze ac-cording to manufacturer's directions (this may have to be done in 2 batches if your machine has a small capacity). Or pour into a shallow nonaluminum pan and freeze 1 hour. Stir with a fork and freeze 1 to 2 hours longer or until frozen.

4. To serve, scoop into parfait glasses and sprinkle a little vodka over each serving (about ½ teaspoon per ½ cup serving).

Makes about 1 quart.

Cantaloupe and Honeydew Compote

. . .

CANTALOUPE—a principal commercial crop in the Carolinas, Georgia, Alabama, Arkansas, Florida, Mississippi, and Virginia—appears on the Southern table throughout the summer, usually for breakfast or dessert. Some sprinkle it with salt, others with lemon juice, still others like their cantaloupe savory, with lots of black pepper. Honeydew melon is not quite as prevalent as cantaloupe, but nevertheless grows well all over the South.

Choose your topping for this simple, refreshing dessert. The tangy sour cream accompaniment has the unexpected kick of curry; the coconut-flavored whipped cream has cream of coconut as its sweetener. Serve with plain cookies, such as Cornmeal Sugar Cookies (page 425).

¼ cup freshly squeezed lime juice
1 teaspoon superfine sugar
2 cups honeydew melon balls or bite-sized pieces

2 cups cantaloupe balls or bite-sized pieces
Mint sprigs, to garnish (optional)

CURRIED CREAM

½ cup sour cream

1 teaspoon curry powder

COCONUT CREAM

½ cup heavy cream

3 tablespoons cream of coconut

1. In a large bowl combine lime juice and sugar. Stir until sugar dissolves.
2. To make the melon pieces: Quarter the melons; discard seeds. Working with one quarter at a time, with a long, sharp knife, cut melon flesh away from the rind. Discard rind. Cut the crescent of melon lengthwise into 2 or 3 1-inch-wide strips; cut strips crosswise into bite-sized pieces.
3. Add melon and its juices to the lime syrup; toss to coat. Cover and chill at least 1 hour.
4. To make the toppings: For curried cream, in a bowl combine sour cream and curry powder. To make coconut cream, in a bowl whip cream until stiff;

fold in cream of coconut. (Use remaining cream of coconut for piña coladas.)

5. To serve, divide melon and the juices into 4 dessert glasses or compotes. Top with either curried cream or coconut cream.

Serves 4.

Syllabubs, Fools, Custards, and Creams

THIS CATEGORY of desserts is one of the richest, both in terms of ingredients (cream is usually a fundamental component) and in terms of history. Some of these sweets have roots in French medieval cooking; others in seventeenth-century English cuisine. Recipes for syllabubs, fools, custards, and creams traveled to the New World where they played a steady role in stylish eighteenth-century Southern entertaining. Their popularity lasted through the early twentieth century.

The dictionary says the word "syllabub" may come from the word "silli-bouk," meaning "happy stomach." "Flummery" is described as meaningless compliments or silly talk, and "trifle" as something of little value or importance. The very onomatopoeic quality of the words "syllabub," "flummery," and "trifle" suggests frivolity and lightheartedness. Garnished with fruit, flowers, sweetmeats, and cream these quivering, shimmering composed dishes enhanced the dessert table—like sparkling jewels on a plain black dress. The savvy hostess adored them since they impressed even the most discriminating guests.

Of all the dessert creams, blanc mange—also known as blanc manger—has perhaps the most illustrious history. Created by the noted fourteenth-century French chef, Taillevent, blanc mange was originally a savory dish that consisted of a capon cooked with broth and ground almonds, and garnished with fried almonds and pomegranate seeds. (Chaucer—Taillevent's contemporary—immortalized blanc mange in the prologue to his *Canterbury Tales*.) By the nineteenth century in England, France, and the American South, blanc mange had evolved into a dessert. Basically, blanc mange was a sweetened custard with a jelling agent added. It was flavored with almond paste or almond milk (a lingering reminder of the original dish), rosewater, cinnamon, or peach water. If the mixture was flavored with lemon juice or zest, it was then called jaune mange or lemon blanc mange. Sometimes arrowroot, rice, cornstarch, potato starch, or tapioca was used to thicken or set the mixture in place of the costly isinglass or the time-consuming calves'-foot jelly. A less-refined dessert resulted, but it saved the cook money and time.

Jellies also added drama to the eighteenth- and nineteenth-century Southern dessert table. Southerners were already familiar with the aspics and meat jellies of their English heritage, so dessert jellies were easily accepted. Dessert jellies were basically a mixture of dissolved gelatin in a liquid such as citrus juice, liqueur, sherry, or Madeira. Jellies were often colored: saffron infusions, violet syrup, spinach juice, and cochineal were used to make gold, blue, green, and red jellies. But while colored jellies may have been all the rage in the seventeenth and eighteenth centuries, in the nineteenth century, Marion Cabell Tyree, author of *Housekeeping in Old Virginia* (1879), wrote that ". . . jelly is considered more wholesome when not colored by any foreign substance, no directions will be given in the subsequent pages for coloring it." She considered "the palest amber jelly, clear and sparkling . . . more beautiful and palatable." In addition to colorings, flavorings changed, too. In the seventeenth century, jellies were flavored with mace, saffron, licorice, raisins, or rose petals. Later, jellies were flavored simply with Madeira, sherry, or lemon juice and lemon zest. Who would have thought that these elegant, glittering desserts would eventually lead to the congealed "salads" and desserts so popular in the South (and the rest of America, as a matter of fact) flavored with everything from cream cheese to maraschino cherries.

Today's packets of dry, unflavored gelatin are speedy in comparison to jelling agents of the past. In the seventeenth century, elephant's tusks were often used to set jellies and other similar desserts; in the eighteenth century, hartshorn (deer's antlers) shavings, isinglass (gelatin made from sturgeon's bladder) and calves' feet were used. Isinglass was the purest, but many cooks felt that calves'-foot jelly provided better consistency. (It was also cheaper than isinglass.)

Making a clear jelly from calves' feet was laborious, indeed. The task began with boiling the calves' feet in water, straining the liquid, then cooling it until solid. The fat was skimmed off and only the clearest part of the jelly was used to make the dessert. Wine, lemons, sugar, and egg whites were added, then the mixture would be beaten for half an hour. It would be poured through a jelly bag to clarify it, then the clear, pure liquid was cooled in a mold to set. But the

Desserts

∎

hostess evidently thought the results worth the time, money, and trouble, because of the color and drama they added to the party table. Jellies reflected candlelight and never failed to impress guests. In 1894 granulated gelatin made the cook's job infinitely easier.

Flummeries were apparently not as popular as jellies or blanc mange but they were easier to prepare. Jelly, cream, and wine were boiled together (or the jelly and cream were boiled together and the wine was added later when the mixture had cooled), then the mixture was sweetened and flavored with orange-flower water or rosewater. The flummery, according to Karen Hess in her transcription of the seventeenth-century *Martha Washington's Booke of Cookery and Booke of Sweetmeats*, was cooled in a mold and served with flavored cream. This old English dessert was originally a sweetened, gelatinous dish made of the liquid of successive soakings of cereal, usually oatmeal, but by the mid-eighteenth century in England, flummeries were set with gelatin instead, a practice adopted by nineteenth-century Virginians.

Southerners in the eighteenth and nineteenth centuries also enjoyed English dessert puddings, trifle, floating island, and Charlotte Russe. South Carolinians seem to have been particularly fond of Charlotte Russe, a dessert made by lining a bowl or mold with lady fingers, then filling it with sherry-flavored custard filling set with gelatin. With the exception of flummeries, these rich desserts are still somewhat popular in the South. In the last fifty years, other frothy desserts—mousses, soufflés, Bavarians, whips, and fluffs—have begun to compete with the old favorites in popularity.

Frozen Banana Syllabub with Sauternes

. . .

And if the house caught fire
and things began to burn,
The First I'd try to rescue
Would be my syllabub churn.

—Colonel John A. May
in *Mrs. Hill's New Cook Book* (1873)

SYLLABUB is something of a symbol of Southern hospitality. A traveler from Canada to New Orleans in the late 1820s described a dinner that he attended in South Carolina thusly: "For a second course [this followed ham, turkeys, chickens, corned beef, fish, vegetables, potatoes, etc.] we had eight pies down the side of the table, six dishes of glasses of syllabub and as many of jelly, besides one or two 'floating islands,' as they denominate what we called whipped cream."

Syllabub is a frothy dessert that probably first appeared in England around the sixteenth century. One of the earliest recipes consisted of sweet cream boiled with nutmeg. The cook was then instructed to stand high on a table and pour the cream into a mixture of white wine, rosewater, lemon peel, rosemary, and sugar. The wine acted as a clabbering agent and the mixture would thicken. (An older method was to mix the wine and sugar in a bowl and add milk by squeezing it directly from the cow's teat.) The first method, at least, was practiced through the nineteenth century in both England and the American South as can be seen in a recipe for syllabub in *Mrs. Beeton's Book of Household Management* (1859) which says "Warm milk may be poured on from a spouted jug or teapot; but it must be held very high" and another in *Housekeeping in Old Virginia* (1879), which says to pour the sugar and wine into the cream "from a height and slowly, so as to cause the milk to froth."

As syllabub evolved, so did the various techniques for making froth. Sometimes the ingredients were shaken in a bottle for ten minutes, then set aside overnight to thicken. Another method was to whisk the mixture to a stiff foam then place it in a sieve. The liquid that drains off is beaten again, although, in serving, the mixture usually separates to form a foamy head with a liquid layer beneath. Syllabub churns resulted as a labor-saving device. They resemble pumps somewhat, being hollow tin cylinders with longhandled, perforated plungers inside.

Today, in the best of all possible culinary worlds, we have heavy cream ideal for whipping, a selection of domestic and imported sweet wines, electric mixers, and freezers. We don't have to wait until milking time—or stand on the kitchen table—to enjoy syllabub.

The frozen syllabub here is refreshing and simple. I like to serve it with Coconut Tuiles (page 429), or Homemade Vanilla Wafers (page 428), a nod to the combination in that favorite of all Southern banana desserts, banana pudding.

½ cup sugar

½ cup sweet white wine such as a
    Sauternes, a Barsac, or a California
    late-harvest Gewürztraminer

1 tablespoon lemon juice

2 medium-large ripe bananas

1 cup heavy cream

Cinnamon or freshly ground nutmeg,
    to taste (optional)

1. In a small saucepan over medium heat, combine sugar, wine, and lemon juice. When sugar has dissolved, remove from heat and cool completely.

2. In a food processor or blender, purée bananas until smooth. Add the cooled lemon-wine mixture and stir to blend. Transfer to a large bowl.

3. In a separate bowl beat the cream until stiff. Fold cream into banana mixture.

4. Pour into 6 6-ounce custard cups or parfait glasses and freeze 1½ hours or until semi-frozen, but not rock hard. Grate a little nutmeg or cinnamon over each serving, if desired.

Serves 6.

Gingered Honey-
Persimmon Fool

• • •

"FOOLS" are old-fashioned desserts that were popular in the eighteenth and nineteenth centuries in the New World. Fools are usually made of a combination of whipped cream, sugar, and fruit and sometimes soft custard. Occasionally fools would be topped with frothed cream or meringue. In some old cookbooks, recipes that are actually fools are called "creams," a term that is more often reserved for molded cream-based dishes (like Bavarian creams) or what we know as ice cream.

As is the case with the amusingly-named "slumps," "grunts," and "trifles," the origins of the name are open to speculation; it may come from *fouler*, French for "to crush." And indeed, the fruit that goes into flavoring the fool is usually crushed. Berries are the most commonly used fruit for a fool, with gooseberries a particular favorite of early Americans. (Although John Adams was said to have preferred whortleberry fool to any other kind.) The persimmons used here may seem an unlikely candidate for a fool, but their honey-like sweetness is nicely perked up by the ginger and mellowed by the cream.

The native American persimmon, *Diospyros virginiana,* grows wild throughout the South and Midwest. This variety is small—cherry-tomato size— dark-orange to purplish, and when ripe, fragrant, and flavorful. The Native Americans dried them like figs, or formed the pulp into bricks and dried it, like jerky, to eat during the winter. The Algonquins called persimmons *putchamin* or *pessemin,* from which we get the modern-day word. It was from the Native Americans that the colonists learned about the fruit. It took a bit of trial and error, for as Captain John Smith observed, "If it [is] not ripe, it will drawe a man's mouth awrie with much torment; but when it is ripe it is as delicious as an Apricock." Wild persimmons are usually ripened naturally, that is, they are not picked (or picked up) until after a hard frost, when they fall, mushy and sweet, to the ground. Some Southerners call persimmon trees, " 'possum trees" because the animals love the fruit.

Persimmon pudding is the most popular American use for the fruit. In the South this dessert is often made with a combination of persimmons, brown sugar, flour, cornmeal, butter, and spices. Since the flavor of persimmons can be quite subtle, it's the flavor of the spices that comes through more than anything. I find that the fruit is really best with the briefest cooking, or no cooking at all.

But since most of us can't get wild persimmons, I've called for the Asian variety, which are cultivated in some regions of the South but are more widely grown in California. The most common type of Asian persimmon is the Japanese Hachiya. It is plum sized, deep orange, and, like the American fruit, needs to be ripened—to the point of squishiness—before eating. The Fuyu persimmon, more widely available now, is imported from Israel and is starting to be grown in California. It is smaller, paler, more tomato shaped than the Hachiya, milder in flavor, and may be eaten while still slightly crisp.

6 very ripe Asian persimmons
1/2 cup honey
2 tablespoons finely chopped candied
   ginger

1 1/2 teaspoons grated lemon zest
2 teaspoons ground ginger
1/2 cup heavy cream
4 ginger snaps, to garnish (optional)

1. Working over the bowl of a food processor or blender, peel the persimmons, scraping all of the soft pulp from the skin. Purée pulp until smooth; discard skins. Press through a sieve set over a medium bowl. Add honey, candied ginger, zest, and ground ginger and mix thoroughly.

2. Transfer 1 cup of the mixture to a small bowl; cover and refrigerate. Cover the remaining mixture and freeze 3 hours or until semi-frozen; it should be very cold and beginning to freeze around edges of bowl. (Note: Do not freeze completely or mixture will discolor.)

3. In a separate small bowl, whip the cream until stiff. Fold cream into the refrigerated persimmon mixture and set aside. Divide the semi-frozen mixture evenly among 4 parfait glasses or bowls. Then, divide the persimmon-cream mixture among each glass, spooning it on top of the semi-frozen mixture. Garnish each with a ginger snap, if desired. Serve immediately.

Serves 4.

Baked Maple-Pecan Custard

. . .

CUSTARDS have been on the American table since the 1600s, but they weren't served as desserts until the eighteenth century. Prior to that, custards traditionally accompanied the second of two main courses. Called crèmes by the French—a word that describes their delicate flavor and texture—the custard category includes simple baked custards (also called "hard custard" by some), boiled custards (or, "soft custard"), custard sauce—what the English call "pouring custard" and the French call crème Anglaise—to the richer and more elegant pot de crèmes, crème brûlée (burnt custard), flans, and crème caramel (caramel custard).

In the South, boiled and baked custards were—and still are in some households—common and frequently made desserts. Custard is the foundation for pie and tart fillings and of elegant desserts like Bavarians and blanc mange and it also is the base for some ice creams.

The making of custard goes back at least to the first century, according to John Edwards, who translated the culinary guide by Apicius, a first-century Roman gourmand. Apicius instructed that an egg, milk, and honey mixture be cooked in a "terrine from Cumae." The word custard comes from the French *crustade,* a custardy medieval meat pie made both in England and the continent. In 1387, Crustade Lombarde was served at a feast to King Richard II. This savory pie—which combined dried fruit, cream, eggs, sugar, parsley, and beef marrow baked in a pastry shell—was typical of sixteenth- and seventeenth-century English *crustades*. The English settlers must have brought their recipes to America, since cookbooks include them as late as the nineteenth century.

Meatless custards—which are closer to the dessert we eat today—also appeared in seventeenth-century England and America. One flavored with cinnamon, nutmeg, mace, rosewater, bay, and almonds was baked in a crust. Other recipes for baked custards and stirred custards are very similar to what we cook today.

Another Early American use of custard—a practice that dates back to medieval cookery—was to make a kind of cheese out of it. The egg and milk mixture was curdled by the addition of citrus juices or other curdling agent, then the whey was drained off. These "custard curds," as they were called, were sometimes sweetened, sometimes not, and were served at least until the nineteenth century in Virginia. I imagine the texture must have been something like ricotta cheese or tofu.

The crème brûlée that became the darling of trendy restaurants in the mid-1980s is at least 300 years old! A recipe for "grilled cream" appears in a seventeenth-century English cookbook. Virginians had a predilection for this dessert too, apparently, since we find a recipe for "Burnt Cream" in a nineteenth-century cookbook.

Nineteenth-century baked or boiled custards prepared in the South were flavored with nutmeg, cinnamon, almonds, lemon, vanilla, coconut, or chocolate. And like all good cooks who make use of what is at hand, Southerners also used an infusion made with peach leaves or peach kernels.

The custard here, flavored with maple syrup and pecans, is as simple to make as it is delicious. I find that really fresh, good-quality pecans have a maple-like flavor, so the combination was a natural one. Serve this with Homemade Vanilla Wafers (page 428) and fresh pears or tangerines.

1 cup pecans	4 large egg yolks
6 tablespoons sugar	1 large egg
Pinch of salt	2 cups half-and-half (or milk),
¼ cup good-quality maple syrup	scalded

1. Preheat oven to 350° F.

2. In a food processor or blender, process pecans, sugar, and salt until finely ground. Add maple syrup and process until a thick paste forms. Set aside.

3. In a large bowl, beat yolks and whole egg. Whisk in the pecan paste, then whisk in hot half-and-half.

4. Pour into 8 6-ounce custard cups or soufflé dishes. Place cups in a shallow baking dish. Pour enough water into the baking dish to reach halfway up sides of custard cups. Bake 30 to 40 minutes or until set. Serve at room temperature or lightly chilled with Cornmeal Sugar Cookies (page 425), or Rye and Indian Stars with Cinnamon Sugar (page 427).

Serves 8.

Sweet Potato Ice Cream

• ■ •

IN THE EIGHTEENTH CENTURY, a dish of ice cream was cause for amazement and delight. In 1744 a dinner at the governor's mansion in Annapolis, Maryland, was described by one diner thusly: "Among the Rarities . . . was some fine ice cream which, with strawberries and milk eat [*sic*] most Deliciously." George Washington was known to have a "Cream machine for Making Ice," and so did Thomas Jefferson.

Ice cream was to become much more commonplace, but no less pleasurable, by the 1870s when hand-cranked ice-cream makers became a common household item. Today's pop-it-in-the-freezer mini-ice-cream makers, or the totally electric, self-refrigerating machines that require virtually no effort at all, make homemade ice cream a cinch.

Now that exotically flavored ice creams are ubiquitous, it might seem silly to make ice cream at home. But where else will you get sweet potato ice cream? If anywhere, in the South: "If you ask for potatoes in the South you get sweet potatoes . . . But once you have tasted some of Charleston's sweet potato dishes you will never again even think of white potatoes." This sentiment, from the authors of *Two Hundred Years of Charleston Cooking,* might well apply to the whole of the South. Old-fashioned sweet potato pudding, traditionally flavored with ginger, mace, or nutmeg is the inspiration for this ice cream. Serve this ice cream after an autumn meal.

2 large sweet potatoes, scrubbed
2 cups milk
4 egg yolks, from large eggs
⅔ cup firmly packed light brown
  sugar
Pinch of salt
1 teaspoon ground cinnamon
½ teaspoon ground ginger

1 teaspoon ground nutmeg
1 cup heavy cream
⅛ teaspoon vanilla extract
1 cup coarsely chopped pecans or
  black walnuts (optional)

1. Preheat oven to 400° F.

2. To cook the sweet potatoes: Prick the potatoes, place on a baking sheet, and bake 40 to 60 minutes or until very soft. Cool until easy to handle, then remove and discard the peel. Purée the flesh in a food processor or blender, then press through a sieve. (Or, cook potatoes in a microwave oven: Prick, wrap in paper towels, and cook on high 5 to 8 minutes, or until soft, turning once. Remove paper towel, wrap potatoes in foil, and let stand 3 to 5 minutes. Proceed as directed.) Measure out 1 cup purée (use any excess for making Sweet Potato Pasta with Pepper and Nutmeg, page 279, or to add to soups or stews) and set aside.

3. In a small saucepan, scald milk and set aside.

4. In a bowl, beat egg yolks well. Beat in sugar, salt, and spices, Add hot milk slowly while whisking constantly. Pour mixture into the top of a double boiler and cook over barely simmering water, stirring constantly, 5 to 8 minutes or until mixture coats back of a spoon.

5. Off the heat, whisk in the potato purée. Cool to room temperature; stir in cream and vanilla. Freeze in an ice-cream maker according to manufacturer's directions. Fold in nuts, if desired.

Makes about 3 cups.

Banana Soufflé
with Bourbon-Butterscotch Sauce

. . .

THE AIRY-SOUNDING DESSERTS in *Housekeeping in Old Virginia* (1879), include Puff Pudding, Balloons, and Feather Pudding, but the modestly-named Delicious Pudding sounds most like a soufflé: Six eggs, separated and beaten, three tablespoons of flour, a pint of milk, and a tablespoon of melted butter. This pudding is baked "quickly," and served promptly: "Make this pudding half an hour before dinner, as it must be eaten as soon as done." The wine sauce recommended with it is one of several simple butter-based pudding sauces she gives.

The soufflé seems to have become popular in the South in the twentieth century, judging by more recent cookbooks. *North Carolina and Old Salem Cookery* offers a recipe for Marmalade Soufflé that is the essence of simplicity.

Soufflés collected in *Out of Kentucky Kitchens* (1949) by Marion Flexner include a banana soufflé that is topped with meringue halfway through the baking, a chestnut soufflé, a sherried prune soufflé, and a caramel soufflé. *Charleston Receipts,* compiled in 1950, contains a macaroon soufflé served with chopped fresh fruit and whipped cream and a wine soufflé suggested for after Christmas dinner or any other heavy meal. Sherry, nuts, and raisins give it seasonal flavor.

Dessert sauces have appeared in Southern cookbooks since the beginning, probably as a spin-off of the English hard sauce or brandy sauce served with plum pudding. Southerners, however, unlike their ancestors, are more likely to use bourbon than brandy or rum for flavoring. The sauce here is a grown-up version of a childhood favorite. It complements the mellow banana flavors and can be made up to three days in advance and reheated.

BOURBON-BUTTERSCOTCH SAUCE

½ cup firmly packed light brown sugar

2 tablespoons unsalted butter

Pinch of salt

½ cup heavy cream

2 tablespoons (or more) bourbon

SOUFFLÉ

4 egg yolks	*½ cup milk*
⅔ cup sugar	*3 medium-sized ripe bananas*
3 tablespoons unsalted butter	*1 tablespoon lemon juice*
3 tablespoons unbleached all-purpose	*6 egg whites*
flour	*⅛ teaspoon salt*

1. To make bourbon-butterscotch sauce: In a saucepan simmer all sauce ingredients except bourbon for 15 minutes, uncovered. Stir in bourbon and cook, stirring constantly, about 1 more minute. Taste and add more bourbon, if desired. Set aside. (Note: This is a very sweet sauce; stir in up to ½ cup additional heavy cream and simmer for a few minutes if you prefer your sauce less sweet.)

2. Preheat oven to 350° F.

3. In a bowl, beat yolks with sugar and set aside. Melt butter in a medium saucepan, add flour and cook 1 to 2 minutes, stirring constantly.

4. Stir in milk and cook, stirring constantly, until smooth and thick, about 2 to 3 minutes. Stir some of the hot liquid into the yolk mixture, and then return the mixture to the saucepan containing the hot liquid. Cook, stirring constantly, until thick and smooth, about 2 to 3 minutes. Cool slightly.

5. Working quickly so the mixture does not discolor, in a food processor or blender, purée bananas with lemon juice. You should have about 1 cup purée. Stir the purée into the saucepan.

6. In a bowl beat the egg whites and salt until stiff but not dry. Fold the egg whites into the banana mixture and pour into a buttered and sugared 2-quart or a 1½-quart soufflé dish. (Or, use 6 8-ounce individual soufflé dishes.) Bake for 35 to 40 minutes according to whether you prefer soufflés soft or firm. (Cook individual soufflés only 10 to 15 minutes.) Serve immediately with Bourbon-Butterscotch Sauce.

Large soufflé serves 6 to 8.

Cookies and Bars

AMERICANS seem to have become cookie-crazed in the last decade and for good reason: these palm-sized treats are relatively simple to bake and easy to eat; they store well, ship superbly, and come in a seemingly endless variety of textures and flavors. And, in my opinion, no other culture can hold a candle to our cookie prowess. Italian almond cookies and French *palmiers* have their place, certainly, but in terms of my own sweet tooth, very few European cookies or bar-like confections even come close to a warm Toll House cookie or a fudgy walnut brownie.

Despite the present-day variety and popularity of cookies, the word itself—which comes from the Dutch *koeptje,* meaning "small cakes"—was not widely used until the 1900s. In seventeenth- and eighteenth-century cookbooks used in the South, recipes for what we would today call cookies are usually referred to as "cakes" (a term also used to describe what we call "candy"). In *Martha Washington's Booke of Cookery and Booke of Sweetmeats,* the author gives several cookie-like recipes. There are three for Sugar Cakes (these are essentially sugar cookies). Two of the recipes are flavored with rosewater, the third with cinnamon. The author also gives a recipe for Shrowsbury (Shrewsbury) Cakes, which are small, round, butter cookie–like sweets that are a specialty of Shrewsbury, near Wales. Shrewsbury Cakes, like so many other English sweets, eventually made their way to the New World and recipes for them abound in eighteenth-century American cookbooks. Martha Washington's book also includes four recipes for Jumbles, a simple sugar cookie flavored with such things as aniseed, caraway seeds, lemon juice, rosewater, almonds, ambergris, or musk. The term "cakes" was used for cookies even as late as 1879 as can be seen in *Housekeeping in Old Virginia.* Recipes for Almond Macaroons, Gingerbread, Drop Cakes, Spice Nuts, Wafers, Sweet Crackers, Ginger Snaps, Cinnamon Cakes, and a powdered sugar–coated fritter-like confection called Nothings are grouped under the heading "Small Cakes." Even gingerbread cookies are called "ginger cakes." Only one recipe—a simple egg-butter-sugar-flour dough—is called a cookie.

South Carolina benne seed wafers and the paper-thin Moravian spice cookies made in North Carolina are perhaps two of the best-known Southern cookies. But my own first cookie memories are of my paternal grandmother's big, warm, farm-style sugar cookies and my maternal grandmother's elegant crisp wafers made in a waffle-like iron. Sugar cookies and wafers continue to be made in the South, as are cookies featuring locally grown ingredients like pecans, peanuts, and black walnuts. Let us not forget another favorite: the Moon Pie. Not exactly a cookie, but surely a "small cake," this Southern institution is pure nostalgia for a number of us. Growing up, my favorite way to eat a Moon Pie—a sweet, gooey, chocolate-coated marshmallow-graham cracker round—was to wash it down with an ice-cold RC Cola. I know it sounds like a cliché. Oh, sometimes, I'd have a Tru-Ade instead, but it was the caffeine in the RC combined with the sugar in the Moon Pie that really gave one a burst of energy on a hot North Carolina summer day.

Unfortunately, Moon Pies can't be made at home. But the recipes that follow will fill your cookie jar with a taste of the South.

Whole Wheat Sesame Seed Cookies

. . .

SESAME SEED, or benne, cookies have been a part of Southern life ever since the seeds were brought over on slave ships. The transplanted Africans scattered the seeds (called "benne" in their Nigerian language) in their doorways to bring luck, and used them in their cooking as well.

White mistresses welcomed and adapted the cookies from their black cooks, since they were familiar with biscuits and cakes flavored with seeds—such as aniseed and coriander—from their own European backgrounds.

The mingled African and European traditions have given rise to a variety of benne cookies; some thin and wafer-like, some thicker and denser. The cookie is particularly identified with Charleston, South Carolina, and is sometimes known as the Charleston Benne Wafer. Moving northward, a recipe adapted from the second edition of *The Virginia House-wife*, published in the 1954 *Monticello Cookbook*, is for a rolled cookie sprinkled with lightly toasted seeds and cut with "small fancy cutters."

President Andrew Jackson, like Jefferson, served the cookies and when Martin Van Buren's daughter-in-law, a South Carolinian, became his hostess at the White House, she revived the popularity of this Southern specialty.

Sesame seeds have not always been as widely available as they are now. In the 1930 book *Two Hundred Years of Charleston Cooking*, the introduction to one Mrs. Rhett's Benne Brittle recipe sadly comments that "benne seed cannot be procured in many places, but the candy made with it is so delicious and so characteristic of Charleston that the recipe is here included." Since then, sesame seeds have become a major U.S. import.

½ *cup tahini (sesame seed paste),*
  room temperature
½ *cup (1 stick) unsalted butter,*
  room temperature
½ *cup granulated sugar*
½ *cup firmly packed light brown*
  sugar

1 egg
½ *teaspoon vanilla*
¾ *cup unbleached all-purpose flour*
¼ *cup whole wheat flour*
½ *teaspoon salt*
½ *teaspoon baking soda*
¾ *cup untoasted sesame seeds*

1. Preheat oven to 350° F.

2. In a bowl, cream together tahini and butter until smooth. Beat in sugars; add egg and vanilla and beat until well blended.

3. Beat in the flours, salt, and baking soda until just blended. Do not overmix. Fold in seeds.

4. Drop by teaspoons onto greased baking sheets. Press lightly with a floured fork to form a tic-tac-toe pattern. Bake 10 minutes or until golden brown. Cool on racks. Store in airtight containers.

Makes about 5 dozen 3-inch cookies.

Black Walnut–Buckwheat Squares

• • •

BUCKWHEAT is the seed of a plant, technically a fruit (related to rhubarb), which was first found in Asiatic Russia. Buckwheat was first planted in America by Dutch colonists in the Hudson River area, and is still grown in New York State. A small amount is also grown in West Virginia, and at one time there was a small commercial production in North Carolina. The robust-flavored blue-gray flour that the plant yields is rich in B vitamins. Its strong flavor does take some tempering with white flour, but it is a good match for earthy-tasting black walnuts. Black walnuts are popular in the South, particularly in Spencer, West Virginia, where a four-day celebration honoring the black walnut harvest takes place each October. Favorite recipes for the nuts include Moravian Magnolia Cake, a rich butter cake with pecans and black walnuts in the batter, and Black John Cake, dark, spicy layers with coconut, raisins, and black walnuts in the frosting.

½ cup California walnuts
½ cup black walnuts (see page 481 for mail-order source)
½ cup sugar
½ cup unbleached all-purpose flour
¼ cup buckwheat flour

¼ teaspoon salt
6 tablespoons cold, unsalted butter, cut into small pieces
1 tablespoon grated lemon zest
1 tablespoon brandy
Confectioners' sugar

1. Preheat oven to 300° F.

2. In a blender or food processor, process nuts and sugar until finely ground. Add flours and salt and process until just mixed. Add butter and pulse just until crumbly. Add lemon zest and brandy and pulse until mixture just holds together. Pat the dough into flat cake, wrap and chill at least 2 hours.

3. Fit the dough evenly into a nonstick or lightly buttered 8-inch by 8-inch baking pan. Using a sharp knife, score the dough into 16 2-inch squares. Bake for 45 minutes. While still warm, cut through the scored lines to separate the squares and remove them carefully with a narrow flexible spatula. Cool on a rack. Sprinkle with confectioners' sugar before serving.

Makes 16 squares.

Sweet Potato–Walnut Cookies

• • •

OVEN ROASTED, baked in the coals, frittered, glazed, mashed, made into pones, chips, waffles, puddings, or pies—sweet potatoes are served up in a wealth of Southern cookbook recipes. The sweet potato in these drop cookies gives them a golden color and a moist texture. They are soft, comforting, not-too-sweet cookies in the tradition of Hermits, Lizzies, and Rocks—homey spiced drop cookies reminiscent of an earlier, simpler time. These cookies are particularly flavorsome in autumn, as they have a kind of "harvest" quality about them. Serve on a cool fall afternoon with a mug of strong tea or a glass of chilled, late-harvest Gewürztraminer.

COOKIES

1¼ cups unbleached all-purpose flour
1½ teaspoons baking powder
1½ teaspoons baking soda
½ teaspoon salt
¼ teaspoon nutmeg
¼ cup (4 tablespoons) unsalted butter, room temperature

¾ cup firmly packed light brown sugar
1 large egg, room temperature
1 cup puréed, cooked sweet potato (about 1 large sweet potato)
¼ teaspoon vanilla
Grated zest of 1 orange
½ cup chopped walnuts

GLAZE

1 cup confectioners' sugar
2 tablespoons orange juice

Walnut halves, to garnish (optional)

1. Preheat oven to 400° F.

2. To make the cookies: In a bowl, sift together flour, baking powder, baking soda, salt, and nutmeg; set aside.

3. In a separate bowl, cream butter and sugar; beat in egg, sweet potato, vanilla, and zest. Beat into dry ingredients; fold in nuts.

4. Drop by tablespoons 1½ inches apart onto buttered baking sheets. Bake

for 12 to 15 minutes or until golden-brown. Cool slightly on racks while you prepare the glaze.

5. To make the glaze: In a small bowl, mix confectioners' sugar with orange juice. Spread on warm cookies. While glaze is still moist, gently press a walnut half onto each cookie. Cool completely and store in 1 layer in airtight container.

Makes about 3 dozen 2-inch cookies.

Cornmeal Sugar Cookies

. . .

MY GRANDMOTHER, Mother Belk, made the best sugar cookies I ever had, but she never wrote down the recipe. But then, a recipe wouldn't have mattered, anyway, since the secret was in her hands. She instinctively knew just how much butter and sugar to add, and just how long to mix the dough. These cornmeal sugar cookies are my variation of those early childhood sweets.

We usually think of sugar cookies as the simplest of baked treats, but consider the recipe for "Sugar Cake" in *Martha Washington's Booke of Cookery and Booke of Sweetmeats*: The first ingredient is a pound of sugar, "beaten and searced [sieved]." Her inherited family recipe reflects the difference in household staples in eighteenth-century England and colonial America to those today. Sugar came in large blocks or cones and had to be scraped, pounded, and sieved (searced) before it was usable for baking. Then the sugar had to be clarified by boiling it with egg white before it could be used for preserving. Powdered, or confectioners' sugar, which gives a tender texture to baked goods, was often called for in nineteenth-century cookbooks in cake, meringue, and icing recipes (the English name for it is icing sugar).

Adding cornmeal to sugar cookies gives them a hearty taste and rustic texture. Sweet cornmeal baked goods may seem novel, but in 1847 *The Carolina Housewife* included a cinnamon-scented, Indian Pound Cake made with no white flour but with "the weight of eight eggs in sugar, and the weight of six in cornmeal, sifted."

Serve these cookies with your favorite ice cream, sherbets, or poached fruit. Or, cut them into holiday shapes and give as Christmas presents or pierce a hole in each dough cut-out, bake, then thread a ribbon through and hang on the tree or tie on packages.

1 cup plus 2 tablespoons unbleached all-purpose flour
1 cup yellow cornmeal
¾ cup plus 2 tablespoons confectioners' sugar
¾ teaspoon salt
½ teaspoon baking powder
8 tablespoons (1 stick) cold, unsalted butter

1 large egg
1 large egg yolk
1 teaspoon vanilla
1½ tablespoons grated lemon zest (optional)
Vanilla sugar—combine 2 cups sugar with 1 whole vanilla bean that has been split lengthwise. Cover and let stand 1 week (optional)

1. In a bowl, mix flour, cornmeal, confectioners' sugar, salt, and baking powder. With your fingertips, a pastry cutter, or two knives cut in the butter until mixture resembles coarse meal. Add whole egg, yolk, vanilla, and lemon zest, if using. Knead 2 or 3 times or until just blended. Pat into a flat cake, wrap in waxed paper, and chill 30 minutes.

2. Preheat oven to 375° F.

3. On floured surface, roll out dough ⅛ inch thick. Cut into 2-inch circles, stars, or other shapes and place on buttered baking sheets. Bake for 8 to 10 minutes or until bottoms are golden-brown. Transfer to a rack and sprinkle with vanilla-sugar, if using, while still slightly warm. Cool completely and store in airtight container.

Makes about 4 dozen cookies.

Rye and Indian Stars
with Cinnamon Sugar

. . .

SINCE THE NATIVE AMERICANS taught the settlers how to grow and cook maize, cornmeal came to be called "Indian meal" or simply "Indian"; the name survives in Indian pudding. Rye, brought here by the Europeans, grew better than wheat in both the Northern and Southern colonies, and was combined with the native corn to make what was known as rye 'n' Injun bread. Boston brown bread, still popular today, is made with this combination of flours.

Rye flour cookies are probably Northern European in origin (rye is a favorite flour in Scandinavia and Germany); cinnamon stars or wreath cookies—Zimtsterne or Zimtkranze—are a German Christmas specialty. The star shapes are of course ideal for the holidays, but let today's endless variety of cookie cutters inspire you to make them for any occasion.

½ cup (1 stick) unsalted butter, room temperature

¾ cup plus 2 tablespoons firmly packed light brown sugar

1 large egg, room temperature

1 large egg yolk, room temperature

1 teaspoon vanilla

¾ cup plus 2 tablespoons unbleached all-purpose flour

¾ cup rye flour

¾ cup cornmeal

¼ teaspoon cinnamon

½ teaspoon salt

½ teaspoon baking powder

¼ teaspoon baking soda

Cinnamon sugar—4 teaspoons granulated sugar mixed with ½ teaspoon ground cinnamon (optional)

1. In a bowl, beat butter and brown sugar until very light and fluffy. Beat in the egg and egg yolk and vanilla until very well blended.

2. In a separate bowl, mix dry ingredients, except for the optional cinnamon sugar. Add to the butter mixture while beating slowly until dough just comes together. Do not overmix. Knead dough 2 to 3 times on a lightly floured work surface (dough will be somewhat sticky). Do not overwork the dough. Pat into a flat cake; wrap in waxed paper and chill at least 2 hours.

3. Preheat oven to 375° F.

4. Roll out dough on lightly floured work surface to a ¼-inch thickness and cut into 2-inch stars with floured cutter. Place ½ inch apart on buttered baking sheet; sprinkle with cinnamon sugar, if using. Bake in the center of the oven for 10 to 12 minutes or until golden on bottom. Cool on rack. Store in airtight container 3 to 4 weeks.

Makes about 40 2-inch stars.

Homemade Vanilla Wafers

. . .

AMERICAN BAKERS owe a great debt to Thomas Jefferson, who brought vanilla here from France. Without vanilla there would be no vanilla wafers; without vanilla wafers, no banana pudding; without banana pudding—well, just ask any Southerner.

Southerners have been making banana pudding with vanilla wafers for years. Where was this perfect marriage made? Bananas—now one of America's most popular fruit—were not regularly imported to the United States until the 1840s, and distribution was not widespread until the turn of the century. Perhaps some Southern cook turned to her time-honored recipe for trifle and thought to try it with the exotic new fruit. She would have layered sherry-soaked ladyfingers, custard, and cream, but replaced the usual jam or berries with sliced bananas. Maybe this inspired her to make it for the children (leaving out the sherry) and the rest is history. Or pure speculation, of course. Although we know that vanilla wafers have been made commercially at least since 1906, we can't pin down the date of their first use in banana pudding.

These homemade vanilla wafers may elevate your next banana pudding back to trifle status. They are also wonderful with Frozen Banana Syllabub with Sauternes (page 410) and almost any ice cream, mousse, or fresh fruit dessert. I like to make these in long, oval shapes, like ladyfingers or the French, *langues de chat* (cat's tongue). But you can make the more classic round shape if you prefer.

1 cup (2 sticks) unsalted butter,
   room temperature
3/4 cup sugar
2 teaspoons vanilla

3 large egg whites
3/4 cup unbleached all-purpose flour
1/4 teaspoon salt

1. Preheat oven to 375° F.

2. Butter 2 large baking sheets. Line the sheets with parchment paper, then butter and flour the parchment paper. Set aside.

3. In a medium bowl, beat together butter and sugar until light and fluffy. Beat in vanilla. Add egg whites slowly while beating constantly. Beat in flour and salt until just mixed.

4. Fit a pastry bag with a plain round tube (approximately ½ inch in diameter). Fill the bag ⅔ full with the batter.

5. Pipe out 3-inch-long "fingers" 1 inch apart on the prepared baking sheet. (Note: Hold the pastry bag almost vertical and very close to the baking sheet to get very thin strips.)

6. Bake in the center of the oven for 7 to 10 minutes or until edges have browned slightly but centers are still pale. Remove immediately from baking sheet and cool on racks and store in airtight container.

Makes about 5 dozen wafers.

Coconut Tuiles

• • •

IN OLD SOUTHERN COOKBOOKS, coconut is used in macaroons, kisses, cakes, and even gingerbread. Brought in through seaports like Charleston, this exotic product entered the Southern cook's repertoire early on. However, adding coconut to the French almond cookies called tuiles—so named for their curved shape reminiscent of roof tiles—is a relatively new idea.

Tile-shaped cookies are made in Italy and Spain, where they are called *tegoline* and *tejas,* respectively, and curled cookies also have a long history in the American South. In *Martha Washington's Booke of Cookery and Booke of*

Desserts

■

Sweetmeats, the old family cookbook inherited by Martha Washington, the author speaks of "cracknells"—a very old English name for tuile-type cookies. These are flavored with "caraway cumfits" (sugar-coated caraway seeds) and rosewater. Karen Hess' annotations to that cookbook suggest rolling the baked cookies over a broom handle to curl them, which is precisely how Broomstick Crunch Wafers are made in *Out of Kentucky Kitchens* (1949).

Tuiles are sensitive to humidity, so bake these treats only in dry weather, then store them in airtight containers. Serve Coconut Tuiles with ice cream, sorbet, mousse, custard, or any poached or stewed fruit dessert.

3 tablespoons unsalted butter, room temperature
½ cup finely ground almonds
½ cup sugar
2 egg whites, room temperature
¼ cup unbleached all-purpose flour

¼ teaspoon vanilla
1 cup shredded coconut, lightly toasted (place on a baking sheet and bake in a preheated 325° F. oven, tossing frequently, for 10 minutes)

1. In a bowl, cream butter, almonds, and sugar until light and fluffy. Beat in egg whites until well blended. Sift flour over mixture a little at a time stirring well after each addition. Stir in vanilla and then coconut. Chill 15 minutes.

2. Preheat oven to 425° F.

3. Generously butter 2 baking sheets. Drop batter by level tablespoons 3 inches apart. Spread batter to a diameter of 2 inches with the back of a spoon dipped in cold water. Bake for 5 to 7 minutes or until well browned on the edges and golden-brown in the center. Remove from oven and immediately lift cookies off the sheets with a metal spatula, being careful that cookies do not tear. Place warm, flexible cookies over a rolling pin to cool into a curved shape. Store in airtight container.

Makes 12 to 15 cookies.

Gingerbread Sandwiches
with Fresh Ginger Filling

• • •

GINGERBREAD is one of the most classic American desserts. Dried ginger was brought to this country from the time of the first English settlement. The fact that molasses—ginger's natural flavor complement—was the most available sweetener in the colonies may have helped make gingerbread as popular here as it had been in the Mother Country, where it was made with honey or sugar. The first English gingerbread recipe is said to have appeared in print in 1430.

In old New Orleans, coarse slabs of gingerbread called "stage planks" were sold in the streets. The *Picayune Creole Cook Book* (1900) gives this sturdy snack—made without softening ingredients, like butter or eggs—the Creole name, "Estomac Mulatre," because "it was only fit for the stomack of a mulatto to digest." Other old gingerbread recipes boast more appetizing titles, from ginger crisps to ginger-nuts to ginger snaps. Lafayette was honored with a gingerbread named for him.

Both the cookies and filling here are pungently flavored with juice squeezed from fresh gingerroot—not ground dried ginger. The procedure for extracting the juice from fresh gingerroot is easy, and you may find other uses for this novel ingredient in savory as well as sweet dishes.

COOKIES

10- to 12-inch piece of fresh ginger-root to make ginger juice
2/3 cup firmly packed light brown sugar
1/2 cup molasses
3/4 teaspoon cinnamon
1/2 cup (1 stick) unsalted butter

3 tablespoons ginger juice
2 1/2 cups unbleached all-purpose flour
1 1/2 teaspoons baking powder
1/2 teaspoon baking soda
1/4 teaspoon salt
1 egg, beaten
Grated zest of 1 lemon

FILLING

1 tablespoon butter, melted and cooled
2 cups confectioners' sugar, sifted

2 tablespoons grated peeled fresh gingerroot (from about 3 to 4 inches fresh gingerroot)

1. To make the cookies: Peel the gingerroot and discard the peel. Mince or grate the gingerroot very finely. Extract the juice by squeezing the gingerroot in your hand over a bowl (or place gingerroot in cheesecloth and wring it). Measure out 3 tablespoons juice for the cookies and 4 tablespoons (¼ cup) juice for the filling. Reserve.

2. In a saucepan, bring sugar, molasses, cinnamon, and butter slowly to a boil; cool to room temperature. Stir in 3 tablespoons ginger juice.

3. In a bowl, sift flour, baking powder, baking soda, and salt. Make well in center and add egg, molasses mixture, and zest; beat liquid ingredients together then incorporate flour until a dough forms.

4. Turn out onto a lightly floured surface and knead 30 seconds or until dough is soft and slightly sticky to touch. Divide dough in half. Pat each half into a flat cake; wrap in waxed paper and chill at least 3 hours.

5. Preheat oven to 325° F.

6. Working with one portion of dough at a time, on a lightly floured surface, roll out dough ⅛ inch thick. Cut into 2-inch rounds with cookie cutters. Place on lightly greased baking sheets and bake 10 to 12 minutes or until lightly browned and set. Cool on racks.

7. To make the filling: In the top part of a double boiler over simmering water melt the butter, then add sugar, ginger, and the rest of ginger juice. Heat the mixture for 10 minutes, stirring occasionally. Remove from heat and beat with electric mixer 8 to 10 minutes or until mixture is light and fluffy. If mixture is too thin to spread, add a little more confectioners' sugar, a tablespoon at a time, until stiff enough to spread.

8. Spread a thin layer of the filling on bottoms of half the cookies; top with remaining cookies. Store in airtight containers.

Makes about 25 to 30 sandwiches.

Maple-Walnut Stickies

• • •

Almost every mountain farm had a grove of . . . sugar maple trees which they called sugar orchards . . . In the early spring months, usually in March after a hard freeze when there would come a warm spell or thaw as they call it, the sap would begin to rise . . . The sweet water [sap] was carried to large kettles or pots. Some folks cooked the water in a cane molasses boiler . . . When it was thick enough for syrup, it was poured into pitchers, crocks and jars. The syrup would keep indefinitely.

—Elizabeth Hedgecock Sparks, *North Carolina and Old Salem Cookery*

ROBERT BEVERLEY recorded "the harvesting of 'sugar trees' " in seventeenth-century Virginia, and the tradition continues today in Highland County, Virginia, where a Maple Festival is held every March. Alice Vance's *Sugarin'-off in the Bullpasture Valley,* a recipe booklet published in connection with the festival, describes the syrup-making process and the festival itself, which is complete with square dancing, "sugar dancing," and pancake eating. The Vance family has been making maple syrup for over fifty years; he still uses a horse-drawn sled to collect the sap, and an iron boiler over an open fire to cook it down. The recipes in Mrs. Vance's booklet include Southern favorites such as sassafras tea and pralines, as well as North-South hybrids like maple syrup pecan pie and Indian pudding made from cornbread crumbs.

Maple sugar is made from maple syrup and is available in specialty food stores. Like the French palmiers, which make use of leftover puff pastry dough, stickies were the Southern cook's way to create something delicious from leftover biscuit or pie dough.

Both of my grandmothers made stickies from biscuit dough scraps and flavored them with butter and granulated sugar. When my mother sent me the family recipe, she added a note saying, "Please, *please*—no gourmet additions, like spices or nuts. These are best plain . . ." Sorry, Mom, but I prefer my version; the original is good in its own pure and simple way, but I find the maple sugar and nuts add delicious texture and flavor. Serve stickies warm for breakfast, brunch, or tea.

1 recipe Basic Biscuits dough (see
    page 23)
6 tablespoons unsalted butter, room
    temperature
6 tablespoons granulated sugar

½ cup maple sugar (or firmly packed
    light brown sugar)
½ cup chopped walnuts

1. Prepare biscuit dough as directed. On a lightly floured surface roll out ⅛ inch thick to a rectangle about 11 inches by 13 inches. Trim edges to make a neat rectangle.

2. In a bowl, cream butter with all but 2 tablespoons granulated sugar and all the maple sugar. Dot mixture evenly over the dough and spread as smoothly as possible. Sprinkle with nuts. Roll up tightly lengthwise like a jelly roll. Wrap and chill 45 minutes or until firm.

3. Preheat oven to 400° F.

4. With a very sharp knife, cut into ½-inch-thick slices and place ½ inch apart on a very lightly buttered jelly roll pan. Sprinkle with remaining sugar. Bake 15 to 18 minutes or until golden-brown on top and crisp on the bottom. Store in airtight container up to 1 week.

Makes about 12 stickies.

"Praline" Blondies

• • •

CHOCOLATE-FREE bar cookies may well have existed before the brownie was ever conceived, but the latter's popularity was such that the nonchocolate squares came to be known as blond brownies—or blondies. Due to the small amount of flour used in this recipe the chewy texture is similar to pralines and the flavor is just as intense, with pecans and butter predominating.

¼ cup unsalted butter
½ cup sugar
½ cup firmly packed light brown
   sugar
2 large eggs, beaten
1 teaspoon vanilla

½ cup cake flour
½ teaspoon baking powder
½ teaspoon salt
1 cup finely chopped (but not
   ground) pecans

1. Preheat oven to 350° F.

2. Melt butter in medium-sized sauce pan; stir in sugars; cool to room temperature.

3. Beat eggs and vanilla in a medium-sized bowl. Beat in the butter mixture. Stir in the flour, baking powder, and salt until just incorporated; do not over-mix. Fold in nuts.

4. Turn mixture into a well-buttered or nonstick 8-inch-square baking pan and bake for 20 to 25 minutes or until just set. Cool slightly; cut into squares. Serve warm or at room temperature with ice cream or lightly sweetened whipped cream. Store in airtight container.

Makes 16 2-inch squares.

Brown Sugar–
Peanut Butter Shortbread

■ ■ ■

MORE THAN HALF the peanuts grown in the United States are processed to make peanut butter, and Americans consume over 700 million pounds of the stuff every year. While most of it goes into sandwich making, some is used in baking. I love the flavor it gives this shortbread. Serve it with Sweet Potato Ice Cream (page 416), peach ice cream, or any sorbet, mousse, or soufflé.

¾ cup unbleached all-purpose flour
¼ cup firmly packed light brown
  sugar
¼ cup granulated sugar
¼ cup cornstarch
¼ teaspoon salt

8 tablespoons (1 stick) cold *unsalted*
  butter, diced into ½-inch cubes
¼ cup *good-quality* cold *lightly*
  salted smooth peanut butter
½ *teaspoon vanilla*

1. Preheat oven to 325° F.

2. In a food processor, mix flour, sugars, cornstarch, and salt. Add butter, peanut butter, vanilla and pulse 15 to 18 times until dough just comes together when pressed. (Note: Dough will be crumbly. Do not overprocess.)

3. Pat dough into a nonstick or lightly buttered 9-inch cake pan. Prick dough all over with a fork at 1-inch intervals.

4. Bake for 35 minutes or until deep golden-brown. Mixture will look bubbly. Cool in the pans on a rack 5 minutes. Then, cut into 8 wedges while still warm. Cool to room temperature. Keeps up to 2 weeks in an airtight container in a cool place.

Makes 8 wedges.

Candy

I must now say something about St. Valentine's day. Missives flew back & forth the whole week. Rob & Mil. each received & sent at least a dozen. Most of them original without much regard to rhyme or metre. Sister had a good many too. Annie & I considered ourselves much neglected I only had one. But the quality of this one! I was compared to sugar—clarafied [*sic*] at that, molasses, honey, & all things sweet. It was easy to discover the Author, as he had first written his name & then erased it so badly I could make it out. But the youth was so much overcome afterwards & apparently so shocked that I was not, I never mentioned it to him.

—Agnes Lee, from *Growing Up in the 1850's: The Journal of Agnes Lee*,
edited by Mary Custis Lee deButts

EVEN THOUGH THE WORD CANDY (from the French, *candi* and the Arabic, *quand,* which means sugar) has been part of the English language since the 1400s, in seventeenth-, eighteenth- and even some nineteenth-century English and American cookbooks, the word is generally used as a verb, not a noun. "To candy" meant to bring sugar syrup to the hard-crack stage (220° F). The category of sweets themselves were usually called sweetmeats (the word "meat" meant "food" at one time) or cakes. According to Karen Hess, transcriber of *Martha Washington's Booke of Cookery and Booke of Sweetmeats,* the "Mint Cakes," for example, are not cakes, but essentially mint-flavored hard candies, made by boiling a mint infusion with sugar and fresh chopped mint.

This category of sweets is one of the most joyful and frivolous, evoking memories of Christmas-stocking treasures, Valentine's Day gestures, and of Mary Janes, jawbreakers, and red licorice consumed with abandon at an age when cellulite and cavities were not a concern.

My aunt Edith was the candy maker on my father's side of the family. As a young girl, she loved to close herself off in the big farmhouse kitchen and concoct her favorite sugary things that included divinity, taffy, and several kinds of fudge. She preferred being alone so she could concentrate on her work with no one (specifically her brothers) to bother her.

My grandmother was the confissiére on the other side of the family tree. At Christmastime, I loved "helping" her dip handrolled buttercreams into shiny melted chocolate and dusting the bourbon balls in powdered cocoa. Her bourbon balls always took me by surprise; they looked so benign, but they were shockingly strong with bourbon and clearly not meant for children. Other popular old-fashioned Southern sweetmeats include caramels, butterscotch, toffee, lemon drops, and of course, pralines and peanut and benne brittle. But today, except for the annual flurry of kitchen activity between Thanksgiving and New Year's, the days of home candy making are numbered. To most people, "candy" is more likely to mean "candy bar" or some other store-bought sweet. Perhaps the best-known commercially made Southern candy is the *Goo-Goo Cluster,* which was first produced in 1912 in Nashville, Tennessee. Whenever I'm in the South I always pick up a good supply of these milk-chocolate-coated caramel and pecan patties to share with my Yankee friends. *Goo-Goo Clusters* have pecans instead of peanuts.

Desserts

■

Honey-Walnut Pralines

• • •

LITTLE DID the Marechal César du Plessis-Praslin know, when he was advised to eat his almonds sugar coated in order to ward off indigestion, that he was giving his name in perpetuity to a great Creole candy. French chefs came to call almost any sugar-coated nut *praline,* and the word *pralinée* sometimes refers to a dessert ingredient or garnish of crushed, sugared nuts. But the classic New Orleans pralines we enjoy today are soft, rather crumbly, melt-in-the-mouth patties of pecans, sugar, and butter.

In New Orleans, pralines and other Creole candies were sold by the so-called Pralinières, who waited outside the schools with "their great salvers, on which were laid snowy napkins and rows upon rows of beautiful white 'Candi Tire,' or 'Pulled Candy,' as the name indicated . . ." Each school had its regular "Candy woman," who made it her duty to be there exactly as the clock struck twelve. Many a faithful old negress helped to support her former mistress in the broken fortunes of the family after the war by her sale of Molasses Candy Pralines, Candi Tire, La Colle, or Maïs Tac-tac. (Candi Tire is molasses taffy; La Colle appears to be like a divinity made with chopped pecans and molasses. Maïs Tac-tac is sugared popcorn candy, the obvious prototype of Cracker Jack.) Offer these tiny honey-walnut candies as you would truffles or petit fours with strong espresso after a rich dinner. The walnuts and orange zest help cut the sweetness somewhat; the honey adds a distinctive flavor.

¾ cup granulated sugar
¼ cup firmly packed light brown
   sugar
½ cup heavy cream
Pinch of salt
1 tablespoon honey (or substitute
   maple syrup)

1 tablespoon orange zest (from 1 medium orange) (optional)
2 tablespoons butter
½ cup lightly toasted coarsely
   chopped walnuts

1. In a large saucepan, over medium-high heat, bring sugars, cream, and salt to a boil, stirring occasionally.

2. Cook until mixture reaches the soft-ball stage (235° F to 240° F on a candy thermometer), about 10 to 15 minutes. Stir in honey and zest, if using, and return mixture to 240° F.

3. Remove from heat, stir in butter. Cool 1 minute, then beat vigorously a few seconds. Stir in nuts and continue to beat 2 minutes or until the mixture thickens.

4. Immediately, drop by slightly rounded teaspoons onto buttered foil-lined baking sheets. Let stand 3 to 4 hours or until hardened. Store in airtight container, separating layers with waxed paper, in cool place.

Makes about 30 to 35 pralines.

Bourbon-Chocolate Squares

■ ■ ■

THINK OF SOUTHERN CANDY. Now think of bourbon. The logical conclusion: bourbon balls and other bourbon-scented chocolates. The Rebecca Ruth Candy Shop in Frankfort, Kentucky, makes Bourbon Whiskey Cremes their specialty. Browse through the charitable cookbooks compiled by the good ladies of Kentucky and you will find a wealth of recipes for these potent confections, variously called Bourbon Candy Bonbons, Yuletide Bourbon Balls, Bourbon Candy, and Kentucky Colonels. With slight variations, they feature butter, confectioners' sugar, and either ground pecans or crushed vanilla wafers mixed with bourbon. This filling is rolled into balls, dipped into chocolate, or rolled in cocoa and then placed in decorative tins for a popular Christmas offering.

Tradition that they are, it is hard to fault bourbon balls, but the uncooked whiskey can give them quite a harsh, raw taste. In the candy here, the baking tempers the alcoholic impact of the whiskey, while the chocolate and cream mellow its flavor. The result is rich, chocolate candy with the spirit of bourbon balls and a texture that lies somewhere between a truffle and a brownie.

Chocolate candy does not have the long history of some other Southern sweets. Cocoa had been brought here from the West Indies since the time of the arrival of Dutch immigrants, but in the form of cocoa powder it was more suitable for decocting into a drink than for cooking. Eighteenth-century recipes for chocolate cakes are often for baked goods meant to be eaten with chocolate or cocoa and do not themselves contain the flavoring.

Chocolate candies were not produced on a commercial scale in the South until relatively recently, since heat and humidity made chocolate not only difficult to work with but made storage nearly impossible. Thanks to air-conditioning and the availability of good-quality bittersweet chocolate, you can make these bourbon chocolate candies an institution at your house all year round. They're easy to make, they keep well, and, like classic bourbon balls, they make fine Christmas presents.

1 pound, 2 ounces good-quality semi-sweet or bittersweet chocolate
8 large egg yolks

1¾ cups heavy cream
¼ teaspoon salt
2 tablespoons good-quality bourbon

1. Melt chocolate in a large double boiler over—not in—hot water. (Or, melt chocolate in microwave-proof bowl in microwave oven.) Cool slightly.

2. Preheat oven to 300° F.

3. In large bowl beat egg yolks until smooth. Beat in cream and salt until well blended. Beat in bourbon and the cooled chocolate until smooth.

4. Pour into a lightly buttered foil-lined 9-inch by 13-inch baking pan and smooth the top with a spatula. Bake for 25 to 30 minutes or until sides have puffed, tiny cracks appear on the surface, and center appears set.

5. Cool completely on a rack, then chill thoroughly. With a knife dipped in hot water and wiped dry, trim edges (discard or give to the children). Cut the trimmed chocolate into 1-inch squares, triangles, or diamonds, keeping the knife hot as you cut by dipping it into the water frequently. Store between layers of waxed paper in an airtight container in a cool, dry place for up to 2 weeks.

Makes 60 1-inch squares.

White Chocolate–Coated Truffles
with Bourbon-Chocolate Centers
• • •

TRUFFLES cannot claim a Southern heritage, but they are as well loved there as anywhere. These make good use of two of the South's most famous ingredients: pecans and bourbon. Serve after dinner with espresso or wrap and give away as Christmas presents.

BOURBON-CHOCOLATE CENTERS

5 ounces best-quality bittersweet or semisweet chocolate, finely chopped

1 ounce unsweetened chocolate, finely chopped

¼ cup heavy cream

¼ cup unsalted butter, room temperature

1 large egg yolk, room temperature

2 tablespoons best-quality bourbon

WHITE CHOCOLATE COATING

1½ pounds good-quality white chocolate, such as Callebaut

½ cup heavy cream

½ (1 stick) unsalted butter

3 large egg yolks, room temperature

3½ cups coarsely ground pecans, toasted

1. To make the centers: In a double boiler over hot (not boiling) water, melt bittersweet and unsweetened chocolates with cream while stirring constantly until chocolate has just melted. Remove from heat; whisk in butter and egg yolk until well blended. Mix in bourbon. Cool to room temperature, then cover and chill 2 hours or until easy to shape.

2. Make chocolate centers by forming ½-inch balls with clean hands or with a ½-inch melon baller. Place on waxed paper–lined baking sheet as you work. Chill until firm.

3. To make white chocolate coating: Heat white chocolate and cream in double boiler over hot (not boiling) water while stirring constantly. When chocolate has melted, immediately beat in butter and yolks. Cool to room temperature, then cover and chill at least 2 hours or until easy to shape.

4. Working with clean hands, take 1 tablespoon of white chocolate mixture and press it between your palms to form a pattie about ¼ inch thick. Wrap this around a cold, dark chocolate center, pressing and molding gently so that white chocolate covers dark chocolate completely. Repeat procedure with remaining chocolate. (Do not worry if shapes are irregular; this is part of a truffle's charm and one of the reasons they are so named!) Place on waxed paper–lined baking sheets as you work and chill briefly to harden slightly. Roll truffles in pecans to coat. Chill in airtight container up to 2 weeks or freeze up to 2 months. Bring to cool room temperature before serving.

Makes about 50 2-inch truffles.

Chocolate-Dipped Truffles
with White Chocolate–Pecan Centers

• • •

WHEN I MAKE TRUFFLES, I like to offer two kinds for the sake of variety. These are easy to make and keep well.

WHITE CHOCOLATE CENTERS

*¾ pound good-quality white choco-
  late, such as Callebaut
5 tablespoons heavy cream
4 tablespoons unsalted butter, cut
  into small pieces*

*2 egg yolks
1½ cups toasted pecans, finely
  chopped*

DARK DIPPING CHOCOLATE

*8 ounces good-quality semisweet or
  bittersweet chocolate, finely
  chopped*

*1 ounce unsweetened chocolate,
  finely chopped
1 tablespoon vegetable oil*

1. To make the white chocolate centers: In a double boiler, heat white chocolate with cream, stirring constantly over barely simmering water until melted. Immediately beat in butter and egg yolks. Stir in pecans. Chill 2 hours or until firm and easy to shape.

2. Roll the white chocolate mixture into 1-inch balls using clean hands or a melon baller. Place on waxed paper–lined baking sheets and chill thoroughly.

3. To make the dipping chocolate: In a double boiler over simmering water, melt 6 ounces of the semisweet chocolate and ¾ ounce of the unsweetened chocolate with the oil. Reserve the remaining chocolate in a bowl. (Take care that no water comes in contact with the chocolate or it will "seize.") When the chocolate in the double boiler has melted and is warm to the touch, remove from heat. Stir to cool slightly.

4. Stir in the reserved bittersweet and unsweetened chocolate by tablespoons. Stir until melted. Using a candy dipper or a fork, dip the cool, white chocolate–pecan centers into the melted dark chocolate, letting excess dark chocolate drip back into double boiler. Place truffles on waxed paper–lined baking sheets as you work. Chill until set. Refrigerate in airtight container up to 2 weeks or freeze up to 2 months. Bring to cool room temperature before serving.

Makes about 45 to 50 truffles.

Beverages

Beverages

WHEN WE THINK of Southern beverages, what usually comes to mind are tall glasses of iced tea, chicory-laced coffee, RC Cola, mint juleps, and just about anything made with bourbon. But the South's potable past includes a wealth of other drinks—from frontier-made beer and cider and hair-raising moonshine made in backyard stills to fancy, frothy eggnog and syllabubs. And then there was tea. Following the English custom, many New World settlers— particularly the well-to-do—made a fuss over brewing and serving tea imported from India. Although medicinal teas concocted from native herbs, roots, and fruits were not actually considered "beverages," they were regularly sipped to heal everything from appendicitis to the vapors. Fresh milk was a popular drink, but prior to refrigeration, milk spoiled easily in the South's warm climate so much of it was churned into butter. The by-product, buttermilk, became a popular beverage during the warmer months and, to this day, Southerners consume above-average quantities of it. This tangy, healthful thirst quencher becomes a satisfying supper when cornbread is crumbled into it, for a meal-in-a-glass that Southerners have enjoyed for hundreds of years.

The consumption of coffee, beer, soft drinks, and tea—hot and iced—has remained steadily high in the South. (The quantities were particularly high during Prohibition.) However, the popularity of other potables has ebbed and flowed with time. For example, the caudles, possets, and meads inherited from our English ancestors have fallen out of favor. (Although some Southern wineries make a modern day version of mead.) Icy mint juleps are primarily reserved for summertime, Derby Day, and special occasions. Eggnog—thick, rich, and generously spiked with bourbon—makes a once-a-year appearance during the holidays. And that frothy, egg-and-milk concoction, syllabub, has become all but a memory. The old, nonalcoholic favorites—like acids, shrubs, and "beers" made from fruit—have given way to soft drinks. Beers made in the South today are brewed from malt and barley rather than the persimmons and sassafras of yesteryear; well-made moonshine—if you're lucky enough to find any—has lost its rough edge and can be as smooth as fine French eaux-de-vie. Herbal infusions—which were at one time some of the only medicines around—are making a gradual comeback both as "cures" and as relaxing beverages as local herbalists revive the art of natural remedies. Another onetime medicine, the cordial (particularly blackberry cordial), today is sipped as an after-dinner liqueur rather than as a cure for an upset stomach.

Perhaps the biggest evolution in Southern drinking habits has been in the area of wine. Thomas Jefferson's dream—that good-quality wine would be made in the New World—has become a reality. Southerners aren't likely to completely give up their bourbon or iced tea for a glass of Virginia Chardonnay or Alabama Blush, but as the region's winemakers perfect their art, wine consumption will surely continue to rise south of the Mason-Dixon line.

The Early Days: Beer, Wine, and Whiskey

MUCH OF THE WATER was unfit to drink in seventeenth-century Europe, so, by tradition and habit, European settlers in the New World often considered wine and beer the safer beverages. On both continents alcoholic beverages were considered essential for good health. They were thought to aid digestion, to ward off chills, and to take away all manner of aches and pains.

Beer was the first alcoholic beverage to be brought over to the New World in substantial quantity. While the alcohol in it undoubtedly helped ease the burden of the long voyage, more important, beer didn't "foul" like water (or other nonalcoholic beverages, for that matter) so it was considered necessary for survival.

Once ashore, the demand for beer was high, so right away brewing began in the New World. By 1629, Virginia had two brewhouses but beer was also made in the home. Colonial wives incorporated brewing into their household tasks: beer making was a daily chore that went along with cooking, cleaning, sewing, and childcare. While beer imported from England was indeed available, locally made beer was less expensive and easier to get.

During this time, cider was popular throughout the New World. European settlers brought their knowledge of pomiculture, and apples flourished as far south as Virginia. Apples grew poorly farther south, so cider enjoyed in other Southern regions had to be shipped from the North.

Wine was only mildly popular in the seventeenth century. Since the majority of the first settlers were of British descent and had no heritage of viticulture, most wines served in New World homes were not locally made but, rather, were expensive imports. Consumption, therefore, was limited to the wealthy. In Virginia the newly settled French Huguenots made one of the first attempts at colonial grape growing, but the vines were soon replaced with tobacco plants for which there was a greater demand.

Although wine was not as important as beer or cider at this time, other distilled beverages were quite another matter, especially the most prevalent form of hard spirits, brandy. It was popular in Europe and valued by the colonists because of its high alcoholic content. In addition, it kept longer than beer. Imported distilled spirits were costly, as was the case with imported beer, so colonial households often made their own. Backyard stills began to proliferate and a taste for these domestically made "hot waters" (or "strong waters," as they were called) grew. People began distilling all manner of grains and fruits, and drinking became a daily habit. (Peaches, for peach brandy, were a particular favorite in the South.) As in England, most colonial drinking was, by and large, family and community oriented, taking place at work, at meals (cider and beer were the usual mealtime beverages), and at celebrations and rites of passage (weddings, funerals, baptisms, etc.).

Demon Rum and Grain Distillates

BY THE MID-SEVENTEENTH CENTURY, the colonists were drinking rum—which was made from molasses, a by-product of sugar refining. The settlers drank rum straight, spiced, hot and buttered, in punches and in eggnog, and by the dawn of the eighteenth century, they had fallen in love with hard liquor. But grain was plentiful in the New World and so about the time of the Revolution, grain whiskeys were growing in popularity and they soon eclipsed rum as the preferred distilled alcoholic beverage. Several things other than the abundance of grain hastened the decline of rum. In 1764 the Sugar Act forbade the importation of rum and spirits from foreign sources, one of several acts that ultimately led to the Revolution. During the Revolutionary War, American ports were blockaded by the Royal Navy and both rum and molasses from the predomi-

Beverages

∎

449

nantly British-colonized West Indies became scarce. After the war, trade was not completely restored with the West Indies. In 1807, the Embargo Act prohibited commerce from the West Indies and cut off the supply of molasses. Then in 1808, Congress abolished slave trade with Africa and, thus, the commerce of rum. (Rum was an important trading commodity and was traded in Africa for slaves. Some smuggling of both molasses and slaves resulted, but the increasing cost to freight rum from the seaboard over the Appalachian mountains hastened the decline of rum.)

In the 1730s whiskey-loving Scotch-Irish immigrants began pouring into the Southeast's western frontier. These newcomers brought their distilling skills with them and right away began concocting spirits from the local grain. The first distinctly American whiskey was rye whiskey distilled from rye, corn, barley, and malt. (Today, rye whiskey must be made with at least 51 percent rye.) Much of it was made in Pennsylvania by that region's Scotch-Irish settlers. Distillers further south used the more available corn to make their spirits—they called it corn whiskey—which was composed of about 80 percent corn with a balance of rye and barley. The first whiskey made from corn is said to have been made along the James River in Virginia by Captain George Thorpe in the seventeenth century. Corn whiskey was simple to make, and brought a greater profit than the sale of corn as food.

Bourbon Is Born

Nothing is so musical as the sound of pouring bourbon for the first drink on a Sunday morning. Not Bach or Schubert or any of those masters . . .

—Carson McCullers, *Clock Without Hands*

OUT OF CORN WHISKEY grew bourbon, which was about 65 to 70 percent corn with a balance of rye and barley. Bourbon takes its name from Bourbon County, Kentucky, where it is said to have been first produced in 1789 by the Reverend Elijah Craig, a Virginia Baptist who was an active distiller in the late eighteenth century. (Frontier churches at this time, it is interesting to note, were not necessarily protemperance.) By the early nineteenth century, bourbon had become an important regional industry.

Like Brunswick stew—whose origins are claimed by both Virginia and Georgia—bourbon's birthplace is claimed by two states as well: Virginia and Kentucky. Prior to 1776, Kentucky was part of Fincastle County, Virginia. In 1776, it became Kentucky County, but it was still in the state of Virginia. Kentucky became a separate state in 1792, three years *after* the Reverend Craig's first distillation. Virginians like to claim bourbon as their creation, not only since Kentucky was still part of Virginia in 1792, but because Craig was a born Virginian and probably learned to distill before going to Kentucky County at age forty-four.

This new whiskey was called "Kentucky bourbon," distinguishing it from Pennsylvanian rye. The special characteristic of bourbon whiskey was a unique combination of corn (for strength and body) and rye (for a smoothing, mellowing effect), plus the aging in charred barrels (which added richness). It was Elijah Craig, in fact, who is said to have first used charred barrels. The use of charred barrels may have come about accidentally. One theory has it that the barrels were used to store salt pork, fish, vinegar, or flour and may have been charred inside to rid them of their strong odors. Accidental or not, the charring added a distinct flavor to the bourbon, and became an integral part of its making.

Bourbon Today

TODAY'S BOURBON is smoother and more refined than its rough, corn-based ancestors because its production is regulated by law. First, it must be at least 51 percent corn (some distillers use more) with a balance of rye, wheat, or other cereal grains. Second, these ingredients are cooked to convert the grain starch to sugars. This mixture, called the mash, is then cooled to around 70° F, transferred to tubs, and injected with yeast. As this warm mixture ferments sugars are consumed by the yeast and converted to ethyl alcohol, resulting in "distiller's beer," which is approximately 10 percent alcohol. The "beer" is then distilled by passing through a continuous still. The alcohol vapors and flavoring agents vaporize and are removed, condensed, or reliquified in the form of "new whiskey," which is clear in color, sweet in taste, and raw in aroma. (Some distillers

Beverages

redistill the "new whiskey" in a pot still for refinement.) The third stage for bourbon is aging. It must sit for at least two years in new charred white oak barrels. Since aging affects the taste, color, proof, and smoothness of bourbon, any that is aged less than four years must be so labeled. After aging, bourbon is mixed with pure distilled water to lower the proof for bottling. It is filtered—sometimes as much as thirty-five times—to ensure purity. Then, the amber-colored whiskey is bottled. After meeting these required criteria, individual distillers may vary other techniques to make their own "signature" taste or house style.

Craig's whiskey may have been called "the whiskey from Bourbon," or Kentucky Bourbon (referring to Bourbon County) but bourbon is now not only made in Kentucky but also in Virginia, Indiana, and Missouri.

Kentuckians remain chauvinistic about their bourbon. The early distillers discovered that the limestone and iron-free water in Kentucky were ideal for making whiskey. So in the days before mechanical pumps, distilleries were always built at the foot of a hill that fed water to them from a spring. Kentucky naturally had many such locations. Today more than 90 percent of all whiskey produced in the United States is made in Kentucky. Federal law prohibits the use of the word Kentucky on the label of any whiskey not made there. Although Kentuckians often credit the high quality of their bourbon to the local limestone, much of the water actually used today in bourbon making is distilled from the public reservoir.

What makes one bourbon fiery, another velvety smooth, depends on variations in the classic formula, such as how much corn or rye is used, its alcoholic strength, and its length of aging. Four of the smoothest are Rebel Yell, Old Grand Dad 100, Maker's Mark, and Ancient Age. If you don't care whether the label says "bourbon" or not, one of the newest bourbon-type whiskeys out is also one of the smoothest. Gentleman Jack, a Tennessee Whiskey, from Lynchburg, Tennessee, made by the Jack Daniels people is more like a fine brandy than a whiskey. Like Jack Daniels, Gentleman Jack is filtered through charcoal. In charcoal filtering, hard maple charcoal is placed in vats. The whiskey slips through the charcoal, and it takes about ten to twelve hours for one drop to seep from the top to the bottom.

Basic Bourbon Terms

Sourmash Bourbon The distiller saves a little of the mash from each distillation and adds this old mash to each new batch. It acts as a kind of starter, as in making sourdough bread. Despite its name, there is nothing sour about the taste of sourmash whiskey. In fact, all bourbon is rather sweet tasting (as opposed to the smoky, peaty flavor of scotch) as a result of the natural sugars in the corn.

Straight Bourbon Whiskey Bourbon that has been distilled off at no more than 160 proof, aged in new, charred white oak barrels for at least four years, and reduced in proof by the addition of water at the time of bottling to at least 80 proof.

Tennessee Whiskey and Kentucky Whiskey Bourbon-like whiskeys that are made under less-restricted government specifications than bourbon. Two examples are Jack Daniels and Early Times. Jack Daniels—a Tennessee whiskey—can't be called bourbon because at distillation it is filtered through charcoal, a step that is not part of the classic bourbon-making process. Early Times, a Kentucky whiskey, is aged in *used* (rather than new) charred white oak barrels, so it cannot be called bourbon, which only uses *new* barrels.

The Mint Julep

> "How about a mint julep," asked Ralph Quick.... "A mint julep by all means," said Clare.... Ralph rose from his chair and began the complicated ritual once more. As he wrapped ice cubes in a dishtowel and solemnly crushed them with a hammer . . .
>
> —Gail Godwin, *A Southern Family*

GODWIN WASN'T THE FIRST great writer to write about juleps: Milton, Pepys, and other greats have also waxed enthusiastic about this elixir. The word "julep" is at least 500 years old and may have come from the Arabic *julab* or Persian *gulab,* meaning "rosewater." According to Karen Hess in *Martha Washington's Booke of Cookery and Booke of Sweetmeats,* in sixteenth- and seventeenth-century England the word julep referred to a drink that was often sweetened as a vehicle for medication. Early American juleps—which were made with brandy or rum—were often taken at breakfast as an eye-opener. But the bourbon-and-mint potation that we know today as a "mint julep" is probably only about 100 years old. Although it is usually associated with Kentucky and Derby Day celebrations, the earliest mint juleps were probably born in Virginia.

Like the recipes for gumbo or barbecue sauce, there are many strong opinions about what the authentic mint julep recipe really is. Some say the mint leaves must be crushed. Others claim the best way to make a mint julep is to mix bourbon, sugar syrup, and shaved ice and to add a mint sprig just before serving. Some fill the glass with shaved ice and let it stand for up to half an hour to let the glass "frost" before adding the bourbon and mint. Whether crushed, bruised, frosted, or not, the sterling-silver julep cup (which has been around since at least the early 1800s) is the traditional vessel. When it is properly frosted, and garnished with a fresh mint sprig, the mint julep is as refreshing visually as it is gastronomically.

Wine Grape Growing and Winemaking in the South: A Brief History

THE FIRST REFERENCE made to winemaking in the Southeast is in a 1565 report by Captain John Hawkins of his voyage to Florida. Hawkins found a colony of French Huguenots near the St. John's River and although they were on the verge of starvation, Hawkins says they had made twenty hogshead of wine. If the story is true, the wine was probably made from the native Scuppernong grape.

According to Thomas Pinney, author of *A History of Wine in America,* more current theories believe that this early Huguenot settlement made no wine at all. Instead, the first effort to make wine in America was more than likely by Spanish colonists in 1568 in what is now Parris Island, South Carolina.

Sixteen years after these first attempts at winemaking in the New World, reports from Sir Walter Raleigh's expedition refer to a veritable Eden of grapes—

muscadines probably—growing in what is now eastern North Carolina. In 1607, the Jamestown settlers also reported on an abundance of grapes in the New World. These combined reports gave the English great hope that in time they would no longer have to be dependent on the French for wine.

According to Captain John Smith's writings, Virginia's first "crush" was in 1609 and produced about twenty gallons of wine made from native grapes. A Dr. Laurence Bohune is noted as being the first New World winemaker. Bohune's wine—made in Jamestown—was said to have been drunk five to six days after crushing; it must have been a tangy, acidic, drink indeed. Other than this early, rather crude New World wine, much of the wines drunk in the early days were European imports. Seventeenth-century settlers followed the general English preference for sweet, heavy wines, like Madeira and sherry. Some of these imported wines, it should be noted, were reportedly of poor quality. Beer, cider, and later, distilled spirits, were the more popular seventeenth-century beverages, so the earliest attempts at viticulture were only halfhearted. Both the Anglican and Puritan churches used communion wine, but it was not until after the Civil War that wine had even a modest growth, and even then, viticulture lagged behind distilling and brewing in popularity.

But the dream continued. Captain John Smith, Lord Delaware, and other officials of the Virginia Company wrote about Virginia's potential as a wine-growing region and urged the London Company to diversify into wine. By 1619, eight French *vignerons* (wine-grape growers) laden with vine cuttings made from *Vitis vinifera* (European wine grapes) were sent to Virginia to develop a wine industry. Their efforts, however, were unsuccessful.

In 1622, French *vigneron,* John Bonoeil, provided a manual—as per orders from the King—for every householder in Virginia, on the cultivation of silk and the vine. Bonoeil's manual provided general instructions for winemaking, including how to crush the grapes with bare feet and a "recipe" for making wine.

Enthusiasm was maintained throughout the seventeenth century with various experiments and theories on New World winegrowing. One such enthusiast was William Berkeley (governor of Virginia from 1642 to 1652 and again from 1662 to 1677) who cultivated a vineyard of native American grapes. Another was English physician Thomas Glover who, after a journey to the New World, reported that "claret-grapes" were growing in Virginia and with proper care he felt they might produce a claret as good as one from France. Another Englishman interested in New World grape growing was Edward Williams, who sug-

Beverages

■

455

gested that Greek vines be planted instead of French. In 1658, the government stepped in. An act of assembly was passed to encourage wine grape growing in Virginia by offering a prize of 10,000 pounds of tobacco to whomever made two tons of wine from a local vineyard. Further south, in 1663, the proprietors of Carolina (it would not separate into North and South until 1712) proposed that the colony concentrate on producing wine, silk, and oil. In 1680, a group of Huguenots settled in South Carolina, and by 1682, they reportedly made wine, probably from native grapes.

In the eighteenth century, John Fontaine, along with other members of a group called the Knights of the Golden Horseshoe, crossed the Blue Ridge mountains—a journey that was part of Lieutenant Governor Alexander Spotwood's efforts to explore and open up the western frontier. In the fall of 1716, Fontaine wrote in his journal:

> We had a good dinner. After dinner we got the men all together and loaded all their arms and we drunk the King's health in Champagne ... the Princes's health in Burgundy ... and all the rest of the Royal Family in Claret. ... We had several sorts of liquors, namely Virginia Red wine and White wine ... Brandy, Shrub ... Champagne, Canary, Cherry Punch, Cider, Water, etc.
>
> —Thomas Pinney, *A History of Wine in America: From the Beginnings to Prohibition*

If the "Virginia red and white" were indeed red and white wines made in Virginia, they were more than likely made from native grapes.

The eighteenth century witnessed several determined wine-growing efforts. In the 1720s, William Byrd, brother-in-law of Virginia historian Robert Beverley, is noted for his efforts with wine grape growing at Westover, his estate in eastern Virginia. In the late 1720s, Byrd planted over twenty European varieties, but in 1736, his crop was destroyed by spring frost, a meteorological recurrence which still plagues southeastern viticultural areas.

In 1759, Virginia planter and statesman, George Mason, proposed a project for growing German vines along the Potomac. Mason found a German vineyardist, Maurice Pound, and acquired funds (George Washington was one of the investors), but the project failed. Three years later, Charles Carter, who had been growing grapes on his estate in King George County on the Rappahannock

River in eastern Virginia, sent a dozen bottles of his wine to London as part of the London Society for the Encouragement of the Arts, which promoted the cultivation of wine grapes in Virginia.

In 1769, the House of Burgesses passed an act "for the Encourageing [*sic*] the Making of Wine", as a result of petitions from Frenchman André Estave. Estave received money and support for his efforts, and he grew both native and European varieties at his vineyard near Williamsburg. The House of Burgesses also funded the vine growing efforts of Colonel Robert Bolling, Jr., a Virginian and Francophile living in Buckingham County. Bolling wrote one of the earliest treatises on American viticulture.

During this same era, General James E. Oglethorpe, the founder of Georgia, ordered the first settlers there to plant grapes to ship back to England.

What was gleaned from all these early experiments was that the European varieties, *Vitis vinifera,* could not easily adapt to the cold winters, spring frosts, and hot, humid summers of the mid-Atlantic region. In addition, drought, black rot, mildews, phylloxera, and pests proved to be problematic. While *Vitis vinifera* efforts continued, the early American settlers had begun making wine from native American grapes and fruits of various sorts.

By the 1800s wine was made from strawberries, gooseberries, dewberries, and blackberries. The latter two in particular were believed to have medicinal value. In the nineteenth-century South, recipes appeared for wines made from elderberries, gooseberries, raspberries, cherries, and currants. In her *Housekeeping in Old Virginia* (1879) the author gives four recipes for blackberry wine and eight recipes for grape wine. Of the grape wine recipes, one specifies Catawba, another, "fox grapes," a third wild black grapes, and another calls simply for "native grapes." The author also gives recipes for wines made with gooseberries, oranges, cherries, strawberries, tomatoes, and for cider wine. Other sources mention wines made with pokeberries, pumpkin, even rice; later, homemade wines were made from plums, rhubarb, as well as corncobs, potatoes, carrots, and parsnips.

Many of the eighteenth- and nineteenth-century homemade "wines" no doubt grew out of similar English homemade concoctions. In *Martha Washington's Booke of Cookery and Booke of Sweetmeats* (written in England but reflective of the eighteenth-century South), there are several recipes for wines made from cherries, lemons, gooseberries, blackberries, elderberries, currants, cowslip, and birch sap, all of which seem to be for medicinal purposes.

Some of the New World wines, like their English predecessors, contained ingredients other than fermented fruit juice. The recipe in *Mrs. Beeton's Book of Household Management* (London, 1859) for cowslip wine calls for sugar, lemon and orange rind and juices, and brandy. Her elderberry wine had spices, raisins, and brandy added. In a like manner, in *The Virginia House-wife,* author Mary Randolph's gingerwine has raisins, lemon sugar, and brandy; her lemon wine, malt wine, and rhubarb wine also had additives. These fortified wines were probably sweeter and higher in alcohol than most of today's table wines.

Jefferson and the Birth of Southeast Viticulture

That as good wines will be made in America as Europe, the scuppernon [*sic*] of North Carolina furnishes sufficient proof. The vine is congenial to every climate in Europe from Hungary to the Mediterranean, and will be found in the same temperatures here wherever tried by intelligent vigerons [*sic*]. The culture, however, is more desirable for domestic use than profitable as an occupation for market.

—Thomas Jefferson in
Jefferson and Wine: Model of Moderation,
edited by R. de Treville Lawrence III

GEORGE WASHINGTON was interested in developing wine in the New World, but it was not until Jefferson's day that fervent efforts were implemented. As minister to Paris (he was appointed in 1784) Jefferson enjoyed the finest European wines and, throughout his life, his letters reveal an ongoing interest in every aspect of wine, from the vine to the table. Jefferson's love for wine determined his travel itinerary. Like a modern-day gourmand, he carefully plotted his European trips so that he would go through the major wine regions. But despite his passionate interest, Jefferson was a moderate drinker. He is said to have never had more than three small (3-ounce) glasses—cut with water—at any one sitting. And following the English custom, he took his wine *after* dinner. (Cider and malt beverages were, however, served sometimes during the meal.) Jefferson also believed that wine had medicinal properties.

Although at Monticello Jefferson had viticultural problems (insects, diseases, and humidity were the primary causes of crop failure) he continued his efforts and encouraged his Tuscan horticulturist, Dr. Filippo Mazzei, to do the same. In 1773, Mazzei planted thousands of *vinifera* cuttings on a 2,000-acre plot near Monticello given to him by Jefferson. Unfortunately, the venture was unsuccessful, due to lack of experienced help in the vineyards and Mazzei's long absences.

For about thirty years Thomas Jefferson continued trying to grow European *vinifera*. He finally admitted defeat when he suggested in a 1809 letter to John Adlum, one of America's earliest wine-grape growers (he is known as the "Father of American Viticulture), that native vines might fare better than *vinifera*. At this point, Jefferson turned his grape-growing enthusiasm toward native American varieties like *Vitis labrusca* and *Vitis aestivalis*. In 1819, when he was seventy-four, Jefferson sipped a native American wine made by Adlum. The wine, which Jefferson compared to a Chambertin, was made with a *vinifera-labrusca* cross, a hybrid that was later called the Alexander grape. Labrusca grapes flourish in northeastern Arkansas, southeastern Missouri, and most states east of the Mississippi. The *Vitis labrusca* and labruscana-like (labrusca hybrids) grapes—such as Concord and Niagara—have a strong flavor that is referred to as "foxy." Adlum championed the Catawba, a native American grape believed to be a natural hybrid of wild, indigenous varieties. Adlum's successes surely sparked an interest in viticulture, for the Catawba was the leading wine grape in America for over fifty years.

By 1859, nine out of ten of the vineyards east of the Rockies were planted with Catawba grapes, except in the South, where Scuppernong—the chief white Muscadine variety—was the favorite. In 1822 Jefferson wrote fondly of the Scuppernong: ". . . her Scuppernon [sic] wine, made on the southside of the Sound [in North Carolina], would be distinguished on the best tables of Europe, for its fine Aroma, and crystalline transparence."

It is believed that the Scuppernong originated in Tyrell County in northeastern North Carolina, at least as early as the mid-eighteenth century. It is said to be a direct offspring of the Muscadine grape *Vitis rotundifolia,* which includes other varieties such as Magnolia and Noble. *Vitis rotundifolia* grows in southeast Missouri, southern Illinois, southwest Kentucky, southeast Virginia, and all the South Atlantic and Gulf states. By 1810, 1,368 gallons of wine from native grapes were said to have been made.

The word "Scuppernong" is a corruption of the Native American word *ascuponung* from *ascupo, ascopo,* or *askopoo,* their word for the Sweet Bay Tree (*Magnolia glauca*), which is abundant along the Scuppernong River in North Carolina. The popularity of Scuppernong wine grew during the 1800s. It was the first native American grape to be cultivated. It fell out of favor in the early 1960s when wines made from new Muscadine varieties were released.

One of the most important stages in the growth of Southeastern viticulture occurred in the 1830s when Dr. D. N. Norton of Richmond, Virginia, domesticated an American hybrid called "Virginia seedling" and later, the Norton grape. Wine made from this grape became known as "Virginia Claret." By 1880, 230,000 gallons of wine made from the Norton grape were made. Virginia Claret won several awards at the Paris Exposition of 1900.

Just before Prohibition, another Southerner made heads turn. North Carolinian Paul Garrett created a wine called Virginia Dare, a blend of Scuppernong, Concord, and, much later, neutral-tasting California *vinifera*. It was the most popular wine in the country from the turn of the twentieth century until Prohibition in 1919. This North Carolina winemaker loved the big, full, fruity flavor of the Scuppernong, and he created his wine so that the unique flavor of this Muscadine grape would predominate. Garrett was probably the first Southern winemaker to make a nationally successful wine.

In the early twentieth century, Prohibition devastated the American wine industry. Most wineries met their demise, but some fermentation continued to be practiced in the home. When Prohibition was repealed in 1933, the wine industry was in great disrepair. Not until the late 1960s and early seventies did new life come to the winegrowing industry in the Northeast, which ultimately inspired winegrowing in the Southeast.

After Jefferson:
Seven Eastern Winemaking Experts

FOUR WINE-GRAPE GROWERS in the North contributed to the evolution and growth of Southeastern winemaking. In the early 1930s, Phillip Wagner of Baltimore, Maryland, began cultivating native Eastern grapes such as Delaware, Norton, and Clinton. Later, dissatisfied with the wines they produced, he experimented with *vinifera* vines from California. He later propagated French-American hybrids. By 1945 he and his wife were producing French-American varietal wines at their Boordy Vineyards, which today remains one of the most successful mid-Atlantic wineries. Wagner's books, *Grapes into Wine* and *A Wine-Grower's Guide,* continue to introduce many hobbyists and would-be winemakers to the art. One Canadian winemaker was particularly inspired. Adhemar De Chaunac of Brights Winery in Ontario began growing French-American and *vinifera* grapes. In 1959 Brights released the first Canadian sparkling wines made from their vineyards' own *vinifera* grapes.

In New York state, Konstantin Frank and Charles Fournier also advanced winemaking in the East. Fournier, a French winemaker, left the noted Champagne house Veuve Clicquot-Ponsardin in Reims to make wine in Hammondsport, New York. Fournier hired viticulturist and Russian emigré Konstantin Frank, who was to successfully grow *vinifera* grapes in New York. With them, Fournier made the first wines from *vinifera* grapes sold commercially in the eastern United States.

Three writers have also nurtured the growth of the Eastern wine industry. Leon Adams, a wine historian and journalist, and the author of *The Wines of America,* founded the California Grape Growers League in 1931 and the Wine Advisory Board in 1938. His endeavors educated Americans about wine, encouraged research in California universities, helped set standards for quality in wine—in the East as well as the West—and saw to it that political issues concerning wine were handled in a fair and just manner.

More recently, Lucie T. Morton, a Virginia-based viticultural consultant, educator, and writer, has translated and adapted Pierre Galet's *A Practical Ampelography—Grapevine Identification* and later wrote her own book, *Winegrowing in Eastern America: An Illustrated Guide to Viniculture East of the Rockies.* Morton's scholarly endeavors helped to clarify the history and classification of wine-grape growing in the East. Her books are useful guides for the winemaker, enologists, students of viticulture and wine enthusiasts in general. Morton's scientific approach lifts Southeast winemaking out of a mere hobbyist activity into another realm: that of a bonafide viticultural region worthy of serious study and commitment to winemaking.

Thomas Pinney, author of *A History of Wine in America: From the Beginnings to Prohibition,* has thoroughly researched the topic and in his book has explained in great detail the evolution of our country's winemaking.

Basic Southern Viticulture

ALL GRAPES belong to the genus called *Vitis*. This genus is made up of many species. *Vitis vinifera* is the species of grapevines native to Europe and includes, among others, Cabernet Sauvignon, Chardonnay, Merlot, and Sauvignon Blanc.

When *vinifera* at first failed to survive in the New World, attention turned toward the hardier native American *Vitis* species. These include *labrusca, riparia, aestivalis,* and *rotundifolia.* Both deliberate and incidental hybrids between native species and *Vitis vinifera* became the stock and trade of eastern grape growing.

Over time, some *vinifera* were successfully crossed with native species to create hybrids. Some of these hybrids are Concord, Catawba, Delaware, Dutchess, and Niagara.

The most important native American species in today's Southern vineyards worth noting in terms of winemaking is *Vitis rotundifolia* whose grapes are highly disease-resistant and are generically referred to as the Muscadines. Rotundifolia includes Carlos, Magnolia, Scuppernong and Noble. States in the deep South—Florida, Georgia, North Carolina, and South Carolina—grow mostly Muscadines, some of which are used for winemaking and also for jams, jellies, pie fillings, and juice.

The University of Florida at Gainesville experts have developed non-Muscadine varieties that are resistant to Pierce's disease—such as Stover, Blanc du Bois, and Lake Emerald—all of which may replace Scuppernong.

In general Southeastern winter weather can be erratic. Some areas have such mild temperatures that the vines never go completely dormant, so they are vulnerable to sudden winter freezes and spring frosts. Summer hail is also a problem in Southern vineyards. High humidity in summer makes the grapes subject to bunch rot and Pierce's disease. But with increased knowledge and experimentation, grape growing and winemaking in the Southeast is becoming more stable and successful.

Grape Terms, and the Primary Grapes Cultivated in the Southeast for Winemaking

Aestivalis (Vitis aestivalis) A small, dark grape family that grows wild throughout most of the Eastern United States. Norton and Cynthiana are varieties of the *aestivalis*. It is the best adapted native grape for winemaking since it has sufficient sugar but lacks labrusca's foxy aroma.

Baco Noir A French hybrid of *Vitis riparia* and *Vitis vinifera* that grows well in the eastern United States. It was created in 1902 by François Baco and was the first French-American variety to be planted extensively in the United States. This grape yields dry, "unfoxy," full-bodied, high-acid, French-style wines and triggered a new generation of Eastern wine-grape growing. Baco Noir grows from Mississippi to as far north as Wisconsin.

Blanc du Bois A white grape developed by the University of Florida at Gainesville. Blanc du Bois is resistant to Pierce's disease.

Cabernet Sauvignon The principal grape from which red Bordeaux wines are made. Cabernet Sauvignon grapes are grown extensively in France and California. Because it is not terribly subject to fungus or fruit rot, and since it buds late in spring and usually escapes frost damage, this grape is grown with some success in the Southeast, particularly in Virginia and North Carolina.

Carlos A white muscadine grape.

Catawba America's most popular wine grape of the nineteenth century. Catawba originated on the Catawba River of North Carolina and was the first native American grape used to make still and sparkling wine on a commercial scale. This red grape produces pale rosé or white wines with a *labrusca*-like aroma and flavor with spicy overtones. Catawba wines should be drunk young.

Chambourcin A French-American cross that ripens late and is well suited to areas with a long growing season. It is cultivated in Pennsylvania, Virginia, Tennessee, and South Carolina and produces a light-bodied red wine similar to Cabernet Franc.

Chancellor A French-American hybrid that produces a dry, medium- to full-bodied clean, fruity red wine. The Chancellor is relatively easy to grow and is cultivated throughout eastern America.

Chardonnay A white *vinifera* grape from which the famous white wines of Burgundy are made. Chardonnay is quite winter-hardy, but warm winter weather can cause early bud break, so it is threatened by spring frost damage. Chardonnay grapes are being grown and vinified in parts of the Southeast.

Chelois A Seibel variety, this red wine grape is used in making varietals as well as in blending.

Conquistador A purple grape that was released in 1983 by the University of Florida and which produces a fruity red table wine.

Cynthiana This grape—a sister variety of the Norton, to which it is almost identical in the vineyard—is thought to be an American hybrid of *labrusca* and *aestivalis*. Cynthiana was first discovered in Arkansas in the 1800s. It produces a dry, delicate, often spicy red wine. Wine made from it won the top award at the 1873 Vienna World Exposition. It is currently grown for commercial purposes in Missouri and Arkansas.

Gewürztraminer Used to make famous white wines of Alsace, this pinkish *vinifera* makes a crisp, spicy white wine.

James A variety of *Vitis rotundifolia* discovered in North Carolina in 1866. It is one of the most widely planted and most popular black grapes in this species.

Lake Emerald A *vinifera* hybrid developed by the University of Florida at Gainesville. Lake Emerald is resistant to Pierce's disease.

Magnolia This light bronze (or "white") Muscadine grape used to make a sweet white wine was introduced in 1961 by the North Carolina Agricultural Experiment Station and the USDA. The Magnolia, along with Carlos and Dixie, is replacing Scuppernong in most Southeastern vineyards.

Maréchal Foch A French-American hybrid that produces red wines said to be similar in style to French Burgundies. Often simply called Foch, this grape variety is the most widely grown French-American hybrid in the Southeast. It is grown from New England to New Mexico and Virginia to Minnesota. It is vigorous, moderately disease resistant, and ripens early, so it can be grown where growing seasons are short. Foch makes a light- to medium-bodied red or rosé wine that has a fresh, berry-like aroma and flavor.

Merlot This vinifera from Bordeaux is used in making varietal wines as well as in blending. It is not winter hardy and therefore is cultivated successfully only in relatively temperate climes.

Muscadine This family of grapes peak in late summer or fall along the Gulf and the lower Piedmont areas of the Southeast. It is native to the Southeastern states and is classified as *Vitis rotundifolia,* so named for its large, round berries. (Another Muscadine species, *Vitis munsoniana,* grows only in Florida, eastern Georgia, and the Gulf states.) Muscadine grapes, like *labrusca,* have a pronounced fruit flavor and unique aroma. Muscadines are known as the Southern "fox" grape (the Northern "fox" grape is the Concord). Southerners have been making homemade wine with Muscadines for years. The making of drier, nonsweet wines on a large scale in the Southeast is a relatively new phenomenon. Muscadines are thick skinned (literally) and resistant to most indigenous diseases, including Pierce's disease. Until recently the entire *rotundifolia* family went colloquially by the name Scuppernong, which, along with Carlos, Noble, and Magnolia, actually are varieties within the family *muscadina*. The term

Muscadine is sometimes used to label wine from any of those grapes. The Muscadines have intense fruity aroma and flavor. Muscadines are purplish-black, reddish-black, or bronze (also called "white").

Niagara A white hybrid that yields a wine with an assertive, sweet, fresh grape taste. Niagara is grown in Arkansas as well as Ohio, Michigan, Pennsylvania, and Missouri.

Noble This black Muscadine was crossed in 1946 at the North Carolina Agricultural Experiment Station and was introduced in 1971. It grows in Florida and other parts of the Southeast and produces light, fruity red or rosé wines. Noble is the most popular black-berried Muscadine in the Southeast for winemaking.

Norton Also called Cynthiana or Virginia Seedling. Dr. D. N. Norton of Richmond, Virginia, is credited with introducing this grape in the 1830s. This pre-Prohibition variety was enthusiastically planted in Virginia where it was the base for so-called Virginia "clarets." Norton is one of the few American varieties that has no "foxy" flavor. It is grown commercially in Arkansas.

Pinot Noir A red *vinifera* grape from which many Champagnes as well as the famous reds of Burgundy are made. A small amount of Pinot Noir is grown in the Southeast.

Riesling This *vinifera* grape is used in producing the great white wines of Germany and is also known as White Riesling or Johannisberg Riesling. It is grown in nearly every wine-growing state in the United States. It grows well in cooler climates, is winter hardy, and has a late bud-break; thus it is at reduced risk for spring frost damage. Rieslings are made in a varying range of sweetness from bone-dry to honey-sweet.

Sauvignon Blanc A white *vinifera* used in making the famous wines of the Loire, such as Pouilly-Fumé and Sancerre.

Scuppernong Best known of the Muscadines, the Scuppernong is widely planted throughout the Southeast. This North Carolina native has been important to Southern winemaking since the early nineteenth century. In recent years, it has begun to be replaced by other Muscadines, such as Carlos, Dixie, and Magnolia. Scuppernong wine is usually semisweet. "Scuppernong" has become synonymous with the white Muscadine grape.

Seyval Blanc A white French-American hybrid developed in the 1920s, grown east of the Rockies. It produces wines dry to medium-dry as well as sweeter, late-harvest styles. Seyval Blanc is partially responsible for defining a new Eastern American wine style. Seyval Blanc adapts well to many different climates and regions. It has two distinct types. The Seyval that grows in the Northeast and Michigan has high acidity and is light, with apple and citrus tones. Seyval Blanc grown in the Southeast generally produces a wine that has lower acidity, but is still rather dry and crisp.

Stover A white hybrid wine grape released in 1968 by the Florida Agricultural Experiment Station. The Stover grape produces a lightly fruity white wine, sometimes blended with the more assertively flavored Muscadines.

Suwannee In 1983, the University of Florida released this grape for commercial production. This white grape has a flavor similar to Stover with a slight muscat taste.

Vidal Blanc A French hybrid that is fairly sturdy and disease resistant. It is cultivated in almost all of the Eastern wine-growing states and produces dry to medium-dry fresh, fruity white wines.

Villard Blanc A hybrid that grows well in warm climates and produces a fruity white table wine.

Villard Noir A French-American hybrid grown in relatively warm parts of the East.

Welder A bronze Muscadine grape developed by a grape grower of the same name in Lake County, Florida. It is vigorous and high yielding.

Selected Wineries
of the Southeast
and Their Wines

Most of the wines produced by the following wineries are made from grapes grown by the wineries themselves. Some wineries also buy grapes from nearby vineyards, and occasionally a winery will create a blend that combines their own wine with those from another state such as California or Texas.

Alabama

Braswell's Winery
7556 Bankhead Highway
Dora, Alabama 35062
205-648-8335
The Braswell Family

Wines produced
Scuppernong, Muscadine, Concord, Niagara, Wild Grape (also called Opossum Grape), Red Grape (a blend of Catawba and other native American red grapes), White Niagara (a blend of Niagara and Lake Emerald), Fredonia, and fruit wines (apple, blackberry, blueberry, cherry, elderberry, peach, pear, persimmon, plum, and strawberry)

Bryant Vineyard
1454 Griffitt Bend Road
Talladega, Alabama 35160
205-268-2638
The Bryant Family

Wines produced
Villard Blanc, Seyval Blanc, Dixie Gold (a blend of white Muscadines), Dixie Blush (a blend of red Muscadines), Red Muscadine, and blueberry wine

Arkansas

Cowie Wine Cellars, Inc.
Route 2, Box 799
Paris, Arkansas 72855
501-963-3990
The Cowie Family

Wines produced
Cynthiana, Burgundy, Extra Dry Niagara, Dry Muscadine, Semi-Dry Niagara, Chablis (a secret blend), Blush (a blend of Vidal and various hybrids), Catawba, Niagara, Golden Muscadine Sipping Wine (a dessert wine), fruit wines

(blackberry and strawberry), and Meade (a honey wine blended with citric acid and water)

The Eureka Springs Winery
The Eureka Street House Restaurant
124 Spring Street
Eureka Springs, Arkansas 72632
501-253-8558
The Cowie Family

Wines produced
Bachman Port (a blend of Stark Star and Cynthiana), Burgundy, Chablis (both are blends), and Spring Blush (made from French Hybrids)

Mount Bethel Winery
U.S. Highway 64
P.O. Box 137
Altus, Arkansas 72821
501-468-2444
The Eugene Post Family

Wines produced
Niagara, Concord,
Delaware, Dry Red (made
from Cynthiana), Red Port
(made from Concord),
White Port (made from
Golden Muscat), Rosé
(made from Concord),
Red Muscadine, White
Muscadine, and fruit wines
(wild plum, blackberry,
strawberry, peach)

Post Familie Vineyard
and Winery
Route 1, Box 1
Highway 186
Altus, Arkansas 72821
501-468-2741
The Post Familie

Wines produced
Chardonnay, Vignoles,
Seyval Blanc, Cynthiana,
Champagne (made from
100 percent Chardonnay),
White Table Wine (a secret
blend), Vin Rosé Sec
(a secret blend), Ozark
Mountain Blush (a secret
blend), Vidal Blanc, Ives
Noir, Champagne Brüt
(a Seyval blend), Musca-
dine White, Muscadine
Red, Muscadine Blush,
Delaware White, Seyval
Blanc, Aurora Blanc,
Maiden's Blush (an Ives

grape blend), Red Table
Wine, Concord, Catawba
Pink, Niagara, Sherry,
Delawine, Golden Rod,
White Port (the last four
are secret blends), plus
strawberry wine

Wiederkehr Wine Cellars
St. Mary's Mountain Road
Route 1, Box 14
Altus, Arkansas 72821
501-468-2611
The Wiederkehr Family

Wines produced
Johannisberg Riesling,
Gewürztraminer, Muscato
di Tanta Maria (a secret
blend), Wiederkehr Extra
Dry Champagne (a secret
blend), Cabernet Sauvi-
gnon, French Colombard,
Vidal Blanc, Verdelet
Blanc, Pinot Noir,
Niagara, Cynthiana, Pink
Catawba, Chardonnay,
Rosé de Cabernet

Florida

Chautauqua Vineyards
and Winery, Inc.
Interstate I-10 and
U.S. 331
P.O. Box 1308
DeFuniak Springs, Florida
32433

904-892-5887
Paul D. Owens, Jr.,
owner

Wines produced
Carlos, Welder, Noble,
and a blush (made from
Carlos and Noble)

Eden Vineyards
Winery
19709 Little Lane
Alva, Florida 33920
941-728-9463
The Kiser Family

Wines produced
Lake Emerald, Edelweiss
(a Semi-Dry white wine
similar in style to Alsatian
Gewürztraminer), the
Cypress Series: Alva
White (a blend of
California Chenin Blanc
and French Colombard
plus Lake Emerald and
Suwannee), Alva Rouge
(a blend of California
Barbera and Chenin
Blanc plus Lake Emerald),
Coral Bell (a blend
of California Zinfandel
plus Suwannee and
Lake Emerald), Eden
Spice (a dessert wine of
California Barbera plus
Suwannee and other
natural fruit flavors)

Lakeridge Winery and
Vineyards
19239 U.S. 27 North
Clermont, Florida 34711
1-800-768-WINE
The Cox Family

Wines produced
Stover, Suwannee, Blanc
du Bois, White Musca-
dine, Red Muscadine,
Nouveau (made from the
Noble grape), Plantation
White (made from Welder,
Carlos, and Suwannee),
Blanc de Fleur (a nonvin-
tage sparkling wine made
from Magnolia and
Stover), Sunblush
(a blend of Muscadine,
Carlos, Welder, Noble,
and Magnolia)

Georgia

Château Elan
7000 Old Winder
Highway
Braselton, Georgia 30517
1-800-233-WINE

Wines produced
Sauvignon Blanc,
Chardonnay, Johannisberg
Riesling, White Cabernet,
Vin Rouge (made from
Chambourcin), Cabernet

Sauvignon, Muscadine
Wines: Duncan Creek,
Summer Wine (a blend
of Muscadine and peach
extract), Autumn Blush
(a blend of Muscadine
and raspberry extract)

Fox Vineyards
(location)
Highway 11
Newton County, Georgia
30209
404-787-5402
(mailing address)
225 Highway 11 South
Social Circle, Georgia
30279
The Fuchs Family

Wines produced
Seyval Blanc, Vidal Blanc,
Chardonnay, Chenin
Blanc, De Chaunac,
Cabernet Sauvignon,
Sauvignon Blanc, Antebel-
lum Rosé (made from 100
percent De Chaunac),
Ambrosia (a blend of
Muscat, orange extract,
and Seyval)

Habersham Vineyards
and Winery
3973 State Highway 365
Alto, Georgia 30510
770-641-0160
Tom and Charles Slick

Wines produced
Chardonnay, Riesling,
Sauvignon Blanc, Seyval
Blanc, Vidal Blanc, White
Muscadine, Cabernet
Sauvignon, Scarlett (a
blend of Cabernet Sauvi-
gnon and Chambourcin),
Granny's Sweet Red (a
Concord wine), Granny's
Blush (made from Musca-
dine and Niagara),
Granny's Arbor (a blend of
Muscadine and Niagara),
Granny's Peach Treat (a
blend of Muscadine and
peach extract), Cherokee
Rosé (a blend of Chardon-
nay and Cabernet)

Maryland

Basignani Winery
15722 Falls Road
Sparks, Maryland 21152
301-472-4718
The Basignani Family

Wines produced
Seyval Blanc, Chardonnay,
Cabernet Sauvignon,
Vidal, Merlot, Riesling,
Marisa (a red wine made
from Maréchal Foch and
Chancellor and Cham-
bourcin), Elena (a white
wine made from Villard
Blanc, Seyval, and Burdin)

Berrywine Plantations
Linganore Wine Cellars
13601 Glissans Mill Road
Mount Airy, Maryland
21771-8599
410-795-6432
The Aellen Family

Wines produced
Vidal, Cayuga, Meade
(an English-style pure
honey wine), Colonial
Meade (a honey wine
blended with ginger and
lemon), Seyval Blanc,
Maréchal Foch, Melody
(a New York State variety
of grape), Mountain
White (made with
Niagara), Mountain Pink
(made with Fredonia)

Boordy Vineyards
12820 Long Green Pike
Hydes, Maryland 21082
410-592-5015
The Deford Family

Wines produced
Wassail (a hearty red
wine blend with imported
and domestic spices),
Chardonnay, Seyval Blanc,
Maryland White
(made from Seyval Blanc),
Vidal Blanc, Chardonnay,
Nouvelle (a blend of
Vidal and Riesling),

Sparkling Wine (made
from Chardonnay),
Maryland Red (a blend
of Foch, Chambourcin,
and Chancellor), Maryland
Blush (a blend of Chelois
and Villard Noir),
Nouveau Cabernet
Sauvignon (a blend of
Cabernet Sauvignon,
Merlot, and Cabernet
Franc), Sur Lie Reserve
(made from Seyval Blanc)

Catoctin Vineyards
805 Greenbridge Road
Brookeville, Maryland
20833
301-774-2310
Robert Llyon, Shahin
Bagheri, Ann and Jerry
Milne

Wines produced
Cabernet Sauvignon,
Chardonnay, Johannisberg
Riesling, Eye of the Oriole
(a blend of Seyval, Caber-
net, and Zinfandel), Eye of
the Beholder (a blend of
Seyval and Vidal), Mariage
(a blend of Johannisberg
Riesling and Vidal)

Elk Run Vineyards
15113 Liberty Road
Mount Airy, Maryland
21771

410-775-2513
The Wilson Family

Wines produced
Annapolis Sunset
(a blend of Seyval Blanc
and Cabernet Sauvignon),
Maryland Chardonnay,
American Riesling, and
Maryland Cabernet
Sauvignon

Fiore Winery
La Felicetta Vineyard
3026 Whiteford Road
Pylesville, Maryland
21132
410-836-7605/879-4007

Wines produced
Vidal Blanc, Seyval Blanc,
L'ombra (a blend of Vidal
and Seyval), Rosato (a
Chianti-style wine made
from the Chancellor),
Chambourcin, Cabernet
Sauvignon, Merlot, Ries-
ling, and Chardonnay

Loew Vineyards
14001 Liberty Road
Mount Airy, Maryland
21772
301-831-5464

Wines produced
Cabernet Sauvignon,
Chardonnay, Classic Red

(made from Foch Millot), Harvest Gold (a blend of Seyval and Chardonnay), Harvest Red (a blend of Chancellor and Cabernet Sauvignon), Johannisberg Riesling, Serendipity (a table grape), Seyval Blanc, Seyval Celebration (a blend of Seyval Blanc and Cabernet Sauvignon), Twilight (a blend of Johannisberg Riesling and Seyval)

Mississippi

Old South Winery
65 South Concord Avenue
Natchez, Mississippi
39120
601-445-9924
The Galbreath Family

Wines produced
Miss Carlos, Carlos, Miss Carlos Dry, Carlos Dry, Sweet Magnolia, Southern Belle, Miss Scarlett, Noble, Noble Sweet, Noble Dry, Red Muscadine, Back to America Blush (a blend of red and white Muscadine)

North Carolina

The Biltmore Estate
Wine Company

1 North Pack Square
Asheville, North Carolina
28801
704-274-6333

Wines produced
Cabernet Franc, Chardonnay, Johannisberg Riesling, Merlot, Pinot Noir, Riesling, Sauvignon Blanc, Zinfandel Blanc de Noir, and two sparkling wines: Brüt (made from Chardonnay), and Sec (made from Pinot Noir)

Duplin Wine Cellars
Highway 117
Rosé Hill, North Carolina
28458
910-289-3888

Wines produced
Burgundy, Carolina Red, and Port (all three are blends of Noble and Old James), Scuppernong, Carlos, Magnolia, Sherry (made from Scuppernong), Sparkling Wines: Sparkling Scuppernong Sweet Champagne (made from Scuppernong), Champagne (a blend of Carlos and Scuppernong)

South Carolina

Cruse Vineyards and Winery
1683 Woods Road
Chester, South Carolina
29706
803-377-3944
Ken and Susan Cruse

Wines produced
Chardonnay, Pinot Blanc, Vidal Blanc, Seyval Blanc, Proprietor's White (a blend of Chardonnay and Seyval), Chambourcin, Pinot Noir, Nouveau Rouge, Proprietor's Red (a blend of Pinot Noir and Chancellor), White Pinot Noir

Montmorenci Vineyards
2989 Charleston Highway (Highway 78)
Aiken, South Carolina
29803
803-649-4870
Robert E. Scott and Robert E. Scott, Jr. (owners)

Wines produced
Chardonnay, Seyval Blanc, Chambourcin, Blanc du Bois, Melody, Cayuga, Vidal Blanc, Suwannee, Vin Eclipser (a dessert wine made from Ravat),

Rosé (made from Chambourcin), Triple Crown Blush (a blend of Chambourcin, Cayuga, and Seyval)

Tennessee

Beachaven Vineyards and Winery
1100 Dunlop Lane
Clarksville, Tennessee 37040
615-645-8867
The Beach Family

Wines produced
Chardonnay, Riesling, Cabernet Sauvignon, Gewürztraminer, Muscadine, Beachaven Red (a blend of Foch, Chancellor, and Chambourcin), Beachaven White (a blend of Seyval Blanc and Vidal Blanc), Beachaven Blush (a red and white wine blend), Beachaven Moselle (made from Johannisberg Riesling), Golden Rosé (made from Concord), Strawberry Fête (a blend of red and white wine with strawberry extract), Sparkling Burgundy (a blend of Concord and Fredonia), Champagne (a sparkling wine made from Seyval Blanc),

Cumberland (made from Niagara), Premiere Blanc (made from 100 percent Vidal Blanc), blackberry wine

Highland Manor Winery
Highway 127 South
P.O. Box 213
Jamestown, Tennessee 38556
615-879-9519
Irving Martin (owner)

Wines produced
Alwood (an American variety), Catawba, Concord, Cayuga, Cabernet Sauvignon, White Riesling, Highland White (made from Chardonnay), Royal Rosé (a blend of Catawba, Concord, and Alwood), Muscadine, Southern Blush (a blend of Muscadine and peach extract)

Loudon Valley Vineyards on the River
555 Huff Ferry Road North
Loudon, Tennessee 37774
423-986-8736
Stan and Lucie Dylewski

Wines produced
Zin-Dal Blush (a blend of Zinfandel and Vidal),

Catawba, Tennes-Sippin' (a blend of Seyval Blanc, Vignole, and Muscadine), Vidal Blanc, Red Nouveau (made from De Chaunac), Seyval Blanc, Claret (a blend of Chambourcin, Chancellor, and De Chaunac), Loudon White (a blend of Zinfandel and Vidal), Muscadine, Loudon Red (a blend of De Chaunac, Seyval Blanc, and Riesling)

Mont Eagle Wine Cellars
Highway 64/41
A.P.O. 638
Mont Eagle, Tennessee 37356
615-924-2120
The Marlow Family

Wines produced
Cabernet Sauvignon, Gewürztraminer, Riesling, Maréchal Foch, Niagara, Seyval Blanc, Chancellor, Sweet Muscadine, Niagara, Suwannee White (a blend of Riesling and Gewürztraminer), Assembly Blush (a blend of Concord and Niagara), Cumberland Red (a blend of Concord, Muscadine, and Maréchal Foch)

Orr Mountain Winery
355 Pumpkin Hollow Road
Madisonville, Tennessee 37354
423-442-5340
Sue and Harry Orr (owners)

Wines produced
Hiwassee White (a blend of Rayon d'Or and Villard Noir), Candle Glow (a blush blend of Seyval Blanc and Chambourcin), Bald River Red (a semi-sweet blend of Chancellor and Chambourcin), Villard Blanc, Tellico Rosé (a blend of Dutchess, Chambourcin, and Rayon d'Or), Chambourcin (a blend of Chambourcin and Chancellor)

Smoky Mountain Winery
Winery Square
Suite #2
450 Cherry Street
Gatlinberg, Tennessee 37738
423-436-7551
Everett Brock

Wines produced
Mountain Mist (an asti spumonti–style wine blended with Riesling and

Muscat), Le Conte White (made from Vidal Blanc), Le Conte Red (a blend of Chancellor and Foch), Brookside White (made from Vidal Blanc), Brookside Rosé (a blend of Cayuga and Chancellor), Brookside Red (made from Cabernet Sauvignon), Mountain White (made from Niagara), Mountain Rosé (made from Pink Catawba), Mountain Red (made from Concord), Scuppernong, Muscadine, Peach Blush (a blend of Muscadine and peach extract), Sangria (a blend of red wine and orange, lemon, lime extracts), May Wine (a blend of white wine and Woodruff herb), and fruit wines (blackberry, raspberry and Blueberry Bliss—a sparkling wine made with blueberries)

Tennessee Valley Winery
Hotchkiss Valley Road
Route 3, Box 1595
Loudon, Tennessee 37774
423-986-5147
The Reed Family

Wines produced
Chardonnay, Cabernet Sauvignon, Riesling, Cellar Master Seyval (an oak-aged Seyval), Seyval, Tennessee White (a blend of Seyval and Vidal Blanc), Vidal Blanc, Country White (a sweet blend of Cayuga and Vidal), White Muscadine, Classic Red Private Reserve (a blend of Chambourcin and Ruby Cabernet), De Chaunac, Chancellor, Maréchal Foch, Millot, Mountain Blush (a blend of Vidal, Seyval Blanc, and Chambourcin), Country Red (a sweet blend of Muscadine and Concord)

Virginia

Barboursville Vineyards and Winery
P.O. Box 136
Barboursville, Virginia 22923
703-832-3824
The Zonin family

Wines produced
Chardonnay, Riesling, Gewürztraminer, Merlot, Cabernet Sauvignon, Pinot Noir Blanc (a blend of Barbera, Pinot Noir, and Chardonnay), Cabernet

Sauvignon Blanc (a blush-style wine made from Cabernet Sauvignon), Vin Rosé (a blend of Malvasia, Barbera, Gamay, Alicante, and Chardonnay), Sauvignon Blanc (a blend of Sauvignon Blanc and Semillon), Pinot Noir Red (a blend of Pinot Noir and Cabernet Franc)

Burnley Vineyards
4500 Winery Lane
Barboursville, Virginia
22923
540-832-2828
The Reeder Family

Wines produced
Riesling, Chardonnay, Cabernet Sauvignon, Rivanna Red (a blend of Chambourcin, Foch, De Chaunac, and Baco Noir), Somerset (a blend of Riesling, Vidal, and Seyval Blanc), Rivanna White (a blend of Vidal Blanc and Riesling), Rivanna Sunset (a blush wine made from 100 percent Chambourcin)

Chermont Vineyard
and Winery
Route 1, Box 59
Esmont, Virginia 22937
804-286-2211

Wines produced
Chardonnay, Riesling, and Cabernet Sauvignon

Farfelu Vineyards
Route 1, Box 23
Flint Hill, Virginia
22627
540-364-2930
The C.J. Raney family

Wines produced
Cabernet Sauvignon, Chardonnay, Dry Picnic White (a blend of Cayuga and Chardonnay), Dry Picnic Red (a blend of Chancellor and De Chaunac)

Guilford Ridge
Vineyard
326 Running Pine Road
Luray, Virginia 22835
703-778-3853
John Gerba and
Harland Baker

Wines produced
Red Page Valley (a blend of Chambourcin, Chelois, Baco Noir and Vinifera), et Delilah (a blend of Chambourcin, Chelois, Seyval Blanc, and Rayon d'Or), Pinnacles (a blend of Seyval Blanc and Rayon d'Or)

Ingleside Plantation
Winery
P.O. Box 1038
Oak Grove, Virginia
22443
804-224-8687
Douglas E. Flemer

Wines produced
Chesapeake Blanc (a blend of Seyval Blanc and Chardonnay), Chesapeake Claret (a blend of Chancellor and Cabernet Sauvignon), Riesling, Chardonnay, Cabernet Sauvignon, Williamsburg Red, Virginia Blush, and two sparkling wines: a Brüt (made from Chardonnay) and a Rosé (a blend of Chardonnay, Chenin Blanc, and Cabernet Sauvignon)

Meredyth Vineyards
P.O. Box 347
Middleburg, Virginia
20118
540-687-6277
The Archie Smith Family

Wines produced
Chardonnay, Sauvignon Blanc, Cabernet Sauvignon, Riesling, Merlot, Seyval Blanc, Maréchal Foch, Harvest Red

(a blend of Foch, De Chaunac, and Léon Millot), Blush (a blend of Villard Noir, Rougeon, and Riesling), De Chaunac, Villard Noir, Delaware (a dessert wine blend of Riesling and Delaware)

Misty Mountain
Vineyards
HCR 02 Box 459
Madison County, Virginia
22727
703-923-4738
Dr. Michael Cerceo

Wines produced
Chardonnay, Riesling, Seyval Blanc, Merlot, and Cabernet Sauvignon, Gewürztraminer, Blush (a blend of Zinfandel and Seyval), and Chablis (a blend of Riesling, Seyval, and Vidal)

Montdomaine/Horton
Cellars
6399 Spotswood Trail
Gordonsville, Virginia
22942
540-832-7440
The Horton Family

Wines produced
Barrel Select Chardonnay

(aged in oak barrels), Chardonnay, Cabernet Sauvignon, Merlot, White Riesling, Blush Wine (a blend of Riesling, Chardonnay, and Merlot)

Morrisette Winery
P.O. Box 766
Meadows of Dan, Virginia
24120
540-593-2866
The Morrisette Family

Wines produced
Merlot, Cabernet Sauvignon, White Riesling, White Burgundy (made from 100 percent Chardonnay), Sauvignon Blanc, Sweet Mountain Laurel (made from 100 percent Niagara), Blush de Virgine (a proprietary blend of Chambourcin), Seyval Blanc, Vidal Blanc

Mountain Cove Vineyards
Route 1, Box 139
Lovingston, Virginia
22949
804-263-5392
The Weed Family

Wines produced
Dry White Monticello (a blend of Villard Blanc and Riesling), Skyline Red (a

blend of Chambourcin, Chancellor, and Baco Noir), Skyline White (a blend of Muscat, Villard Blanc, Riesling, and Cayuga), Skyline Rosé (a blend of Villard Blanc and Chancellor), Harvest Red (a blend of Chambourcin, Chancellor, and Baco Noir), fruit wines (La Abra Peach and La Abra Apple, both made from 100 percent fruit)

Naked Mountain
Vineyard
P.O. Box 131
Markham, Virginia 22643
540-364-1609
The Harper Family

Wines produced
Chardonnay, Sauvignon Blanc, Riesling, Claret (a blend of Cabernet Sauvignon, Cabernet Franc, and Merlot), and Catamount Hollow (a white *vinifera* blend)

Oakencroft Vineyard
and Winery
Route 5
Charlottesville, Virginia
22901
804-296-4188 (weekdays)
804-295-8175 (weekends)

Mrs. John B. Rogan, owner

Wines produced
Chardonnay, Cabernet Sauvignon, and Country-side White (a blend of Seyval Blanc and Vidal Blanc)

Piedmont Vineyards and Winery
P.O. Box 286
Middleburg, Virginia 20118
540-687-5528
The Worrall Family

Wines produced
Chardonnay, Semillon, Seyval Blanc, Hunt Country Wine (Seyval and Chardonnay), Little River White (Seyval and Vidal)

Prince Michel Vineyards
HCR4 Box 77
Leon, Virginia 22725
540-547-3707
Jean Le Ducq, owner

Wines produced
Chardonnay, Chardonnay Barrell Select (aged in French Oak barrels), Blush de Michel (a blend of White Riesling and Cabernet Sauvignon), VaVin

Nouveau (a blend of Cabernet Sauvignon, Merlot, and Cabernet Franc), White Burgundy (a blend of Chardonnay and Pinot Noir), and Le Ducq, Lot 87 (a Bordeaux-style red table wine blend)

Rapidan River Vineyard
Route 4, Box 199
Culpeper, Virginia 22725
540-423-1866
Jean Le Ducq, owner

Wines produced
Dry White Riesling, Semi-Dry White Riesling, Gewürztraminer

Shenandoah Vineyards
3659 South Ox Road
Edinburg, Virginia 22824
540-984-8699
Emma Randle, owner

Wines produced
Cabernet Sauvignon, Chardonnay, Pinot Noir, Johannisberg Riesling, Vignoles, Sweet Serenade (a blend of Riesling and Vidal), Fiesta (a rosé blend of red and white grapes under the Stoney Creek label), Seyval Blanc, Vidal Blanc, Chambourcin, Shenandoah Blanc (a

blend of Riesling, Vidal, Seyval and Cayuga), Shenandoah Rosé (made from De Chaunac), Shenandoah Ruby (a blend of Cabernet, Seyval, Chambourcin, and Chancellor Noir), Blushing Belle (a blend of Vidal, Chambourcin, and Cabernet)

Stonewall Vineyards
Route 2, Box 107A
Concord, Virginia 24538
804-993-2185
Larry and Sperry Davis (owners)

Wines produced
Chardonnay, Dry Vidal Blanc, Semi-Dry Vidal Blanc, Cayuga White, Rosé Chambourcin (made from 100 percent Chambourcin), Claret (a blend of Cabernet Sauvignon and Chambourcin), Vin Clochard (a blush wine blend of Seyval, Rayon d'Or, Vidal Blanc, Cabernet Sauvignon, and Chambourcin), Pyment (a meade-style wine made from honey, white grape juice, cloves, peppercorns, and oil of bergamont)

Beverages

The Williamsburg
Winery, Ltd.
5800 Wessex Hundred
Williamsburg, Virginia
23185
757-229-0999

Wines produced
Chardonnay, Governor's
White (a blend of Riesling
and Vidal), Plantation
Blush (a semi-dry blend of
Riesling and Foch), James
River White (a blend of
Chardonnay and Seyval),
Sir Christopher Wren
White (a blend of
Chardonnay, Riesling, and
Seyval)

West Virginia

Fisher Ridge Wine
Company
Fisher Ridge Road
Box 108A
Liberty, West Virginia
25124

304-342-8702
Wilson E. Ward
(owner)

Wines produced
Chardonnay, Cabernet
Sauvignon, Riesling,
Zinfandel, Seyval Blanc,
Vidal Blanc, Blush Wine
(a blend of Cabernet
Sauvignon and Seyval
Blanc), Maiden's Kiss
(a blend of Seyval Blanc
and Vidal Blanc)

Southern-Grown Tea

ALTHOUGH WE OFTEN THINK of iced tea as something drunk in the South, most tea lovers assume that the leaves themselves are from India. However, tea is also being grown just outside of Charleston, South Carolina on Wadmalaw Island. Since the mid-nineteenth century, agricultural scientists have been interested in growing tea in North America. But it did not develop into a successful domestic industry until recently. In 1795, a French botanist, André Michaux, planted tea near Charleston. Although his plants survive to this day, at that time, no one supported his endeavors. In the 1850s through the 1870s, tea growers in seven U.S. states were subsidized by the Department of Agriculture, which eventually withdrew financial aid. In 1888, a South Carolina chemist grew tea in Pinehurst, and won honors for his tea.

Harvesting tea is labor-intensive, which is one reason it has failed to survive as an industry in the United States. S. Mack Fleming, a native South Carolinian horticulturist, developed a mechanical harvester that plucks tea plants quickly and efficiently. Along with Canadian-born tea taster, William Barclay Hall, Jr., Fleming is growing, harvesting, curing, and packaging tea. Their American Classic Tea is a blend of over 200 teas grown at Charleston Tea Plantation.

Southerners didn't invent iced tea (it is said to have been created at the 1904 World's Fair in St. Louis) but Southerners drink it by the gallons.

To make iced tea that isn't cloudy, use freshly drawn cold tap water. Bring it to a boil in an enameled or stainless-steel pan or kettle. As soon as it comes to a rolling boil, pour the water over the leaves or tea bags. Cool to room temperature, then strain if necessary and serve over ice.

I love the above iced tea, but sometimes I like to make the following iced teas for variety.

Minted Ice Tea Combine 3 cups very strong (triple strength) herbal mint tea with 1 cup regular tea. Sweeten to taste and serve over ice. Garnish with fresh mint sprig. Serves 2.

Black Currant Tea with Cassis (inspired by a recipe created by Karen Mac-Neil): Combine 4 cups strong black currant tea with 2 to 3 tablespoons superfine sugar and ¼ cup crème de cassis. Serve over ice as a cocktail or afternoon apéritif. Serves 2.

Lemon Tea Combine 3 cups very strong (triple strength) herbal lemon tea with 1 cup regular tea. Sweeten to taste with superfine sugar and serve over ice. Garnish with lemon wedges. Serves 2.

Iced Honey Vervein Tea Make 4 cups double strength verein (lemon verbena) tea and while still warm, add 4 tablespoons of honey. Cool, then serve over ice. Garnish with a sprig of fresh lemon verbena. Serves 2.

Other Southern Beverages

Sazerac Named after the tavern where this cocktail was made famous. Today, the Sazerac Company won't say what is in their cocktail, but it can be approximated by the following recipe: 1 teaspoon sugar, 1 teaspoon water, 2 dashes Pernod or Ricard, 1 dash aromatic bitters, 1 dash Peychaud bitters, 2 ounces bourbon whiskey.

Southern Comfort Said to have been named by Louis Heron, a bartender in St. Louis, Missouri. Although Missouri is not actually in the South, it *is* on the banks of the Mississippi. And the liqueur *is* made with bourbon and peaches, two of the South's most popular commodities. Besides, Southern Comfort (the drink was called Cuff and Buttons—meaning white tie and tails—in the 1870s) is one of the South's most popular drinks.

Peychaud Bitters A blend of herbs and flavorings added to cocktails and soda water. It is named after Antoine Amedie Peychaud, an early nineteenth-century New Orleans pharmacist who was famous for his bitters, which were used to aid digestive disorders, among other ills.

Herbsaint Also made in New Orleans and modeled after France's Pastis.

Note: For other Southern foods to order by mail, I highly recommend *True Grits,* by Joni Miller (Workman, 1990), an entire book devoted to the subject.

Black walnuts

The Hammons Pantry,
formerly
Missouri Dandy Pantry
414 North Street
Stockton, MO 65785
800-872-6879

Barbecue Sauce

Tomato-based

Moonlite Bar-B-Q-Inn
2840 West Parrish Avenue
Owensboro, KY 42301
502-684-8143

Vinegar-mustard based

Johnny Harris
Famous Bar-B-Cue
Sauce Co.
2801 Wicklow Street
Savannah, GA 31404
912-354-8828

Vinegar-and-pepper based

Wilber's Barbecue sauce
(mail order only)
c/o WWW Associates, Inc.
4172 US 70 East
Goldsboro, NC 27534
919-778-5218

Dry-cured hickory smoked country ham

S. Wallace Edwards & Sons
P.O. Box 25
Surry, VA 23883
800-222-4267; in
Virginia, 757-294-3121

Smoked Trout

Bucksnort Trout Ranch
622 West Sugar Creek
Road
McEwen, TN 37101
615-729-3162

Unbleached soft wheat flour

Weisenberger Flour Mills
Box 215
Middway, KY 40347
606-254-5282

Goat cheese

Fromagerie Belle
Chèvre, Inc.
26910 Bethel Road
Elkmont, AL 35620
205-423-2238 and
800-735-2238

Brier Run Farm
HC 32, Box 73
Birch River, WV
26610
304-649-2975

Dried cherries

American Spoon Foods
P.O. Box 566
Petoskey, Michigan
49770
800-222-5886

Cider jelly

Vermont Country Store
P.O. Box 1108
Manchester Center, VT
05255
802-362-4667

Quail

Manchester Farms, Inc.
by mail order:
P.O. Box 97
Dalzell, SC
29040
803-469-2588
*(call for the distributor
in your area)*

Bibliography

Adams, Leon D. *The Wines of America.* Boston: Houghton Mifflin Co., 1973.

The American Society of the American Association for State and Local History. *An Historical Guide to the United States.* New York: W. W. Norton & Co., 1986.

Anderson, Jean. *Recipes from America's Restored Villages.* New York: Doubleday & Co., Inc., 1975.

Beard, James. *James Beard's American Cookery.* Boston: Little, Brown and Company, 1972.

Beaufort County Open Land Trust. *Sea Island Seasons: A Collection of Favourite Recipes.* Beaufort: Beaufort County Open Land Trust, 1980.

Beeton, Isabella. *Mrs. Beeton's Book of Household Management.* New York: Exeter Books, 1986.

Bespaloff, Alexis. *Frank Schoonmaker's Encyclopedia of Wine.* New York: Fireside/Simon & Schuster, 1984.

Betts, Edwin Morris, ed. *Thomas Jefferson's Garden Book.* Philadelphia: The American Philosophical Society, 1985.

Betts, Edwin Morris, and James Adam Bear, Jr., eds. *The Family Letters of Thomas Jefferson.* Charlottesville, VA: University of Virginia Press, 1986.

Beverley, Robert. *History and Present State of Virginia.* 1705. Ed. Louis B. Wright. Chapel Hill: University of North Carolina Press, 1947.

Brennan, Ella, and Dick Brennan. *The Commander's Palace New Orleans Cookbook.* New York: Clarkson Potter, 1984.

Burros, Marian. "Reviving the Art and Ritual of Tea," *The New York Times,* May 11, 1988.

Buster Holmes, Inc. *Buster Holmes Handmade Cookin'.* New Orleans: Buster Holmes, Inc., 1980.

Cameron, Angus, and Judith Jones. *The L. L. Bean Game and Fish Cookbook.* New York: Random House, 1983.

Carson, Gerald. *The Social History of Bourbon.* New York: Dodd, Mead & Co., 1963.

Carson, Jane. *Colonial Virginia Cookery.* Williamsburg, VA: The Colonial Williamsburg Foundation, 1985.

Cash, W. J. *The Mind of the South.* New York: Alfred A. Knopf, 1941.

Catton, Bruce. *This Hallowed Ground.* New York: Washington Square Press, 1956.

Censer, Jane Turner. *North Carolina Planters and Their Children, 1800–1860.* Baton Rouge: Louisiana State University Press, 1984.

Coleman, Will H. *Lufcadio Hearn's Creole Cook Book.* New Orleans: Pelican Publishing House, 1967.

Cole, William, ed. *And Be Merry!* New York: Grossman, 1972.

Collin, Rima, and Richard Collin. *The New Orleans Cookbook.* New York: Alfred A. Knopf, 1982.

Colquitt, Harriet Ross. *The Savannah Cook Book*. Charleston, SC: Colonial Publishers, 1978.

Conroy, Pat. *The Prince of Tides*. New York: Bantam Books, 1987.

Cooper, Dorothea C. *Kentucky Hospitality: A 200-Year Tradition*. Louisville: Kentucky Federation of Women's Clubs, Inc., 1976.

Coulling, Mary P. *The Lee Girls*. Winston-Salem, NC: John F. Blair, 1987.

Coulter, E. Merton. *Confederate Receipt Book*. Athens, GA: University of Georgia Press, 1987.

Covington, Vicki. *Bird of Paradise*. New York: Simon and Schuster, 1990.

Cox, Jeff. *From Vines to Wines*. New York: Harper & Row, 1985.

Crane, Verner W. *The Southern Frontier: 1670–1732*. New York: W. W. Norton & Co., 1981.

Crump, Nancy Carter. *Hearthside Cooking*. McLean, VA: EPM Publications, Inc., 1986.

Dabney, Virginus. *Virginia, The New Dominion: A History From 1607 to the Present*. Charlottesville, VA: University of Virginia Press, 1983.

Dalsass, Diana. *Miss Mary's Down-Home Cooking: Traditional Recipes from Lynchburg, Tennessee*. New York: New American Library, 1984.

Darden, Norma Jean and Carole. *Spoonbread and Strawberry Wine*. New York: Fawcett Crest, 1978.

David, Elizabeth. *Spices, Salt and Aromatics in the English Kitchen*. Middlesex: Penguin Books, 1970.

Davidson, Alan. *North Atlantic Seafood*. New York: Viking Press, 1979.

Davis, Nancy, and Kathy Hart. *Coastal Carolina Cooking*. Chapel Hill, NC: University of North Carolina Press, 1986.

Davis, Rich, and Shifra Stein. *The All-American Barbecue Book*. New York: Vintage Books, 1988.

deButts, Mary Custis Lee, ed. *Growing Up in the 1850's: The Journal of Agnes Lee*. Chapel Hill, NC: University of North Carolina Press, 1986.

DeMers, John. *Arnaud's Creole Cookbook*. New York: Simon and Schuster, 1988.

Desaulniers, Marcel. *The Trellis Cookbook*. New York: Weidenfeld & Nicholson, 1988.

Dudden, Faye D. *Serving Women: Household Service in 19th Century America*. Middletown, CT: Wesleyan University Press, 1983.

Edwards, John. *The Roman Cookery of Apicius* (translated and adapted). Washington, DC: Hartley & Marks, Inc., 1984.

Egerton, John. *Southern Food*. New York: Alfred A. Knopf, 1987.

Eldridge, Judith. *Cabbage or Cauliflower?: A Garden Guide for the Identification of Vegetable and Herb Seedlings*. Boston: David R. Godine, 1984.

Elias, Thomas S. *The Complete Trees of North America*. New York: Gramercy Publishing Co., 1987.

Escoffier, Auguste. *The Escoffier Cook Book*. New York: Crown, 1947.

Escott, Paul D. *Slavery Remembered: A Record of Twentieth-Century Slave Narratives*. Chapel Hill, NC: University of North Carolina Press, 1979.

Eustis, Celestine. *Cooking in Old Creole Days*. New York: R. H. Russell, 1904.

Ezell, John Samuel. *The South Since 1865*. Norman, OK: University of Oklahoma Press, 1982.

Farmer, Fannie. *The Original Boston*

Cooking-School Cook Book. (1896). Facsimile: New York, Weathervane Books, 1973.

Favorite Recipes Press, Inc. *La Cuisine Creole*. Louisville: Favorite Recipes Press, Inc., 1885.

Fegan, Patrick W. *Vineyards and Wineries of America: A Traveler's Guide*. Brattleboro, VT: The Stephen Greene Press, 1982.

Flexner, Marion. *Out of Kentucky Kitchens*. New York: Bramhall House, 1949.

Folse, John D. *The Encyclopedia of Cajun & Creole Cuisine*. Donaldsonville, LA: The Encyclopedia Cookbook Committee, Inc., 1983.

Forkner, Ben, and S. J. Samway, eds. *A Modern Southern Reader*. Atlanta: Peachtree Publishers, Ltd., 1986.

Franklin, Linda Campbell, *300 Years of Kitchen Collectibles*. Florence, AL: Books Americana, 1984.

Galet, Pierre. *A Practical Ampelography Grapevine Identification*. Ithaca, NY: Cornell University Press, 1979. Translated by Lucie T. Morton.

Ghodes, Clarence. *Scuppernong: North Carolina's Grape and Its Wine*. Durham, NC: Duke University Press, 1982.

Gibbons, Euell. *Stalking the Wild Asparagus*. Putney, VT: Alan C. Hood, 1962.

Gillespie, Lori, et al., eds. *The Foxfire Book of Wine Making*. New York: E. P. Dutton, 1987.

Glenn, Camille. *The Heritage of Southern Cooking*. New York: Workman, 1986.

Godwin, Gail. *A Southern Family*. New York: William Morrow & Co., 1987.

Grissom, Michael Andrew. *Southern by the Grace of God*. Gretna, LA: Pelican Publishing Company, Inc., 1989.

Grossman, Harold J. *Grossman's Guide to Wines, Beers, and Spirits (6th revised edition)*. New York: Charles Scribner's Sons, 1944.

Hammond-Harwood House Association. *Maryland's Way: The Hammond-Harwood House Cook Book*. Annapolis, MD: The Hammond-Harwood House Association, 1963.

Hardeman, Nicholas P. *Shucks, Shocks, and Hominy Blocks: Corn As a Way of Life in Pioneer America*. Baton Rouge: Louisiana State University Press, 1981.

Harrell, Monette R., and Robert W. Harrell, Jr. *The Ham Book*. Norfolk, VA: Donning Company, 1977.

Harris, Jessica B. *From Pots and Wooden Spoons: Africa's Gifts to New World Cooking*. New York: Atheneum, 1989.

Heat Moon, William Least. *Blue Highways*. New York: Fawcett Crest, 1982.

Hess, Karen, ed. *The Virginia House-wife* by Mary Randolph (1824). Columbia, SC: University of South Carolina Press, facsimile 1984.

Hess, Karen, ed. *Martha Washington's Booke of Cookery and Booke of Sweetmeats*. New York: Columbia University Press, facsimile 1981.

Hill, Mrs. A. P. *Mrs. Hill's New Cook Book*. New York: Carleton, 1872. Facsimile, bound with the *Confederate Recipe Book*. Birmingham, AL: Oxmoor House (Antique American Cookbook Series).

Hooker, Richard J. *Food and Drink in America: A History*. New York: The Bobbs Merrill Company, Inc., 1981.

Hutchinson, Ralph E., Richard Fifiel, and Ted Jordon Meredith. *A Dictionary of American Wines*. New York: William Morrow & Co., 1985.

Janney, Asa Moore and Werner L. Janney,

eds. *John Jay Janney's Virginia: An American Farm Lad's Life in the Early 19th Century.* McLean, VA: EPM Publications, Inc., 1978.

Johnson, Hugh. *Vintage: The Story of Wine.* New York: Simon and Schuster, 1989.

Johnson, Hugh. *The World Atlas of Wine.* New York: Simon and Schuster, 1985.

Johnson, Cathy. *The Wild Foods Cookbook.* New York: Pelham Books, 1989.

Johnson, Greg, and Vince Staten. *Real Barbecue.* New York: Harper & Row, 1988.

Jones, Caroline Murrick. *Gourmet's Guide to New Orleans.* New Orleans: Caroline Murrick Jones, 1967.

Jones, Evan. *American Food: The Gastronomic Story.* New York: Vintage Books, 1974.

Jordan, Terry G. *Trails to Texas.* Lincoln, NE: University of Nebraska Press, 1981.

Junior League of Baton Rouge, Inc. *River Road Recipes.* Baton Rouge: The Junior League of Baton Rouge, Inc., 1983.

Junior League of Charleston, Inc. *Charleston Receipts.* Charleston, SC: The Junior League of Charleston, Inc., 1950.

Junior League of Charleston, Inc. *Mountain Measures: A Second Serving.* Charleston, WV: The Junior League of Charleston, Inc., 1984.

Junior League of Hampton Roads, Inc. *Virginia Hospitality.* Richmond, VA: The Dietz Press, 1981.

Kaufman, William J. *Encyclopedia of American Wine.* Los Angeles: Jeremy P. Tarcher, Inc., 1984.

Keane, Molly. *Molly Keane's Nursery Cookery.* London: Macdonald & Co., Ltd., 1985.

Kimball, Marie. *Thomas Jefferson's Cook Book.* Charlottesville, VA: University of Virginia Press, 1976.

Kluger, Marilyn. *The Wild Flavor.* Los Angeles: Jeremy P. Tarcher, Inc., 1984.

Lawrence, R. de Treville, III, ed. *Jefferson and Wine: Model of Moderation.* The Plains, VA: The Vinifera Wine Growers Association, Inc., 1989.

Lee, Hilde Gabriel, and Allen E. Lee. *Virginia Wine Country.* White Hall, VA: Betterway Publications, Inc., 1987.

Lee, Jimmy. *Soul Food Cook Book.* New York: Award Books, 1970.

Lender, Mark Edward, and James Kirby Martin. *Drinking in America: A History.* New York: The Free Press, 1982.

Lettie, Gay, et al., eds. *Two Hundred Years of Charleston Cooking.* Columbia, SC: University of South Carolina Press, 1982.

Lewis, Edna. *The Taste of Country Cooking.* New York: Alfred A. Knopf, 1976.

Lichine, Alexis. *Alexis Lichine's New Encyclopedia of Wines & Spirits.* New York: Alfred A. Knopf, 1987.

Lippson, Alice Jane, and Robert L. Lippson. *Life in the Chesapeake Bay.* Baltimore: Johns Hopkins University Press, 1984.

Loomis, Susan Herrmann. *The Great American Seafood Cookbook.* New York: Workman, 1988.

Lustig, Lillian, ed. *The Southern Cookbook of Fine Old Dixie Recipes.* Reading, PA: Culinary Arts Press, 1935.

MacNeil, Karen. *The Book of Whole Foods: Nutrition and Cuisine.* New York: Vintage Books, 1981.

Malcolm X. *The Autobiography of Malcolm X.* New York: Ballantine Books, 1964.

Mariani, John F. *The Dictionary of American Food and Drink.* New Haven: Ticknor & Fields, 1983.

Martin, Kirby. *Drinking in America: A History*. New York: The Free Press, 1982.

McClane, A. J. *The Encyclopedia of Fish Cookery*. New York: Holt, Rinehart and Winston, 1977.

McCullers, Carson. *The Ballad of the Sad Cafe and Other Stories*. New York: Bantam Books, 1981.

McCullers, Carson. *Clock Without Hands*. New York: Penguin Books, 1961.

McCullers, Carson. *The Heart Is a Lonely Hunter*. New York: Bantam Books, 1983.

McCullers, Carson. *The Member of the Wedding*. New York: Bantam Books, 1986.

McCulloch-Williams, Martha. *Dishes and Beverages of the Old South*. Knoxville: University of Tennessee Press, 1988.

Mennell, Stephen. *All Manners of Food: Eating and Taste in England and France from the Middle Ages to Present*. Oxford: Basil Blackwell Ltd., 1985.

Mickler, Ernest Matthew. *White Trash Cooking*. East Haven, CT: The Jargon Society, 1986.

Mickler, Ernest Matthew. *Sinkin Spells, Hot Flashes, Fits and Cravins*. Berkeley: Ten Speed Press, 1988.

Miller, Joni. *True Grits*. New York: Workman, 1990.

Mintz, Sidney W. *Sweetness and Power: The Place of Sugar in Modern History*. New York: Penguin Books, 1986.

Mitcham, Howard. *Creole Gumbo and All That Jazz*. New York: Addison-Wesley, 1978.

Moore, Virginia. *Virginia Is a State of Mind*. New York: E. P. Dutton, 1943.

Morris, James McGrath, and Persephone Weene, eds. *Thomas Jefferson's European Travel Diaries*. Isidore Stephanus Sons, 1987.

Morris, Willie, ed. *A Cook's Tour of Mississippi*. Jackson: Mississippi Publishers Co., 1980.

Morrison, Toni. *Beloved*. New York: Alfred A. Knopf, 1987.

Morton, Lucie T. "Robin Hood Grapes of the South," *Eastern Grape Grower & Winery News,* June 1979.

Morton, Lucie T. *Wine Growing in Eastern America: An Illustrated Guide to Viniculture East of the Rockies*. Ithaca, NY: Cornell University Press, 1985.

Neal, William F. *Bill Neal's Southern Cooking*. Chapel Hill, NC: University of North Carolina Press, 1985.

Orton, Vrest. *The American Cider Book: The Story of America's Natural Beverage*. New York: Farrar, Straus & Giroux, 1973.

Patout, Alex. *Patout's Cajun Home Cooking*. New York: Random House, 1986.

Patteson, Charles. *Charles Patteson's Kentucky Cooking*. New York: Harper & Row, 1988.

Payne, Ruth. *Historic Kentucky Recipes: 200 Years of Kentucky Country Cooking*. Harrodsburg, KY: Mercer County Humane Society.

Phillips, Roger. *Wild Food*. Boston: Little, Brown and Company, 1986.

Pinney, Thomas. *A History of Wine in America*. Berkeley: University of California Press, 1989.

Porter, M. E. *Mrs. Porter's New Southern Cookery Book*. New York: Arno Press, 1973.

Price, Reynolds. *Kate Vaiden*. New York: Ballantine Books, 1987.

Price, Reynolds. *Mustian*. New York: Ballantine Books, 1987.

Prouly, Annie, and Lew Nichols. *Sweet and*

Hard Cider: Making It, Using It, and Enjoying It. Charlotte, NC: Garden Way Publishing, 1980.

Prudhomme, Paul. *Chef Paul Prudhomme's Louisiana Kitchen.* New York: William Morrow & Co., 1984.

Rawlings, Marjorie Kinnan. *Cross Creek Cookery.* New York: Charles Scribner's Sons, 1942.

Revel, Jean-Francoise. *Culture and Cuisine: A Journey Through the History of Food.* New York: Doubleday & Co., Inc., 1982.

Rhett, Mrs. Blanche et al., *Two Hundred Years of Charleston Cooking.* Columbia: University of South Carolina Press, 1976.

Rights, Douglas L. *The American Indian in North Carolina.* Winston-Salem, NC: John F. Blair, 1988.

Rombauer, Irma S., and Marion Rombauer Becker. *Joy of Cooking.* New York: Bobbs Merrill Company, Inc., 1981.

Root, Waverly, and Richard de Rochemont. *Eating in America: A History.* New York: Ecco Press, 1976.

Rutledge, Sarah. *The Carolina Housewife.* Columbia: University of South Carolina Press, 1979.

Saint Stephan's Episcopal Church. *Bayou Cuisine: Its Tradition and Transition.* Indianola, MS: Saint Stephan's Episcopal Church, 1979.

Sass, Herbert Ravenell, ed. *A Carolina Rice Plantation of the Fifties.* New York: William Morrow & Co., 1936.

Schmidt, Patricia Brady, ed. *Nellie Custis Lewis' Housekeeping Book.* New Orleans: The Historic New Orleans Collection, 1982.

Schneider, Elizabeth. *Uncommon Fruits and Vegetables: A Commonsense Guide.* New York: Harper and Row, 1986.

Shapiro, Laura. *Perfection Salad: Women and Cooking at the Turn of the Century.* New York: Farrar, Straus and Giroux, 1986.

Shields, John. *The Chesapeake Bay Cookbook.* New York: Addison-Wesley, 1990.

Smart-Grosvenor, Vertamae. *Vibration Cooking: Or the Travel Notes of Geechee Girl.* New York: Ballantine Books, 1986.

Smith, Julia Floyd. *Slavery and Rice Culture in Low Country Georgia 1750–1860.* Knoxville: University of Tennessee Press, 1985.

Sokolov, Raymond. *Fading Feast.* New York: Dutton, 1983.

Sparks, Elizabeth Hedgecock. *North Carolina and Old Salem Cookery.* Kingsport, TN: Kingsport Press, Inc., 1980.

Spurling, Hilary. *Elinor Fettiplace's Receipt Book: Elizabethan Country House Cooking.* London: The Salamander Press, 1986.

Stern, Jane, and Michael Stern. *Good Food.* New York: Alfred A. Knopf, 1983.

Stern, Jane, and Michael Stern. *Real American Food.* New York: Alfred A. Knopf, 1986.

Stevens, Mrs. E. *Home Dissertations: An Offering to the Household.* New York: Hunter and Beach, 1886.

Stieff, Frederick Phillip. *Eat, Drink and Be Merry in Maryland.* New York: Putnam, 1932.

Tannahill, Reay. *Food in History.* New York: Stein and Day Publishers, 1974.

Tatum, Joe. *Wild Foods Cookbook and Field Guide.* New York: Workman, 1976.

Taylor, Joe Gray. *Eating, Drinking and Visiting in the South.* Baton Rouge: Louisiana State University Press, 1982.

Thompson, Terry. *Cajun-Creole Cooking.* New York: HP Books, Inc., 1986.

Time-Life Books. *Dried Beans and Grains.* Alexandria, VA: Time-Life Books, 1982.

Tower, Jeremiah. *Jeremiah Tower's New American Classics.* New York: Harper & Row, 1986.

Trillin, Calvin. *Alice, Let's Eat.* New York: Vintage Books, 1979.

Tyree, Marion Cabell. *Housekeeping in Old Virginia.* Louisville: John P. Morton & Co., 1979.

Voltz, Jeanne A. *The Flavor of the South: Delicacies and Staples of Southern Cuisine.* New York: Grammercy Publishing Co., 1983.

———. ed. *American Cooking: Southern Style.* New York: Time-Life Books, 1971.

Wagner, Philip M. *Grapes Into Wine.* New York: Alfred A. Knopf, 1976.

Weaver, William Woys. *America Eats: Forms of Edible Folk Art.* New York: Harper & Row, 1989.

Welty, Eudora. *Delta Wedding.* New York: Harcourt Brace Jovanovich, 1974.

Welty, Eudora. *The Golden Apples.* New York: Harcourt Brace Jovanovich, 1977.

White, Deborah Gray. *Ar'n't I a Woman? Female Slaves in the Plantation South.* New York: W. W. Norton & Co., 1985.

Wilkes, L. H. *Famous Recipes from Mrs. Wilkes' Boarding House in Historic Savannah.* Memphis: Wimimer Brothers Books, 1984.

Williams, Susan. *Savory Suppers and Fashionable Feasts: Dining in Victorian America.* New York: Pantheon Books, 1985.

Wilson, Charles Reagan, and William Ferris, eds. *Encyclopedia of Southern Culture.* Chapel Hill, NC: University of North Carolina Press, 1989.

Wolcott, Imogene. *The Yankee Cook Book.* New York: Ires Washburn, Inc., 1963.

Wolfe, Thomas. *Look Homeward, Angel.* New York: Charles Scribner's Sons, 1929.

Wolfert, Paula. *The Cooking of South-West France.* New York: The Dial Press, 1983.

Woodward, C. Vann, and Elisabeth Muhlenfeld. *The Private Mary Chestnut: The Unpublished Civil War Diaries.* New York: Oxford University Press, 1981.

Woodward, Sandra Kytle. *Norfolk Cookery Book: The Culinary Heritage of a Southern Seaport.* Norfolk, VA: Donning Co., 1981.

Metric Conversion Chart

Liquid and Dry Measure Equivalencies

Customary	Metric	
¼ teaspoon	1.25	milliliters
½ teaspoon	2.5	milliliters
1 teaspoon	5	milliliters
1 tablespoon	15	milliliters
1 fluid ounce	30	milliliters
¼ cup	60	milliliters
⅓ cup	80	milliliters
½ cup	120	milliliters
1 cup	240	milliliters
1 pint (2 cups)	480	milliliters
1 quart (4 cups, 32 ounces)	960	milliliters (.96 liters)
1 gallon (4 quarts)	3.84	liters
1 ounce (by weight)	28	grams
¼ pound (4 ounces)	114	grams
1 pound (16 ounces)	454	grams
2.2 pounds	1	kilogram (1000 grams)

Oven Temperature Equivalencies

Description	°Fahrenheit	°Celsius
Cool	200	90
Very slow	250	120
Slow	300–325	150–160
Moderately slow	325–350	160–180
Moderate	350–375	180–190
Moderately hot	375–400	190–200
Hot	400–450	200–230
Very hot	450–500	230–260

Index

·A·

acorn squash, 317–18
Adams, John, 413
Adams, Leon, 461
Adlum, John, 459
aestivalis (Vitis aestivalis),
    462, 463
Alabama, wineries in, 468
Alciatore, Antoine, 343
Alexander grape, 459
Algonquins, 31, 262, 413
Alice, Let's Eat, 162–63

alligator, 203
amaranth, 298
American Classic Tea,
    479
American Revolution, 146,
    230, 253, 449–50
anchovy—red pepper but-
    ter, broccoli rabe
    with, 306–7
Anderson, Jean, 45
angel biscuits, buttermilk,
    26–27
angel hair pasta with Vida-
    lia sauce and Ameri-
    can caviar, 286–87
Antoine's Restaurant (New
    Orleans, La.), 343
Apicius, 415
appetizers, 51–78
    see also first courses;
        hors d'oeuvres

apple(s):
    garnish, 193, 194
    glazed, veal scallops with
        cider cream, onion
        confit and, 242–44
    spiced stack cakes with
        cider butter and cream
        389–91
    thyme sauce, medallions
        of pork with, 224–25
    see also cider
apricot:
    orange sauce, bourbon-
        orange pound cake
        with bourbon glaze
        and, 384–86
    pistachio fruitcake, 382–
        384
aquaculture, 145, 152,
    166
Arcadia (New York,
    N.Y.), 76
Aren't I a Woman?, 261
Arkansas, wineries in,
    468–69
artichoke bottoms, braised,
    with eggs and spinach,
    343–44
arugula:
    cornmeal pizza with
        greens and fontina,
        59–61
    duck liver (foie gras de
        canard) on, with wal-
        nut vinaigrette, 73
    wilted spinach and,
        salad with bacon, wild

mushrooms, and
    thyme, 126–28
ashcake, 32
asparagus:
    fettuccine with country
        ham, red-eye sauce
        and, 285
    on toast points with tar-
        ragon butter, 68–69

*Autobiography of Malcolm
    X, The,* 302
avocado(s), 77
    with peach vinaigrette, 77

·B·

bacon, 218
    brown rice and scallop
        pilau with wild mush-
        rooms and, 173–75
    corn, and tomato sauté,
        quick, 312
    cornmeal pizza with to-
        matoes, peppers and,
        61
    and dandelion salad
        with hard cider vinai-
        grette, 131–32
    double-smoked, Bruns-
        wick stew with rabbit,
        mushrooms and, 95–
        97
    dressing, warm potato
        salad with green beans
        and, 125–26

Index

■

cakes, sweet (*cont.*)
spiced apple stack, with
cider butter and
cream, 389–91
sweet potato cheesecake,
391–94
California Grape Growers
League, 461
Callow, Richard, 245
canapés:
olive oil biscuit, with
thyme butter or sun-
dried tomato butter,
65
pimiento-cheese, 53–
54
spiced beef with two
sauces, 232–34
candy, 436–44
bourbon-chocolate
squares, 439–40
chocolate-dipped truffles
with white chocolate
—pecan centers, 442–
443
honey-walnut pralines,
438–39
white chocolate—coated
truffles with bourbon-
chocolate centers,
441–42
cantaloupe, 407
and honeydew compote,
407–8
canvasback duck, 202
caper(s):
lemon mayonnaise, 170–
172
lima beans with garlic
and, 273–74
shad roe with balsamic
vinegar and, 146–47
caramel-peanut sauce, peanut layer cake with
whipped cream filling
and, 387–88

caraway:
ramp and potato soup
with, 83–84
rye biscuits, 29–30
rye biscuits with horse-
radish cream and
smoked trout, 63–64
carbonara, rice (rice with
eggs and bacon), 257–
258
Carlos grape, 462, 463
Carolina blueberries in
black Muscat wine,
403
Carolina Housewife, The,
277, 309, 313, 362,
376, 387, 392, 397,
425
Carolina rice flour pan-
cakes, 354–55
carrot(s), 331, 332
julienned fennel and,
broiled bluefish (or
pompano) on bed of,
149–51
and parsnip "slaw" with
pecan vinaigrette,
135–36
and parsnips with or-
ange butter and cher-
vil, 331–33
Carter, Charles, 456–57
cassis, black currant tea
with, 480
Catawba grape, 457, 459,
462, 464
catfish, 143, 151–52
fried fillets with spicy
red pepper sauce,
152–53
grilled, with two sauces,
154
Catoctin Vineyards, 471
cattle herding, 229–30
caviar:
American, 75–76

American, angel hair
pasta with Vidalia
sauce and, 286–87
buckwheat biscuits with
crème fraîche and, 64
chive cream, mini corn
puddings with, 73–75
field peas with chives
and, 274–75
fresh corn and cornmeal
pancakes with crème
fraîche and, 75–77
processing of, 76
cayenne:
double corn hush pup-
pies with cheddar
cheese and, 50
julienned sweet potatoes
with bacon and, 328
celery, 119
and celeriac salad with
Creole mustard dress-
ing, 119–20
sauce, 154
Chambourcin grape, 464
Chancellor grape, 464
Chardonnay grape, 464
Charles I, King of England,
159
Charleston Receipts, 132,
362, 418
Charleston Tea Plantation,
479
Château Elan, 470
Chautauqua Vineyards and
Winery, Inc., 469
chayote, 319
cheddar cheese:
cream, ham and grits
custards with, 266–67
double corn hush pup-
pies with, 50
and ham spoon bread, 67
layered brunch torte of
sausage, cornmeal
crêpes and, 339–41

chive(s) *(cont.)*
field peas with caviar
and, 274–75
lemon "boiled" dressing,
chicken salad with,
120–21
chocolate, 439–40
bittersweet, chunk—
pecan pie, 364–65
blackest bottom pie,
365–67
bourbon centers, white
chocolate—coated
truffles with, 441–42
bourbon squares, 439–
440
-dipped truffles with
white chocolate—
pecan centers, 442–
443
white, chess tartlets,
367–70
white, —coated truffles
with bourbon-
chocolate centers,
441–42
cider, 448, 449, 455
butter, spiced apple
stack cakes with
cream and, 389–91
cream, veal scallops with
onion confit, glazed
apples and, 242–44
hard, vinaigrette, dande-
lion and bacon salad
with, 131–32
jelly, mail-order source
for, 481
sauce, peanut and
ham—stuffed chicken
with, 192–94
cinnamon sugar, rye and
Indian stars with,
427–28
citron-cranberry "double
decker" pie, 375–77

Civil War, 159, 218, 245,
253, 296, 361

clams, 161
fried, with green tomato
salsa, 162–64
Claret, Virginia, 460
clarified butter, 314
Clinton grape, 461
Clock Without Hands,
146, 450
cocoa, 439
coconut:
butter, 353
cream, 407, 408
tuiles, 429–30
coffee, 447
coleslaw:
carrot and parsnip, with
pecan vinaigrette,
135–36
savoy cabbage, with
sweet and tangy yo-
gurt dressing, 115–
116
collard greens, 298, 299,
301
and black-eyed pea soup
with cornmeal crous-
tades, 100–102
sautéed, with Dijon mus-
tard and sour cream,
301–2
with warm walnut vinai-
grette, 300
Collin, Rima and Richard,
190
Colquitt, Harriet Ross,
107
compote, cantaloupe and
honeydew, 407–8
Concord grape, 403, 459,
460, 462
condiments:
cucumber-melon relish,
166–67

lemon-caper mayon-
naise, 170–72
mustard mayonnaise,
234
onion confit, 242–44
Vidalia "marmalade,"
62–63
Vidalia mayonnaise,
138–40
see also butter(s); salad
dressings; sauces;
sauces, dessert; vinai-
grettes
confit, onion, 242–44
congealed salads, 106,
119
Conquistador grape, 464
Conroy, Pat, 222
conversion chart, 490
cookies, 420–21
coconut tuiles, 429–30
cornmeal sugar, 425–26
gingerbread sandwiches
with fresh ginger fill-
ing, 431–32
homemade vanilla wa-
fers, 428–29
rye and Indian stars with
cinnamon sugar, 427–
428
sweet potato—walnut,
424–25
whole wheat sesame
seed, 421–22
see also bars
Coolidge, Ellen Randolph,
68
Cooper, Anthony Ashley,
Earl of Shaftsbury,
330
cordials, 448
corn, 19, 260–61, 311,
337
and chèvre stuffing,
baked yellow squash
with, 321

fat:
  for biscuits, 22
  rendering, 206, 208
fennel, 109
  julienned carrots and,
    broiled bluefish (or
    pompano) on bed of,
    149–51
  and lamb burgoo with
    garlic biscuits, 98–100
  orange, and pomegran-
    ate salad with rasp-
    berry vinaigrette, 109–
    110
  pasta with shrimp, basil
    and, 282–83
  pork chops smothered
    with garlic and, 221–
    222
  spicy ham and phyllo
    triangles, 56–57
fettuccine with asparagus,
  country ham, and red-
  eye sauce, 285
Few, Colonel, 113
field peas, 270
  with caviar and chives,
    274–75
fig(s), 70, 373–74
  fresh, with Smithfield
    ham and mustard
    cream, 70–71
  and pecan custard tart,
    372–75
  rye muffins with black
    walnuts and, 42
fillings:
  buttermilk, 377
  fresh ginger, 431–32
  whipped cream, 387–88
Fiore Winery, 471
first courses, 65–78
  angel hair pasta with
    Vidalia sauce and
    American caviar, 286–
    287

asparagus on toast
  points with tarragon
  butter, 68–69
avocado with peach vin-
  aigrette, 77–78
broiled soft-shell crabs
  with Vidalia-butter
  sauce, 168–70
buckwheat pasta with
  kale and goat cheese,
  280–81
cold buckwheat noodles
  with cucumbers and
  spicy Virginia peanut
  sauce, 288–89
crab cakes with Smith-
  field ham and lemon-
  caper mayonnaise,
  Lorraine Eppler's,
  170–72
duck liver (foie gras
  de canard) on dande-
  lion greens with wal-
  nut vinaigrette, 71–
  73
fettuccine with aspara-
  gus, country ham, and
  red-eye sauce, 285
field peas with caviar
  and chives, 274–75
fresh corn and cornmeal
  pancakes with crème
  fraîche and caviar,
  75–77
fresh figs with Smithfield
  ham and mustard
  cream, 70–71
fried oysters (or clams)
  with green tomato
  salsa, 162–64
green risotto, 256–57
ham and cheese spoon
  bread, 67
mini corn puddings with
  caviar-chive cream,
  73–75

oysters and leeks on
  corn pancakes, 161–
  162
pasta primavera with
  green beans, peas, and
  herbs, 287–88
pasta roll with country
  ham and three
  cheeses, 290–91
pasta with chicken and
  chicken liver, bacon,
  and fresh sage, 283–
  284
pasta with shrimp, fen-
  nel, and basil, 282–
  283
poached red snapper
  with double tomato
  bouillon, 156–58
shrimp (or crawfish)
  with spicy chile-
  saffron sauce and
  cucumber-melon rel-
  ish, 166–68
spoon bread soufflé with
  fresh corn sauce, 66–
  67
sweet potato pasta with
  pepper and nutmeg,
  279–80
whole wheat spaghetti
  with Bel Paese, cream,
  and pecans, 281–82
ziti with country sausage
  and sun-dried tomato
  sauce, 278–79
  see also hors d'oeuvres;
  salads; soups
fish, 141–58
  baked flounder with four
    peppers, 148–49
  baked grouper with
    mixed herb pesto,
    155–56
  broiled bluefish (or pom-
    pano) on bed of juli-

Index

■

garlic *(cont.)*
  pork chops smothered with fennel and, 221–222
  sautéed okra with red pepper, herbs and, 316–17
  turnips and turnip greens with ginger and, 302–3
Garrett, Paul, 460
geese, 202
gelatin, 409, 410
Georgia, wineries in, 470
Gewürztraminer grape, 464
giblets, in dirty brown rice with chives, 260
gigging, 148
ginger(ed):
  bourbon sauce, steak with, 235–36
  honey-persimmon fool, 412–14
  turnips and turnip greens with garlic and, 302–3
gingerbread sandwiches with fresh ginger filling, 431–32
glazed apples, 242–44
glazes:
  bourbon, 384–86
  orange-molasses, 220–221
  Tupelo honey, 227–228
Glenn, Camille, 124
Glover, Thomas, 455
goat cheese, 339
  buckwheat pasta with kale and, 280–81
  mail-order source for, 481
  see also chèvre

Godwin, Gail, 23, 453
Golden Apples, The, 372, 401
golden buttermilk scones, 47–48
goose fat, rendering, 208
goose with damson-Port sauce, 206–8
grandmother's roast lemon chicken, 183–84

Grapes into Wine, 461
gravy:
  pan, fried chicken with, 181
  red-eye, 347
  roast turkey and, 199–201
Great American Seafood Cookbook, The, 160
green bean(s), 323
  pasta primavera with peas, herbs and, 287–288
  salad with sesame seed dressing, 113–114
  sautéed, with country ham, 324
  warm potato salad with bacon dressing and, 125–26
green risotto, 256–57
greens, 298–99
  beet, and julienned beets with ham, 305–6
  collard, and black-eyed pea soup with cornmeal croustades, 100–102
  collard, sautéed, with Dijon mustard and sour cream, 301–2
  cornmeal pizza with fontina and, 59–61

dandelion and bacon salad with hard cider vinaigrette, 131–32
  frozen, 299
  mustard, with warm walnut vinaigrette, 300
  sautéed watercress and radicchio with pepper vinegar, 304–5
  spring, easy lamb patties with Creole mustard sauce and, 247–48
  turnip, and turnips with ginger and garlic, 302–3
  wild, 298, 299
green tomato(es):
  salsa, fried oysters (or clams) with, 162–164
  sautéed, with rosemary browned butter, 314–315
grilled:
  catfish with two sauces, 154
  chicken paillard with peach salsa, 194–96
  hickory pit pork barbecue on cornmeal buns (or in cornmeal crêpes) with hot sauce, 228–29
  quail with herb butter, 209–10
  squash with parsley vinaigrette, 320
  steak with bourbon-ginger sauce, 235–236
Grissom, Michael Andrew, 15, 315
grits, 263
  fontina, 264
  fried garlic, 267–68

and ham custards with
cheddar cream, 266–
267
grouper, 155
baked, with mixed herb
pesto, 155–56
grouse, 202
Growing Up in the 1850's,
144, 196, 436
Guilford Ridge Vineyard,
475
gumbo, 81

·H·

Habersham Vineyards and
Winery, 470
Hall, William Barclay, Jr.,
479
ham:
cuts of, 226
and grits custards with
cheddar cream, 266–
267
wet-cured vs. dry-cured,
226
ham, country, 225–26
biscuits, chicken maque-
choux on, 190–92
biscuits with chèvre but-
ter, 25
black pepper bread with
herb butter, 39–41
and cheese spoon bread,
67
cornmeal pizza with
greens and fontina,
59–61
fettuccine with aspara-
gus, red-eye sauce
and, 285
herbed hoppin' John
with, 271–73
julienned beets and beet
greens with, 305–6

mail-order source for,
481
pasta roll with three
cheeses and, 290–91
and peanut—stuffed
chicken with cider
sauce, 192–94
pear, and hazelnut salad,
111–12
and phyllo triangles,
spicy, 56–57
poached eggs with cous-
cous and, 341–42
processing of, 226
red cabbage salad with
sugar snap peas, wal-
nut dressing and,
124–25
with red-eye cream,
347
sautéed green beans
with, 324
sautéed hominy with,
344–45
Smithfield, fresh figs
with mustard cream
and, 70–71
Smithfield, Lorraine Ep-
pler's crab cakes with,
and lemon-caper may-
onnaise, 170–72
and sweet potato "pan-
cake," 349
with Tupelo honey
glaze, 227–28
whole wheat cornmeal
pizza with Vidalia
"marmalade," cheese
and, 62–63
Hammond, John, 229
Harris, Jessica, 271
hash, sweet potato, 345–
346
Hawkins, John, 454
hazelnut(s), 111
butter, 259

Louisiana rice with
mushrooms and, 258–
259
pear, and ham salad,
111–12
*Heart Is a Lonely Hunter,
The,* 298, 301
Hendryx, Frank, 202
Henry VIII, King of En-
gland, 326
herb(ed)(s):
butter, black pepper
ham bread with, 39–
41
butter, grilled (or
broiled) quail with,
209–10
buttermilk cornbread,
198–99
chèvre biscuit thins, 55–
56
cornbread dressing, roast
turkey with, 196–99
egg sauce, quick lamb
scallops with, 245–46
and fontina topping,
58–59
hoppin' John with coun-
try ham, 271–73
mixed, pesto, baked
grouper with, 155–56
pasta primavera with
green beans, peas and,
287–88
rice stuffing, breast of
veal with, 239–41
sautéed okra with garlic,
red pepper and, 316–
317
tomato salsa, 154
see also specific herbs
herbal infusions, 447–48
Herbsaint, 480
Heriot, Thomas, 122
*Heritage of Southern
Cooking, The,* 124

Hess, Karen, 20, 38, 231, 392, 410, 430, 437, 453–54

Hewell, Amanda, 224

hickory pit pork barbecue on cornmeal buns (or in cornmeal crêpes) with hot sauce, 228–229

Highland Manor Winery, 473

History and Present State of Virginia, 217

History of Wine in America, A, 454, 456, 462

hoecakes, 32

hominy, 262–63, 344
  corn, and lima bean salad with jalapeño peppers and red pepper vinaigrette, 128–129
  sautéed, with country ham, 344–45

hominy grits, *see* grits

honey, 360, 361
  persimmon fool, gingered, 412–14
  Tupelo, glaze, country ham with, 227–28
  vervein tea, iced, 480
  walnut pralines, 438–439

honeydew and cantaloupe compote, 407–8

Hooker, Edward, 33

Hooker, Richard J., 125, 218, 263

hoppin' John with country ham, herbed, 271–73

hors d'oeuvres, 53–65
  biscuit pizzas with two toppings, 58–59
  buckwheat biscuits with crème fraîche and caviar, 64

caraway-rye biscuits with horseradish cream and smoked trout, 63–64

cornmeal pizza with bacon, tomatoes, and peppers, 61

cornmeal pizza with greens and fontina, 59–61

fresh corn and cornmeal pancakes with crème fraîche and caviar, 75–77

ham biscuits with chèvre butter, 25

herbed chèvre biscuit thins, 55–56

olive oil biscuit canapés with thyme butter or sun-dried tomato butter, 65

olive oil biscuits with spreads, 27–28

pimiento-cheese canapés, 53–54

spiced beef with two sauces on pumpernickel or rye, 232–234

spicy ham and phyllo triangles, 56–57

whole wheat cornmeal pizza with Vidalia "marmalade," ham, and cheese, 62–63

see also first courses

horseradish cream, 234
  caraway-rye biscuits with smoked trout and, 63–64

Housekeeping Book, 405

Housekeeping in Old Virginia, 19, 41, 106, 115, 119, 241, 367, 370–71, 376, 381, 385, 395, 409, 411, 418, 420, 457

Hunter, Betsy, 385

hush puppies, double corn, 49–50

· I ·

ice cream, 416–17
  sweet potato, 416–18

iced tea, 479–80

Ingleside Plantation Winery, 475

International Barbecue Festival (Owensville, Ky.), 98

Isabella grape, 459

· J ·

Jackson, Andrew, 347, 422

jalapeño pepper(s):
  baked flounder with four peppers, 148–49
  butter, 195
  corn, hominy, and lima bean salad with red pepper vinaigrette and, 128–29

James grape, 465

Jamestown, Va., 31, 76, 143, 159, 179, 217, 244, 311, 325, 326, 337, 455

Jefferson, Thomas, 73, 120, 202, 244, 253, 271, 277, 352, 364, 416, 422, 428
  fruits grown by, 70, 109, 111, 134, 373, 397, 401
  salad greens grown by, 105

"marmalade," Vidalia, 62–63

Martha Washington's Booke of Cookery and Booke of Sweetmeats, 84–85, 391–92, 410, 420, 425, 429–30, 437, 453–54, 457

Maryland, wineries in, 470–72

Mason, George, 456

Matlack, Timothy, 111

Mayberry, Alicia Rhett, 380

mayonnaise, 106
lemon-caper, 170–72
mustard, 234
Vidalia, 138–40

Mazzei, Filippo, 459

mead, 447

medallions of pork with apple-thyme sauce, 224–25

melon:
cantaloupe and honeydew compote, 407–408
cucumber relish, shrimp (or crawfish) with spicy chile-saffron sauce and, 166–68

Member of the Wedding, The, 271, 295, 384

Meredyth Vineyards, 475

Merlot grape, 465

mesclun salad, Southern, 116–17

metric conversion chart, 490

Michaux, André, 479

milk, 447
for biscuits, 22

mini corn puddings with caviar-chive cream, 73–75

mint(ed):
ice tea, 480
juleps, 447, 453–54
mixed herb pesto, baked grouper with, 155–56
orange, fresh pea soup with, 84–85
Vidalia butter, lamb chops with, 248–49

mirlitons, 319

Mississippi, wineries in, 472–73

Mrs. Beeton's Book of Household Management, 41, 411, 458

Mrs. Hill's New Cook Book, 376

Mrs. Porter's New Southern Cookery Book, 124, 146, 151–52, 338

Misty Mountain Vineyards, 476

molasses, 360, 361, 431, 449, 450
butter, 353
cornmeal muffins, 44
and lime sauce, light, roast duck with, 203–206
orange glaze, quick pork chops with, 220–21

Montdomaine, 476

Mont Eagle Wine Cellars, 473

Monticello, 105, 109, 114, 307, 313, 352, 373, 397, 459

Monticello Cookbook, 421

Montmorenci Vineyards, 472

Moon, William Least Heat, 149, 159, 168, 170

Moon Pies, 421

moonshine, 447

Moore, Virginia, 55, 341

Morrisette Winery, 476

Morrison, Van, 227

Morton, Lucie T., 461–62

Mountain Cove Vineyards, 476

Mount Bethel Winery, 468

Mount Vernon, 364

mozzarella and pesto topping, 58–59

muffins, 41–44
history of, 41
molasses cornmeal, 44
rye, with figs and black walnuts, 42
whole wheat peanut butter—raisin, 43

Muhlenfeld, Woodward and Elisabeth, 395, 396, 398

Muscadine grapes, 455, 459, 460, 462, 465–466

Muscat wine, black, Carolina blueberries in, 403

mush, garlic cornmeal, 265

mushrooms:
Brunswick stew with rabbit, double-smoked bacon and, 95–97
Louisiana rice with hazelnuts and, 258–59
wild, brown rice and scallop pilau with bacon and, 173–75
wild, wilted arugula and spinach salad with bacon, thyme and, 126–28

muskrat, 202

mustard:
cream, fresh figs with Smithfield ham and, 70–71

oyster(s), 144, 159–61
fried, with green tomato
salsa, 162–64
history of, 159
and leeks on corn pan-
cakes, 161–62
loaf, 163
seasonal characteristic
changes in, 160
species of, 160–61

· P ·

paillard, grilled chicken,
with peach salsa,
194–96
pancakes:
Carolina rice flour, 354–
355
corn, oysters and leeks
on, 161–62
cornmeal, 355
fresh corn and cornmeal,
with crème fraîche
and caviar, 75–
77
sweet potato and ham,
349
parsley:
mixed herb pesto, baked
grouper with, 155–56
vinaigrette, grilled
squash with, 320
parsnip(s), 331
and carrot "slaw" with
pecan vinaigrette,
135–36
and carrots with orange
butter and chervil,
331–33
partridge, 202
pasta, 277–91
angel hair, with Vidalia
sauce and American
caviar, 286–87

buckwheat, with kale
and goat cheese, 280–
281
with chicken and
chicken liver, bacon,
and fresh sage, 283–
284
cold buckwheat noodles
with cucumbers and
spicy Virginia peanut
sauce, 288–89
fettuccine with aspara-
gus, country ham, and
red-eye sauce, 285
introduced to America,
277
primavera with green
beans, peas, and
herbs, 287–88
roll with country ham
and three cheeses,
291–92
with shrimp, fennel, and
basil, 282–83
sweet potato, with pep-
per and nutmeg, 279–
280
whole wheat spaghetti
with Bel Paese, cream,
and pecans, 281–82
ziti with country sausage
and sun-dried tomato
sauce, 278–79
pastry(ies), 361–62
basic, 363
sweet pie, 374
see also pies, sweet; tartlets; tarts
pastry cream, bourbon,
374, 375
pâte de foie gras, 71–72
duck liver (foie gras de
canard) on bed of
dandelion greens with
walnut vinaigrette,
71–73

patty pan squash, 319
pea(s), 270, 309–10
field, with caviar and
chives, 274–75
fresh, purée, 309–10
fresh, soup with orange
mint, 84–85
pasta primavera with
green beans, herbs
and, 287–88
peach(es), 370, 396
cornmeal shortcakes
with cream and, 396–
398
and cream shortbread
tart, 370–72
salsa, grilled chicken
paillard with, 194–96
vinaigrette, avocado
with, 77–78
peanut(s), 387
and ham—stuffed
chicken with cider
sauce, 192–94
layer cake with whipped
cream filling and
caramel-peanut sauce,
387–88
sauce, spicy Virginia,
cold buckwheat noo-
dles with cucumbers
and, 288–89
peanut butter, 435
brown sugar shortbread,
435–36
butter, 353
raisin muffins, whole
wheat, 43
"Peanut Butter Conspiracy,
The," 435
pear(s), 111, 401
bourbon-poached, with
pistachios and cream,
401–2
ham, and hazelnut salad,
111–12

pine nut butter, sweet potato soup with, 94–95
Pinney, Thomas, 454, 456,
462
Pinot Noir grape, 466
pinto beans, 269
smoky maple, 275–77
pistachio(s):
apricot fruitcake, 382–
384
bourbon-poached pears
with cream and, 401–
402
pizzas:
biscuit, with two top-
pings, 58–59
cornmeal, with bacon,
tomatoes, and pep-
pers, 61
cornmeal, with greens
and fontina, 59–61
whole wheat cornmeal,
with Vidalia "marma-
lade," ham, and
cheese, 62–63
planking, 146
Plessis-Pralin, Marechal
César du, 438
plum(s), 404
damson, Port sauce,
goose with, 206–8
and raspberries in Vir-
ginia Cabernet, 404–5
poached:
bourbon-, pears with
pistachios and cream,
401–2
eggs and country ham
with couscous, 341–
342
red snapper with double
tomato bouillon, 156–
158
Poilâne, Lionel, 20
pokeweed, 298–99
polenta, 265

pomegranate(s), 109
fennel, and orange salad
with raspberry vinai-
grette, 109–10
pompano broiled on bed
of julienned carrots
and fennel, 149–51
Ponce de Léon, Juan, 109
pone, 32
pork, 217–29
chops smothered with
fennel and garlic,
221–22
chops with orange-
molasses glaze, quick,
220–21
cornmeal crêpes with
country sausage, 349–
351
cured, 218–19
health concerns and, 219
hickory pit barbecue on
cornmeal buns (or in
cornmeal crêpes) with
hot sauce, 228–29
history of, 217, 218–19
layered brunch torte of
sausage, cheese, and
cornmeal crêpes, 339–
341
medallions of, with
apple-thyme sauce,
224–25
roast loin of, with pears,
222–23
ziti with country sausage
and sun-dried tomato
sauce, 278–79
see also bacon; ham;
ham, country
Port:
-braised red cabbage,
325–26
damson sauce, goose
with, 206–8
Port du Salut cheese, 339

Porter, M. E., 124, 146,
151–52, 338
Pory, John, 150
Post Familie Vineyard and
Winery, 469
potato(es), 330
"creamed," with saffron
and garlic, 330–31
double, Anna, 329
and ramp soup with car-
away, 83–84
salad with green beans
and bacon dressing,
warm, 125–26
spiced shepherd's pie,
Southern style, 237–
238
and steak salad with
Vidalia mayonnaise,
138–40
see also sweet potato(es)
"pot likker" soup, 90–91
poultry, 177–201
roast turkey and gravy,
199–201
roast turkey with herbed
cornbread dressing,
196–99
see also chicken; game
Pound, Maurice, 456
pound cakes, 385
bourbon-orange, with
bourbon glaze and
orange-apricot sauce,
384–86
Practical Ampelography,
A, 461
"praline" blondies, 434–
435
pralines, honey-walnut,
438–39
Price, Reynolds, 95, 382
Price, Richard and Patricia,
254
Prince Michel Vineyards,
477

Prince of Tides, The, 222
*Private Mary Chestnut,
    The,* 395, 396, 398
Prohibition, 447, 460
Prudhomme, Paul, 119,
    221
puddings, mini corn, with
    caviar-chive cream,
    73–75
"pulled" biscuits, Marcene
    Rorie's, 24
pumpkin, 317–18
purée, fresh pea, 309–10
purple-hull peas, 270
purslane, 298

· Q ·

quahogs, 161
quail, 202, 209
    with cornbread stuffing,
        212–13
    grilled (or broiled), with
        herb butter, 209–10
    mail-order source for,
        481
    roasted on bed of aro-
        matic vegetables, 210–
        211

· R ·

rabbit, 202, 203
    Brunswick stew with
        mushrooms, double-
        smoked bacon and,
        95–97
raccoon, 202
radicchio, sautéed water-
    cress and, with pepper
    vinegar, 304–5
raisin(s):
    golden buttermilk
        scones, 47–48

peanut butter muffins,
    whole wheat, 43
pecan biscuits, whole
    wheat, 28–29
rye muffins with black
    walnuts and, 42
Raleigh, Sir Walter, 454–
    455
ramp and potato soup
    with caraway, 83–84
Randolph, Anne Cary, 114
Randolph, John, 307
Randolph, Mary, 38, 68,
    105, 134, 163, 231,
    235, 271, 309–10,
    319, 362, 392, 458
rapeweed, 298
Rapidan River Vineyard,
    477
raspberry(ies), 404
    and plums in Virginia
        Cabernet, 404–5
    vinaigrette, fennel, or-
        ange, and pomegran-
        ate salad with, 109–
        110
Rawlings, Marjorie Kin-
    nan, 19, 77
Raye, 180
Rebecca Ruth Candy Shop
    (Frankfort, Ky.), 439
red beans, 269
red cabbage, 325
    Port-braised, 325–26
    salad with sugar snap
        peas, ham, and walnut
        dressing, 124–25
red-eye cream, country
    ham with, 347
red-eye gravy, 347
red-eye sauce, fettuccine
    with asparagus, coun-
    try ham and, 285
red pepper(s), *see* pep-
    per(s), red
red rice, double-, 255–56

red snapper, 156
    poached, with double
        tomato bouillon, 156–
        158
relish, cucumber-melon,
    166–68
rendering fat, 206, 208
Rendezvous (Memphis,
    Tenn.), 276
Revolutionary War, 146,
    230, 253, 449–50
rhubarb, 399
    sauce, crisp pecan
        "shortcakes" with
        strawberries and,
        398–400
rice, 253–60
    brown, and scallop pilau
        with wild mushrooms
        and bacon, 173–75
    brown, whole wheat
        philpy, 46–47
    carbonara (rice with
        eggs and bacon), 257–
        258
    dirty brown, with chives,
        260
    double-red, 255–56
    green risotto, 256–57
    herbed, stuffing, breast
        of veal with, 239–41
    herbed hoppin' John
        with country ham,
        271–73
    history of, 253–54
    Louisiana, with mush-
        rooms and hazelnuts,
        258–59
    salad with pecans and
        curry vinaigrette, 132–
        133
rice flour, 19, 254
    pancakes, Carolina,
        354–55
Richard II, King of En-
    gland, 415

spoon bread, 66
  ham and cheese, 67
  soufflé with fresh corn
    sauce, 66–67
Spotwood, Alexander, 456
Spratley, Sadie, 182
squash, summer, 319
  grilled, with parsley vin-
    aigrette, 320
  sautéed zucchini "rib-
    bons" with bacon and
    basil, 322
  yellow, baked with
    chèvre and corn stuff-
    ing, 321
squash, winter, spiced,
  317–18
squirrel, 202, 203
stack cakes, spiced apple,
  with cider butter and
  cream, 389–91
stacked pies, *see* double
  decker pies
Stars Restaurant (San
  Francisco), 194
steak:
  with bourbon-ginger
    sauce, 235–36
  and potato salad with
    Vidalia mayonnaise,
    138–40
stews:
  Brunswick, with rabbit,
    mushrooms, and
    double-smoked bacon,
    95–97
  lamb and fennel burgoo
    with garlic biscuits,
    98–100
stickies, maple-walnut,
  433–34
stock:
  duck, 204, 205
  goose, 207, 208
Stonewall Vineyards,
  477

Stover grape, 462,
  467
straight bourbon whiskey,
  453
strawberry(ies), 398–99
  crisp pecan "shortcakes"
    with rhubarb sauce
    and, 398–400
stuffings:
  chèvre and corn, baked
    yellow squash with,
    321
  cornbread, quail with,
    212–13
  herbed rice, breast of
    veal with, 239–41
  peanut, chicken stuffed
    with ham and, with
    cider sauce, 192–94
succotash soup, swirled,
  87–88
sugar:
  brown, peanut butter
    shortbread, 435–36
  brown, pecan crust, 368,
    369
  cinnamon, rye and In-
    dian stars with, 427–
    428
  cookies, cornmeal, 425–
    426
  history of, 359–61
  Southerners' love for,
    359
Sugar Act (1764), 449
*Sugarin'-off in the Bullpas-
  ture Valley*, 433
sugar snap peas, red cab-
  bage salad with ham,
  walnut dressing and,
  124–25
summer squash, *see*
  squash, summer
sun-dried tomato:
  butter, olive oil biscuit
    canapés with, 65

and country sausage
  sauce, ziti with, 278–
  279
supper dishes, light:
  angel hair pasta with
    Vidalia sauce and
    American caviar, 286–
    287
  buckwheat pasta with
    kale and goat cheese,
    280–81
  chicken maquechoux on
    ham biscuits, 190–92
  collard greens and black-
    eyed pea soup with
    cornmeal croustades,
    100–102
  crab cakes with Smith-
    field ham and lemon-
    caper mayonnaise,
    Lorraine Eppler's,
    170–72
  fried oysters (or clams)
    with green tomato
    salsa, 162–64
  ham and grits custards
    with cheddar cream,
    266–67
  oysters and leeks on
    corn pancakes, 161–
    162
  poached eggs and coun-
    try ham with cous-
    cous, 341–42
  ramp and potato soup
    with caraway, 83–84
  shad roe with balsamic
    vinegar and capers,
    146–47
  shrimp and snow pea
    salad with creamy
    chèvre dressing, 117–
    118
  smoked chicken salad
    with dried cherries
    and walnuts, 134–35

Index

■

yogurt, 338
    dressing, sweet and
      tangy, savoy cabbage
      coleslaw with, 115–16
Young, Dianne, 151

· Z ·

ziti with country sausage
    and sun-dried tomato
    sauce, 278–79

zucchini, 322
    grilled, with parsley vin-
      aigrette, 320
    "ribbons" sautéed with
      bacon and basil, 322